Owning Main Street:

A Beginner's Guide to the Stock Market

By
Patrick Pappano

ISBN 978-0-9889127-0-0
Library of Congress Control Number: 2013909228

Published by:
Cardyf Company
632B Heritage Village
Southbury CT 06488
(203) 405-3433

www.owningmainstreet.com

A draft of this book was edited by Brooke C. Stoddard

Author photo on rear cover by Laura M. Reden

Cover design by Zizi Iryaspraha S
www.pagatana.com

In Memoriam

Alessandro "Alex" Ferro
1952 - 2010

Alex was born in Torsa Di Pocenia, (Venezia) Italy and immigrated to Canada in November 1955 when he was 3 years old, accompanying his mother Maria, father Pietro, and older sister Teresa. Alex was founder of Ferro Environmental Ltd. and co-founder of Coastal Controls Inc. Alex was also a friend, a colleague and an avid investor.

Below is an email note from Alex at Thanksgiving 2008, at the time of the market crash.

Happy Thanksgiving.

Hope all is well for you and Laura and life is good in the investment world!!

My investments went down the old tidy bowl, I'll have to work for another 20 years or until death!!

It looks like the land of capitalism has become the land of corporate socialism we must maintain that good old boys network of highly paid CEO,COO,CFO and every VP. Must be nice to get paid tons of money for driving a company into insolvency. I think a lot of people can handle those jobs since you don't need much intelligence or foresight. It's cronyism at its worst!!! As they would say "let the peons eat cake" we'll take the money, we're owed it because of our status/birthright!!!

Bush is gone and Obama is in, wonder if things will get better, hope so.

We're all OK, Marco's working in Calgary in the gas business and Mel is dancing up a storm, lead dancer Claire at this year's Nutcracker show. Pam's busy with the orchids and two dogs now and I'm working, traveling and enjoying life as much as I can!!

Cheers
Alex

This book is dedicated to my boss, Gordon Beatty at Remington-Rand (1966), who taught me to how to read the stock quotes in the newspaper and taught me the value of dividends, starting me on my investment odyssey.

I must also thank my mentors in the financial services industry presented in order of their appearance in my life. Mike Cimaglio, Jeffrey Kitzberger, Ethan Braid, CFA, Jon Wagner, Rick Sofka, Dick Chernus, Lou Telerico, Tommy Stratton-Crooke, Lyle Cox, Wes Crowley, Dan Bragg, Larry Sigler, Jonathan Broadbent, Masaharu Miki, Kevin Crain, Nathan Reyes, Michael Rennels, Kumar Dey (deceased), Aaron Lapp, Eli Lapp, Craig Rosenberg, Steve Stearns, Julian Diaz, Frankie Caolo and Mark Berman. All of these gentlemen are fine people, fine Financial Advisors, and have made an invaluable contribution to my knowledge of stocks and bonds and investment in all of its permutations.

A Note on the paintings contained in this book.

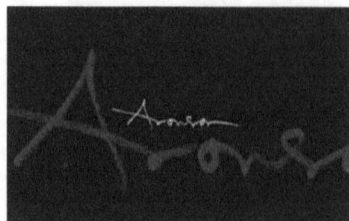

http://www.benaronson.net/

Pictures in the interior of this book are the works of Boston area artist Ben Aronson (born October 1958). Aronson earned a BFA and MFA at Boston University, School of Fine Arts. He has been widely recognized for his expressionistic cityscapes which document the culture of our time. Having won many awards, Aronson's paintings are included in the permanent collections of over 45 museums both nationally and internationally. His work is represented by Tibor de Nagy Gallery in New York City and Jenkins Johnson Gallery in San Francisco.

In his Wall Street series, Ben Aronson's aim was an attempt to 'pull the curtain back' to reveal a fascinating human drama not widely seen, to examine the human response to risk and reward captured by Wall Street actors. Aronson's gallery dealers and friends thought he was crazy, convinced at the very least that the paintings would alienate a large sector of his collector base. Naturally he has strong opinions of his own on Wall Street culture, but there is already plenty of polemic in the media regarding Wall Street. Why simply add to the noise? Objectivity was essential to present balanced and truthful images in the paintings. Aronson's hope was that the "conversation" would go beyond the surface and probe deeper into the human psychology of risk and reward, rather than being instantly dismissed as yet another axe grinder from one camp or the other.

Ben's intention in this case was to reinforce and intensify viewers impressions consciously and subconsciously while simultaneously making a contemporary connection to art history and the old masters. Universal human truths as they relate to the world of finance, objectively portrayed in a painting which has not become obscured by a shallow artist's agenda, will contain all that is base and lofty in the world of the market. This is what Aronson means by truth.

In Aronson's own words, "...*the really interesting responses to my paintings, which I could never have predicted, were the reactions* and feelings from those who saw the exhibition in person. "Main Streeters" looked around and agreed that "YES, these are the unscrupulous individuals who brought the world economy to its knees with their greed." And conversely, right beside them, the private equity guys, brokers, hedge fund managers, and bank CEO's were thrilled saying "YES, this is our world, and this is the energy and excitement we live for!" and purchased the large works for their soaring skyscrapers and grand homes. Both groups were looking at the very same paintings."

Contents

Urban Reflections   *Ben Aronson*
Oil on panel, 60 x 60 inches   *Private Collection*

Foreword

From Matthew Chapter 6

"And why do you worry about clothes? See how the flowers of the field grow. They do not labor or spin. Yet I tell you that not even Solomon in all his splendor was dressed like one of these. If that is how God clothes the grass of the field, which is here today and tomorrow is thrown into the fire, will he not much more clothe you – you of little faith? So do not worry, saying, 'What shall we eat?' or 'What shall we drink?' or 'What shall we wear?' For the pagans run after all these things, and your heavenly Father knows that you need them. But seek first his kingdom and his righteousness, and all these things will be given to you as well. Therefore do not worry about tomorrow, for tomorrow will worry about itself. Each day has enough trouble of its own."

These words of Jesus according to Matthew capture my intent in writing this book. I was a layman up until I reached the age of 61, when I left honorable work and became a stockbroker. Although I possessed no unique knowledge that would equip me to manage other people's money, I went to work in my new profession feeling I would gain the requisite knowledge through training. I had never been able to find a good broker and so my business plan for success was to just be a good broker. How naïve I was!

First is the problem of all the financial products; they go well beyond stocks and bonds to encompass dizzying flavors of bonds and convertibles, which are part stock and part bond. Then there are mutual funds, not to be confused with closed-end funds. There are index funds, and index funds on steroids via weighting differences. There are hedge funds, which are only for "accredited investors,' and private equity for the same group. There are Master Limited Partnerships (MLPs), which may issue both general partner and limited partner shares. There are Business Development Companies and REITs, which like MLPs, are not taxed at the corporate level. There are commodities like grains, precious metals, and hogs. Then there are life insurance products of various flavors, and variable annuities that compose perhaps one of the most complex asset classes available.

All of these asset classes may be held -- with some exceptions -- in taxable accounts, tax deferred accounts, IRAs and Roth IRAs. Tax- deferred accounts require naming a beneficiary but taxable accounts do not, which may require the broker to offer joint ownership with survivorship rights.

Buying into a number of these asset classes may be done in single lumps, regular deferrals, or using a variety of trading stratagems such as going long or short, or putting in stop orders or stop-loss orders. Additionally, a number of asset classes offer derivative products called options, which are available in various flavors.

This list sounds complete but is not, because MIT graduates who used to go into engineering now go to Wall Street for the big paycheck, and they come up with various securitization strategies that yield such exotics as Collateralized Debt Obligations (CDOs) that come in various risk "tranches," including one called "Plain Vanilla." Recent notoriety was earned by one well-publicized new "MIT PhD-inspired" product called Credit Default Swaps (CDSs). Millions, if not billions of dollars in CDOs were guaranteed by the nation's largest insurance company, AIG, using CDSs, almost plunging the company into infamy and bankruptcy and America's financial system into cardiac arrest. Such is the work of the PhDs in mathematics.

As you can readily infer, even the brightest stock broker candidates are not going to master these products in their six-months training period, let alone gain enough familiarity in any one of them to provide good advice.

Granted, the diversity and complexity of America's financial services menu described above is one of the nation's strengths and sets us apart as an incubator of new businesses. The problem is offering access to lay investors who on the one hand are intimidated by any discussion of financial services products and on the other just need to beat inflation and create a retirement nest-egg.

There is no question that this array of products offers many ways for staying ahead of inflation, and using several rather than one seems the prudent thing to do -- but how is are these products to be accessed by the public?

People have a similar challenge in accessing medical services, but doctors routinely refer patients to specialists with no expectation of being paid a commission. In the investment world, however, brokers do not refer clients to specialists because they may lose the client. And because clients are not highly motivated in the first place, brokers have little choice but to claim to be offering a universe of solutions with the expertise that goes with it, when in fact there is no time for expertise. Every day, clients are sold products that are far from optimal, and not so much out of venality as of ignorance. But of course, there is venality as well -- often, breathtaking venality. My guess is that most American investors are not well served by the profession of financial advisor but don't know any better, and will never find out. This book is intended to offer the more curious investors insight into the investment world, and to inoculate them from the more exotic investments which sound intriguing but which generally don't offer returns that are any better than investing in the common stocks of the world's great corporations.

Perhaps the most sophisticated investors are hedge fund managers, who could be considered "the Pros," but they do not, with a very few exceptions, consistently beat the S&P 500 index. So the primary mission of this book is to give the readers the confidence needed to invest in a portfolio of common stocks without being distracted by the empty promises of alternative investments.

Most people are familiar with the story The Tortoise and the Hare from childhood. The lesson parents reading the story wish to impart to their children is that arrogance is such a powerful emotion that it can lead to the upending of even the most certain outcomes, such as a race between a turtle and a rabbit. The story is also intended to promote the core values of hard work, dedication, faith in oneself, sticking to a process no matter how hopeless it looks, and plain old discipline.

I think the story also very aptly serves to teach people how to invest. The hare represents the world commonly referred to as Wall Street, made up of wealthy financiers, stock brokers, financial advisors, brokerage houses, and all of the exotic investment vehicles, etc. The tortoise represents Main Street, those who just plod along totally innocent to what is going on around them in the financial world. And in both the apocryphal story and in real life, the tortoise wins.

Of course you have to have faith, and that is where the system breaks down. Many would-be tortoises hear the siren song of Wall Street and are drawn in to what looks like a no-brainer -- "Of course the hare is going to beat the plodding tortoise, that's not even worth discussing!" And so most of Main Street gets caught up in the apocrypha of Wall Street and thus loses the race. It is for Main Street that this book is offered, to prompt emulating the plodding tortoise, because, just as in the story, in the real-life of investment, the tortoise wins.

The mission of this book is to stress the need in retirement saving to set a process and not a target -- the investments will take care of themselves, as Matthew would say. When retirement time comes, the resources that you will have at your disposal will be the result not of investment gains of careful stock selection, but rather of the reasonableness of the process you put into place and your discipline in sticking to that process. In the end, which stocks you invested in will hardly matter -- what will matter is that you invested in them at regular intervals, over a long span of time.

The reason I wrote this book is that the beginning investor is very likely to be seduced into the Wall Street culture of alternative investments, the hidden gem, or, if common stocks, stock selection and trading. This book is intended to show that active trading strategies are losing strategies. I cite Matthew and the tortoise to guide the beginning investor toward a profitable investment process to that will build a retirement nest-egg -- by letting the market do the work and watching as a generally passive investor.

The Wall Street culture of frenetic stock index watching is a roller-coaster ride to losses. I invite you, the reader and beginning investor, to use instead a "Ferris Wheel" approach, which is much gentler and gives a much more predictable ride. At regular intervals you will have lows and highs: lows to buy more cheap stock and highs to appreciate the unrelenting power of the market -- if only you will allow it to work for you.

Finally I wish to save you a lot of unnecessary reading and contemplation. You can throw this book away right now and do the following: invest 5% of your income in the individual common stocks that make up the Dow 30 a little at a time.

That's it. That is all you have to do to assure yourself of a maximum achievable retirement in 30 years -- just harness the power of the stock market, and it will do the work for you.

But if your penchant for investment adventure is still not satisfied, go to Chapter 12 on portfolio construction, and pick out 15 or 20 common stocks of the world's greatest corporations, put your blinders on, and focus on just that subset you have selected. For young people, putting away just 5% of your take-home pay will in 30 years yield you a good retirement. It is just that simple, and no amount of Wall Street blather will ever change that formula.

Remember, all Wall Street does is create a market to buy and sell shares; the actual creation of those shares and the value underlying them is done on Main Street.

POSTSCRIPT:

On April 1, 2012, The New York Times published an article by Julie Creswell titled "Public Worker Pensions Find Riskier Funds Fail to Pay Off."

Citing research from a firm named Preqin, the article compared investment outcomes between Georgia, which by law is prevented from using alternative investments, and Pennsylvania, which made liberal use of alternative investments. The annualized 5-year return for Georgia was 5.3% at an annual fee of about 0.3% while Pennsylvania realized an annual return over the same period of 3.6% at an annual fee of about 5%. The aggregate return for all public worker pensions over the same period was 4.9%.

What was not reported was what proportion of the pension funds had to be invested in low-return near-cash to provide for current retirees. Nevertheless, an asset management fee of 5% implies a level of expertise needed to manage non-cash assets and a sub-par outcome implies that expertise seems to have gone missing. This is exactly what Jesus was talking about and the central idea of this book: Control of investment outcomes is beyond our reach, so better to set a process that incorporates randomness than to set a target that presumes a level of control which does not exist.

Patrick Pappano
Southbury, CT

57th and 5th   Ben Aronson 2008
Oil on panel, 24 x 24 inches   Tibor de Nagy Gallery

Chapter 1

Economies

Investment begins and ends with economics and everything in between those two points is Wall Street trying to read into economic data what may or may not be there.

When people rise in the morning and go to work they join seven billion other people around the world attempting to create value. At some point that incremental value creation can be measured -- say, in another car rolling off the assembly line – reflecting the value created by financiers channeling money to a successful enterprise, engineers and designers creating the car, and then factory workers converting the paper creation to reality. Then comes the crucial part: Will the public buy it? But long before this point is reached, the stock in the company, needed to attract investment to finance the whole thing, to buy raw material and to pay the workers, will have already grown a life of its own claiming that the stock price tells the story – stock price up, the car will be a success, or stock price down, the car will be a failure.

If the public loves the car and sales rise, the stock price will rise as investors bid up the price trying to cash in on the success. Of course at some point the stock price will surpass even the rosiest of forecasts for future corporate profitability and will begin a fall as everybody stampedes for the exits. This is the world of the stock market, prompted by economic activity but driven by the insatiable drive for a shortcut to riches, a drive that is only contained by the fear that the wrong stock was picked to get to those riches. In order to manage that mercurial state of suspended belief, information is needed, and for that flow of information we have Wall Street.

Eventually the true state of corporate success will be demonstrated by the public's acceptance of the products a corporation produces. But there will be a disconnect between public purchasing behavior and Wall Street expectations. Wall Street wants a clear winner. Wall Street wants one automobile company that supplies the entire global market, without competition, and makes a huge profit by virtue of which they can sell stock with the total certainty that their clients will become rich. This is the promise of Wall Street and you heard it there first.

Free Markets

But in real life things are not so simple. There will be what J.P. Morgan termed "wasteful competition." There will be people not invested or employed in the first car company who think they can do better and will come into the market with another car and muck things up. And the problem will be that sometimes company A is ahead and at other times company B is ahead. And as these two companies duke it out what drives stock price is not the reality on the ground but the forecast floating on the wind. Forecasts differ but are all the same in a core way. Forecasts mine economic data at the point of creation and extrapolate results in a way that is actionable. But there will be multiple forecasts and sometimes conflicting forecasts all drawing upon economic information deemed irrefutable. It is on this air that stock price floats, but it is all undergirded by economic activity.

In a free market, there are few soft landings, because the feedback loops are weak – every supplier thinks they are superior to every other supplier so they keep on supplying. Eventually the market decides who the superior suppliers are and the others go bust. The result is a "mature" market that has discipline, and the surviving suppliers then act more rationally accepting whatever order the market has dealt them – market leader, market follower, niche player or into the dustbin of history.

Sometimes not only individual markets but all markets go into overdrive and then the entire society goes bust once the party is over, always prompted by recognition that they ran out of buyers at the prevailing price: No more demand, so everything goes bust. John Maynard Keynes, the great British economist living through the Great Depression, formulated his "General Theory" during that period and postulated that when demand slumps, government is then the best actor to step in and provide demand to soften the landing. Keynes theory split the economist community into two basic schools: Laissez Faire economists like Friedrich von Hayek who advocate leaving the market alone because in the long run it will correct itself, and Keynesians who argue for government intervention and quote Keynes' famous line: "In the long run, we're all dead."

According to von Hayek, free markets run off the rails when money becomes so cheap that projects which would normally be ignored instead get financed, and without feedback loops the disconnect between investment and demand ultimately leads to oversupply, followed in turn by a crash. So for von Hayek, the money supply, or the velocity of that money supply, is the key to managing economies.

The difference between Keynes and von Hayek is that when the crash comes, Keynes advocates government spending to take up the slack, and von Hayek advocates cutting back spending until it is in sync with saving. Keynes argues for preferring consumption over saving while von Hayek argues the opposite. The two approaches are obviously at 180 degrees of one other.

For better or for worse, the government is a player anyway in setting monetary and fiscal policy, so I doubt we will see Laissez Faire economics in a big way anytime soon.

Laissez Faire economic arrangements are blamed for economic distortions, like investment banker bonuses for bankers who created the great recession of 2008. The fact is that those distortions only exist in the absence of Laissez Faire economic structures. Laissez Faire destroys wealth after it creates it. That is the true Laissez Faire economic cycle.

This is an important point, because the general population will frequently point to Laissez Faire or free markets as the villain in creating distortions that result in what has been characterized as the "1%" or the "0.1%." These are the top American income earners who highlight the lopsided distribution of income that has become characteristic of 21st century U.S. life. The magic of free markets is that they, with rare exception, achieve an optimal allocation of assets such that the greatest good is attained for the greatest number.

In free markets, distortions such as the distribution of U.S. household income would be rare. Where you see income inequality distortions, what is at work instead of free markets is successful "rent-seeking," which is actors finding ways to protect their incomes from free market competition. The nice thing about the stock market is that rent-seeking never succeeds; the market is the great destroyer of wealth. If anything, rent-seeking in the market is punished when overpriced stocks are found out and quickly deflated -- well maybe not so quickly, but eventually and certainly, deflated.

This is worth a paragraph to describe this market behavior. The media will fixate on a stock and begin to talk it up and it will become the darling of the stock market chatter. This will drive buyers in who will bid up the stock price. This is rent-seeking. There will be savvier players who will see this and begin selling the stock with the intention of buying it later, at a lower price, to close out their position. These traders are called "short-sellers," and quickly, or not so quickly, depending on the effectiveness of media hype, will drive down price taking the imperfection out of the market. Needless to say short-sellers are generally reviled by market players trying to cash in on the hype.

National Economies

Despite the global free flow of economic networks, they all come under the control, more or less, of a nation state, giving rise to the characterization of economies by nation: the U.S. economy, the Chinese economy, the French economy, and so on. At one time, the U.S. economy was measured and reported as GNP, Gross National Product. Then it was observed that much U.S.-based economic activity was foreign owned, so the key number then became GDP, Gross Domestic Product, or the totality of that value created within our borders by all entities, domestic and foreign.

Despite the replacement of GNP with GDP, there still are national differences that come with currency differences offering the investor opportunities to beat inflation at attractive risk/reward ratios. According to economic theory, free market normal profits are pretty thin, prompting new, or different, economic activity in pursuit of greater gains, but such activity always comes at greater risk of loss. Within a national economy risk is rationalized, or a set value assumed in all pricing and profit. Because the set value differs across borders, it is possible at times to realize greater gain at lower risk by investing across borders.

A good example of cross-border lower-risk investment is what is called "carry trade." In this game, an investor borrows in a home currency at a low interest rate and then loans (buys sovereign bonds) in a host currency at a higher interest rate. Doing so yields extraordinary profit at low risk, but only so long as the home currency doesn't gain value against the host currency, an event that might well wipe out the gain and produce losses. But the reason for the difference in rates is demand for the currency, so higher rates mean more demand, which should translate into appreciating host currency against the home currency. Thus, investing globally can mean finding higher returns at lower risk than may be found in the home country alone.

There are currency risks and looking at the global currency markets, the U.S. dollar (USD), will float up and down in investor sentiment and demand for the USD relative to other currencies. In the post-war era of the late 1940s and the 1950s, as European and Asian economies recovered from the war, the strong USD made foreign goods very cheap. The cheapness of foreign goods and the European and Asian experience of returning soldiers gave the U.S. market an appetite for foreign goods that did not exist previously. Soon strange new products were offered in the U.S. market, like the Volkswagen "Beetle," that was unlike any American offering. When the first "Beetle" was introduced in 1949, the U.S. economy was almost entirely U.S. based, but over the succeeding 60+ years has evolved into a global economy and since the 1960s into largely an import economy that has accelerated dramatically with cheap imports from China and India.

From an investment perspective, choosing between investing in an electric utility that may derive all of its income in USD, or in, say, McDonald's, which derives income in over

100 currencies, will be a choice of currencies as well as commercial prospects. The global currency question is also raised when it is time to retire. Some retire to places like Mexico in the expectation that the stronger USD will give them a heightened lifestyle with a lower-cost Mexican Peso (MEX). But there can be changes. When the European Union first adopted its unified currency, the Euro (EUR) was trading at 75¢ USD. Since then, the relationship has reversed, and the EUR is trading at $1.29 USD. Nevertheless, the USD is the default global trade currency and used all over the world for both legitimate business, Petrodollars, and not-so-legitimate business, such as Russian oligarchs using suitcases stuffed with $100 USD bills to make their purchases.

Economics, a Study of Scarcity

Economics is the study of scarcity, which may seem an hour's worth of study before moving on to something else. But the human behavior that scarcity prompts affects almost everything human beings do. Shopping for food every week is only the most prosaic. What about a young bride or groom making a "good" marriage. A "good" marriage is one that promises money to ease one's progress through life – no need to budget or budget too carefully. The failure of most people to make "good" marriages is itself an example of scarcity -- scarcity of candidates or not focusing on scarcity until it is too late. In either case, before too long scarcity will become apparent to all actors, even those insulated from it by their trust funds.

Psychologist Abraham Mazlow postulated in a 1943 paper, "A Theory of Human Motivation," what has come be known as Mazlow's Hierarchy of Needs. Scarcity is not felt all at once in all areas; rather scarcity is a stepped affair and occurs in stages, or, as Mazlow states, after a more urgent need is satisfied soon enough a new need comes into focus.

As you might imagine, mere survival is the first need,

giving rise to a drive to obtain food, shelter, and clothing. Once these are achieved, securing or preserving them is the need. Once we have secured our places, we want community and social interaction. Once accepted into a community, we want to feel good about ourselves, and we strive for that by attracting the esteem of others. Finally we arrive at the pinnacle of Dr. Mazlow's hierarchy: We want to feel our specialness. This is called the self-actualization stage and is man's final achievement -- and for many, not achieved until the last hours of life, staring up at the ceiling from the deathbed, contemplating decisions made and paths not taken.

When you combine scarcity with Mazlow's hierarchy, you can imagine the complexity of human behavior, well beyond an hour's casual study. The study of these colliding forces is called economics and fills volumes of books, many with complex formulas to model behavioral outcomes of various economic policies. Take reducing interest rates -- we know there will be more borrowing; we just don't know how much or what for.

The general view of economic activity was perhaps best enunciated by University of Chicago economist Paul Samuelson in his classic 1948 textbook: *Economics.* Samuelson was not only a seminal economic thinker but also a bit of a humorist. Take his famous quote: *"It is indeed true that the stock market can forecast the business cycle. The stock market has called nine of the last five recessions."* This is a sign not only of Samuelson's humor but also his view of the efficiency of the stock market in pricing assets.

In any case, the classical view of economic activity starts with an entrepreneur spotting an un-served need, for example Christopher Columbus being greeted by natives with burning cigars protruding from their noses. If they do it in the New World, why not in the Old, thought Columbus, and brought back a bundle of tobacco to the Spanish economy. The rest is history – tobacco caught on big time. Entrepreneurs then assembled factors of production -- people and machinery -- and began satisfying the market for tobacco products.

Such investments provide broader resources in the form of wages, which act on the supply with demand, further spurring economic activity as the base broadens to encompass larger and larger populations of both suppliers and users, all chasing scarcity and creating an industry. This cycle will inevitably prompt the ramping up of supply ahead of demand as all suppliers seek to climb Mazlow's hierarchy. Unfortunately although supply is unlimited demand is not and eventually the needed demand will go missing at the prevailing price -- and a slump will follow.

The study of economics is also useful in giving the investor a customer-centric view of the investment landscape. Unlike the "chicken and egg" conundrum that is the mainstay reference point for citing unsolvable problems, the problem of economics can be solved. It starts with an entrepreneur discovering a new demand and then taking steps to fill that demand -- usually with a thesis for investors.

The Customer is King

The enabling factor in an economy is not the entrepreneur, however, although he is obviously critical to the process, but rather the persons demanding the product, because it is they that have a need. Buyers decide what gets bought and thus what gets made. The savvy investor focuses on who the buyers are, what they are buying, from whom and why. This is investment -- looking at the destination for goods and services, not their source. A business is a business because it has customers not products. Products are only a means to have a business, not a business itself. Investment is the action of placing surplus money in the hands of an entrepreneur striving to satisfy a market. The entrepreneur will always be biased, but those buying the entrepreneur's products will not be biased, so it is the buyers you want to pay attention to and put your money where they implicitly tell you to put it. Economics is the study of buyer behavior in the presence of scarcity, and investment should be the same.

Our society also tends to over- weigh the role of entrepreneurs in new product development, entirely neglecting the very important role of "early adopters." These are the persons making bets on the new products and by their purchases advance a new product's development to a point where a product can go mainstream.

This book is intended to help the beginning investor gain the confidence needed to buy common stocks of great corporations that are in great businesses, and then hold onto those stocks through the inevitable economic cycles of boom and bust natural to national economies with delayed feedback loops, that is to say, all economies.

There Will Always Be Customers

The purpose of this first chapter is to ground the investor in basic economics to achieve successful investment in an often turbulent market, by understanding that although markets fluctuate man's basic needs stay the same and that is where investment focus needs to be. In America there are about 125 million investing persons and companies; it is their aggregate behavior that determines market outcomes.

There may be pockets of predictability that can be exploited by those closest to the action, but the most reliable economic -- and thus market -- indicator is that global population stands at around 7 billion people and they will purchase goods and services in ever increasing amounts as people have been doing for thousands of years. If you think people will stop wanting better tomorrows, the market is not for you. If you think people's drive for better tomorrows is irreversible, then the market is for you and it doesn't much matter at which point you stick your oar in, as long as you put it in and keep it in.

Once you put it in, keeping it in is the next most important step. This is accomplished by disbelieving that any individual or organization can accurately forecast what 125 million people are going to do on any given day or that people are suddenly not going to wear shoes anymore or stop eating. Over time the global population will work to improve their circumstances. That will cause entrepreneurs to start businesses, and stock prices of the successful ventures will rise over time with advancing population and the human drive to have better tomorrows.

I recently read that a pundit had concluded that mankind had reached a plateau and that we could not expect the types of development breakthroughs that had occurred in the past. This is of course nonsense. There is a wonderful story that took place in the 1930s when Lyndon B. Johnson was a Congressman from Texas' 10th district. He had pushed to have power lines installed in rural areas of Texas. People signed up for the service and lines were installed some time before power could be sent through them. One night as a rural family was trudging home after a day's outing they suddenly saw a bright light where their house was and began running because they thought their house was on fire. But actually the power had finally been turned on and for the first time they saw the power of electric lighting. As Robert Caro, a Johnson biographer, wrote, that year many babies were named Lyndon. People want easier and more interesting lives, and they are willing to pay for it, so there are going to be startling breakthroughs going forward.

Recently a New York Times article by Carl F. Nathan, chairman of microbiology and immunology at Weill Cornell Medical College, wrote that the market failure to incentivize antibiotic development spelled doom for the human species because the bugs are fighting for their lives and will win unless challenged. What impressed me most about Mr. Nathan's article was his unabashed faith in mankind to develop the antibiotics needed if only given enough money to do so, in other words, there are no limits to mankind's resourcefulness given enough money. The point is that any plateaus in man's development propounded by pundits are likely to exist in only the mind of the pundit. We, as a species, can look forward to an unending parade of wonderful new developments and some as game-changing as electricity in rural homes.

These fundamental economic principles explaining human behavior and forecasting business outcomes are central to investment but usually out-shouted by the Wall Street rumor of the day expected to generate a new cash flow for the shouters. Most investors feel compelled to listen to and act upon this "news." While news drives stock price, it is basic economics that determines the success or failure of an enterprise and hence its common stock. And as we have seen, while Wall Street is certain who the winner is, the economic story is not so clear other than to anticipate competition in a growing market with no clear winner until the market matures. The wise investor ignores the Wall Street news and focuses instead on basic needs as described by Mazlow and identifying those companies likely to be preferred by people seeking to satisfy those needs.

I was skeptical when I saw Borders opening up grand bookstores. Who is going to buy all these books, I wondered. Well, I was wrong. The very recent rise of big-box bookstores has been very successful. I thought the same thing about early Starbucks: Who would pay all that money for a cup of coffee? Millions it turned out. What was at work in both cases was an entrepreneur who saw a market nobody else saw. This is investment; it is the interface between people and unmet needs. Even mature companies understand this and have a constant flow of product development to exploit emerging markets. For the investor, identifying those entities doing the best job of spotting unserved markets and offering products in those markets is the key and that information is not contained in any Wall Street "research;" it is more likely contained on the front page of your local newspaper or even in everyday life. I was in a Starbucks in New York City one recent morning and counted over 30 people standing in a slow-moving line to get a cup of coffee. Before the rise of Starbucks this would have been unthinkable. Today it is routine.

So the point of this first chapter on Economics is to drive you to a better way of considering investment candidates. Don't go rummaging through annual reports; they will only tell you what has happened in the past, not the future, and only quantitatively. Don't listen to Wall Street chatter; it is not research but rather a trap baited with data-mining to get your money in order to charge you a "management" fee. Instead, pick out the most comfortable piece of furniture in your house, plop down in it, and begin to ask yourself questions like, which company has done the best job of innovating? The world is constantly growing and changing, these basic economic forces will create chaos. Out of the chaos a winner will emerge. It will inevitably be a nimble player well versed in a changing playbook. In the meantime the Wall Street chatter labeled "research" will be a distraction typically focused on micro information completely disconnected from those issues that determine a company's fortunes. For some, that Wall Street chatter will be a siren song that cannot be ignored, but hopefully for readers of this book, that siren song is instead discordant noise and gets turned off.

Nighthawks   *Ben Aronson 2008*
Oil on panel, 44 x 44 inches   Private Collection

Chapter 2
Inflation and Shifts in GDP

"The adoption of Keynesian and monetarist ideas by central bankers and elected officials subsequently cast the Fed in a proactive macroeconomic role. William McChesney Martin, who served as chairman from 1951 to 1970, said that the job of the Fed was "to take away the punch bowl just as the party gets going." This might have been wise in theory, but it wasn't mandated by the law. In 1977, an amendment to the 1913 Act explicitly charged the Fed with promoting "maximum" employment and "stable" prices. The Humphrey-Hawkins Full Employment Act that followed in 1978 mandated the Fed to promote "full" employment and while maintaining "reasonable" price stability."

Amar Bhide

About 70% or more of U.S. economic activity comes from consumer spending, that is, spending by families at the local grocery store to keep the family nourished for the more arduous task of shopping at the mall for clothes and electronics, and maybe attending a movie and buying popcorn, plus buying appliances and a car every once in a while. This spending then prompts other spending, because the grocer, the shopkeeper, the movie impresario and the car dealer now have income, much of which will be spent buying things that their customers are employed in producing or selling.

This circular flow of money is called an economy and is largely driven by the collective participants' confidence in the future replenishment of their pocketbooks after their spending, plus the perception that inflation will drive prices up going forward. In other words, people don't look at the money in their pocketbooks before deciding to spend; they calculate the prospects for replenishment of that money they will take out to spend and the changing cost of those goods they want to buy. If they see certainty in that replenishment and rising cost in those goods, they will spend. If there is uncertainty about future earning and future costs, they will either postpone or select a lower-cost alternative. If the consumer has no confidence in where that replenishment is coming from, in all likelihood, he or she will put off spending. If the consumer expects deflation, that is goods and services becoming cheaper over time, he or she will put off spending.

John Maynard Keynes, a prominent English economist, creator of Keynesian economic theory, a hero of the author and a successful (later) speculator, proclaimed that as spending proliferated through the economy it caused a multiplier effect, which he calculated to be two times the original spending. Later studies have verified a 1.8 multiplier effect. In other words, a dollar spent produces $1.8 dollars in downstream economic activity.

So in addition to the replenishment dimension on the supply of money, there is also a value dimension in the spending of money. If there is slight inflation, say 2% to 3% per year, people are encouraged to spend immediately before the goods and services they want become more expensive. This keeps the economy moving. If instead of slight inflation there is slight deflation, then goods and services get cheaper over time, and spending will be postponed to take advantage of lower future pricing and the economy will grind to a halt. What drives inflation is not so much how much money there is available for circulation as the velocity of that circulation. It is principally velocity – spending -- that determines inflation and economic health. Incidentally, velocity was first enunciated (as far as I know) by Adam Smith, in his seminal work; *The Wealth of Nations* or more formally, *An Inquiry into the Nature and Causes of the Wealth of Nations*, published in 1776.

Managing Inflation

Most, if not all, economists like to see enough of a dose of confidence in the economy to keep spending velocity constant at an activity level that gives each participant a sense of prosperity without profligacy. In order to accomplish this happy but not exuberant state, governments like to promote a slight sense of prosperity where otherwise it might not exist, and this is done by lowering interest rates. At some threshold level, borrowing picks up – because interest rates are low -- and suddenly there is more money and velocity in the economy; soon consumers are feeling the prosperity and spending. But since the additional money in circulation represents real buying power that has been added to the economy without adding to the supply of goods or services, the existing goods and services must be re-priced upwards to absorb the extra money. As long as the consumers see that additional money in their income, they are perfectly happy to see it go out in their spending, because equilibrium is maintained, albeit at a slightly higher number. The Federal Reserve, tasked to keep everybody happy but not euphoric, likes to see this growth at 2% to 3% annually, and adjusts interest rates in an attempt to maintain this "equilibrium" level.

Compare U.S. postal rates to mail a letter; 30 years ago in 1981 it cost 18¢, today it costs 46¢. That is inflation – same service, higher cost, but not higher purchasing power. Today 46¢ buys what 18¢ would have bought in 1981, or thereabouts.

Calculating the effect of inflation is tricky because the many components that go into the typical American's shopping cart do not all experience the same rate of inflation. In addition, as a national economy we are one inflationary unit within an international network of units all inflating at different rates at different times in response to individual cycles. As time passes, the differences can create significant distortions. There are also fundamental shifts that have dramatic impact on the cost of living, such as the availability of land offering access to a major business center like New York City. In the 1950s an acceptable commute into New York City was anything under 45 minutes. Today, some people commute up to two hours.

To further illustrate the uneven inflationary forces in a society, consider the automobile. In the 1950s a car was pretty well used up at 60,000 miles, which would typically be six years of normal use and would have required five sets of new tires that were typically good for 10,000 miles. Today an automobile can deliver 100,000 miles of service and more, and with only two sets of tires. Also, over those 100,000 miles, today's automobile will deliver largely trouble-free service.

In the 1950s, when a car's mileage exceeded 30,000, you could expect to need new radiator hoses, fan belts, piston rings, and more. Today's automobile is more expensive but the cost per mile is cheaper. Households moved from owning one car to owning several. These changes make it practically impossible to measure the rate of inflation by automobile use and ownership. In the 1950s the idea of driving over 15 miles to work was mind-boggling; today, much longer commutes are routine.

Aside from changing product characteristics, determining the present value of historical sums requires a decision, whether the calculation is based on average inflation or growth relative to GDP.

For example, my 1988 income of $95,000 today would be equal to $175,000 as strictly a change in CPI (Consumer Price Index) but equal to $271,000 as a percent of today's GDP. But, here is the most amazing part for me: I would be happy today to be making $95,000 a year, because I am making half of that. What happened? According to one report, in 1988 I was competing with 500 million developed-world workers and since then the workforce has added two-billion low-wage workers from the Third World. That has done two things: It has driven down wages and it has shifted money from labor to capital, producing a nice GDP number of which I have a much smaller share. So inflation is only part of the story, but the part you can do something about.

You could say that inflation is from government and GDP shifts are from commerce. A $100,000 bond purchased in 1988 would only have about $57,000 purchasing power today. That same amount invested in an S&P 500 index in 1988 would be worth around $810,066 today. Compare this with the CPI calculation over the same period yielding a present value of about $187,167 for $100,000 in 1988 dollars. A calculation of Relative Share of GDP growth for that same amount over the same period has a present value of about $295,000. So just investing in the S&P 500 index over the same period has in the past, trumped inflation and global GDP shifts in wealth. Also keep in mind that over that same period, a house mortgage payment would have been crushed by inflation, while the house appreciated somewhere between CPI growth and the growth of the S&P 500.

Boom and Bust

There is both national and international inflation, and despite the ravages, inflation of a healthy sort keeps things humming. And humming is pretty much what the economy does until a wild-card erupts, like the sudden discovery of a gold mine by one of the participants. When this happens, the gold mine owner suddenly feels much more confident about replenishment and inflation and begins spending more. This in turn triggers a multiplier effect and a general sense of greater confidence in the economic population. Suddenly there is an accelerated rate of spending that in a circular motion creates an upward vortex, and soon everybody is in a state of euphoria.

This euphoria will inevitably cause alarm in the government economic policy community, and interest rates will be raised to cool the euphoria, hopefully at a rate that brings about a "soft-landing," back to just enough confidence to restore inflation down to a 2- 3% range. While this is the theory, the actual practice has not had a good track record, because the cooling measures have mostly been applied out of sync or after the bubble has popped when consumers suddenly see that the mere presence of gold does not of itself create value and that the re-pricing which must be maintained among the available goods and services is out of reach for most of the consuming public. So prices collapse and euphoria turns to depression and, of course, spending drastically declines. Or as von Hayek said, spending outstrips available savings leading to a hard landing.

Because of the inevitability of these out-of-control cycles, government economists spend much time figuring out ways to monitor inflation and keep it in check. In normal times this is not too difficult, but times are seldom "normal" and given the range of human enterprise, you can be sure that as you read this, some operative, somewhere, is hatching a plan to produce the next "gold mine," and when that gold mine goes public and then viral, the economy again becomes a roller coaster.

This is what happened in the Roaring '20s, which produced a historic plunge from high euphoria to the depths of depression that lasted from October 29th, 1929 until December 7th, 1941 – 145 months or 13 years and 1 month. While this was the most severe depression in U.S. history, recessions are regular phenomena as economies expand and contract in response to consumer sentiment, and incidentally, consumer sentiment that desperately strives for euphoria on a daily basis. Just in recent years, we had the tech bubble burst of 1999 and the housing bubble burst of 2008.

The following is a list of market blowups and panics for the period before 1929: 1819, 1832, 1836, 1837, 1857, 1869, 1873, 1893, 1901, 1907 and of course the one we call the big one – 1929.

In 1819, oversupply of farm products in response to earlier shortages caused not only commodities to fall precipitously but also highly overpriced rural real estate as well.

The goldmine in the tech bubble was the belief that the Internet would revolutionize the economy overnight, which it did, but unevenly. Euphoria led consumers to the belief that any Internet businesses could not fail and so there was a proliferation of Internet businesses. But many failed, prompting rather sudden dissipation of euphoria. In the meantime, the Federal Reserve (government economists) as they saw a sour mood setting in after the burst, lowered interest rates to near zero and suddenly people who lost money in the Internet bubble saw they could remake their money in the housing market with cheap mortgages; they went at it.

Interest rates remained low and eventually pulled in migrant workers, who were at the bottom of the economic ladder and saw an opportunity to own a fine home, for a few weeks anyway, and then sell at a profit that would dwarf their regular earnings. That process eventually led to a housing bubble which eventually collapsed in December 2008, producing the largest economic collapse since 1929's that led to the Great Depression.

There are a number of lessons to be taken from this cyclical, natural and never-ending phenomenon, but the lesson proposed here is the lesson of change. Things do not have an intrinsic value separate from the valuation given them by market forces. During periods of euphoria, things will be worth more, perhaps a lot more, than during periods of consumer pessimism. How to manage in this inescapable sea of change is what this book attempts to illustrate, so that when portfolios of common stocks go in the tank during a bust, rather than panic, the reader of this book will look upon the bust as an opportunity to accumulate cheap shares of favored companies.

To help understand the boom and bust cycle, it is helpful to identify the main actors that produce these out-of-control market forces. We start with you, the reader. You are the market for those things you buy. You set the price even when you don't buy, because that tells the merchant that perhaps his price is too high. When you buy, you reaffirm a proper price point at that point in time.

The Market is Everywhere

Sometimes you hear people say they avoid the market because of its randomness. This is nonsense, because it is impossible to avoid participating in the market. When someone takes a job, it is a market decision that the new employer will fare well in a competitive market. Buying a house is a strong pronouncement that the buyer feels the housing market will grow during the term of his ownership. So everybody is in the market all the time in ways they might not realize.

The core lesson centers on the role of inflation, and inflation fighting in the ebb and flow of economic activity. As we have seen, a steady, low, and healthy rate of inflation is often upended by an outsized market development that wreaks havoc before it is tamed -- often the taming doesn't succeed -- and there is the inevitable self-immolation of the latter-stage participants. Early participants, those that get in and out early, can do very well, but they will be very few. And just as there are victimless crimes, where the victim suffers no damage, at the other end of the spectrum is the collapsing bubble that takes down even the innocent bystanders. So learning to be a bystander in a stormy world is an important skill!

As has already been stated, many people have a fear of the market and take great pains to avoid being "in the market," and then feel that they are immune from market forces having taken those steps. The opposite is true. The steps people take to avoid market forces results in a minor reduction in their exposure. Their biggest assets -- their job, their house, their cars, as well as all dependent family members -- are all in the market, rising and falling with the ebb and flow of supply and demand. Such people, and indeed all of us, may think we are operating from a solid platform we call terra firma. Actually that terra firma is a pitching platform rising and falling on an inflationary sea, and our financial decisions must be made with that pitching platform in mind.

Just as the economy is a circular flow of cash, each of us is a micro-economy taking in and doling out cash. Sometimes that cash is in lumps and at other times it is in flows. If the cash, in or out, is in a flow, then some assessment of inflationary effects must be considered. Take a life insurance policy. The life of the policy might be, say 60 years. On day one, the policy may have a death benefit of $100,000. That is a fixed number that will be $100,000 in 60 years. The number will remain fixed, but the purchasing power of the $100,000 lump will erode with time, probably cut in half at least twice, yielding a purchasing power in today's dollars of $25,000 by the time the insurer pays off. That amount is nice to have, but won't come anywhere near making up for a lost salary. The theory of life insurance is that as time passes and children leave, expenses recede and therefore insurance coverage may be reduced. This reduction is done by inflation.

Inflation Effects on Cash Flows

A life insurance policy is paid for in a cash flow over the same 60-year period, so the premiums that come towards the end will also be much smaller (in purchasing power compared to that at the beginning of the policy) and easier to bear. This highlights that life insurance is a tremendous bargain on day one, at which point the life insurance company is on the hook for $100,000 while having received maybe one premium payment amounting to $500.

But on the last day, even in death, the payoff of $100,000 will have come from well invested premium payments. The first premium of $500, over a 60-year period becomes $28,973 at 7% interest. Using the 9.5% returned by the S&P 500 index, that $500 turns into $115,828. This illustrates the difference, over time, of being in the market, where $500 becomes $115,828, versus being out of the market where $100,000 becomes $25,000. This is the pitching platform we are all standing on. So the smart thing to do is grab the market with both hands and hang on -- you're going for a ride.

Even financial decisions people face daily need to be made with inflation in mind. This is because, as noted, target inflation is often exceeded dramatically by actual inflation, and then there are changes in per capita GDP. With this as our foundation, all assets and liabilities may be thought of as either floating with inflation and GDP shifts, or as fixed. If we take money from salary, which is floating with inflation and GDP, and put it into a fixed security, such as a passbook savings account, we are applying a drag unless the passbook interest rate beats inflation, which is seldom the case. The upside is that if the market collapses, the passbook savings account will be unaffected because it is a fixed income instrument. Fixed income instruments are essentially loans from the saver for which interest is earned and for which the loan amount may be demanded back in full at some future time.

So to battle inflation, investors have two classes of tools: 1) floating or market instruments and 2) fixed-income instruments. You may assume that each instrument may only be bought, which means buying a fixed instrument or buying a floating instrument, but two additional positions can be built by selling rather than buying. If you take out a loan, you are selling a fixed income instrument. If inflation takes off, your loan value will get crushed and you will wind up paying back a lot less than you borrowed. If you buy a fixed income instrument by opening a passbook savings account, as the years pass, inflation will eat away at your savings so at the end of an inflationary term, you might find yourself with less money than when you started, in purchasing power. See chart below.

	BUY Side	SELL Side
MARKET	Buy a House Buy Hard Assets Buy Stocks	Sell a House Sell Hard Assets Sell Stocks
FIXED-INCOME	Buy Bonds Deposit Savings	Take out a loan

The shaded boxes are those that flourish for you with inflation because assets rise and liabilities (loans) fall or get inflated away. In a deflationary market, the opposite occurs: Your house devalues and your mortgage becomes harder to pay as you struggle with more challenging income. During deflation, salary raises will be postponed and there may even be salary cuts. Interest on savings and returns of investment will be reduced, all leading to declining incomes while loans and other financial obligations remain fixed and harder to pay.

People who need to save for retirement need to stay ahead of inflation and the most reliable way to do this is through investment for gain, which is called capital gain, a gain in your capital. Investing in real estate, as in your house, has been pretty much accepted as a "no brainer" – but perhaps without the understanding that it merits.

As described above, over a 30-year period, during periods of normal inflation of 2%-3%, purchasing power of money gets cut in half. Purchasing power of bonds will be cut in half whereas traditionally stocks will not. A house is a hybrid that takes advantage of both characteristics. The bank loans you money for 30 years to buy a house. From the bank's perspective this is a bond they bought from you; it is a fixed-income instrument whose purchasing power will be cut in half over a 30 year period – the life of a mortgage. This means that the mortgage payments you make will decline in value over time, eventually falling to about half their original purchasing power -- and probably a lot more depending on intervening rates of inflation. At the same time, your house value will rise with inflation with a reasonable expectation that it will double in value over a 30-year term. So what starts out at parity on Day One – loan-to-house value of 1:1, becomes after 30 years loan-to-house value of 1:4 if an interest only mortgage loan is used to finance the house. The buyer gains fourfold because the house doubled in value and the mortgage got cut in half. This, of course, is theory only because the mortgage payments are a 30-year cash flow with a wide spectrum of purchasing power from a high on day one for the first payment to a low for the last payment. So the exchange of a fixed income asset, a mortgage, for a market-based asset, a house, for a term that may last 30 years, is one of the most significant measures one can take to build wealth, even at a 2%-3% annual rate of inflation.

The actual average annual inflation numbers have been much more volatile – see chart below.

YEAR	INFLATION %	S&P 500 %	GDP %
1980	13.5	32.5	8.9
1981	10.3	-4.9	12.1
1982	6.2	21.5	4.0
1983	3.2	22.5	8.7
1984	4.3	6.3	11.2
1985	3.6	31.7	7.3

1986	1.9	18.7	5.8
1987	3.6	5.3	6.2
1988	4.1	16.6	7.7
1989	4.8	31.7	7.5
1990	5.4	-3.1	5.8
1991	4.2	30.4	3.3
1992	3.0	7.6	5.8
1993	3.0	10.1	5.1
1994	2.6	1.3	6.3
1995	2.8	37.6	4.7
1996	3.0	22.9	5.7
1997	2.3	33.4	6.3
1998	1.6	28.6	5.5
1999	2.2	21.0	6.4
2000	3.4	-9.11	6.4
2001	2.8	-11.9	3.4
2002	1.6	-22.1	3.5
2003	2.3	28.7	4.7
2004	2.7	10.9	6.4
2005	3.4	4.9	6.5
2006	3.2	15.8	6.0
2007	2.8	5.5	4.9
2008	3.8	-37.2	1.9
2009	-0.4	27.1	-2.5
2010	1.6	14.3	4.2

Also shown on the chart for comparison, annual change of the S&P 500 in % and the growth rate of the GDP in % (all goods and services produced within the United States).

Keeping Ahead of Inflation

Over this 30-year period, S&P 500 average annual price return adjusted for inflation was 9.14%. Average GDP growth, also adjusted for inflation, was 5.95%. Over the same 30-year period, $1 would have grown to $9.91 adjusted for inflation. This is a dramatic demonstration that modeling outcomes using Fed targeted inflation rates of 2%-3% is often woefully inadequate for planning particularly over shorter terms. Such a model using 3% annual inflation rate would have grown $1 over a 30-year period to $2.43 instead of the actual $9.91. So the lesson here is that the S&P 500 index, invested in and left alone, will stay well ahead of inflation and is your ticket to a secure retirement.

A note must be inserted regarding the casual use of the term S&P 500 index. The index is generally felt to be a proxy for the broader market made up of well over 10,000 stocks. If someone asks: "What did the market do today?" The answer is found by looking at the S&P 500. Sometimes the Dow 30 (Dow-Jones Average) is cited but the S&P 500 is more universal for the entire market.

The index itself is composed of 500 common stocks of what are felt to be the world's most prominent corporations with a bias toward American companies. The tenure on the S&P 500 list has dropped to 18 years, down from about 60-years during the 1950s. Companies come and go and only the most prominent are added to the index. When their fortunes fall, they are replaced with new entrants. But there are some companies that have been in the index for many, many years and others that only stay a few years. Over the last ten-years, half of the index has been changed.

John Bogle, referred to at other points in this book, reportedly calculated the long-range difference in total return (with dividends) and price return (without dividends) of the S&P 500. According to Bogle, the difference over an 81-year period (1926 to 2007) between total return and price return was annually 10.4% vs. 6.1%. To put that into perspective, a $10,000 investment would have had a total return of $33,100,000 whereas the price return would have been only $1,200,000. Of course the actual ownership results would have been identical since in a price return scenario, the investor is receiving dividends as they are distributed, just not reinvesting them. But it is "Total Return" and not "Price Return" that tells the whole story. The point is that the difference between total return and price return can be substantial and most return data as well as charts are price return only.

Another analysis of the S&P 500 over 80 years (1930-2010) found total return to be 9.4% and price return to be 5.2%. In both cases, over a span of 80 years the difference was about 4%. See chart below.

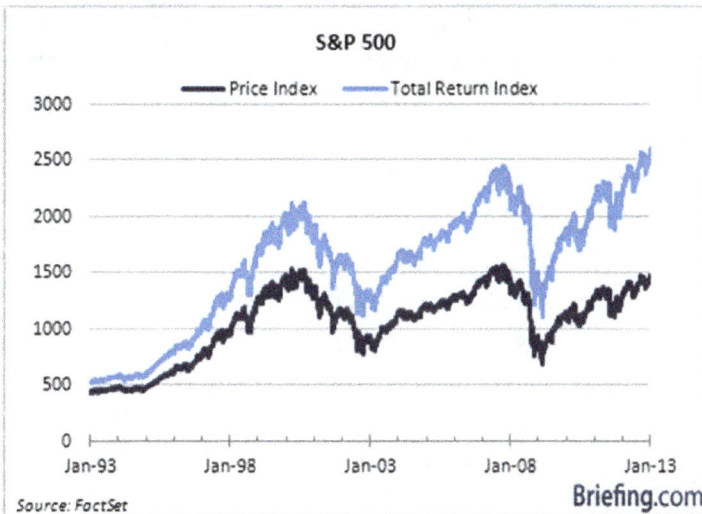

The use of estimating figures over long periods like 80 years may imply that markets are perfectly cyclical with a regular and predictable inhalation and exhalation of the business cycle, but this is misleading; there are secular movements, which are stock price conditions or trends that last for 10 years or more. So be careful in making assumptions over shorter periods or in thinking that all 80-year periods are pretty much the same; they are not. But regular periodic investments made from outside of the market, from salary or income for example, will smooth cyclical and secular effects. Cash flows are different from cash lumps.

Also be warned about stock charts, they typically show price return only and miss the heavy contribution of dividends. This can lead investors to believe that non-dividend paying stocks are performing equally with dividend paying stocks.

In other parts of this book, I refer to the seminal investment book, *A Random Walk Down Wall Street* by Dr. Burton Malkiel. Malkiel draws the conclusion that since the market is entirely random, it is all but impossible to beat, and the best course is to just invest in the S&P 500 index, which essentially is the market.

Mortgages and Inflation

Houses, particularly homes used as everyday residences, offer an exceptional way to harness the power of the market, leverage and inflation. This is because a house purchase is first of all, highly leveraged when people typically put down only 10% to 25% of the current value of the house. Next a house purchase is a transaction that takes place over a long period and possesses characteristics of both floating and fixed-rate instruments. In an inflationary environment, floating assets rise with inflation while fixed assets get crushed by inflation.

As has already been stated, target annual inflation in the U.S. typically ranges between 2% and 3%. Typically inflation is measured from the Consumer Price Index (CPI) that measure the change in price from a typical family market basket. But a house mortgage payment makes up a big chunk of the family budget and that will get fixed with a house purchase and not rise with inflation. So a homeowner's CPI, with a level mortgage payment, will be lower than a renter's, for instance, in an inflationary period.

Also the original mortgage amount remains fixed meaning the bank's asset, your mortgage, is fixed and will erode with time taking the mortgage payment down with it. In the meantime the house will float with inflation and may well appreciate a point or two above inflation. A lot depends on the individual house.

So when a typical 30-year mortgage is paid up, inflation has crushed the mortgage payments while more than doubling the value of the house. So what starts out on day one at parity, equity in house equaling the down payment plus loan, becomes after 30-years, house value at twice the acquisition cost and mortgage payment at half the original value. Plus you can live in it.

To really do this analysis one would have to calculate the present value of all the mortgage payments over a 30-year period and compare that with the present estimated value of the house. That calculation is routine, but beyond the scope of this book.

Rule of 72

One very useful rule in assessing the dual role of inflation, that of inflating values of floating assets and crushing values of fixed assets, is the Rule of 72. According to this rule, a rate of inflation or return may be divided into 72 and the result will be the number of years for the asset to double in value from inflation or get cut-in half from inflation. At an annualized inflation rate of 3%, a Mortgage will be cut in half every 72/3=24 years. A house appreciating at 4% would double in value every 72/4=18 years.

Buy Low; Sell High

But also keep in mind, that because house values float with the market, they are subject to upward and downward market forces, so before buying, take the market pulse and be careful about buying during market highs. Perhaps the best way to gauge buying opportunity in the housing market is to look at mortgage rates. Like any product, the price of money is metered to reconcile supply with demand. If there is high demand for money, usually fueled by a housing boom, mortgage rates rise, signaling a seller's market. If the housing market slumps, signaled by banks practically giving money away, housing prices are in the tank, making a buyer's market. If prevailing rates are around 5% or lower, it probably signals a market low and a good time to buy. If mortgage rates are up around 8% or higher, it probably signals housing prices are too high, and it is better to wait. So while using the bank's fixed money to buy a floating asset is fundamentally a good strategy, it does require refinement in purchasing a generally appreciating property at a reasonable price. Unwise purchases can defeat much of the benefit of locking in a fixed rate. Also keep in mind that much of the value in a real estate property is the land that if in a neutral location will appreciate ahead of inflation. The house on the land will also appreciate, but at the expense of ongoing maintenance and upgrading.

Inflation and the Public Debt

To provide another perspective on inflation, at an average annual inflation rate of 4.2% between 1946 and 1955, 40% of the U.S. public debt incurred to finance U.S. military operations during WWII was inflated away – 40% gone, disappeared. So staying on the right side of the inflation fight is elemental to the subject of investing and is the core reason to invest in the first place. Investing to stay ahead of inflation by buying a house is only the start of an inflation fighting program. Next up is investing in good companies. Like houses, the price of stock in a good company will keep pace with inflation, because the company will price its products to stay ahead of inflation – this is a requirement for survival, like eating the next meal.

Bonds

Sometimes you hear that investing in companies is dangerous and the best investment is in bonds. Such advocates also point out that buying company bonds is safer than buying company stock because eventually the bond must be repaid. But for a moment, let's look at another seminal work on the subject of investing, *Security Analysis,* first published in 1934 by

Benjamin Graham with David Dodd.

Graham and Dodd make the point that bonds are no safer than stocks because if the company closes, bondholders line up behind creditors and usually a company that closes is so far in debt that not even the creditors will be paid. In the meantime the bondholder closed off for themselves any possibility of cashing in had the company become successful. So the lesson Graham and Dodd wish to impart is this: Safety is not in the asset class -- stock or bond -- but in the soundness of the business issuing the security. Graham and Dodd point this out for another reason and that is they are presenting stock analysis and not bond analysis, for the very reason that bonds are generally not inflation fighters. For Graham and Dodd, keeping ahead of inflation is essential or you will find yourself paying 46¢ in postage from a drawer stocked with 18¢ stamps.

The Non-Safety of Bonds

Let's look at how the bond market works. A bond is a loan instrument that usually describes the amount of loan called the "face value," term of loan, and interest rate, usually called "coupon." Bonds are issued by institutions needing to borrow money for a variety of reasons, always central to the borrower's operations. Companies borrow to finance expansion, which may be done by issuing stock or bonds. If the company feels their stock is overpriced in the market, they will more than likely issue more stock, feeling they are getting a larger inflow of cash for giving up a smaller portion of ownership. If they feel the stock price is too low, they will issue debt in the form of bonds. In all cases, companies will balance their financing needs with both stocks and bonds in what is called "Capital Structure."

Because stock doesn't have to be paid back, companies are relieved of the burden of interest payments, though by sacrificing ownership. Debt does not require giving up ownership and because it uses other people's money as a lever to grow the business, it is called "leverage." Companies sometimes get into trouble by over leveraging in a capital structure that takes on too much debt and burdens the company with interest payments they struggle to make. Investors routinely look at capital structure in evaluating the safety of an investment; what they look at is the "Debt/Equity" ratio and sometimes the "Quick Ratio," which tells them the ability of the company to pay its debts, even in a downturn in business. If a company can't pay its bills, it either goes into liquidation or saves itself at a very high price.

Investors can save themselves the trouble of calculating debt/equity ratios from company annual or quarterly reports just by visiting the websites of bond rating agencies like Moody's, Fitch, and S&P. These agencies have not agreed on a code, so you will be faced with a cascading array of letters and numbers that defies easy memorization except by serial bond buyers. A rule-of-thumb is that all "A" rated bonds are called "investment grade," with AAA or Aaa having the highest rating. Triple "B" rated bonds are also investment grade. Double "B" marks the divide into the lower rungs of "non-investment" grade all the way down to single "B" which are labeled "highly speculative." This is "junk bond" territory. Then "C" ratings are extremely speculative and "D" ratings usually mean the bonds are in default. In any case on "A" rated companies you need not concern yourself with debt/equity ratios.

Other debt issuers are governments: state governments for state operations and to finance colleges, roads and other public works. Cities also issue debt for public works projects. State and city debt is called municipal debt, and the bonds issued are called municipal bonds or simply "Munis." Champions of Muni bonds argue that they are safe because the issuer has taxing authority. The "safest" of all financial instruments are thought to be debt instruments issued by the U.S. federal government, called "Treasuries." Here, the safety comes from not only taxing authority, but printing authority as well. At some point, of course, taxing and printing authority becomes meaningless, as it did in the hyperinflation experienced in Germany after WWI. The real source of soundness and safety is the confidence of the population in its national currency. Also keep in mind that the federal debt that got inflated away after WWII had two sides: the federal government paying off the debt and the bond holders seeing their face value losing purchasing power while they collected their very "safe" coupon.

The Bond Market

As is clear to any beginning investor, the stock market offers liquidity, which is the opportunity to convert stock shares into cash at any time. But what about cashing in bonds before their term is up? For that, there is a bond market. But as stocks are priced directly because they don't pay interest, bonds are priced according to the interest they pay rather than only their face value. This is called "yield" and measures the value of the bond in terms of interest payments expected over the remaining life of the bond. With a bond, the holder of the bond, even when not the original owner, will get back the face value of the bond when the term is up and the bond matures. So in buying and selling bonds, the market price has to be adjusted to reflect the value of the interest it will earn over its remaining life (also called term) in addition to its face value.

A typical bond has a face value of $1,000 and is issued with an interest rate, called coupon. The interest rate is determined by several factors but the most important is marketability, that is how much interest the institution has to pay to borrow money from the public. As you might imagine, the relative safety of Treasuries means that the U.S. government can pay a lower interest rate than a company that perhaps might have to pay very high interest to entice a risk-averse lender. Also, once the bond is issued, conditions change.

The Federal Reserve may raise interest rates to cool the economy, and suddenly the interest rate your bond pays is not all that great. Perhaps in irritation you decide to sell the bond and you are offered $980 instead of the $1,000 you paid for it just the day before. What's going on? You haven't received any interest payments yet and already you lost 2% of your investment. The reason is that because interest rates are now higher, the price of your bond has to be reduced to produce the same yield as a new bond with the higher coupon. So the market calculates the interest payments over the remaining term of the bond and makes an adjustment to the price in order equalize yield. And the longer the term of the bond, the greater the adjustment must be to reflect the difference in yield over a longer period.

This is very frustrating for people who just bought a bond because it was "safe." In addition, bond prices also reflect risk and as the perception of risk changes toward a particular issue, price is adjusted up or down to adjust yield to the new understanding of the soundness of the issue. These pricing issues are crucial to understanding bonds and raising aware-ness among new investors of the relative non-safety of bonds. U.S. government "bills" are sold at a discount and then pay off at a quicker maturity and may be thought of as a "zero-coupon" instruments. U.S. Series EE Savings Bonds are purchased at a discount and pay off full face value at maturity and are the classic zero-coupon bond. All bonds all the time are priced to produce a market yield, and the only time face value counts is when a new bond is issued and when it matures. Everything in between those two points is at the fickleness of interest rates and the market.

On the next page is a table of yields for various Treasury bills, notes and bonds and Munis. What you are seeing is how risk is priced. The short-term Treasury T-Bills have almost no risk and so pay almost nothing. As the term extends out to 30-years the spectre of inflation plays a role ramping up interest rates. Munis are not risk-free and so command and interest premium.

Security	Yield
1-month T-bill	-0.01
6-month T-bill	0.03
2-year T-note	0.24
5-year T-note	0.81
10-year T-note	1.85
30-year T-bond	2.86
Municipal bonds	4.90

The yield spread between the Treasury bond and the muni bond is a measurement of the bond market's appetite for risk. In this case, that appetite is low because the spread is quite wide and people are willing to lose money -0.01% for the security of a Treasury or T-bill. That is a very low tolerance for risk.

The real safety issue with bonds is what happens over time. Bonds are called fixed-income instruments and as such, the income they produce is fixed. As has just been illustrated, however, what is not fixed is the value of the bond during its term. The value fluctuates driven by the interest rate environment it lives in, as well as the attractiveness of the issue relative to other lending opportunities. At maturity however, regardless of the prevailing interest rates or the perceived attractiveness of the issue, the bondholder gets full face value. This is what is meant by safety in bonds. You will always get your money back if the borrower is solvent.

But that maturity will be at some future date, giving inflation a chance to eat away at the purchasing power of your bond redemption. If you are holding a 30-year Treasury -- the "Long Bond" -- you are looking at getting back half your original purchasing power and that is during "normal" inflation – inflation is rarely "normal." But there are exceptions. In 1981 U.S. Treasury interest rates for the 10-year bond peaked at over 15%. I presume the 30-year bond was paying that or more, so having a "riskless" asset that locked-in a 15% coupon for 30 years would have not only provided a very nice income, but also as interest rates declined, holders of a 30-year bond would have seen their bond's value rise in the secondary bond market as the bonds were re-priced on yield. Thirty years later, toward the end of 2011, the 10-year bond coupon was around 2%. So in peak interest rate environments, the Treasury Long-Bond is worth investigating.

So who would buy bonds? Typically wealthy people who are happy to pay the inflation premium, knowing their money will be there when they need it. Some of the wealthiest people purchase munis, because they are sheltered from federal taxes, and they can save considerable money in the tax avoidance. In addition, interest from U.S. Treasury securities are exempt from state and local tax. Also remember the wealthy don't have to cash in their bonds prematurely because they need money – they keep their bonds for the full term and always collect the face value. And for the wealthy, that tax avoidance may make up some or a lot of the inflation premium.

But for the non-wealthy, bonds are not a good idea. Although the "safety" of bonds can never be matched, you can come close with a broadly diversified stock portfolio of carefully selected companies, or as Burton Malkiel suggests, just buy the S&P 500 index.

My suggestion is to buy the individual stocks in the Dow 30, because the 30 top stocks are much more selective than the top 500 stocks of the S&P 500 and by owning the Dow 30, you will accumulate dividend earnings and may even experience stock splits, most of which are not captured in mutual fund ownership. Or, if your wish, don't restrict yourself to U.S. companies; look at a subset of the 100 greatest global corporations (listed in chapter 12).

What I have not covered in this section is the use of bonds for capital gain. Although Malkiel suggests just buying the S&P 500, he does acknowledge there are actors who, perhaps by instinct, can consistently outperform the broader market. But these people are both hard to find and perhaps harder to identify. This is also the case with bonds. There are people who through diligent study of capital structure and other factors can consistently forecast the growing attractiveness of some bonds and are able to capture a capital gain from a bond's appreciating market price. It would be very unlikely, however, that a retail investor would encounter such an actor and that such an actor would be willing to take on a retail account. For one thing just the liability exposure would discourage the most intrepid bond analyst. Sophisticated investors take their lumps; but retail investors have been known to sue or their lawyers sue on their behalf.

Securitization of Mortgages

In my training to become a stock broker I had to study mortgage backed securities (bonds) that were called CMOs, Collateralized Mortgage Obligations, or CDOs (Collateralized Debt Obligations). These were baskets of homeowner mortgages bundled up into notes which could be sold like bonds that would pay interest as homeowners made their monthly mortgage payments. The process of aggregating many mortgages into one security is called "securitization," and the term "collateralized" refers to the fact that the notes were backed by collateral, in this case, houses. If the homeowner defaulted, you got a house, or a piece of a house.

Now not all mortgages are of equal quality. Some are for loans that are almost certain to be paid off and others are for sub-prime mortgages that as it turned out had little chance of getting paid off. These disparities were separated into what are called tranches, allowing investors some menu options with differing risk/reward characteristics. They were all sold as collateralized so the inference was that they were backed up by hard assets, and therefore "safe." As the housing market, in response to extraordinarily low interest rates (incidentally managed by the Fed, led by the "Maestro," Alan Greenspan, who no longer goes by that moniker), advanced, it eventually went into overdrive and then into orbit. CMOs/CDOs followed the housing market skyward and of course it was all unsustainable. But as in the Madoff case, people kept buying. This is characteristic of all bubbles -- no matter how crazy, people will fight to get in on it.

In the midst of this madness there was one cool customer, John Paulson of Paulson & Co., a hedge fund. Paulson not only felt the housing market was in orbit, he decided to do something about it. And this will give a real flavor of who it is you are betting against in the market. Paulson went to Goldman Sachs, the most prestigious broker/dealer on Wall Street, and asked to either help out with the securitization or examine the securitization of some of the CDOs being assembled. Paulson then took a short position on some selected CDOs he felt from his examination had a likelihood of collapsing, CDOs backed up with large sub-prime mortgages of highly leveraged homeowners. These same CDOs were then sold to Goldman customers, but without the provenance of their securitization or the short side of their trade, held by John Paulson.

The housing market did eventually collapse, which was not a surprise to many, except maybe to Jamie Dimon of Chase and a few other Wall Street CEOs, who defended themselves in Congressional hearings with the defense that the popping of the housing bubble could not have been anticipated. But when housing collapsed, John Paulson closed his open position for a cool profit of $1 to $3.7 billion depending on the report.

Regardless of what you think of Goldman or Paulson, the fact is that looking beyond an overheated market to a strategy for cashing in on it is closer to investment, as opposed to the buying of the CDOs by presumably shrewd Goldman clients who apparently couldn't think beyond the next market close. Investment is thinking and that always means longer-range thinking than is current in the market. And that comes from listening to market noise only for the purpose of detecting the next bubble to short, or as John Maynard Keynes stated, "Don't look at the stocks, look at the people looking at the stocks." If you don't want to go short, and I never have, then ignore the financial media, go into your room, close the door, sit down, and think about what is going on around you, what trends are emerging. That is the beginning of investment.

There are other hedge funds that obtain capital gain like returns in the bond market, but, they are in it for the gain and not the coupon. A post-script is in order in Paulson's case, however. Apparently John Paulson lost a big bet on Sino-Forest after the mortgage triumph. Rumor puts the loss at around $500 million. Paulson still is a winner, but the market is a challenge for him as for anyone else. *The New York Times* on October 23, 2012, however, reported that John Paulson of Paulson & Co., made a $100 million gift to the Central Park Conservancy of New York City. As a young child the park had been an important destination for Paulson and he lamented the graffiti and poor maintenance that had changed the experience. He wanted to change the park back to the place of refreshment it had been in his youth and he had the money to put up $100 million. So maybe the market is a challenge for Paulson, but a manageable challenge.

As you accumulate assets, it won't be long before you learn there is no foolproof place to put your money such that in 30 or 40 years, it will be there when you need it. If you put your money in bonds it will be ravaged by inflation, and if you put your money in stocks, it may be ravaged by market forces.

Given this choice, you must choose stocks, because the risk of loss in stocks is a probability between 100% and 0%. The probability of loss in bonds to inflation is nearly 100%. In both cases the loss need not be total, but in stocks, there is the potential for gain, and the possibility for gain over and above inflation. In fact the likeliest outcome for stocks, if left alone, is the inflation-trouncing result of the broader market, the same market you and 50 million American households work and shop in.

Remember, as you survey the very uncertain landscape called investment in common stocks, the most certain outcome in all of the myriads of moving parts is inflation. Inflation is something you can assign an almost 100% probability to.

Behavioral Finance

Amos Nathan Tversky and Daniel Kahneman collaborated on a field of study that may be thought of as the risk-averse behavior of people or perhaps called "Prospect Theory," explaining irrational human economic choices. One finding was that people feel greater pain in loss than euphoria in gain. This means effort at avoiding of pain will be greater than effort directed toward gain. It also means people will give outsized attention to risk and miss an equal and offsetting research into gain. This may also explain why stock prices rise more slowly than they fall. When a stock is perceived to be a loser, it is dumped in totality. When a stock is perceived to be a winner, it will be purchased in stages.

This bias toward loss is healthy, but is does at the same time obstruct a clear conception of the risk of ownership of common stocks. I will state unequivocally that despite probabilities that capture a very wide spectrum of results, *there is nothing safer than the ownership of a well-diversified portfolio of the common stocks of the world's great corporations.* And if an investor can cite losses from their ownership, it is because they were sold prematurely in what is inevitably panic selling in response to Tversky and Kahneman's finding of the overarching pain of loss. Panic selling is the act of acting irrationally in what Tversky and Kahneman identified as loss bias – fear of loss driving out all thought of the possibility of gain in a lopsided assessment of risk. As one wag once stated, risk is not in the market, it is between the ears of the investor.

Chapter 2: Inflation and Shifts in GDP

To put the purchase of common stocks into perspective, think of all the purchases you have made over the years. Consider marriage, which is a purchase decision of sorts. How many marriages wind up in divorce? Or of all the car purchases you have made, how many would you repeat? How many times have you walked out of a restaurant feeling the money was well spent? And what about all those clothes hanging in your closet that no longer fit -- were they enduring purchases? Now pick out a dozen major U.S. corporations and look at their appreciating stock prices over the last 10 or 20 years, and compare how those purchases would have worked out for you compared with the purchases you did make. There you will find the answer to your question; how risky are common stocks? The Tversky-Kahneman pain bias should then be directed not at buying stocks but at the act of refraining from buying stocks. That is where the real loss lies – what could have been but isn't.

There is one other dimension to this unsupported fear of purchasing common stocks, and that is the exertions of the professional investment community known as Wall Street. The fact is that the selection of common stocks can be done by anybody by just experiencing the everyday life of shopping, using shopped for products, reading the daily newspaper, and just generally remaining alert to investment candidates from everyday life experiences. Wall Street players would have you believe that stocks are dangerous, and that it is only by opening an account at their office and following the advice on what stocks to buy from their "research" departments that one can avoid catastrophic loss. How can I pop this balloon? Well, the best way is to point out that the people actually determining the future course of a company, that is, the employees and their customers, aren't even aware and don't even care what the Wall Street research is and for one reason, the "research" will be obsolete in another few months. It is not research that is cranked out by Wall Street; it is sales fodder. So given the scaremongering of Wall Street, for your investment health it is best to ignore Wall Street altogether.

You are investing in people's natural proclivity to multiply, and financing that multiplication by daily labor that creates value for everybody.

The subject of this chapter has been inflation. The core concept is that inflation is a good thing if you are on the right side of it, and a wealth killer if you are on the wrong side. The simplest and perhaps most effective strategy is buying the common stocks of companies that make up the Dow 30, or a subset of the S&P 500, or a subset of the greatest 100 global corporations. To the popular expression "The only certain things in life are death and taxes" you might well add "...and inflation."

Common stocks of the great global corporations float on a sea of inflation. Owning those stocks keeps you ahead of inflation.

POSTSCRIPT:

The S&P 500 index is the default index used as a stand-in for the broader market because it has been tracked since 1957, is the most highly tracked index, is comprised of 500 of the most notable global corporations that trade in USA markets, contains both "value" and "growth" stocks and is slow changing.

If one does not want to select individual stocks from the Dow 30, the S&P 500 or the S&P 500 High-Quality index, then investing in several indices besides the S&P 500 would be the more opportunistic thing to do. But be aware, the S&P 500 can be tracked back to 1957, the Russell indices only go back to 1983. Beating the S&P 500 over 50 years must still be demonstrated.

The table below includes the market crash of 2008, five years ago. If one is just beginning to invest in an index fund, than you will be missing the 2008 market crash in your data, making much of the data in the accompanying table not very relevant.

Market Indices as of 6/30/2013				
INDEX	12-Mo	3-Year	5-Year	10-Year
T-Bills	0.11	0.11	0.29	1.72
S&P 500 Total Return	20.60	18.43	7.00	7.29
Dow Jones Industrial Av.	22.36	17.07	9.43	8.04
Russell 1000 Growth	17.05	18.66	7.47	7.39
Russell 1000 Value	25.32	18.49	6.67	7.78
Russell Midcap	25.39	19.50	8.27	10.64
Russell Midcap Growth	22.89	19.51	7.61	9.93
Russell Midcap Value	27.64	19.50	8.86	10.91
Russell 2000	24.20	18.65	8.76	9.52
Russell 2000 Growth	23.66	19.93	8.87	9.61
Russell 2000 Value	24.75	17.31	8.59	9.29
MSCI International	17.61	9.95	-0.34	8.35
MSCI Emerging Markets	3.23	3.71	-0.11	14.01
DJ Wilshire Real Estate	8.38	18.28	7.03	10.87

Inside the Machine   Ben Aronson 2010
Oil on panel, 50 x 40 inches   Tibor de Nagy Gallery

Chapter 3
Investing vs. Gambling

"Good judgment comes from experience.
Experience comes from bad judgment."
A 13th century aphorism

When most people are confronted with the word "investment" they think of a sophisticated, well-heeled gentleman making a quiet phone call to his broker and putting in an order based on savvy judgment on information largely inaccessible to the general public. That image may be useful for a number of reasons, most urgently because this is the gentleman you are betting against every time you place an order. The image is incorrect, however, if we are speaking about investment broadly. Investment in its broadest meaning is any bet that opens a position to be closed at some future time, at buyer discretion, with the expectation of profit. Sometimes the life of an investment is very short, minutes for day-traders, or very long, as in the case of a house purchase that is left to a beneficiary in a will. Also, investment is an activity engaged in by people in all walks of life.

Before proceeding with a discussion on investment, it is worth taking a short detour to address the perennial question; What is the difference between gambling and investing? Gambling is a formal contract of a position taken on one of many or one of two possible outcomes on an event with a definite and foreseeable decision point, which may be in a minute or two, or perhaps a year or more, but always within a single cycle. In other words, gambling is an event taken during a period where further outside influences are not expected, or if they do, the wager is voided. An example is a wager placed on a horse race; if one of the horses withdraws from the race, the bet may be voided.

Gambling by and large is a single-event phenomenon in which there is perceived total visibility to the end result. Investment is also a gamble, but undertaken for a period that may involve several cycles or an indeterminate number of cycles, but in all cases, will have no set future decision point and very little visibility into that future. A horse race or a presidential election are examples of wagering opportunities over single cycles with finite periods and with definite and discrete outcomes. Betting on a race horse in a single race is gambling; buying the race horse instead is investing. In betting there is visibility into the outcome and – before that outcome -- a difference of opinion in how it will play out. In investment there is no visibility, there is only judgment, but judgment perhaps on numerous variables.

Investment

Investment could be defined as what people do with excess money they don't need right away, but people sometimes borrow money to make investments, as in getting a loan to buy a house or buying stock on margin. So investment money is not always so discretionary, but it may have been at the beginning of civilization when investment started. Investment may have started with trade, where an individual had to buy a quantity of goods to be transported some distance and hopefully sold at a profit. And since trade goods are ubiquitous we can say that investment is ubiquitous and engaged in by all people pretty much all the time. This is not to be confused however, with money used to buy wasting assets, like cars, that will only lose value over time. That is consumption and not investment, although it may entail just as much research and thought. So investment has three key dimensions: opening a position that will be closed at a future time; expectation of profit; and discretion over when the position will be closed.

This definition is so broad that it admits almost all human activity and does little to help focus a beginning investor on those rules that might offer guidance. A problem is that the investor is then vulnerable to everything that is ever printed and broadcast by not only the financial media but also the popular media. How do you deal with all this information? I think it is useful right at the outset to point out that our sophisticated investor quietly calling his broker to enter a trade has absolutely no structural advantage over the beginning investor and over a lifetime will turn in a performance that will lag that of grandma, who doesn't give two hoots about the market. In other words, effort is not a prerequisite for success. And I would go further and state that *it is not the opening of the position that determines success, but the closing of the position.* This is important because invariably people agonize over making investment decisions, but sell without any thought at all.

My experience has been that most losses occur due to

premature closing of a position, thus placing the emphasis not only on what position is opened but also the process for closing it. So to complete this counterintuitive rule, don't be so concerned with what you buy; focus your attention on restraining yourself from closing a position before it has become profitable. And since the market will always rise over time, waiting is often the best action to take, something that grandma can do a lot better that our sophisticated investor talking to his broker. Remember, when you are in the market, there are two moving parts: the market and you. If you use a broker, there are three moving parts. In general, and particularly in investment, the fewer moving parts, the better off you are. If you can restrict your investing to one moving part, the market, you will probably have no problem beating inflation provided you are diversified.

Another trait of investment that sets it apart from almost all other human activity is the education required to become a good investor. There are no fixed courses, although there are organizations that claim their course as a prerequisite to successful investment. The most notable is the Chartered Financial Analyst (CFA) Institute, which holds out their CFA designation as a coveted and crucial knowledge set. Indeed, the CFA is devoutly to be wished for, but is well beyond the capabilities of most investors and it falls short of the life experiences needed to perfect an investment activity. In short, investment goes far beyond the technical training offered by the CFA Institute or any other formal program, and will draw upon all experience the investor has ever had. This is because when all is said and done, the prescription of Helmuth von Moltke about war will prevail: the only plan you will ever have is whether or not to go to war, because once in a war, everything is chaos and all prior plans are out the window. Or to quote the prizefighter Mike Tyson: *"Everybody has a plan until they get punched in the face."*

This is true in investment as well, because once committed

to a position, control over the investment is lost to fortune, and most inaccessible fortune at that, future fortune. So as per von Moltke and Mike Tyson, only open investment positions you mean to hold regardless of changing transient conditions. The challenge of investment is that there are no rules, although investors will spend a lifetime looking for them. So the first rule is that there are no rules, and the practical application of this lesson is to instruct investors to focus on what they have invested in to the exclusion of all other investments. If you are invested in XYZ Company, then for you, that should be the only stock in the universe.

As has already been mentioned, Burton Malkiel, a finance professor at Princeton University, wrote a book which is one of the mainstays of the investment world, *A Random Walk Down Wall Street*. Burton Malkiel believes that market outcomes are totally random and therefore cannot be gamed, except by a very few talented individuals who typically do not hold themselves out to be investment professionals serving the public, presumably because they are content serving themselves. A very few may serve the public, but the public's ability to identify such actors is non-existent, or very rare.

Burton Malkiel developed his thesis by investigating the "efficient market" theory of open and free public markets where all are equally empowered by the same information. According to this theory, where information is freely available the market becomes very efficient at pricing and very quick also, removing for the most part any bargains because stock price incorporates all available information.

In a graduate class in finance at an Ivy League business school, I witnessed a highly respected professor stating that the stock market was a perfect market because of the free flow of information. This caused some murmuring among the students in the class, but it quickly died down as it was digested into rote acceptance. This gives us another dimension to add to the process of investment, which already includes 1) opening a position that will be closed at a future time, and 2) expectation of profit. This added dimension is the notion that the stock is accurately priced. It is true that price contains all available information, but that information is a poor predictor of the future, as Burton Malkiel affirms, and the future will ultimately determine value and therefore price (recall our definition for investment including the aspect of time, over several or more cycles) reducing to almost zero an investor's future view.

In addition, how the market prices a stock is worth noting. The market is forward looking, so stock price does not represent present value, but future value. The stock price is a price expected to be repaid by future earnings. How far into the future? That is an open question and may vary with the volatility of the stock in question. But when news comes out that a particular company has just won a large contract, the stock price will move up almost immediately, although the earnings from that contract are a long way off. The important thing is that the earnings are booked, and therefore certain to accrue to the owner of the stock at some future time.

The biggest investment decision people face is selecting an occupation, because an occupation will pretty much determine the life that they will live. In my case, as in the case of most people, my occupation was selected for me by an 18-year-old boy. I leave it to the reader to decide how much forward thinking went into that decision. The next big investment is marriage, and again a crucial life decision often left to whims of youth. Some may object to citing occupational and matrimonial choices as investments, but they are -- and done without any formal training.

Now why is it that the two most crucial decisions people face are not supported with any formal training? The reason is undoubtedly because these decisions are so complex and far reaching that any training at all would only serve to obstruct rather than inform. These decisions rise up from the total experience of the individual and are difficult to qualify in any way as due to particular experiences or influences – they touch on too many points. And to suggest that a rigorous research effort should be undertaken before making these decisions is laughable, because you couldn't do enough research to approach the intelligence actually used. When mental organization is overwhelmed, intuition kicks in, using the totality of the mind's experience to organize thought and emotion into a decision. And it is at the intersection of organized thought and intuition where investment occurs.

(It might be noted that a UCLA professor named Lloyd Shapley has taken on the study of matrimony as game theory in what is called the "Stable Marriage Problem.")

Wall Street vs. Investment

As I will describe repeatedly in this book, investment has been hijacked by an investment industry that holds itself to be investment professionals, able to apply highly sophisticated measures to arrive at investment selections that are both successful and beyond the ability of the untrained and unconnected. This then gives rise to a media industry that purports to educate the individual to make investment decisions "like the pros." All the layman has to do is subscribe to the papers, the magazines, the newsletters, and tune in on all the Wall Street chatter, and then, and only then, does the casual investor have any chance at all at "successful" investment. The thinness of this proposition can be seen in the numbers, with the explosion of online "do-it-yourself" investment websites, myriads of stock investors have arrived at their screens mostly driven by the realization that the Wall Street wizards are more "Wizard of Oz."

The frantic nature of Wall Street culture and media may be dated from the panic of 1907. In 1896 Charles Dow had begun publishing the Dow Jones industrial average by adding up the closing prices of twelve stocks and dividing by twelve, with the intention that consulting the average every few months and serving as a useful guide to stock market sentiment. Then the panic of 1907 hit and grew into a national run on the banks and, of course, mass hysteria. The Dow Jones average then became the default pulse of the return of confidence and began to be consulted daily if not hourly. Since that time, the "pulse" of the market is taken every moment and given such respect that those not plugged in feel at a disadvantage. That moment-by-moment market movements are in any way connected with rational investment has been one of the great frauds of Wall Street. Most "civilians" (those with no connection to Wall Street) feel that without a broker they have no access to the investment potential of common stocks. The thesis of this book is to unravel that ball of yarn.

Doing so, however, does not provide direction, only a cautionary tale of what to avoid. I point people toward Burton Malkiel's book, but it, like virtually every book on investment I have ever read, *deals only with the one moving part, the market.* My intention in this book is to deal more thoroughly with the other two moving parts: the investor and the investor's advisor.

The Investor in Investment

I have devoted a chapter to the investment profession so will spend the remainder of this chapter on the moving part that is the most difficult to control, the investor. Fortunately the problem is a simple one, keeping the needle stable somewhere between euphoria and panic. Euphoria is that state of blindness experienced by people who are discovering that stock positions taken have appreciated beyond their wildest dreams, signaling a need to buy more with the expectation of even greater riches. This is a very frequent tale and nobody is immune from it, as evidenced by the many bubbles in the history of investment, perhaps first being recorded in the tulip mania of 1637.

My favorite witness to euphoric bubbles is the most learned and revered scientist Sir Isaac Newton. During the South Sea bubble, Sir Isaac invested and when he thought that South Sea

Company stock value had reached a reasonable level, sold his holdings. But the stock kept rising in an upward spiral of euphoria. At first Sir Isaac blew off the intemperate behavior of the masses, but when the stock kept going up, he got in again not wishing to miss out on the riches. Shortly afterward the stock collapsed and he took losses. In despair Sir Isaac wrote, and this is a paraphrase, *"I can calculate the movements of the heavenly bodies, but how can I calculate the madness of men?"* What Sir Isaac conveniently leaves out is the calculation of his own contribution to the madness by buying during the euphoric period like everybody else. So if Sir Isaac, one of history's most brilliant men, not only got caught up in investment euphoria, but neglected his own contribution to the "madness," how is the ordinary investor to protect himself from the same disease? There is no vaccine for this. All are vulnerable.

Another way to think about this problem comes from the comedian George Carlin. In the 1980s there was a popular bumper sticker proclaiming the Green injunction: "Save the planet." Carlin's riff was that the Earth was going to do just fine; it was mankind that was on the planet that was in trouble. Likewise, in the investor/investment relationship keep your eye on the investor; that's usually where the problem is.

The other side of the euphoria coin also causes blindness; it is panic. Whereas euphoria causes unbridled buying, panic causes unbridled selling. Panic selling has never received the same level of criticism that attaches to euphoric buying, apparently because you get into trouble when you buy into a euphoric ascent and cease the trouble by selling out of it. This is certainly true, but it has the unhappy consequence of promoting selling as a default sign of good judgment. This is unfortunate because although in gambling where only a single-cycle event is in play selling is usually a good thing, this is not the case with investment, particularly those that extend over many cycles. In fact the opposite is true: premature selling is the leading cause of losses. How many times have you heard:

"....if only I had hung on a little longer." And there are even well publicized investors like Warren Buffett who has been quoted as saying things like, "never" is a good time to sell out a position.

The Nature of Investments

In general there are two types of assets, wasting assets and appreciating assets. Wasting assets are assets that are used up, like an oil well, or a gold mine, or a car. At some point, wells and mines run out of assets and are used up and abandoned, and cars definitely have finite lives even when not used. You should certainly sell out of those positions. But other assets are appreciating assets, like land, timber, and common stocks in some companies. Other hard assets such as commodities are generally appreciating, but due to the volatility in both supply and demand may fluctuate too dramatically to be thought of as always an appreciating asset.

One asset that is always appreciating due to the declining global supply is water. The shortage of clean potable water is increasingly becoming a global threat to agriculture and hence global security. The U.S., despite perennial shortages in the Southwest, has a plentiful supply of water in the Great Lakes, but even there, attempts to export that water to areas experiencing shortages has been blocked owing to its value to the region. So, putting the concept of investment together with appreciating assets, you might want to give serious thought to water, and then the challenge will be hanging onto that position through years of apparent inactivity. This is when gamblers are separated from investors. Gamblers will bail out without the immediate "big hit," and will miss out on the dramatic appreciation which is sure to follow. The only development that will get in the way of the successful investment in water is a scientific breakthrough, when science develops a substitute for water. Although it cannot be ruled out, it is highly unlikely. Most popular stocks are like water; if left alone, they will appreciate.

I focus on water because gold is being mined all the time. Land, as Will Rogers pointed out in his famous quote, "They ain't makin' it anymore," is a finite supply, but still not on a collision course with the expansion of humanity, and timber is a renewable resource. Water is none of those and therefore a more certain investment, but its scarcity is still far enough off to act as a litmus test for investment stamina. And if I could find one word to separate investment from what purports to be investment, that word would be "stamina." And I think if people consider the role stamina will play in their success, they will make sure going in that the investments they make will be ones on which they can employ their stamina with the least amount of discomfort.

Investment is a lot like shopping. As you wheel your shopping cart down the aisle, you make selections pretty much based on experience. Occasionally you try something new, but often because a new product failed to satisfy, you stick to the "tried and true." It is also true that in shopping for food, trial is substituted for judgment (which involves research), because trial is cheaper – there is a cost to research, a steep cost. As the products you buy become more expensive, the relative cost of the research declines and research is engaged in to try to arrive at the optimal solution, one that balances cost of research with benefit of a better performing product. But even in the most expensive purchases, research is largely dependent on "by example" anecdotal data.

For example, a house is a major investment, and a house inspection by an engineer is common, yet there are technical aspects to a house that cannot be uncovered by such an inspection, like the impending failure of a well, or sub-soil settlement. The buyer takes such risks on faith at best, and in most cases doesn't even consider the possibility. This is "by example," because these things would be checked, or considered if they had occurred in the buyer's experience or if it came out during the house hunt that such an event had occurred on another property. Of course the probability of duplicating this event on a house of interest to the buyer has not changed by the buyer learning about it, but it suddenly becomes an area of energetic research. In the end, no matter how much research is undertaken, the risk is not materially diminished. But what does occur is a demand for greater benefit to balance out the risk. The cognizant buyer simply becomes more demanding. So balancing the need for research with the cost of research is a key component of investment. If you invest in well-known companies, much of your research is done for you.

Investments need to be thought of in the same way. Is the potential reward worth the risk? Investment, however, has one characteristic that may be missing from a house – appreciation due to inflation. While land is not a wasting asset and will appreciate as long as there is a growing human population to use that land, that is not true of the house on the land, which is a wasting asset. You might argue with this by citing houses that have appreciated with time, or appreciating condominiums that have no legal claim to land, but houses appreciate at the expense of upkeep and upgrading, and condominiums occupy collectively land that appreciates. So the difference between an investment and a house is that the investment does not require upkeep and upgrade. Also, in most cases, the risk in the investment declines over time. When an investment is first made, it is usually at market prices, and markets are subject to intermittent declines that may reduce the value of the asset below acquisition price, but over time, inflation will take over, and the intermittent declines will not dip below acquisition price. The spread between acquisition price and current price will then widen even further with time, reducing risk as it goes.

Occasionally an investment will be found that will produce a smooth ride into the profit zone, but more typically the early period will be a rough and uncertain ride, causing the less committed to abandon their position, often at a loss, only to cry in despair many years later: "If only I had hung on." The purpose of this chapter is to help the investor build a practice of approaching every investment with the need not to only assess the promise of an investment, but also to assess the risks. And as Benjamin Graham pointed out, a major risk is risk of abandoning the investment due to lack of commitment owing to insufficient thought and research. Know beforehand that the function of research is not to eliminate risk, which cannot be done, but to reduce risk to below the threshold of panic that leads to preemptive selling, which is thoughtless selling.

The Role of Instinct

Among the disciplines, investing stands apart as a process rather than mastery of a body of knowledge, and part of that process must be the incorporation of losses. For one thing, an investor who always wins learns nothing. It is only in loss that lessons are drawn.

And those lessons will inevitably revolve less around the extent of the loss or the choices leading up to the loss than around managing the investor through the loss. It is only in managing and converting emotions into actionable process that losses produce their palliative effect – a better investor. After a string of victories that led to more and more war making, King Frederick of Prussia was dealt his first big loss. He wrote: "*Good fortune is often more fatal to princes than adversity: the former intoxicates them with presumption; the latter renders them circumspect and modest.*" Take a lesson from a King who wound up being called Frederick the Great.

One of the great companies is Motorola, a family run affair guided from $290 million in sales in the late 1950s to $10.8 billion about 30 years later by the son of one of the founders, Robert W. Galvin. Later when the company made a bad bet on satellite phones trumping cellular phones and lost billions of dollars, Robert Galvin used one of his stock aphorisms: "If it's intuitive, it's probably wrong." My take on Galvin's aphorisms is that intuition will inevitably play a role in decision making under uncertainty, but also that intuition must be the product of research and thought, not a flight of fancy disconnected to the decision at hand. It may even be true that a well-developed intuition is an ingredient of successful investment and the more investment experience the better the intuition. What the investor needs is development of an internal gyroscope to keep balance through what appears to be a perilous market but is in fact nothing more than the daily interplay between buyers and sellers on the thinnest information, mostly rumor.

The best way to think of risk in investment as being either forward-looking or backward-looking. Going forward, risk always looms very large, larger than life. Looking backward, we can all see that our past assessment of risks has been grossly overblown. Somehow all those huge problems in life that seemed insurmountable going forward got diluted down to nothing more than important life lessons seen in our rear-view mirrors. Perhaps the difference between successful and unsuccessful investment can be distilled down to successful investment being the product of good risk assessment, which will invariably mean watching and waiting rather than acting precipitously.

Statistics and "Distributions"

Most events may be thought of as offering a variety of possible outcomes, from upper and lower extremes of unlikely outcomes toward a more central and larger list of probable outcomes. If the distribution of outcomes follows a formula, where 95% of results occur between the two tails of a bell curve and the 95% in the middle follows a roughly 68%/27% split, we can say that the outcomes follow a "normal distribution." A normal distribution may be tall and narrow for results that are in tight pattern of agreement or low and wide for highly variable results, but the distribution will be symmetrical and always with 68% hovering around the center or the mean. It is generally felt that S&P 500 historical returns follow a normal distribution. Using statistical measures to consider the probability of outcomes often discounts almost entirely the probability of the outcome falling in one of the "tails" of the bell curve, the leading or trailing tail. It is easy to discount the tails when you look at the huge mountain of probabilities in the middle. But recent tsunami events have led to a number of books being written on the phenomenon of "fat tails," tails that are fat because they represent extreme outcomes that are probable enough to happen. Another term for this risk assessment is called Black Swan, because black swans are very rare but do occasionally occur in nature. Writers like Nassim Nicholas Taleb, who coined the term "Black Swan Theory," point out that Black Swan events occur more frequently than people realize or allow for.

Investment relies heavily on statistics, and a healthy respect for Black Swan events would be an important discipline to develop. For example, my mother's generation lived through the Great Depression, and my mother made frequent reference to the next depression. I missed the first one and blew off any notion of a second one, and then came 2008 and what to some felt like a Black Swan event. As was described earlier, John Paulson did see a coming collapse in the housing bubble and reaped about $1 billion or more profit from that prescience.

Heads of major banks, who might have been expected to have had the same prescience, when grilled by a Senate committee, defended themselves by saying the collapse of the housing market could not have been anticipated. Logic backs them up in the presumption that random events, like market outcomes, are normally distributed, and that therefore the tails are highly improbable. But Benoit B. Mandelbrot, a Yale University professor, points out that such events are much more probable than they are given credit for, and further postulated that market outcomes do not follow a normal bell curve distribution.

Shorting the real estate bubble

It may be worthwhile to examine the risk taken on by John Paulson who shorted mortgage backed securities at or near the top of the bubble. In a shorting investment, the investor sells first and then buys later to close the position. When virtually everybody was buying these securities, the contrary investor has to disassociate himself from the crowd, go against the crowd, and then gather up his winnings. The chart below is one view of the level of risk Paulson took, some would say, no risk at all. As shown, house prices followed a gently sloping upward trend and then began a dramatic climb that outstripped the growth of income. Who could possibly buy houses at those prices? That is what Paulson saw that few others on Wall Street did.

In the chart the rent line grows at around the pace of inflation but home prices tend to be volatile. Home prices begin a dramatic rise starting in 2000 and start to collapse in 2008. So that is a nearly 8-year run-up.

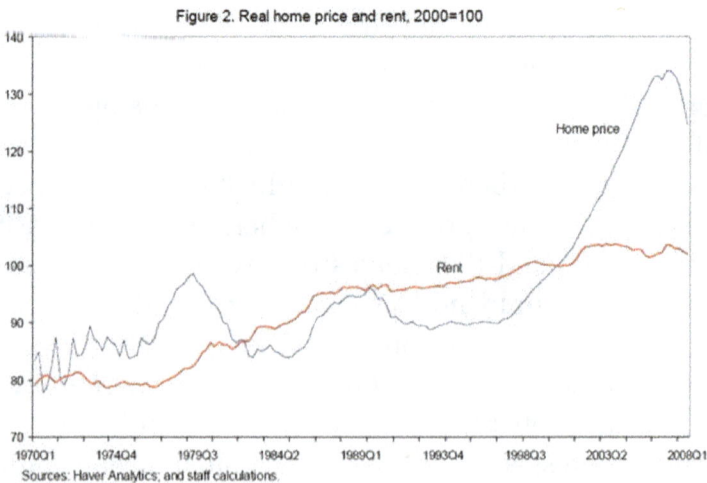

Figure 2. Real home price and rent, 2000=100

Sources: Haver Analytics; and staff calculations.

I present this as an example of investment because the outcome was not dependent on any single event and it required an assessment of fundamental value and a prognosis of what happens when market values differ widely from perceived fundamental or intrinsic values.

For a vivid example of investor assessment of intrinsic value, let's look at the internet or tech bubble that popped at the end of 1999. At that time, any company that had "dot com" in its name was literally skyrocketed into the stratosphere of stock price.

Most of the revenue generated from these companies would be derived from advertising at their websites, made popular by the essential service they would be providing for free. When contrarians began questioning the conclusions of rosy revenue forecasts based on little evidence of pricing power, those promoting the investments fought back with the reasoning that revenue could be calculated from "eyeballs," that is people who visited a site and thus were exposed to the advertising. At least the optimists had the restraint to count each visitor as one eyeball, perhaps giving rise to the "eyeball" expression. The dot com bubble eventually popped and anyone looking at the housing bubble with tech bubble experience might have reason to think the housing bubble would pop too. But just as in the tech bubble, the housing bubble had its champions as well, and one argument used was that a house was tangible and had real value, that is you could live in it, whereas sites like DrKoop.com was all smoke & mirrors.

In both the tech bubble and the housing bubble, bets in either direction could be considered "investment" in that they were not single event situations but rather based on forecasts over a longer term. However, after looking at the chart on the previous page, only the most passive investor could have been very enthusiastic about going long at the top of either market -- by going long, I mean buying rather than selling short. So investment is not necessarily successful and does not of itself increase the likelihood of success. Successful investment is actually a lonely quest pursued in the depth of the individual mind while the market gyrates in response to the clamor of the public, euphoria on the way up and panic on the way down, all attended by shouting and herding.

Most successful investment is contrarian, which is to say moving opposite to the herd, not for the sake of being different, but by way of arriving at a different view from thinking outside the Wall Street box.

The normal or not so normal distribution curve may be used to graph market outcomes for a population of investors. Imagine a normal/near normal distribution where the vertical coordinate is number of investors and the horizontal coordinate is gains, beginning with big losses at the left and finishing up with big gains to the right.

The right tail would be a small subset profiting by getting in and out early and by selling at a profit to those more to the left. The mounting demand of the greater number of investors to the left drives up price and profits for the earlier investors. But at some point, the population of new investors lags and price begins to fall, and then at some point panic may set in precipitating a dramatic fall, because price seems to always fall faster than it rises.

A "Normal Distribution" (on the next page, left) is defined by how much of the population is clustered around the center. In a "Normal" distribution, around 68% of the total population is contained within one standard deviation from the center and 95% of the population is contained within two standard deviations from the center, leaving 2½% in each tail. The "Non-Normal" distribution shown to the right could illustrate the price movement in the South Sea Bubble, gradually moving up and then tumbling in the ensuing panic. The Non-Normal curve models stock price over time in the South Sea Bubble, but it could be any bubble. A few investors profited early-on by selling to the later entrants. This is called "The Greater Fool

Theory," and the lesson it teaches is that no matter how distorted price gets, as long as there is volume and upward "lift" to stock price, you can safely buy and then soon after sell to later entrants eager to get in on the good times.

The curves below depict a "normal" distribution and a "Non-Normal" distribution where the bulk of the population is skewed to the left.

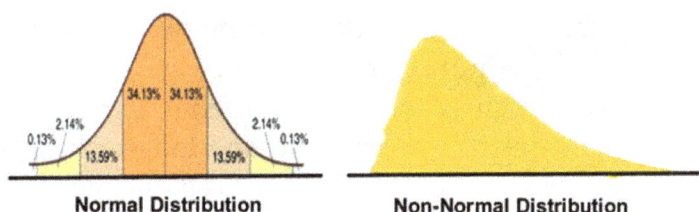

Normal Distribution   **Non-Normal Distribution**

What is intended to be illustrated in these curves of statistical outcomes is that one may invest in stocks or gamble in stocks, gambling would be getting a call from your stock broker (Financial Advisor) that the "*word on the Street*" is that Ajax Inc. is going to acquire Consolidated Widget and Consolidated presently at $40 per share is expected to hit $60, or go even higher. This is a single event wager and those who get in early may realize a quick profit by selling to those coming to the feast a little later. This is illustrated by the curve on the right. The stock price rises slowly and then collapses. But what is lost is any examination of the enterprise itself and any sense of participation in what the companies do, and so if the stock price ever goes down, it is unloaded at a loss to get out of something that was never understood in the first place.

The Role of Price in Investment

Price becomes the rationale for investment selections. You can imagine what life would be like if you made all your purchasing decisions not on utility, but on price. Imagine if you went grocery shopping with the intention of buying the Thanksgiving turkey but came home instead with hot dogs because they were on sale and a better buy. That is trading, and occasionally you will get a good buy on turkey, but only very occasionally. So as silly as that looks, it is a good approximation of much of the "liquidity" in the stock market.

The silly behavior of buying stocks for short-term gain is really more like what could be called trading rather than investing. Trading is a very robust industry and I suspect accounts for a lot of the liquidity that exists in the stock market. Trading can vary anywhere from day-trading, which may hold a position for minutes if not seconds, to owning a stock all the way up to a year, which is the term the federal government uses to discriminate between short-term and long-term capital gains. If you hold a position for one-year plus a day, your gains from that position are taxed at the much lower long-term capital gains rate, at one time about half the short-term or ordinary income tax rate.

By trading in an upwardly spiraling market, the investor is surrounded by references to the runaway market and stories of riches already realized -- mostly paper riches because if the riches had been booked, as in selling, it would signal the end of the opportunity, and investment scuttlebutt is all about opportunity, not caution. The investment that has been creating riches is generally referred to as a "good" investment. The prospect of easy riches inflames the passions, so from *thinking* about investing for riches to actually *feeling rich* makes the action part easier: Just buy and wait for the money machine to start spewing out its riches.

It is a very rare investor who uses the thinking phase to really investigate the buzz, and to even follow threads that are contrary to the bandwagon's direction. It is not that successful investment relies on thought and unsuccessful investment on emotion -- both thought and emotion are present in all gambles and investment. The difference is how familiar you are with your purchase – are you purchasing because the price is low or because it is a company you want to own?

Very few investments are smooth rides to the top, and those who haven't thought about the negative characteristics of an investment are left unprotected from the inevitable volatility as stock price responds to dislocations of supply and demand. Where a stock price has already spiraled into the stratosphere, thought would almost certainly uncover the possibility that the opportunity had already been missed and the stock should be passed up for the present.

Decision Making under Conditions of Uncertainty

I am always amused when I see ads for salespeople with the phrase, "...closers wanted." This always conjures up an image of a high pressure salesperson shaming a prospect from climbing back up the slope he has already slid down, at least in the eyes of the salesman, and succeeding frequently enough to refer to himself as a closer. This would be a pitiable thought except for the fact that the conflicted buyer may not be prone to making a better decision than the un-conflicted buyer. How many high-pressure life insurance salesmen sold policies that made the difference to a widow and her children? – A lot is my guess. We don't know the future and that is why we are conflicted. If conflict led to more thought, that would be one thing but often conflict leads to inaction. In this way, investment is not only a learned skill, but also recruits the totality of the individual to arrive at a decision always made under uncertainty. "No brainers" are seldom found in investment decisions and should be vigorously questioned when they are.

Although the distinguishing traits separating successful and unsuccessful investment occur in the thought stage, you cannot discount instinct – feeling -- that contributes to finally pulling the trigger. Sometimes we say, "it doesn't feel right," when we are still in the thought stage. This is an example of instinct being felt when nearing the transition from thought to feeling. Such anticipatory feelings may be a warning that it is too soon to enter the feeling zone, that there is time for more thought this brings up another aspect of contemplating investments: the divide between research and thought. Research is not thought; it is research and its objective is to identify issues to think about. Once enough research has been accumulated to start the thinking (processing) part, thinking can become so open-ended that it doesn't lead anywhere but rather to "paralysis by analysis." In this instance it may be better to structure the thinking toward answering some questions. One way to do this is a chart of the terrain as seen below.

In this matrix the vertical coordinate is Growth Rate and the horizontal coordinate is Market Share that translates into Profitability. Although the lower right "Dog" quadrant could conceivably be very profitable due to lack of competition in a declining market – all the competitors left already.

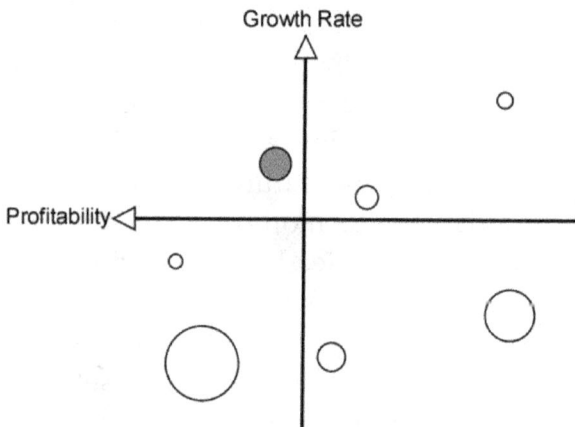

In this matrix there are seven investment candidates in the same market, presumably with only partial overlap; in other words they are not direct competitors but share a market with some or all of their product mix. This is pretty typical of markets. The largest competitor (lower left) is more profitable presumably due to larger size from larger market share trans-lating into pricing power – think of Coca-Cola commanding a premium price over generic colas.

The competitor farthest to the right is gaining market share judging from the size and position, but apparently at the cost of profits. The small competitor nearest the market leader in the lower left is doing a nice job of keeping profits up while growing the business but may not be growing fast enough to remain a force. The single competitor in the upper left quadrant is the investment I favor based on growing market share while remaining profitable. My calculation is that this mix of growth and profitability will win out. The fastest growing competitor (upper right) shows very nice growth rate but not enough profit to grow the business – in fact this company might be a candidate for shorting. This analysis is by no means exhaustive or perfect, but it does show structured thinking that can lead to actionable ends instead of paralysis and provides a structure for after-purchase monitoring – *"Is the investment playing out the way I thought it would?"* The above Figure applies to companies, but a similar matrix can be equally useful in shopping for houses or even cars. Pick three variables you feel are crucial, then plot them using two coordinates and size to illustrate how the choices are related to each other. If you are looking at houses, use the vertical coordinate to graph Condition, the horizontal coordinate to graph Attractiveness of Location and use bubble size to portray price, or any other combination that helps you focus on key factors.

It's important to note that feeling has just as important a role as thinking, and perhaps even a greater one. Once the trigger has been pulled on the investment, further thinking, or "second-guessing," is a waste of effort and time. Now is the time for the stamina for holding on, and stamina comes from feeling. It is within the strong emotions part of your character that lies the stamina to stay with an investment as it bobs on choppy seas until eventually attaining a permanently profitable height, which will continue to advance and retract, but over time with a widening margin of profit. Yet in most cases such stamina is not enough, and the best option is to ignore what you have invested in. Once the investment is made, forget it and move on to the next investment candidate. Think about shoes. In the shoe store all shoes are examined very critically, giving very great attention to each detail. After the shoes are purchased, they receive no further thought. Stocks should be acquired in a similar process.

Investment vs. Trading

Now let's look at "horizon." Everybody generally has two horizon points of greatest interest: a far-in-the-future point, like retirement, when size of asset accumulation will determine lifestyle; and closer, vague time when an emergency might need a lump sum of money. A fundamental precept of investing is that the sum held for emergencies be liquid or near liquid and thus typically not contribute significantly to future asset size. Rather it will be invested in near-cash assets that can be converted quickly to cash and so will earn little more than the rate of inflation, if that. This is where one form of risk enters in. Too much in near cash and there is not enough growth. Too much devoted to long-term investment, and you run the risk of having to take losses to get liquid. This is a balancing act that may not draw much on investment skills per se, but could have a profound effect on where you wind up. In general, the farther out your investment horizon, the more you can expect to accumulate, provided you actually plan and execute an investment program for that horizon.

If you obtain an asset at a deep discount due to some transient upset that you have found from your research, and sell it when it recovers, you may realize an attractive short-term gain, but have squandered your effort on something that immediately presents another challenge, what do you do with the proceeds? A series of short-term opportunistic plays may give the illusion of building wealth, but you are not letting time and the market do their work, which gives a much larger and more certain result than finding a series of attractive opportunities. Also, tax is likely due on the gain, which means taxing and tax reporting.

The Power of Compounding

Einstein is reported to have said that *"....compound interest was the most powerful force in the universe."* Whether he said this or not, I am not certain, but few take issue with the meaning of it – there is nothing like time when your money is in a machine that makes money from money. Accordingly, you want to find a money machine that has a 100-year or 50-year design, not something that is only good for a few months or a year. Using a long horizon, like Rip Van Winkle, you will find when you wake up a very pleasant surprise, and usually a much larger surprise than you expected. There are studies that show a dramatic reduction in return if you missed the five highest growth days in the market. To get market returns you must be in the market, not trading in and out of it.

To illustrate, take a $1,000 investment at 5% for 30 years. It becomes $4,467.74. That is a 446% gain for no additional effort other than leaving it alone. Now imagine a 401(k) plan where you defer $1,000 per year for 30 years at 5% compound interest. In 30 years, that 401(k) plan would be worth $71,246.51. If the plan instead were 100% invested in the S&P 500 from say 1980 to 2010, the plan in 2010 would be worth $101,347.71. This is from only $1,000 per year, and from a low-impact investment, the S&P 500. Of course remember that at typical inflation rates, purchasing power gets cut in half every 24 years, so in purchasing power, the above figures of $71,246.51 and $101,347.71 become $35,623.25 and $50,673.85 respectively. This shows both the power of compounding and the destructive power of inflation. It also demonstrates the life determining role investment decisions have over our lifetimes. Slight course adjustments have enormous consequences.

Smith College Economics professor Randall Bartlett cites

Benjamin Franklin's 1790 gift of $500 to the City of Boston, the city of his birth. Franklin's stipulation was that the money be invested conservatively and not touched for 200 years. In 1995 the account was worth $6.5 million. The growth rate was 4.8675%. Had the growth rate been 5% the account would have been worth $8.6 million. This is a great example and illustrates both the power of compounding and the power of small interest rate changes.

The stock market can be a vehicle for long-term wealth creation, meaning money is made from money over time without additional capital or labor. But for that to work, you must leave your investment alone and in order to do that you must select investments that are likely to survive.

Wall Street Culture

The culture surrounding Wall Street will have you believe two things that are false, or perhaps more accurately, a distraction: 1) that Wall Street professionals possess some advantage over non-professionals in realizing wealth from investing in stocks; and 2) that frequent trading is the key to wealth creation.

I'll start by debunking those two red herrings by pointing out that they are connected. Once you buy into the idea that frequent trading is necessary to success, you must eventually wind up believing that the closer to Wall Street you are, the better off you are. This is true, but think about this: once you purchase a stock with the intent on disposing of it after the next rise in price, you are placing yourself on the other side of a bet against a Wall Street professional trader, someone who spends his day using a proprietary computer program to follow real-time market action and who has done this for years and in a team environment.

In the early days of the market before there were trading software programs and proprietary traders, there were great speculators who would lose more bets than they would win, sometimes by a 5:1 ratio, but when they hit a winner they would load up as the stock price rose and sell at or near the peak, making the 5:1 ratio work for them because the losers were dumped before they could build losses. These speculators had a rule: "*Cut your losses and let your winners run.*" But that was before proprietary traders with computers. Betting against these professional traders is not for you and it isn't even for your retail broker, and yet that professional trader is who you are going up against every time you make a short-term play usually based on some short view of a catalyzing event that in the long run will have little if any bearing on the value of the stock, even just a year later. Betting against such professionals is not a way to create wealth.

The Relationship of Stock Price to Corporate Performance

Elsewhere I have alluded to stock price being disconnected from corporate performance, of exhibiting a life of its own. To say disconnected is really not accurate -- a better phrase would be remotely connected. Think of earthquakes that erupt where there has been a long period of inactivity. The tectonic plates are not inactive, but all the time are at work absorbing a regular increase of pressure, until finally the plates cannot hold any longer and they slip, causing an earthquake. This is the way the stock market works. A long period of national economic growth will have little impact on the aggregate valuation of the stock market and then in a matter of months or even weeks, great price advances are made as the market catches up with the value that industry has produced. Sometimes the lag can be years. But what is certain is that value is being created daily and that this value will ultimately be reflected in the stock market. Moreover, this tectonic analogy is applicable not only to the broader market but to individual stocks as well.

Stock market theory is that the stock market is an efficient market in that it correctly prices assets, which as we have just pointed out is wrong. It is the mis-pricing of assets that creates much of the liquidity in the market. Another stock market theme is that it is a level playing field, that laws against insider trading are vigorously enforced, as is front-running, which is the act of brokers buying ahead of their customers. But this is misleading also because brokerage houses routinely fill customer orders from their own inventory rather than market purchases. But one must go a step further to assess how level the stock market landscape is. Consider this: the six largest broker dealer banks had combined profits in 2010 of $75 billion, of which $56 billion (75%) was earned from proprietary trading, that is professional traders trading for the house. This means that when you put a trade in, you are putting yourself in competition with professional traders who are producing the bulk of their institution's profits and who can fill your orders from inventory or the market. You can only imagine the resources that go into this activity.

Recent articles have appeared about banks finding ways to preserve these assets in the face of rising criticism. More interesting, however, is the defense of proprietary trading by one of the biggest beneficiaries of prop trading, Jamie Dimon of JPMorgan Chase, who was quoted as follows at a Chamber of Commerce event: *"To people who say the system would be safer with smaller banks doing traditional banking, well, the system would be safer if we also went back to horse and buggies. That is a quaint notion that won't work in the real world."* At any rate, lame as it is, we are in Jamie Dimon's "real world," at least as of the year 2013, and trading in and out of stocks in pursuit of gains left on the table by professionals probably will not be a winning strategy for most people, even most retail brokers.

On the other hand, if you purchase a stock, the same stock the professional trader is selling, with the intention of holding onto it for years, you are no longer betting against that trader, but betting on the global economy and its ability to create wealth by creating goods and services that people want to buy. If you pick a portfolio of 20 or 30 stocks of companies that provide goods and services that people want to buy and hold those stocks for 30 years or so, you will have built a level of wealth that will have far greater influence on how you live than the aggregate impact on your lifestyle of all the purchases foregone to make those investments. And at such time that you are enjoying the spoils that industry and the market have produced, you will have a better understanding than most of what it means to invest, and incidentally you will probably have performed at or above the S&P 500, the target most pros try and fail to beat consistently.

There is one other data point that needs to be covered – national economies vs. company economies. Elsewhere I have observed the decline of the U.S economy, much of it due to a gradual shift of wealth from the entrepreneurial class to the non-entrepreneurial class. The "Rags-to-Riches" examples of yesteryear are fading, if they haven't faded altogether. There are still success stories, but they are not broadly based, as evidenced by the rise of unemployment, under-employment, and abandoned employment by those who in prior periods might have been employed in producing value in our common national economy yet in today's economy have given up.

This adds up to a U.S. economy in decline and with no foreseeable change agent. This is not true of corporate economies that still do a pretty good job of allocating money where it will do the most good. This means that when investing in companies, even U.S. companies, investment should be viewed not from a U.S. perspective, but from a global perspective, even for companies doing business almost exclusively in the U.S. While the fortunes of the U.S. economy may be inexorably on a downward trend, corporate economies trade in a free market and are free to succeed strictly on their own merits. The future fortunes of American companies will not necessarily be the same fortunes experienced by their home country. You must separate country risk from company risk.

A stark example of this is the Indian software company

Infosys (Nasdaq INFY). While you might hesitate to invest in India due to systemic corruption, Infosys has demonstrated a culture based entirely on merit and has even been active in attempting to turn the tide of corruption in corporate accounting. India is a rising giant with almost four times the population of the U.S. and perhaps the only place in the world where you will see billboards advertising *"Degrees in Physics,"* but it is hemmed in by a culture of corruption. Nevertheless, an investment in Infosys is not an investment in India, but rather an investment in the natural productivity and value creation embedded in the genes of *Homo Sapien Sapien* wherever they may happen to be. Traders rely on the worst dimension of mankind -- looking for a quick profit for no effort -- while investors rely on mankind's most noble dimension -- using human effort to create value so the rising generation can have better lives.

My objective in writing this book is to inspire the reader to develop a personal investment process that won't be hijacked by media noise on some transient condition. I ask readers to steel themselves against the Wall Street siren song of quick riches. In my effort I cite Burton Malkiel's advice to just buy the S&P 500. That is good advice because it gets you plugged into the power of the market is a very passive way. My advice is to be a little more engaged and diversify into several of the Russell indices, but better yet, buy the discrete common stocks that make up the Dow 30 and thus avoid the fees of an S&P 500 and Russell index funds, or even better, select a subset of the 100 greatest global corporations. In either case, if you follow through on this, you will handily outperform Wall Street while at the same time gaining the luxury of ignoring this chapter's discussion on probability, risk, and selecting individual investments from a field of candidates – useful information perhaps but entirely superfluous to building wealth.

Alchemist   *Ben Aronson 2010*
Oil on panel, 67 x 48 inches   Private Collection

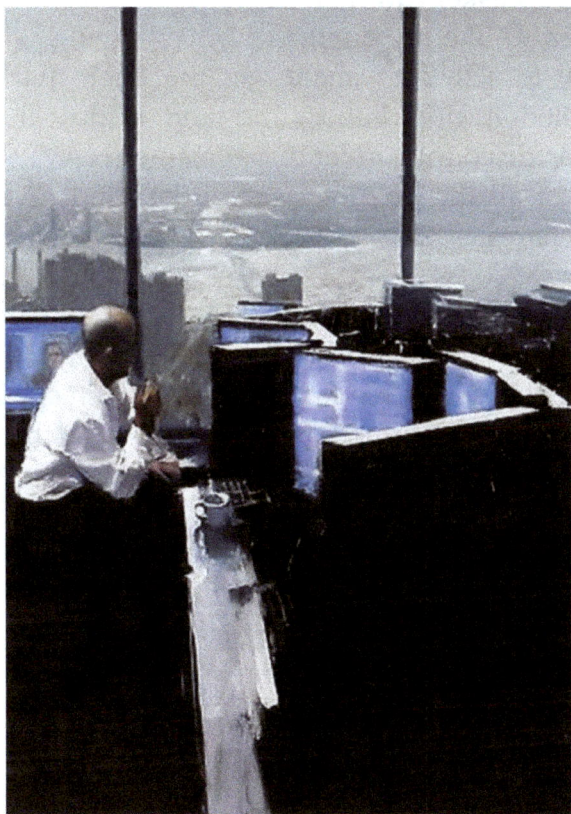

Chapter 4
Mutual Funds

Mutual funds trace their origin back to Belgium or the Netherlands of the 18th century, where they catered to a public that had neither the time nor inclination to engage in market research but wished to gain market returns on capital. There were, apparently, people devoted to assembling pooled baskets of the securities of joint-stock companies for public offering.

The question might have been raised whether the basket needed continuing management. If the basket is fixed at the start and unmanaged after its assembly and distribution, then shares in that basket can float in the secondary market and be traded openly like a single security, giving investors an opportunity to sell their shares on the open market. Such a fund is called a closed-end fund and trades at either par, premium, or discount to Net Asset Value (NAV). NAV is the total value of all the holdings inside the fund divided by the number of shares.

Active or Passive Management

One might well wonder how market pricing could possibly depart from NAV. This seeming oddity is often cited whenever market efficiency arguments are made – if the market is efficient, why do closed-end funds seldom trade at NAV? It's a good question to which there may not be a good answer. However, before going out and buying a fund at a deep discount to NAV – thus to collect the upside recovery -- bear in mind that the discount may persist for a long period or possibly get even wider. As a general rule, discounts don't go beyond 20%, at which point some entity is expected to come in and buy the entire fund out and sell off its contents for a 20% gain, before fees of course. It is generally thought that discounts less than 20% will be allowed to linger on indefinitely, and nobody seems to know why.

An opposite school of thought is that funds need to be actively managed, and this notion gives rise to open-end funds called mutual funds. In this asset class, fund managers -- or fund management teams -- continuously buy and sell positions to keep the fund "healthy." Naturally such active management is going to cost money, not only for the trader's salaries, but also for the trades as well and the recordkeeping and of course, the huge remuneration for money managers deciding which stocks to buy and sell. One reason this is done is to attract investment. As new investment comes in, additional shares must be created, which adds cost, and when shareholders sell, shares must be redeemed, adding more cost. Mutual funds are sold to the public based on the perception of both gain from market action and safety brought about by multiple positions and active management.

Because mutual funds were conceived to reduce risk, it might be well to look at risk and see how this works. In buying a stock of an individual company, an investor is immediately afloat in a sea of risks. First there is country risk if the stock earns all of its revenue within one country. Then there is sector risk if the company earns its revenue exclusively from a single market sector, for example, Exxon-Mobil, which is almost exclusively dependent on the market for consumption fuel rather than GE, which operates in many sectors, including finance. There is company risk, which is affected by management or by luck that a company experiences in a competitive market.

The riskiest investment would be in a single company deriving all of its revenue in a single sector in a single country, for example, a telecom company or utility, although these are fairly immune to sector risk because they provide a service which is inelastic – that is, consumers have little choice in how much they buy regardless of fluctuating economic conditions. A better example would be an elastic company that operates in only one country and one sector and is subject to the full impact of economic swings. These are called cyclical companies, examples being found in airlines, steel, appliances, furniture, clothing, paper, heavy machinery, and real estate, especially hotels and theme parks or any other provider of goods or services that are demanded in proportion to the state of the economy – up in good times and down in bad times. Mutual funds, as well as closed-end funds, reduce risk by diversification; that is by spreading the various sources of risk over many positions.

Investing in a basket of stocks that contains only cyclical companies in a single national economy may not offer much of a hedge against a tanking economy. So mutual funds, while offering the perception of reducing risk, may do so in varying degrees, or not at all. The advantage, presumably, of an open-ended fund, is that the managers might react positively to a coming economic storm, while a closed-end fund would be fully exposed. How critical are these differences? Mutual funds charge fees on AUM (Assets Under Management), and cash is not considered an asset you can charge much of a fee on, so mutual funds, as far as I have been able to determine, remain invested at all times. So the difference between open-end and closed-end fund's performance during market upset will probably not be very great, if detectable at all. But if active management gives an investor the confidence to ride out a storm without resorting to panic selling, then the open-end fund is a better choice. I prefer the lower fees and greater transparency of closed-end funds and the opportunity to gain on discount to NAV. Also, in a closed-end fund I know how I am invested. In a mutual fund, try to identify the turnover rate and you might be surprised at what you find – 100% turnover in a year is not unusual. That amount of turnover misses dividends and stock splits and of course, turns upside down any mutual fund selection based on holdings at the time of purchase.

Mutual Fund Rules

The unscrupulous sales practices that led up to the market crash of 1929 included "pump & dump" activities on individual stocks, where unscrupulous syndicates would quietly take a large position in a target company's stock, then start rumors of impending good fortune and when the stock had reached a high point as a result of a buying frenzy that had been prompted by "rumor" of a "hidden gem," when no new investors could be reeled in, the stock would be quickly sold off by the syndicate leading to its inevitable crash as sellers overwhelmed buyers, but not before the syndicate had largely gotten out with their outsized profits.

During this same period, mutual funds began being marketed as a safer investment, but were just as likely to be merely another unscrupulous syndicate product. But this history is prophetic and as relevant today as it was in 1929 because most "investment" decisions are driven by near-term price expectation and not any sober contemplation of a company's long-term prospects. It is this very bifurcation this book attempts to address.

After the crash of 1929, the Roosevelt administration, hiring a thief to catch a thief, put Joe Kennedy, one of the syndicate ringleaders, in charge of creating legislation to "clean up" the market. The result was the Securities Act of 1933, the Securities and Exchange Act of 1934, and the Investment Company Act of 1940, wherein mutual funds, among other stipulations, were required to provide a prospectus to prospective investors, in which details of the fund were documented, including the investment strategy of the fund, for example, cyclical/non-cyclical, market sector, etc. In this way investors could be assured that they understood how their money was invested and that it would in reality be so invested.

Jean Dalrymple, a New York City theatrical producer, Director of City Center during to 1950s and '60s and an extraordinary woman, described early in her career working unknowingly in a "bucket shop." She quit as soon as she learned the way the game worked was that customers' margin orders were routinely never executed (but rather thrown in the bucket), and the original margin money just pocketed by the firm. A margin order is an order paid for with a margin deposit and a loan from the brokerage firm, and as long as the order is profitable there is no problem, but if the position goes down, then the firm sends out a "margin call" for more money to prop up the client's equity in the position. If the investor fails to meet the margin call, the position is sold out at a client loss and the firm reimburses itself for any losses by selling out other client positions. In the few cases where margin calls for more money were honored with more money or where the stock did appreciate, the firm would have to make good on the margin orders. But most of the margin orders were losers, netting the firm not only the commission but the investment deposit as well. In Jean's own words from September's Child, here is how bucket shops worked:

"Thinking it over I found it logical. One of the reasons I had had to work late so often was to help in sending out those "margin calls," and it had sometimes seemed odd to me that many of the men appeared in better spirits when the market went down than when it went up. In the latter event, when and if the client came through with the additional margin, then and only then did the firm have to buy the stock. It was all suddenly quite clear."

During the run-up to the tech bubble of the late 1990s, some funds began to undergo "style drift." This is a condition where a large cap fund, being left behind by the stampede toward the tech sector, would then begin to direct their investment activity to the tech sector as well, despite the fact that the fund was sold as a big cap fund. The Investment Advisers Act of 1940 limited, but did not eliminate, this "style drift," as it is called. Naturally style-drift is usually not a threat to closed-end funds which have their investments fixed for the life of the fund at the start.

Mutual Fund Fees and Fiduciary Cover

The active management of open-end funds immediately burdens them with activities and fees not required of closed-end funds. Closed-end funds are created at inception with a defined basket of stocks and set number of shares for distribution.

Once the distribution is complete, the public shares are then traded in the open market as if they were a single stock such as GE. In the case of Unit Trusts, the basket has a time limit after which the fund is liquidated, but closed-end funds, theoretically, can last forever, trading at some differential from NAV. Closed-end fund investors look to the market itself to provide liquidity, offering them a place to sell their shares if they have a "liquidity preference," in economic-speak.

Open-end funds didn't take off for a long time, being a step-child to closed-end funds, but that began to change in 1950s and accelerated quickly with the emergence of 401(k) plans, the mother of all investment vehicles for non-investors. The theory here is, and it is only theory, that actively managed funds protect their investors because they are run by professional money managers. While it may be argued that in a calamitous market the mutual fund managers in place may take steps to head off calamity, market collapse as well as recovery cannot reliably be anticipated, and so the best response is usually to do nothing and allow the market to recover. Nevertheless the growth of 401(k) plans, which are joined at the hip with mutual funds, has pretty much pushed mutual funds to the forefront as investment vehicles. Moreover, investment advisory services and brokerage houses like the liability protection actively managed funds provide.

If a client suffers losses, a hunt for the cause of the losses will inevitably end with the money managers at the fund. If the losses are produced by a closed-end fund, there are no active managers to blame except the advisor who suggested the fund to the client in the first place – that is who the client sues. Obviously professional advisors have a preference for active management as targets other than themselves for their client to sue should things go wrong.

Companies who sponsor 401(k) plans are vulnerable to suits from unhappy plan participants as well, but they also get protection by using actively managed funds. In my view, liability protection for the professional investment profession is the key driver in the emergence of open-end funds as the default investment vehicle for 401(k)-style retirement plans and variable annuities (to be discussed in a later chapter). Also, mutual fund companies are the primary providers of packaged 401(k) plans.

Marketing Mutual Funds

There is one other key player in the rise of the mutual fund industry, and that is the funds themselves. Once a management team is in place, what is their mission? To get more money, of course, on which to charge more fees. So a mutual fund may start out with a modest capital base, but then the team goes to work to attract capital, or "gather assets," as the expression goes in the industry. So an army of salespeople armed with credit cards are then dispatched to the brokerage houses and investment advisories of America to buy lunch and distribute lots of very glossy literature extolling the benefit of the fund. The asset gathering is further tweaked by offering funds with different styles: large cap value, small cap growth, etc., eventually creating a mutual fund "family." Then a number of these fund families provide administrative services for 401(k) plans, so that any stock broker may instantly become a 401(k) plan provider to his clients. If this asset gathering activity is successful, and it almost always is, then the fund managers have a new mission: keeping the money they have gathered.

The promotional activity of these mutual fund companies has led to the term "data-mining." It refers to the practice of putting spin on a fund's performance, such as taking the period of rising values and pointing out that the core competency of the fund is the ability, say, to outperform the market during some particular market upset, and then proving it with actual numbers. This is strong sales fodder. Another technique I witnessed was a fund claiming it put a floor on losses by pointing out that in past market downturns its numbers showed less loss than the overall market. There is just enough truth in data mining to make a good case out of almost anything. But it works. As a broker, I sat in on countless lunchtime presentations of mutual fund companies that had developed partnerships with brokers. After lunch, the brokers would peddle the new wonderful product to their clients. Meanwhile I got a free lunch for listening!

Imagine being the manager of a mutual fund and you come into the office one day, and in your in-box are new orders for $1million in shares. What do you do? In order to satisfy this demand you create the requisite number of new shares to absorb this capital inflow, and you have all day to do it, because mutual funds are priced at the end of each day. This daily pricing gives funds the flexibility to inflate or deflate calmly while the markets are roiling. Say the market is bullish and the following morning the in-basket contains $50 million in new orders. Oh dear, it's time to get cracking. And so it goes, day after day. Then the market turns and suddenly redemption orders fill the in-basket. This constant market gyration prompting the need for creation and redemption of shares is a bother, and so dampening the inhalation and exhalation becomes a priority.

Using 401(k) plans is a big aid to dampening volatility in supply and demand, because 401(k) plan participants rarely change their elections once they are made. And most if not all funds are "benchmarked" to an index. For example, if an investor is looking to mimic the performance of the S&P 500 index, he or she will look for a mutual fund that is "benchmarked" to the S&P 500. In fact, the fund aims a little higher that the S&P 500 so that after fees, the client sees S&P 500-like returns. If a fund does substantially better than the index against which it is benchmarked, the fund managers may expect an inflow of cash to be invested, which is the object of the game. But inevitably the fund will lag the benchmark, and then it is redemption time. I leave it to the reader to decide how the fund deals with this tiresome inflow and outflow. I suspect the best strategy is merely to mimic the index itself.

Index Construction and Proliferation

Enter John Bogle. At one time a darling of the mutual fund industry, Bogle headed the very highly regarded Vanguard group. After Bogle left Vanguard he got to thinking and calculating and discovered that most mutual funds, after fees, lag the indexes they are benchmarked against. Why not just invest in the indexes? Of course, John missed the part about advisor liability and mutual fund fees, but he was focused on investor outcomes. Presto, the emergence of a new asset class, index funds.

Index funds needed fund managers, too, not to create and redeem shares, but to create, manage, and record-keep the fund, but at least those expensive money managers were gone and so were most of the fees. So what John Bogle wrought was performance without the fees. But what if the market tanks, then what? Just hang onto your hats and it will all come back. Of course there was the next graduating class at MIT and they needed jobs. No problem. Index fund entrepreneurs sprung up, hired the kids from MIT to create index funds on steroids, and out they came. How do you enhance an index? Easy, through weighting.

In 1651, Thomas Hobbes published his seminal view into mankind titled Leviathan. The title page of the publication was illustrated with his vision of the Leviathan that regulates mankind, a King, created by figures of little people. In other words, the sovereign is not an individual but the collective will of many people. Hobbes felt that people were naturally brutish and therefore a sovereign was needed to control their (our) behavior. This idea never caught on this side of the Atlantic, where individual freedom is given, may I say, free reign. Well, nowhere is this seen more clearly than in the stock market Leviathan, which I have once heard, is made up of 125 million separate investing entities. Total U.S. trading volume may be very roughly estimated at 3 trillion shares per day, which works out to each of the 125 million investing entities trading at 24 shares per day. More likely, volume over the trading population is normally distributed, so an average of 24 is a meaningless measure!

In 1896, Charles Dow set out to capture the behavior of the

Leviathan in his Dow Jones Industrial Average. Dow assembled a basket of 12 stocks of the most prominent industrial companies, added up the value of one share of each, took the average and declared that the index. What Dow was after, however, was not the value of the index, but the daily changes that would signal optimism and pessimism and be an investment guide for his subscribers.

I'll digress for a moment to offer just a brief word on construction of indexes, a subject that is worthy itself of a book. If one of Dow's index stocks split, and the index was composed of one share each of the participating companies, the index, post-split, would fall, forcing investors to a pessimistic view when all that had happened was a split, which is good sign. Dow may have just tied the index to the opening value and adjusted for splits, but the other prominent way to construct an index is by "capitalization" weighting, wherein each company in the index is weighted by the size of its total capitalization. The criticism of these two methods is that Dow's stock-price or "equal-weighting" over-represents smaller company's performance, while capitalization-weighting over-represents large company's performance, and therefore both styles fail to capture the mood of the market very well.

Stock Splits, Indices and Charts

This needs a little more explanation. There is general agreement that an ideal stock price is around, say, $30 to $40 a share. At that price, investors feel the stock is "affordable," whereas at $100 they may feel they can't afford it and buy into something else. As stock price rises with the general rise of the market, some issues will rise faster and get "out of reach" for many investors. When that happens, companies often split the stock, typically two-for-one and one share of a $100 stock becomes two shares of a $50 stock. This will then be reflected in the stock price chart for that stock by dropping the trace going back, making it look like going back in time the stock was much cheaper than it really was. Charts are usually logarithmic anyway, so must be used carefully. The best way to use a stock chart is to compare the stock of interest to another stock or the S&P 500, just as currencies are always examined in pairs.

A note on charts is needed. If someone said that say GE is up $2 for the day, that wouldn't mean anything except for people who follow GE and can translate that into, say, a 9% gain for the day. Consequently price movements are usually quoted in percentage, which is more meaningful. GE is up 9% for the day. So charting that assigns equal weight to a $2 gain for a $20 stock and an $80 stock would probably not give a very true picture. We are really only interested in percent gain, not absolute dollar gain. To chart more usefully, the vertical axis in stock charts are routinely made logarithmic to show that a $2 gain on a $20 stock is much more dramatic than a $2 gain on an $80 stock. Or you could say stock prices move logarithmically and therefore stock charts should do the same. The horizontal axis is linear. All days are exactly 24 hours and so each day is exactly 100% equal to the day before, no day ever stands out as being longer than any other, so the horizontal axis is always linear. And as discussed elsewhere, charts record price only, not price-plus- dividends on dividend paying stocks.

One other note on charts is needed. Never assume a graphic outcome to be illustrative of a mathematical outcome. Graphic outcomes can be distorted in both over-representing and under-representing returns even in logarithmic scaling. Much better is to use interactive charts, note the starting and ending prices of the term you are interested in, and then use a compounding calculator to find the true return. This will often be a much different picture than illustrated by a chart.

Getting back to stock splits and indices, adjusting stock price for marketability bears no relationship to the overall capitalization of the company issuing the stock. Accordingly, a small company may be trading at $50 per share, while a company ten times larger may be trading at $30 a share. So stock price says nothing about the size of the issuing company. An equal-weighted index assigns a weight within the index by stock price, which fails to account for dramatic differences in overall capitalization and results in over-representation of smaller companies. This would seem to be a distortion, so many indices are capitalization-weighted, wherein each stock is proportioned within the index by its relative weight considering capitalization. The criticism of this solution is that large capitalization companies are over-represented.

The purpose of an index is to track change, and the only generalization that may have some validity is that in low-interest environments, equal-weighted indices will probably outperform capitalization indices, as smaller companies thrive with easier access to money. In a rising interest rate environment, these differences are likely to reverse. But you can check this yourself by comparing the charts for the S&P 500 (SPX) and the Equal Weighted S&P 500 index (EWI). You will find dramatic differences, but it may be a stretch to attribute the difference to interest rates. Like all price history, the insight offered is often illusory, except for data-mining purposes.

It is also interesting to compare the capitalization-weighted S&P 500 (SPX), representing 500 of the most prominent companies, with the Dow Jones Industrial Average (DJIA), an equal-weighted index made up of 30 of the most prominent companies. Obviously the top 30 should handily outperform the top 500 and that is what you see in comparing those two indices. However, to really add interest and perhaps insight, compare all three indices: the capitalization-weighted S&P 500 (SPX) and the two equal-weighted indices, the equal-weight S&P 500 (EWI) and the Dow Jones (DJIA). In this comparison you can begin to see the relative roles played by weighting, and greater discrimination that comes from the top 30 vs. the top 500.

Perhaps Benjamin Graham's admonition fits here: In the short term the market is a voting machine and in the long term it is a weighing machine, or words to that effect. In other words short-term changes are meaningless but a change over a five-year period, say, reflects actual corporate performance. Ed Easterling, in his seminal work, *Unexpected Returns*, presents the thesis that there are three sources of return in stock price appreciation: actual corporate growth, dividends, and increase in P/E (Price/Earnings Ratio). During inflationary or deflationary periods, which are destabilizing, P/E will decline. During sustained periods of annual inflation of 3%, or slightly less, P/E will rise in response to perceived stability. When times are stable, investors bid stocks up. In any case, this digression into the history and construction of indices is needed to understand the benchmarks against which funds are measured and to understand index funds.

Getting back to those kids from MIT and the subject of weighting in indexes, the MIT kids were hired to make a product out of index funds for which fees might be charged. The result is index funds on steroids, which is accomplished by weighting, so that individual components offering the greatest promise are given greater weight and those components thought to be a drag are down-weighted. Note that when applying advanced mathematics for such shenanigans the algorithms can become quite complex, thus defying pirating by competing firms, but in all cases index funds on steroids still meet the very loose qualification for being called "index" funds. One company that was a pioneer in this work called their index funds, "Power-Shares."

The Power of Oratory

Another means on playing with indexes came to my attention during a presentation by a mutual fund money manager while I was a stockbroker at a major firm. Occasionally fund families rolled out their top money manager for a road show and I was privileged to attend a number of these sessions. In most cases, the money managers convinced me they were brilliant and in most cases possessed egos to match. Nevertheless I never let the ego get in the way of appreciating what they were saying. These kids were brilliant. One, "Dr. Bob" from a fund family now lost to my memory, was particularly insightful about a macroeconomic view. He had no overblown ego and was a big hit with brokers in the office. "Dr. Bob" was the exception, however.

But getting back to the money manager who referenced indices in his talk – he had a huge ego and he paced slowly back and forth gently waving his arms and rolling his hands to emphasize a point, giving the impression of carelessly lobbing genius out into the audience. The performance, designed to gather assets by the way, was mesmerizing and each lob of insight and truth was received with telling effect through the assembled congregation, including me. At one point he denigrated index funds by saying that beating the index was a trivial exercise in just removing the obvious dogs and allowing the remaining participants to follow their natural course. I don't recall his name, but I was rebuffed when I asked for his card, and he did gather major assets at our office that day. It was magic! I never forgot it. But it was not magic enough to propel me into offering mutual funds to my clients, and from the cool perspective of time, I doubt if his funds did much better than the S&P 500 -- but he was a great performer.

I wish to subject my readers to another digression on the power of oratory by quoting Benjamin Franklin. Franklin, incidentally, was a notorious tightwad, and wealthy one, too, so what you read will be doubly insightful and perhaps troubling.

"This I [Franklin] *advis'd; but he was resolute in his first project, rejected my counsel, and I therefore refus'd to contribute. I happened soon after to attend one of his sermons, in the course of which I perceived he intended to finish with a collection, and I silently resolved he should get nothing from me. I had in my pocket a handful of copper*

money, three or four silver dollars, and five pistoles in gold. As he proceeded I began to soften, and concluded to give the coppers. Another stroke of his oratory made me asham'd of that, and determin'd me to give the silver; and he finish'd so admirably, that I empty'd my pocket wholly into the collector's dish, gold and all. At this sermon there was also one of our club, who, being of my sentiments respecting the building in Georgia, and suspecting a collection might be intended, had, by precaution, emptied his pockets before he came from home. Towards the conclusion of the discourse, however, he felt a strong desire to give, and apply'd to a neighbour, who stood near him, to borrow some money for the purpose. The application was unfortunately [made] to perhaps the only man in the company who had the firmness not to be affected by the preacher. His answer was, "At any other time, Friend Hopkinson, I would lend to thee freely; but not now, thee seems to be out of thy right senses."

So beware of the silver-tongued money managers, they usually don't deliver anything beyond their oratory, but what oratory!

Mutual Funds, the Default Investment Vehicle
Mutual funds are viewed as "safe" or "safer" by not only beginning investors, but pretty much the larger Wall Street community. When I first began my professional investment career at a major brokerage, it was assumed by the management that I would assemble mutual fund portfolios for my clients. I looked at the funds but found nothing in them that would allow me to feel inspired enough to promote them as a way to gain new clients. Mutual fund providers are aware of this, prompting them to default to data-mining presentations in very glossy mutual fund handouts. As my career progressed I continued to spurn mutual funds, gathering ammunition to shoot them down as I went. I was a maverick it seems, and even found many "grey heads" (highly experience brokers)

who retreated in terror when I told them I was using individual stocks instead of funds.

But mutual funds are the prevailing default investment and the inertia behind them is very great. First, almost every day, at every brokerage, a luncheon speaker is brought in who supplies lunch (a very reliable formula) -- a hot lunch in some offices -- and presents his "family" of funds, which might be like Alger for small cap, or Davis, for the very popular Davis New York Venture Fund, or ING, The Hartford, John Hancock, etc., and then focus on the fund du jour, hoping to stimulate some immediate buys on the new data-mined thesis. I evidently had the firmness of Hopkinson's friend in the Benjamin Franklin episode cited above. I attended the lunches every day but never bought any of the funds, although other brokers bought, and so the lunches were well paid for -- by the clients of course.

Benchmarking Mutual Fund Performance

Before leaving mutual funds I will give a plug for Alger funds. Alger specializes in small cap and growth areas, both of which are fast moving and difficult to predict long term. Even large cap "value" stocks, which are non-cyclical and for which research is readily available, are difficult for the investor to research thoroughly enough for an investment decision. To do this for small cap and growth is impossible in my view. Alger, at least at that time, required their analysts to call every company they were covering every six months and question them on their operations and prospects. The analysts then met in committee and challenged each other over their findings. From this process, they managed their portfolios. So to fill the small cap growth area of my personal matrix, I am perfectly satisfied to use an Alger fund or two or three. Otherwise, I find mutual funds rather a bore in that all they do is keep up with the indices by constantly trading in and out of positions on short-term news. Doing so, of course, embeds real drag on performance in both fees and failure to capture dividends and exploit stock splits.

It has become custom among mutual fund managers to benchmark their performance against an index which then aids the financial advisor in diversifying a portfolio by style – large cap value, small cap growth, etc. Many mutual funds have fanciful names that tell you absolutely nothing about how they are invested. For example, Davis New York Venture might lead you to think you were getting into some high powered hedge-like fund. The top holdings of the fund were, when I looked, American Express, Costco Wholesale, Berkshire-Hathaway, Wells Fargo, Bank of New York Mellon, and other similar holdings that don't smell anything like some early stage tech effort. Moreover it appears that they benchmark against the S&P 500, which is hardly a venture group, but more cash cows. Presumably the fund is so named to give it some sex appeal, but it should be mentioned that this fund was a favorite among brokers for reliable performance. In my examination, it pretty much kept pace with the S&P 500, something many funds try but fail to do, regardless of capitalization or strategy.

As part of my training, I was required to call up mutual fund offices and interview home office personnel to get inside views. It was good training and I was lucky to have called Davis, because at the time I had no idea who they were. I was told that the scion of the family, Christopher, had been in Ireland studying for the priesthood when he got the call to come home and join the family business. I could not confirm this on Google, but it's an interesting story, and worth retelling. I don't know what kind of a priest Christopher would have made, but he turned out to be a pretty good fund manager.

Getting back to the subject at hand, mutual funds became the default investment vehicle for most non-professional investors and their advisors, perhaps because they were more vigorously promoted than any other asset class and were perceived to meet the "safety" requirements for fiduciary oversight of 401(k) plans. Incidentally, fiduciary oversight means escape route for the responsible party, as in a Financial Advisor being able to point his index finger at a third-party money manager as being responsible for losses. The upside of "fiduciary" oversight is that it removes the more egregious practices that can develop in "managing" participant investment accounts, like steering them to high-commission funds. A broker can do this whereas a fiduciary cannot, which may steer people toward using an RIA (Registered Investment Advisor) who is a fiduciary. A broker is a Registered Representative and has no fiduciary responsibility to the client other than the "suitability" requirement. The RR is expected to know the customer and suggests only suitable investments.

Now 401(k) plans are increasingly offering index funds, and I am not sure how they manage the fiduciary issue unless it is to lay the blame on the aggregators of indices. And incidentally, there used to be only a handful of indices, the Dow Jones Industrials, S&P 500, and a few others. Today there are seemingly a gazillion indices which slice and dice the market in every which way. And while I generally frown on funds, I am attracted to the simplicity of just buying a fund for gaining exposure to a sector that is difficult to access in any other way. But bear in mind that different market sectors have different velocities of change. For example the Dow Industrials, the largest companies trading in the U.S., will be much less volatile than an emerging market fund investing in tech start-ups. For this reason, I prefer the vigilance of actively managed funds in small cap, micro-cap, and Far-East markets that don't trade on the NYSE, although I notice that index funds are increasingly exhibiting what I call "active management creep." The reason for this is to hijack the sizzle of the word "index" and then give the illusion of adding extra sizzle with active massaging.

For large cap stocks trading on U.S. exchanges, an index fund or picking individual stocks makes much more sense. However, be aware of the basic statistics involved in any basket of moving parts. The total performance of the basket will be an average of all the individual performances inside the basket. The average will fall somewhere in the middle, meaning that half the stocks in the index did better than the average and half the stocks did worse. You would think that a highly paid money manager at a mutual fund, with a highly paid staff of junior analysts working a 40- or 50-hour week, would be able to bias the fund holdings toward the higher performers, but John Bogle (a founder of Vanguard Funds) pioneered the use of index funds, pointing out that active management lagged the indexes in performance and so imposed fees for no value, failing to figure out which half not to invest in. Even the whiz kids adding steroids to index funds can't reliably figure out which constituents need to be over-weighted or under-weighted. This is because the market is random and the definition of random is "unpredictable," over the short-term anyway.

Mutual Fund Fees

We began this chapter looking at all funds and discriminating between mutual funds and closed-end funds, pointing out that mutual funds are actively managed and sometimes come under fire over fees. Of course, fees are why the mutual funds and mutual fund families exist in the first place, fees and liability. Nobody likes fees and nobody likes to talk about fees, so considerable trouble is taken to remove them from the landscape. First, fees are obscured by divisions of fund shares into "classes:" Class A shares, Class B shares, Class C shares and "I" shares, or investment shares. Class A shares charge a fee up front, but are generally without fee afterward. Class B shares have no fee until sold, and class C shares have an annual ongoing fee. Investment shares are used in 401(k) plans and typically have lower fees. All of these shares are identical in every other way except in the fees they charge.

At one brokerage house where I worked, a memo came out

that after a certain date, Class B shares would be off-limits, evidently heading off what the management felt would be SEC (Securities and Exchange Commission) scrutiny of a potentially predatory practice. I am guessing the predatory practice was getting clients into funds without an up-front fee but then earning a fee when getting the client to trade out of the fund on "new information." I rarely sold mutual funds, but when I did, I followed the lead of most brokers and opted for C shares so that I would get a regular income from the sale.

The fees are meant to cover share creation and redemption, trading fees (most mutual funds trade frequently enough to be thought of as day-traders), administrative fees, money management fees and marketing fees, which includes all the fancy glossy literature and the lunches I was attending. Promotional fees are called 12b -1 fees in the trade. Each of these fees differ by share class, rendering the entire subject so arcane that nobody wants to look at it, except John Bogle, when his examination led to the emergence of index funds.

Notwithstanding all of this fund bashing, in the absence of performance, fees really do matter, as Bogle showed, but there are funds that are very expertly managed and, in my view, well worth the fees. For small cap I would examine Alger, which I described earlier. For real estate, Cohen & Steers has been very good in the past. For international, Franklin Templeton used to be good, at least when operated by Sir John Templeton. Sir John was perhaps the first to dispatch employees to the far corners of the earth to observe up close the companies he was recommending in his funds. And then there are the proven money managers like Bill Miller, Maggie Patel, Bill Gross at Pioneer and of course, the poor man's hedge fund, Warren Buffett at Berkshire-Hathaway. But again it must be pointed out, long-term, it is hard to beat the plain old S&P 500 or the Dow 30.

Hedge Funds

Buffett brings us to the subject of hedge funds. In the wake of the 1929 stock market crash, the Roosevelt administration put into place oversight and regulation designed to protect the unwary investor from the worst excesses of unscrupulous securities marketing. While these measures have helped to avert disaster for many, the same regulations are a constraint to more sophisticated investors who have access to more skillful advice. Gradually, this subset of the investment community was finding a variety of alternatives that are broadly categorized as hedge funds, but are in fact a variety of strategies pursued on behalf of clients by top tier asset managers, who really are able through research and instinct to sometimes identify faster growing asset pools. Research at this level is always bespoke, in very great depth, which may and often does include meetings with not only company executives, but their customers as well, to synthesize an actionable view if one can be arrived at. Sometimes the research leads to a negative decision, but also frequently to a competing company, which may be in a better position to exploit a changing market structure.

In the world of hedge funds, the idea of mimicking the S&P 500 or any other index is a non-starter – the objective is always, absolute return, that is to say, positive return under all market conditions. This heady return forecast does not come cheap; fees are high, typically 2% of assets, and may reach 20% or more on earnings. SAC Capital Advisors, one of the most successful hedge funds, has in the past, reportedly, charged as much as 3% plus 50% of earnings. But hedge funds are for "accredited Investors," those earning $200K per year with $1 million in liquid assets and theoretically well able to take care of themselves, or as illustrated above, possessing enough sense not to be swayed by silver-tongued preachers as Benjamin Franklin was. Hedge funds are not even permitted to promote to the general public and many don't even have websites. However, this asset class is no different from any other in underperforming expectations, and most hedge funds have trouble keeping up with the indices.

In addition to Berkshire-Hathaway, called by me a poor man's hedge fund because anybody can buy it (you don't have to be an Accredited Investor), there are others that are not hedge funds per se but offer a hedge fund like experience, and on the cheap. This class of assets are Master Limited Partnerships called Business Development Companies (BDC), which make a business out of financing start-ups and early term companies with expensive debt. Prominent firms in this category are:

American Capital Strategies (ACAS)
Ares Capital Corp. (ARCC)
Apollo Investment (AINV)
Fifth Street Finance Corp. (FSC)
Gladstone Investment Corp. (GAIN)
Hercules Technology Growth Capital (HTGC)
Kohlberg Capital Corp. (KCAP)
Pennant Park Investment (PNNT)
Triangle Capital (TCAP)
BlackRock Kelso (BKCC)
Prospect Capital (PSEC).
Blackstone Group (BX)

A Master Limited Partnership (MLP) is not taxed at the corporate level, but only at the investor level in the form of capital gains taxes with some twists. One disadvantage of these investments is that you are not likely to get your tax statement until well after tax day, and so you will be filing an extension. As an investor in Blackstone, I didn't get my tax statement until July. But if you can live with this inconvenience, BDCs offer a good absolute return, hedge-fund like experience for the plebes or proletariats of our society of which I claim to be one.

Finding a Good Financial Advisor

A discussion of mutual funds must inevitably include the reason for their existence. As described earlier, funds came into existence to serve the general public as a distinct group of investors separate and different from wealthy sophisticated investors. Wealthy sophisticated investors have access to better advice because people holding themselves out as investment advisors will naturally want to increase their earnings by serving wealthier people, more able to afford more expensive advice. Also, wealthy investors tend to be more sophisticated and understand the limits of advice, and don't automatically sue when advice leads to losses. The general public holds investment advisors to a higher standard of performance than do sophisticated investors, and so lawsuits are more likely when serving the general public. This, along with the lower fees, makes serving the general public something successful advisors try to avoid if possible.

But for many advisors it is not possible to avoid serving smaller investors, at least in their early years. So because serving the public is a necessity, the public should be served with mutual funds to protect the investment advisors and their employers. Wealthy people, in contrast, have access to theoretically more able investment advisors charging higher fees. But this is a gross generalization. The uncovering of the Bernie Madoff scandal also uncovered the surprising lack of sophistication in what are categorized as Accredited Investors. What we learned was that these wealthy investors were not sophisticated at all and just blindly gave their money to people characterized as successful investment managers without the least bit of scrutiny. And of course, they are now suing, throwing up their hands with the question: "How were they supposed to know?"

This may sound outrageous, but that is the way hedge funds work -- the clients are not supposed to know. The investment formula is secret, and so all the investor sees is the results. But the difference between most hedge fund investors and Madoff investors is that sophisticated investors using hedge funds are diversified, limiting the allocation to each fund organization. Madoff investors gave it all to Bernie. So although wealthy, they were not sophisticated investors at all – babes in the woods as far as that goes.

The reason I left a career as a sales engineer selling technical equipment to engineering firms was because I had never been able to find a good investment advisor and thought there was a need. Although I had tried for a number of years, interviewing a number of advisors and investing with a subset of that number, from my experience I came to the view that investment advisors came in two flavors: 1) venal and very quick to take your money without any thought of serving you, or 2) inept. Those were the alternatives: venal or inept. Since being in the business for six years at two major brokerage houses I have not changed my views very much, other than to conclude that the venal ones are also inept – they are just better talkers.

However, there are a small number of investment advisors who understand the limits of their profession and will serve their clients with that admission, and do their clients a lot of good by explaining the limitations of actionable information and presenting a variety of investment vehicles and how their operation may be of benefit. But the clients are invariably as unsophisticated as the Madoff investors and assign to their advisors a level of expertise that does not exist. Investment advisors who really do have the talent and instinct and drive to get out ahead of the market become hedge fund managers or analysts at a financial services firm – they will not become retail investment advisors.

Wealthy and sophisticated investors have a network to learn about and access to the very best in investment advice, but that access comes with conditions: the investment must be substantial and no carping in bad years - take your lumps or go elsewhere, and no suing. So my experience as a professional investment advisor left me with the view that truly effective investment advisors are extremely rare, and that they are unrecognizable to the public. This means that should a truly talented and effective investment advisor contact a jaded retail investor to offer help, the investor in all likelihood will reject the initiative being unable to discriminate between good and bad advice. And this is where the financial services industry is today, with a growing need to serve a growing but unsophisticated public that cannot recognize good advice, and responding with products that are more focused on protection from lawsuits than on capital gain.

Useful Closed-End Funds

Closing out this chapter I wish to return briefly to closed-end funds. Closed-end, like index funds, are a way to access otherwise inaccessible markets, like Singapore, for example -- there is a Singapore Fund. These are actively managed funds but they generally have very low fees, perhaps because they trade freely on the open market and do not burden management with creation and redemption of shares. I rate Singapore to be perhaps the most fiducially conscious and best managed market offering access to Southeast Asia. To access the world of closed-end funds, point your browser to www.cefconnect.com.

China is somewhat different. It is difficult to gain exposure to the China market, which is exploding , through a reliable third party, without either using a mutual fund with attendant high fees, and high ego to go with it, or a closed-end fund, which looks to me to be the better choice.

I will close with a final recommendation on the China market and funds. China is a totalitarian state and the market there exists at the pleasure of the leadership. I learned this when I invested in China toll roads and expected a windfall when storms hampered rail. I correctly figured that truck traffic would pick up on the toll roads, thus providing some capital gain and dividend distribution. Not so. The train freight was offloaded onto trucks, and the trucks did use the toll roads, but no tolls were levied on freight that otherwise would have been conveyed by state-owned railroads. So while your investment thesis may add up in an open market country, this is not the case in countries like China and Russia, where government officials use profitable companies like their own private ATM machines.

But there are options for getting in on the "China Trade." The East India Company monopolized British trade with China until a couple of very savvy Scots really ramped up the trade in 1844 by establishing a head office in Hong Kong. The company was named Jardine Matheson after the founders: William Jardine and James Matheson. By 1900 Jardine Matheson had become the largest trading company in the Far East and had expanded from tea into textiles, shipping and railway construction.

At one point the tea trade became so successful that Great Britain began suffering a great imbalance in the China trade and was having difficulty coming up with products the Chinese would buy, until they hit upon opium, which grew in India. That did the trick and soon the Chinese emperor found himself presiding over a nation of opium addicts. There were hostilities and Britain ended up with a chunk of China – Hong Kong. They gave it back not too long ago. But amazingly, Jardine Matheson Ltd. is still there, and nobody knows the China trade like this company. It is worth visiting their website, www.jardines.com, and buying a few of their shares periodically (JMHLY.PK). This is another fund I can comfortably endorse for access to the China growth engine.

To have encouraged the reader to focus on the common stocks of the Dow 30 would not have served the reader well without a discussion of alternatives. When an investors seek professional investor help, they will be presented with mutual funds. The rationale offered will be "safety." The point I wish to make is that while closed-end funds will capture dividends and stock splits, mutual funds will miss in most cases due to active trading.

When looking at a mutual fund, check the turnover number and you will undoubtedly see figures of 100% or more. That is a lot of trading, which runs up the fees, misses dividends and splits, and in the end, provides no value. Closed-end funds usually pay higher dividends, but I have had it pointed out to me that sometimes those dividends are juiced up to build demand. In other words funds from other sources are re-characterized as dividends. This is just more fund management chicanery.

For optimal growth balanced with safety, it is difficult to beat a well-diversified portfolio of common stocks, like the Dow 30, a subset of the S&P 500, or even better, 15 or so stocks from a list of 100 great global corporations. You will be told by your investment professional that this is dangerous, but the danger is to his purse, not yours.

Alchemist II   *Ben Aronson 2011*
oil on panel 64 x 48   *Jenkins Johnson Gallery*

Chapter 5

Wall Street

At this point, my book becomes a bit of a tell-all, because it gives insight into why in most cases avoiding a broker is the beginning of a sound investment program. Although there are some very good brokers, the pressures upon them may result in less than stellar performance, particularly for the smaller clients. Moreover, discriminating between good and bad brokers is a real challenge and is usually done by trial, and then the question arises, How many trials can an investor survive?

In the continuum of occupations, that of financial advisor is difficult to place. In order to offer financial services products to the public, the most prominent hurdle facing an entrant is passing exams mandated by the Securities and Exchange Commission through its enforcement arm called FINRA (Financial Industry Regulatory Authority). The basic exam is called the Series 7 and that may be followed by a number of others depending on the career choices a beginning broker makes.

There is also the Series 66 exam (or Series 63 plus Series 65), which covers state regulations and regulations that cover acting as a fiduciary or holding one's self out as a practitioner with the client's interest placed ahead of his own. In addition, a Life & Health exam must be successfully completed to sell products with insurance characteristics, like variable annuities, which will be discussed later.

Of the Series 7 and 66 exams, only a lesser fraction concerns itself with product knowledge; rather the focus is on ethics regulations, like a proscription against "front-running." Front-running is a broker buying a position for his or her own portfolio before offering it to clients. And there are numerous other proscriptions to practices the broker must learn to steer clear of, and these are considered much more urgent issues than product knowledge, which nonetheless is given considerable space.

In reality, a broker wishing to serve a wide audience, which all brokers hope to do, must engage in a daily comprehensive round of research to be well informed on any issue a client may wish to discuss. The gathering and digestion of market information is central to the occupation of financial advisor and has always been so, although the profession is changing. There has been a gradual shift from the occupation of "stock broker" to "financial advisor," reflecting several changes, but all rooted in a fight for assets on which to charge fees. Up until the '70s, stock brokers were just that, charging their clients commissions to make trades. Each time a client acted on a broker's direction to get out of ABC and into XYZ, two commissions were involved, a sell out of ABC and a buy into XYZ. Commissions at that time were hefty by today's standards and were fixed by regulation – there were no discount brokers and no online trading.

Evolution of the "Financial Advisor"

From the early 1970s to 40 years later, commissions dropped from 80 cents per share to 4 cents per share. Naturally the brokerage industry had to find new ways to make money and that was done by morphing persons from "Stock Brokers" into "Financial Advisors," expert on all things financial. The industry also widened the market from serving only the wealthy to the millions of people in middle America.

As opposed to a stock broker or "Customer's Man" who at 80 cents per share could advise sophisticated investors on late breaking moves in the stock market, Financial Advisors today serve an unsophisticated audience, much more prone to blame losses on bad advice, and sue over it, all for 4 cents a share. This has pushed the industry into offering a wider range of products that are more immune to disgruntled client suits and have the added advantage of fees that are difficult to discern. But perhaps the biggest sea change, is the general character of the client base from sophisticated to unsophisticated. And this comes at a time when the increasing longevity of the general population has put a new strain on finances. In an earlier era, people retired and died about 10 years later. Today people can look forward to 30 years or more of retirement followed by very expensive terminal care. How is this going to be paid for? Enter the Financial Advisor.

There are two threads to this story: getting financial advisors enough of an income to survive and matching up clients with needed products. This sounds like a rather easily surmountable challenge but it faces a fundamental disconnect: gaining the trust of skittish and lazy clients by advisors who will not survive unless they succeed in making a sale. The New

Yorker magazine, known for its wonderful cartoons, recently had one that can be noted here. The picture is an interview scene in which the candidate is leaning forward making a point, and the interviewer is laid back and very relaxed, taking in the scene at his leisure. The caption is: *"You're desperate. I like that."* Well, skittish and lazy clients do not like to entertain desperate pleas loaded with technical jargon that they are expected to understand and act upon. So the clients engage in all sorts of subterfuge and procrastination. Into this void enter Bernard Madoff the Ponzi scheme king. Bernie Madoff made significant contributions to the operation of Wall Street brokerage and rose to become Chairman of the Board of Directors of NASD (National Association of Securities Dealers); he also played a prominent role in the formation of NASDAQ, a computer trading platform that offered an alternative to the New York Stock Exchange and other established exchanges that use people rather than machines to conclude the transactions. From this vantage point, Bernie was able to gain the trust of a wide following and from that trust, built a very large book of brokerage business. Among the faithful, the mantra became: *"Just give it to Bernie."* This is the interface between the financial advisory community and the world of prospective clients. Clients are urged to not even try to understand what a financial advisor is explaining, bypass that fruitless exercise, and so *"just give your money to Bernie"* and be done with it.

This underscores the laziness of most clients. Bernie's clients were wealthy, and even they had no interest in financial product discussions -- so what is the average person expected to do? Madoff was eventually uncovered as a Ponzi fraud, paying off early investors with inflow from newer investors, with a loss estimated for his clients at between $12 billion and $20 billion. Of course the losses were attended with much hand-wringing by the shorted clients who took no responsibility whatsoever for their losses, claiming that people have a right to be protected from scams by the federal government, regardless of their inattention.

I am reminded of a gentleman who was horrified to learn that his girlfriend was pregnant, claiming that she had told him she was on the pill when she wasn't. She wanted to get pregnant, it seems. He was fighting child support. He lost. The court, in so many words, asked what responsible adult was close enough to the situation to make an informed decision. Well, nobody was closer than he was. For some reason this does not apply to investment; apparently clients are not informed adults who need to absorb losses as an outcome of their choices. Court action to restore those losses seems to indicate that clients believe they are only responsible for gains, and not for losses, at least in the Madoff case.

I can't help but point out that in phase two of the Madoff affair, a new set of characters then entered the scene to enrich themselves but under the cover of doing good – clawing back assets for the "innocent" losers. I refer to the Irving Picard circus that elicited the following from the New York Times:

"So far, Mr. Picard's efforts have created a whopping $554 million in legal and other fees. How much have Mr. Madoff's victims actually received from all of the cases and motions he's made? Only $330 million. And how much does Mr. Picard estimate the fee spigot will pour out by 2014? A mere $1 billion."

This is not unexpected and was very well caricatured by the French author, Guy de Maupassant in his short story: That Pig of a Morin. Mr. Picard merely updates an old story.

There is also another thread to the Madoff story that bears upon not only the culpability of clients, but also the unmasking of "expert" financial channels: feeder funds. Some Madoff clients did not know they were Madoff clients, having given their money to other "trusted" advisors such as Fairfield Greenwich Group, a prestigious Connecticut investment advisory firm. The following is "An Important Notice from Fairfield Greenwich Group," that appeared on their website along with office closing notices for New York City, London and Madrid.

> January 8, 2009
> To Our Investors:
> We have had many requests for further detailed information from our investors. We are working to collect these questions and to respond to them in an orderly fashion. We understand that many investors, along with the many other investment firms and private investors, share our shock and dismay at the December 11 news of the arrest and charging of Bernard L. Madoff with federal securities laws violations. It appears to be a highly sophisticated and massive fraud – perhaps the largest in history.
> As we have said previously, we are currently assessing the extent of potential losses and will pursue on behalf of our investors the recovery of all assets associated with our accounts related to Bernard L. Madoff Investment Securities ("BLM"). We noted that as of November 1, 2008, assets under management at FGG totalled approximately $14.1 billion, of which approximately $6.9 billion was invested in vehicles connected to BLM.
> BLM is in federal receivership and federal authorities are pursuing their case against Mr. Madoff and BLM. We are seeking to gather all facts, work diligently with counsel to determine the appropriate course of action toward recovery, and stand ready to assist the authorities with their investigation.
> We will communicate with our investors as we have pertinent news. For now, we must ask for your patience during these difficult times and thank you for your continued support.
> Sincerely,
> Fairfield Greenwich Group

Clients of Fairfield Greenwich Group thought they had found a work-around to the onerous job of investment analysis by becoming clients of an investment advisory firm that had all the trappings of exclusivity and success. While it is not known what sales proposition the group offered, another feeder fund was Medici Bank opposite the opera house in Vienna, also with the trappings of exclusivity and success, and the sales proposition there was access to Bernie.

It has been said that Medici Bank founder, Sonja Kohn, would take a suite at Claridge's Hotel in London, and hold court, condescending to act as an intermediary for the elect, which she was able to do due to her close personal relationship with Bernie Madoff. It was then up to the supplicants to state their cause, which presumably would include not only need, but wherewithal and perhaps a good dose of inattentiveness or lack of interest in the arcane detail of investments. To help on the trust dimension, Sonja Kohn apparently roped in some high powered trustees to her board, such as former Austrian Ministers of Economics and Finance. In any case, the proposition was that if you wanted access to Bernie, you had to go through her and she wouldn't take just anybody. Apparently she did take some Russian oligarchs who have a reputation for knowing how to take care of business the old fashioned way, and when the scandal broke, she dropped out of sight, or as Damon Runyan would have put it, "She took a powder."

The New "Customer's Man"

The Madoff case has been used as a poster child for Ponzi schemes, but I think it is more useful to think about it as the poster child for client/advisor interface. People seek advice on three services they have no prospect of understanding sufficiently for making an informed decision: medical advice, legal advice, and financial advice. How do doctors and lawyers handle this disconnect? They propose a solution to the client's problem and then describe the probable outcome of adopting the advice and the probable outcome of not adopting the advice. The second option is usually so terrible that the proffered advice is almost always taken and of course once that happens, the client is in bed with the advice giver and adoption is total. Moreover, medicine and law are backward-looking and merely apply tried and true prescriptions. In medicine the tried and true solution is called the "gold standard" of care. Investment is forward-looking into the murky unknown future.

This may sound like a lame process but what is at work is that enough doctors and lawyers are expert enough to provide the promised outcome because they are simply repeating what they have done hundreds of times before. We can say doctors and lawyers are expert at what they do. There is also one other dimension that prompts people to seek out medical and legal advice; this is when the problem as stated by the client is not in the practitioner's "sweet spot," the client will be redirected to a more appropriate practitioner. This is because doctors and lawyers are generally not desperate for new clients, or not as desperate as stockbrokers. There is also the possibility that doctors and lawyers are ladies and gentlemen who will reciprocate on referrals. As a rule, stock brokers do not reciprocate.

Financial Advisors do not have the luxury of studying a set curriculum to gain mastery over what prospects are looking for – gains. There are no rules in financial services as there are in medicine and law. There are a myriad of financial instruments, each accompanied by a daunting curriculum, but even mastery of that curriculum only addresses the past and not the future. Medicine and law is the application of tried and true remedies, and the effectiveness of those remedies follows closely upon their application: The patient lives and the law client avoids jail. Financial advice is peering into the future of a volatile and random process and the outcome will not be known for years. So what proceeds from this conundrum of trying to win desperately needed new clients on a promise that if delivered will not be visible for years? Well, Wall Street. And that is a Wall Street that includes characters as diverse as John Bogle, who worked to reduce fees for investors, and Bernie Madoff, who sought to earn fees by defrauding investors.

Since discriminating between the John Bogles and Bernie Madoffs is so daunting, some work-around had to be found just to make the market work. That work-around is called "assets under management" or AUM. Once an advisor has any critical mass whatsoever, say $30 million, AUM becomes the mantra: "I have $30 million under management," declares the advisor, that then might attract a $1million relationship. An advisor with $100 million under management might win a $30 million relationship. Where is performance or expertise in this? There is none; it's irrelevant. The only thing that counts is trust that the money is in the "right" hands. And this is how Madoff worked and it is how his feeder funds worked.

Madoff had $20 billion under management and that put him in the big leagues and the bigger the league it seems, the less the scrutiny, by all players. Well, not all, but most players. Witness the story of one gentleman who apparently earned 50% in four years at Madoff Securities, pocketing over $1 million in profit, but closed out his account after being told by his accountant that such returns were not credible. So this is one of the few who was able to rise above the "bandwagon" effect and take constructive action. All others were on the bandwagon or schlafwagen (sleepwagon) on the German railroad.

The SEC Schlafwagen

It turns out that the SEC may have been on the schlafwagen as well. A report faulted the SEC for missing "repeated and obvious signs of trouble." The report cited obvious flaws, such as the fact that in general the securities inside a Madoff fund were not doing as well as the fund itself, a clear invitation to further scrutiny. If the SEC was on such a schlafwagen, what is a retail investor to do?

One could argue that Madoff, due to his pioneering work in the securities industry, would naturally been given a pass by the very industry he was part of. But in 2003, Société Générale, a prominent French bank, took Madoff off their investment menu after conducting due diligence. A few years later, in a separate action, Bancaire Privée, a Swiss bank, took similar action. But the inertia embedded in financial advisory relationships is so great, that even in the face of strong evidence, action is not always taken. Witness the case of the ownership of the New York baseball team the Mets. The ownership partners of the Mets were heavily invested with Madoff, and apparently were challenged on at least two occasions, one being by advisors at Merrill Lynch which said that Madoff's performance was suspect. This would be inexcusable but for the fact that even the SEC, whose mission is regulatory, couldn't break through the inertia of the status quo either and that is what they are paid to do.

The way the investment business works is that the SEC recognizes the New York Stock Exchange (NYSE) and the National Association of Securities Dealers (NASD) as self-regulated organizations (SROs) to exercise oversight on the securities industry they operate in. This style of regulation was prompted by the proliferation of financial scams that lead to the great crash of October 1929. It took a few years for Franklin Delano Roosevelt to get into the White House and begin cleaning up the mess. But when he did, the SEC was created by the Securities Exchange Act of 1934. This is the genesis of the requirement for all persons offering financial services products to the public to pass the Series 7, Series 66 (a combined Series 63 and 65), and Life & Health exams. The NYSE and NASD merged their enforcement arms into a new SRO called the Financial Industry Regulatory Authority (FINRA). FINRA now rules.

But the existence of FINRA does very little to bridge the gap between the public and the financial services world. The fundamental problem is this, buying and holding a basket of common stocks of companies that are household names will provide all the growth that is needed to outstrip inflation and, bolstered by a savings rate of 5% of income, will provide a secure retirement, however, you cannot make an industry out of such action – there is not enough to do. Given the choice between holding "Blue Chip" stocks to retirement and beyond or trading on "research" that anticipates price-appreciation spurts, enough of the investing public chooses the latter to make an industry, and what an industry. The industry is so loud, cacophonous and all enveloping that the idea of just holding stocks long term isn't even a talked-about option, and in fact is characterized as dangerous. The envelopment is so complete that the term "investment" is understood to mean trading in and out of stocks on what is cited as "research." It is research of the most transient kind, not leading to any long-term assessment of company strengths or weaknesses but rather on some arcane aspect that is thought to propel stock price in the near future. The world is made of news junkies and for them we have the Wall Street "research" machine. Wise investors will head for the exits. But, there would be no exits if there wasn't a Wall Street to create them through a regime of trading.

It would not be surprising to find that the public views this culture with skepticism, not informed skepticism but just a kind of skepticism created by apathy. I believe this apathy is created by Wall Street's hijacking of the term "investment" to mean trading, forcing ordinary people to confront a world of trading protocol they have no affinity for and no interest in. *"Just give it to Bernie"* becomes the default mantra. There is also another dimension to this phenomenon - affirmation. Often when an individual finds a financial advisor who seems to be succeeding for them, they will promote use of that advisor to others as a way to gain affirmation for their selection. This behavior also helps to promote the client/advisor relationship perhaps in hopes of prompting better service. Of course none of this has anything to do with a clear evaluation of suitability of advisor or investment method. It is merely what happens in a vacuum.

The Client/Financial Advisor Interface

But most of the public doesn't have access to Bernie so they are afloat on a sea of Financial Advisors, each with a story of investment expertise. But it is the kind of expertise prospective clients are unable to evaluate because, for one thing, there is no expertise for a market that is totally random. So the public defaults to performance and assets under management (AUM). A skittish client may be reeled in by an advisor who has a big book of business, like Madoff. Moreover, because clients are unable or unwilling or both to explore the soundness of the advice they are being offered, what is the incentive to offer sound advice? Would a butcher offer pork when beef is demanded?

Another example of this conundrum has to do with the required practice of calling clients before placing trades. Brokerage houses will not accept written or emailed instructions to execute trades; only the spoken word from the client, is acceptable. When I was a new broker, I asked a veteran how the client could judge a recommended trade without doing the same research the broker had done. The look I received in return told me that was a taboo question.

The U.S. economy, perhaps the most sophisticated in terms of financial engineering, has never solved the problem of serving the public need for financial services. What follows is a look at how it is done in this inexplicable vacuum. But the core reality is that since retail investors cannot digest financial services information, the financial services industry defaults to sales pitches designed more to obfuscate than educate. The role of FINRA is to place limits on the obfuscation. All historical performance charts, for example, must be accompanied by the qualifier: "Past performance is no guarantee of future results." One might well ask why then show the chart in the first place?

How Financial Advisors are Created

I will use my own case to illustrate the minting of a Registered Representative. Mine is a typical recruitment by the financial services industry and will serve to illustrate the relationship between know-how and the practice of advising clients either for a commission (non-fiduciary role) or for a fee (fiduciary role). But first I must go back farther in time to an incident in graduate school.

At the age of 40 I decided to go to graduate business school and get the coveted MBA that was supposed to put my career on steroids. Since I worked full-time, I decided on an executive MBA and was accepted at an Ivy League school. In the last semester we students were given the opportunity to take some elective courses and I chose Investment Banking. It had been my dream to be a merchant banker in the mold of Mayer Amschel, the first Rothschild, and now I had my chance. On the first day of class, a gentleman entered the room, who I understood was from a Wall Street firm. He walked up to the front, stood, and addressed the class with this question: *"What happened today?"* What happened today? I couldn't think. I was expecting a lecture on investment banking and this guy wanted to know what happened. I tried to think back about the morning headlines and couldn't come up with anything notable. I then thought that maybe there had been some event on campus, but I hadn't heard about anything on campus either. By this time, there were some boys toward the front who were waving their hands in the air, and the professor called on one. When the student stood, I could see he was formally dressed in a suit, with the jacket carefully hung over the back of his chair, and wearing a tie and suspenders. I then noticed that a great many of the students were similarly clothed. I was wearing a sport shirt and slacks, maybe even jeans.

The student stood and recited the event: *"There is a drought in Ethiopia and I am buying grain futures on the Cairo exchange."* *"Good!"* shouted the professor and then called on another who had a similar tale to tell, followed by another *"good!"* By this time I had gone faint and knew I was in the wrong class.

After that little warm-up exercise we went into interest rate swaps; we had to calculate the present value of cash flows associated with two loans and then price a swap. Well, I have always been math challenged and was completely befuddled by this game. Finally, relief. The class was over. I didn't walk; I ran down to the registrar's office and withdrew from the class. I just couldn't think in terms of looking at all of life's events as sources, or not, of profit.

This story then became part of my repertoire when entertaining others at cocktail parties, and then one day, well after I had become a stock broker, I repeated the story in abbreviated form to my wife, who said, *"That's the way you think today."* Well, I had to admit, that when I read my favorite source of information, The New York Times, a secondary objective is finding investment opportunities. For example, I read the other day that Fiat, the Italian automaker, is bringing their iconic small car, the 500 (Cinquecento) to the United States. Because the U.S. market is many times larger than the Italian market, I immediately made a note to buy Fiat shares, well ahead of the market. If I had been in class that would have been my story: *"Fiat is bringing the iconic Cinquecento to the U.S. auto market and I'm buying Fiat shares. "Good!"* the professor bellows out in my imagination. Ah. I have finally arrived.

It was another 20 years before I used my business school education. I was 60 years old at the time with a long career as a sales engineer calling on heavy industry with a fair amount of international work. I had posted a resume on the internet and received an unexpected response, which began: *"Dear Sir, We think your experience would be a good fit for our business…"* When I saw that it was a brokerage house, I laughed it off and deleted the email. Well, long story short, I had heard that stock brokers make a lot of money and the firm had an incredible history going back to the 17th century, and being an avid investor and admirer of Mayer Amschel, the first Rothschild, I bit. I bit with dreams of becoming an American Irish-Italian Rothschild.

There were several interviews and tests, and I was soon

seated at a desk in the "bullpen." My job was to spend the next 6 months studying for the Series 7 and 66 exams, and for the Life & Health exam and do the daily online product and industry drills I found on my computer screen. I was given a workbook to complete the online drills, which would train me on products.

There were sections on stocks, bonds, mutual funds, etc. Also, at 7 a.m. every morning there was squawk box, which was an opportunity to listen in as analysts presented their reports. Analysts seemed to be MBAs from prominent schools who had perhaps worked under a senior analyst, and were tasked to "follow" about half-a-dozen stocks and report regularly on them. They were undoubtedly the students who had so unnerved me in graduate school. It soon became my perception as I made my way into this strange new field that the purpose of the squawk box was to give brokers sales ideas with the chatter to go along with it.

After squawk box, the next task was filling out various sheets reporting various national and global indices and various interest rates over various terms. The idea here was to prepare every broker to field client questions on market performance for both stocks and bonds. A client calling in with some arcane question on where the DAX was that day would very quickly get a precise answer, which would inspire confidence that he was talking to the "right" person and the "right" firm.

I was also in training during the emerging housing bubble and had to learn the securitization of mortgage backed securities called Collateralized Mortgage Obligations (CMOs), which were split up into "tranches" of varying risk/return characteristics -- with the main tranche dubbed "Plain Vanilla." Of course in my training I spent a few hours on this subject and then moved on, and maybe there was one question on it on the Series 7, which, by the way, is a six-hour exam taken in two three-hour sessions. And incidentally, the standard test-taking reminder -- "There are no trick questions" --does not apply to brokerage testing, because every question is a trick question.

Each day of the six-month training was taken up with a new subject that had to be mastered well enough to pass a thorough quiz. Keeping up the pace was a struggle. I worked from 7 a.m. to 9 p.m. daily and put in weekend hours.

Most of the people who were hired passed the very challenging Series 7 and Series 66 examinations because the major brokerage houses would administer a test that would select out those candidates unlikely to pass. There were a few failures and, in one house, failure meant dismissal whereas in another house, one failure was tolerated but not two. But the pass rate was surprisingly high.

When the exams were passed, newly minted brokers were sent to a training facility for two weeks of practical training, where product specialists would make presentations and then answer questions. The idea was to give the new people a chance to see how things worked in the real world. Several evenings over the two-week session, cold-calling laboratories were held to acquaint students with cold-calling techniques. While I had no problem with this at all, many students did and some wound up calling friends and family. Later cold-calling would develop into my core competency and lead to some success, but at my peril as I will explain later.

The Loss of Innocence

There occurred an incident worth relating because it gives a flavor of how the population of financial advisors works, which will give insight into the Madoff affair and other less than edifying behavior at the hands of brokers. After my six-month training and passing all securities exams, I traveled to corporate training headquarters and joined a company-wide class of about 200 trainees. One morning in assembly, it was announced that a very high ranking muketymuck would be visiting to make a brief motivational speech. We expected the gentleman to take questions and so we were prompted to rehearse "good" questions. I have always been big on class participation and so devised the following question: *"Are you contemplating any bolt-on acquisitions in retail brokerage?"* By this question, I meant was the company planning to acquire another brokerage house, like a Morgan Stanley or Smith Barney. I was rewarded with an *"atta boy"* -- our instructor liked this question.

On the day of the event, sure enough the high muketymuck showed up, gave a motivational speech and then took questions. I thought I would hold back with my question. Then I heard someone ask: *"Are you contemplating any bolt-on acquisitions in retail brokerage?"* Well, I'll be. Someone had stolen my question. This would be an omen for things to come. When assets are too difficult to bring in from the outside, advisors sometimes look for assets on the inside – from their fellow brokers. I read somewhere that Hammerhead sharks give birth to live young but some of them emerge half eaten by their siblings. I was beginning to see I was emerging a new-born broker in Hammerhead shark country. This eventually caused me to leave the brokerage world. But during the assembly, not to be left speechless, I asked: *"Our logo of crossed keys is obviously very European. Do you think this will be a headwind in the American market?"* After the meeting the instructor caught up with me and said: *"Hey Pat. You really threw him a hardball."* It was a hardball and the high muketymuck had stumbled over it, but in the end, it made no difference -- when it comes to money, European is just as good as American.

Gathering Assets

At the end of two weeks, I returned to my sponsoring office, was told I was now "in production" and had to go to work "gathering assets" as the terminology went. I then undertook a cold-calling campaign and reeled in several accounts over the next six months, but it wasn't enough and so I was dismissed.

Over time I learned that the attrition rate is about 90%, that is, only 10% who are hired by the major brokerage houses are still working as brokers a year or so later. The sticking point is building a book of business by attracting clients. It also became apparent to me that most of the 10% who survived had a connection to either an outside source of client money or to an established broker.

The brokerage houses, aware of the tremendous challenge of gaining new clients, offered ongoing training and motivation. These were typically one-day sessions with about a dozen speakers who were mainly motivational or focused on the sales aspect of the business. The closing ceremonies inevitably included prizes for brokers who had brought in the most assets. And since charging fees on assets is the name of the game, the focus was on bringing in the assets, and nothing else.

During lunch at one of these sessions, I got into conversation with a young woman who admitted being new to the production end of the business, having spent about five years as a client associate (CA). Client Associates actually did most of the work required by clients. The broker was responsible for acquiring the client and periodic reviews, but the day-to-day service work was performed by the CAs. Some CAs were licensed and those that were, actually entered the orders and in many cases had a closer relationship with the client than the broker. But sales trumps service, so it is the broker's client and the difference in pay is astronomical – where a CA might make $50K the broker made $300K or more. When we went into production, we were told to give the CAs a bonus from our earnings to help them out. I must also add that the CAs worked like dogs.

The CA-turned-broker I was on the lunch line with, described inheriting a book of business because the broker she had worked for retired. Actually the deal was planned in advance and the broker waited for her to get her licenses before retiring. She didn't say what size the book was but it was clear that prospecting or cold-calling was not in her future.

At the end of the day, the brokers who had brought in the most assets were publicly identified and rewarded, obviously as incentives for the rest of us. These awards were also attended with much prompting of the general audience to get in the groove and bring in those assets the way these stars had done. One of the major stars of the day was the young woman I had met in the lunch line. She had brought in big assets, and was given a huge box as a prize, which I presumed to be high end electronics of some sort. There were about five or six others similarly identified and rewarded. I was of course, experienced enough by that time not to be surprised by the use of such props to motivate others. In fact, in a later meeting I became such a prop. But this underscores the culture at the brokerage firms: What matters is assets and not how you acquire them or how you manage them.

When a broker is dismissed it usually signals the end of the brokerage career so I was quite surprised to receive a recruitment call to work for another major firm after my first dismissal. *"Why would they want me,"* I asked. *"Well, I can get you an interview. Do you want it or not?"* I was asked. Accordingly, I went on the interview and was hired. I learned that what they liked was my work ethic and sturdy cold-calling; they wanted a strong cold-caller, they said.

I had a rather funny incident soon after. It was early morning before most of the office was in and I was in the men's room when one of the largest brokers in the office entered. *"Who are you?"* he asked. I replied that I had just come over from XYZ. *"Why did you leave them?"* the broker asked. *"I didn't,"* I replied, and with a leg and foot motion said, *"I was kicked out."* *"Well, why would they want you here?"* he asked. Then, bending down to make sure there were no others in any of the stalls, I whispered: *"Beats the hell out of me, but I ain't askin."* The broker just rolled his eyes and walked out.

Later I became quite friendly with this broker, viewing him as one of the real people in the office and also one of the very few stock-pickers, spurning the default to mutual funds for his clients. He made a very fine living, I'm guessing well over $300K and he had a large boat, on which I was hoping to have an outing sometime.

One day, again early in the morning, we again fell into conversation, and he told me he had taken his nephew out in the boat over the weekend, and the nephew being very impressed began pressing his uncle to take him on in the brokerage business, but the uncle only offered discouragement. He said the business had become so difficult he would discourage anybody from attempting it. Good advice, I later learned.

Accounts under $100K are pretty much treated with contempt except by new brokers trying to build a business. Larger brokers typically will not take an account under $250K because of the risk/reward ratio – liability-to-income. Brokerage houses are targets for lawyers specializing in financial chicanery and the awards can be mind-boggling even in cases where there was little to no provable malfeasance. I will relate a case that came to our attention at an annual compliance meeting, attendance of which is always mandatory.

Big Money and How it is Invested

A wealthy gentleman died leaving his wife a portfolio of stocks that was not highly diversified. This gentleman, it seems, had a preference for a particular company and had about $6 million of its common stock in the portfolio he left his wife. In this case, the broker allowed the CA to do most of the contact work because over the years, the CA and the wife of the deceased client had developed a close working relationship. Well, the market tanked, and the wife's holdings went in the tank with the market. A savvy lawyer got a hold of this incident and brought suit on behalf of the wife for not diversifying her holdings, as a hedge against market volatility. The brokerage, on the hook for millions of dollars, got a deposition from the broker in which he testified to having discussed diversification with both the husband and the wife after the husband's death, but because there were no notes and no letters the brokerage lost the case and had to pay up. This is in spite of the fact that because the broader market had tanked any diversification would have offered little protection, plus the fact that if they had waited, the stocks would have recovered. So this gives insight not only on the hazard of serving clients, but also the short market outlook taken not only by lawyers in search of rich settlements, but also major brokerage.

Another story relating the myopic view taken by sophisticated and professional investors may be illustrated with the well-publicized case of Martha Stewart, Sam Waksal, and their Merrill Lynch broker, Peter Bacanovic. As reported, Sam Waksal, co-founder of a pharmaceutical company, ImClone Systems, was awaiting results of an FDA approval application on a new drug called Erbitux. Sam apparently got word that the FDA was turning down the application, and as is the way with pharmaceutical stocks, which rise and fall dramatically on the success or failure of R&D efforts, this development was sure to sink the stock when the information went out to the public. In SEC-speak, this was material, non-public information, and to trade based on this information is illegal. Trading without the information is not illegal. But Sam apparently got the word and put in sell orders with his broker, Peter Bacanovic.

Peter then apparently advised Martha Stewart, a friend of Sam and another key client who was holding a large position in the stock and also who, incidentally, had been a licensed broker earlier in her career. Martha sold her position in the stock and avoided about $45,000 in near-term paper losses. She drew prison time for apparently lying to authorities. My guess is that because all she knew was that Sam was selling and concluded she should sell, too, her action did not rise to the level of "insider trading." Presumably, Sam Waksal avoided a much larger figure, but again, in short-term paper losses.

A year later, the stock rebounded to a healthy gain, and eventually, Sam Waksal, after spending five years in prison for insider trading, sold ImClone Systems to Eli Lilly for $6.5 billion, and Erbitux was generating $1.5 billion in annual revenue. Peter Bacanovic incidentally, was fired by Merrill Lynch and was banned from the securities industry for life. Had all of these players, all of whom can be characterized as sophisticated and experienced and "accredited" investors, taken a broader view, they could not only have avoided the draconian consequences of transgressing regulations on "insider-trading," but also realized a handsome profit. Perhaps no other case better illustrates the myopic view of market insiders and the lack of expertise attending the highest levels of an industry holding itself out to be indispensable to the public.

The lesson is that the constant daily, if not hourly flow of information is so compelling, that even sophisticated investors and professionals are prompted to act on that information for no other reason apparently, than that it exists. For professionals, there is one other reason the information flow is actionable, it is sales fodder for gaining new clients, and of course the news media caters to this "need."

Building a Book of Business

When I completed my licensing and training and went into production, I was faced with the question of what to tell people when I got on the phone. One of my first clients was a Chinese woman from Washington, D.C., and I acquired her business by being the first to point out to her that as a resident of the capital, she had access to municipal bonds from all states on a Federal tax-free basis. Muni bond interest is free of federal taxation to residents of home states, the point being to allow the state and city government agencies to raise money more cheaply by offering lower interest that is also federal tax-free interest. Also, Muni bonds are considered safe because governmental agencies enjoy taxing powers, which may be used to pay the bondholders. Residents of the nation's capital may consider all the 50 states to be home states. This woman was unaware of this and rewarded me with some business, but she was exceedingly wary and gave me only a small starting capital amount.

I then had to figure out what I was going to do for her. I felt uncomfortable proposing Munis and so focused her attention on stocks. I was faced with the information onslaught and had to diligently pick my way through it. Remember that six months earlier I had been a sales engineer with absolutely no intimate knowledge of the stock market, and here I was, six months later, deciding how to invest money for a client who could only surmise that I was a professional and an expert. Nothing could have been further from the truth; I was already a member of the smoke and mirrors club.

Elsewhere in this book I describe the bond market of which the Muni market is a subset. I had the good fortune later in my stock broker career to work next to a former bond trader and so got some insight into bond trader analytical methods, but bonds are generally considered within the broker community a special case reserved for "bond people," and better left to those specialists. Looking back now, if I had to do it all over again, I would have skipped stocks and focused entirely on bonds, because bond salespeople are viewed by the public with a level of respect not given to "stock brokers." As it was, I was ignorant of this at the time and proceeded down the stock channel.

I began an internal campaign among my fellow brokers, querying them on what I should do, and for the most part I was given lists of mutual funds. It turns out that with the rise of the unsophisticated retail investor who was reliant on others for "advice" and would sue if that advice resulted in a near-term significant loss, there arose action on the advice side to forestall suits and this action was a flight to safety offered by mutual funds. First, as a fund of multiple stock positions, volatility was largely dampened, but even so, if a fund did tank, which occurred from time to time, the broker would simply point his client to the fund as being the villain.

Brokers are also insulated from suit by calling a client to get approval before entering a buy or sell order. In this way, the suit-prone client need only be reminded that he approved purchase of the fund, and ignorance is no excuse – if a client approves a purchase, it is assumed the client has given informed consent. So the diversifying character of mutual funds and offloading of culpability along with informed consent has reduced dramatically -- though not eliminated -- the suing dimension of serving an unsophisticated public. I looked at the mutual funds and was totally non-plussed by their performance and their fees. In general, performance lagged the S&P 500 index and typical fees for this underperformance was 1½%, though it wasn't for lack of effort, annual turnover in most funds is 100% or greater. Now the fee issue did arise for me, because, after all, I had to earn a living at this.

A broker has two choices for earning a living by acting as a "Registered Representative," which is the official SEC and FINRA title of a licensed broker. A broker may put his client into mutual funds and collect an ongoing fee that is embedded in the funds, which is the low impact solution, or a broker may be "transactional" and buy and sell discrete stocks and bonds for trading commissions, which is the high impact solution. A typical trade might generate a $100 commission, 60% of which goes to the brokerage firm, leaving the broker with $40 per trade as income. If a broker does 10 trades a day, that's an income of about $100K a year. Brokerages, of course, want assets, so they skew the commission "grid" to incentivize the gathering of assets. Accordingly, small brokers might only get to keep 25% of their trade commissions while the largest brokers might get to keep 75%. I decided on a third way, a "wrap" account. This type of account permitted the charging of a blanket fee for all trades as long as the trading activity was kept moderate, but the fee was charged on assets under management and quarterly, whether or not any trades had taken place. Incidentally, wrap accounts came under fire from the non-Series 7 community, which is made up of non-wirehouse practitioners (wirehouses are firms that have a "wire" to the stock exchange and can enter orders directly) who offer their advisory services for a fee and act as fiduciaries rather than brokers. They are called Registered Investment Advisors (RIA) and must pass the combined Series 66 or the Series 63 and Series 65, which are the State regulations and regulations governing fiduciary relationships.

The RIA community argued that they were at unfair disadvantage because they were not paid fees by the mutual fund companies as the wirehouses were and therefore had to charge their clients their personal management fee on top of the mutual fund fees. Mutual fund fees that range from about ½% to 1½% contain distribution and sales commissions that are paid to the wirehouses but not to "for fee" RIAs outside of the wirehouse world. This agitation on the part of the fee-only community led to changes, but did not entirely eliminate wrap accounts.

Now that I had my first client in a wrap account and had solved the fee problem, I decided to avoid mutual funds and pick stocks. In our office there were about 20 brokers of varying success, experience level, and style, but only one stock and bond picker, a guy named Mike, who incidentally also owned 23 race horses, several of which he raced at the Meadowlands and Yonkers and occasionally at Northfield in Cleveland, Ohio. I shared my skepticism of mutual funds with Mike; an instant friendship formed and he cheered me on. He was also the largest broker in the office and the loudest.

Transactional business, as Mike's was, depended on commissions and so he was on the phone every day with the story of the day. But Mike got his own story; he never tuned in to any corporate blather. Instead Mike followed what he called "break out" stocks by lying on his couch at home every evening and watching the ticker on a financial news network. Days were spent talking to clients, mainly about baseball, or presidential election prospects. He was sort of like Rush Limbaugh, never at a loss for words and keeping up a constant and loud dialogue interspersed with a particular stock he was peddling for the day. The clients almost always bought what Mike was selling. He was successful, but I once told him that he would never be able to sell his book of business, because there wasn't anybody who could replicate his style, a style his clients had come to expect. He didn't disagree.

I also didn't feel I could promote Mike's stock picks because I was more of a buy-and-hold guy and didn't feel comfortable with the transactional model and the fast moving stocks that a transactional model entails. It was also becoming increasingly clear that my time devoted to prospecting had to ratchet up from 50% to 150%. I began working from 7 a.m. to 9 p.m., the ending time dictated by regulations on outbound cold calls, and most of that time was spent prospecting rather than studying stocks.

I was still listening to squawk box in the mornings but felt that as a neophyte I should start out with large cap stocks. These were not sexy and therefore not good sales candidates. "*Mister, I have some information on GE that you might want to know about*" is a non-starter, for one because the listener might well already own GE, and for another because information on GE is ubiquitous. This is not how one attracts new clients. Nevertheless I focused my attention on selling large cap stocks and put my first client, the Chinese woman, into the Swiss pharmaceutical company Novartis.

The "Research" Department

I needed another stock for my Chinese client and one day got my wish. I had signed up for a corporate email service called "International Stock of the Day" and one day the stock of the day was a Chinese coal mining company with a big dividend. According to the attached report, the stock was trading at $60 per share and the analyst felt the stock was headed to $90. Because my client was Chinese, I thought this was a slam dunk. I bought the stock for her.

Well, several weeks later the stock started heading down dramatically and I became spooked and in a panic called my client for approval to sell, which I got. I then sold out the position and emailed the analyst to learn what happened. He emailed me back from China: *"You have to expect some volatility."* But he had rated the stock at low volatility in his report, I emailed back. He emailed another response: *"There was an IPO,"* and then the channel went dead. I then began a search on my own on this stock and learned that a much larger coal mine just went public, which of course would depress competing smaller stocks. I then downloaded the annual report and found the mouth-watering dividend was also a mirage – it yielded around 1%. I didn't have to think about it, I had gotten out well before it settled around $30 per share.

You can imagine my surprise when about a month later out came a new report on this coal mine stock, from the same analyst, forecasting low-volatility with a target price of $60 from the present $30. I finally decided that this analyst was probably required to issue regular reports whether merited or not and that this mine was simply the best thing he was covering.

For this book I reviewed how Yangzhou Coal Mine had fared since this episode. Since I bought and sold my client's position, the stock split 5-for-1 and today is trading at $14.98 while appearing to have a yield of about 2%. So if I bought it for $60, a five-way split would value each share at $12.

Considering the present $14.98 price, this represents an appreciation of about 2.5% per year. The dividends, of course, would have helped. This was the international stock of the day from our "research" department.

When I was dismissed, my Chinese client did not follow me to my new post. I presumed the reason was because she knew very little about me other than that I pushed the panic button on the Chinese coal mine. I learned my lesson, no more "Stock-of-the-Day" from headquarters research analysts who have to come up with a stock, any stock, every day. No more Chinese coal mines and no more rosy research reports. This also propelled me further away from brokerage firm chatter and doing my own research on blue-chip stocks. The term blue-chip incidentally comes from the casino practice of assigning blue colored chips the highest value, originally $10, while red chips were worth $5 and white chips $1. Presumably blue was also the color for royalty as in the term "blue-bloods."

Long before my dismissal I knew I was in trouble, but hope springs eternal and I always thought, right up to the time of my dismissal, that the next call I made was going to be to some clueless heir who had just inherited millions and was desperate for help. I also was becoming aware of what a struggle for assets there is on Wall Street and became privy to office gossip of how this or that broker was angling to take over a book of business when a retirement came up. Brokers can also buy a book of business from retiring brokers but this is dicey because many clients have several brokers and when one leaves the business, they just shift their assets to other relationships they already have. Consequently most sales are paid over time on retained assets. This also applies when brokers leave one wirehouse for another.

Office Management

While brokers are tasked with bringing in new assets, office managers are tasked with the same agenda and carry it out by recruiting brokers from competitors. If a broker, for example, has $100 million under management, and that business is producing, say, $1 million in fees a year, about $250K of that goes to the sponsoring office. If a competing manager can successfully recruit such a broker, his office can expect $250K in annual fees to come into his office, so he might offer the broker $500K or more to move his business, but the pay-out will be on retained assets. For this reason, many large brokers periodically move their businesses, and what gets left behind is typically business they don't want anyway. Small accounts, those under $100K, are liabilities in that the fees generated don't outweigh the risks of suits, which are more likely to be brought by smaller clients who don't understand the volatility of the market and don't have the resources to weather a storm. As a matter of fact, occasionally brokerage firms will dismiss a number of smaller brokers for the same reason. They are given perhaps five years to build a sizable book of business and if they can't do it they are dismissed.

An exception to small broker dismissals would be a broker who has a small book, but also one sizeable client. The brokerage firm doesn't want to lose a client like that because large clients often beget other large clients. In the office I was in, there was such a broker and when her client got into the news for alleged illegal activity, the firm pulled the plug on the client and she lost her job. It is quite possible that she could reopen with that client at another firm, which is probably what happened.

When brokers left, all of their clients were distributed to the other remaining brokers, typically by pecking order. This then prompted a cat-fight between the departing broker fighting to move his clients to the new brokerage house and the newly assigned brokers at the former house fighting to gain the trust of new clients and convince them to stay. Over the years I was in the business, I inherited a number of clients under $100K in assets and was encouraged to hand them over to a central office that managed smaller relationships, and then focus on bringing in the bigger clients. But I liked the experience of managing the assets and clients afforded from these smaller inherited accounts.

One day I had an interesting experience relating to working with small clients. I was asked to meet with the compliance officer who had in his office a newish broker. The broker had a client who was threatening to sue this very large brokerage firm because she thought she was being billed inappropriate fees and neither the broker nor the compliance office was able to do a thing with her.

Evidently their next step was to give her account to me. I accepted because I was desperately in need of assets to keep my job. I studied her file, noted that she owned two annuities and arranged a meeting with her at a coffee shop near her home. It turned out that previously she had owned fixed annuities and that the two in her account at present were her first variable annuities. There are no fees on fixed annuities because the firm takes the earnings from the investments and is on the hook to the client for only the small fixed income that is a fraction of the profit. The fees are the spread the firm realizes between investment profits and the fixed rate they pay the client, so no fees on fixed annuities, the annuity provider takes the spread. I then explained that on variable annuities the roles are reversed and the client takes the lead position and gets the big payday while paying the financial firm a small pittance (the fees) out of the winnings. She was starting to see that she had been sold a different animal, and generally liked what she saw and for the first time began to view her original broker and the compliance officer as maybe not crooks after all. I then asked her what she would like me to do with the assets inside her annuities. *"Isn't that your job?"* she asked. *"Well, yes. Do you think I should be paid for it?"* I responded. *"Oh. So those are the fees,"* she said. So she got it and I had a new client -- and the brokerage didn't get sued.

The suit never would have gotten any traction anyway but probably would have prompted a payoff to make her go away at a fraction of the cost of an attorney.

Smaller brokers, always faced with dismissal, have another option. This is teaming up with a larger broker to form a larger entity that has the added advantage of offering greater service resources, allowing team members to specialize and offer clients greater depth. These, too, can be troublesome in that sometimes team members prove unreliable or begin recruiting other team member's clients. For this reason, many of the teams are made up of family, if even extended family members. The eventual hope of those who weren't able to partner up, is to become a junior partner to an older broker, without family, who can be expected to exit and leave his book behind, perhaps for a fee or an ongoing piece of the action.

There is one incident worth citing to give a view into the working of an office. A trainee had recently gone into production, and one day happened to be at his desk during lunch when a prospect came in off the street and wanted to speak to a broker. This trainee was the only one available, so he got the client opportunity. Usually a "Broker of the Day" is named for call-ins or walk-ins, but the rules are you have to be on station, or if not the available broker gets the client -- and that's what happened in this case.

The trainee won the investor's trust and opened up a $1.5 million account. This was breathtaking, but didn't last. When the office manager returned from lunch and found out about it, he directed the trainee to share the account with one of the veteran brokers whom the manager selected. Not long afterward, the trainee, who may have been dismissed for failing to hit the asset target, was at a competing wirehouse, but had failed to bring the account over. The client, faced with the ordeal of moving the account, just kept it with the experienced broker who had been brought in by the manager. My guess is that in fact the manager anticipated the departure of the trainee and took anticipatory steps to keep the assets in his office by bringing in a proven long-time broker. But it points out the futility of becoming a stock broker if you are not connected to some asset pool.

After I was dismissed in my first job for failing to gather the requisite assets, I decided that trying to build a book of business with retail clients was too daunting, particularly since I didn't have a network to money. I knew of one quite good broker, for example, who had started from scratch, but had a mother-in-law who was well connected and brought her son-in-law most of his clients. He had been a portfolio manager in Israel and had deep experience, which I'm sure helped. That wasn't my situation so I had to find another way. I finally decided to prospect companies for their 401(k) plan business. This might seem like a stretch from a service and advisory point of view, plus it would force me into the mutual fund world which I was very jaded on, but it would also mean meeting assets targets and keeping my job.

The service dimension of 401(k) plans would be handled by a "provider" like The Hartford, who backed up brokers with packaged 401(k) plans. My job would be to find the client and then pick the funds for the program menu. People from The Hartford would come out and help me do the selling. Given that plan sizes can range from $500K up to $500 million and higher, it looked like a fast-track to what in the industry was called "making it" or achieving a large enough book of business to make a living. A popular expression among the new brokers was: *"You fake it until you make it."*

Top "Experts" and "Partners" in the Potemkin Village

Accordingly I shifted my business entirely to the institutional market, but soon ran up against new challenges, as will be seen.

I prospected and set up a meeting with a business manager who was uncomfortable with the management of his company's $500 million pension plan. A major bank had acquired the bank holding the plan and had fired the advisor on the account. It was several months before a new advisor from the acquiring bank contacted this business manager and, as the manager told me, he had lost contact with $500 million he was responsible for, for several months. In a preliminary meeting I had with him, I learned that he was the top manager and that his father had saved the company after WWII by sourcing raw material from China. So I was talking to the right person. I told him I would bring in the experts to meet with him and further there was no danger of our firm being taken over since we had been in business since 1913 -- he would not lose access to his assets.

When I began exploring who to work with on this project, which was clearly well beyond my own experience and capabilities, I learned there were two possible tracks. I could either work with our corporate Retirement Group, who would treat me like a step-child while they managed the account and paid me accordingly, or I could work with an institutional level retirement plan broker and share the business. While I was pondering this decision, the obvious broker candidate called me and opined that he would be able to find revenue in the relationship that the Retirement Group institutional people could not, because they were almost like government employees, staffer types, and didn't have any commercial sense. This gentleman's practice was the only large enough "institutional" level broker team in the state and had been profiled in a prominent retirement plan magazine, and had also been the broker of record on a strictly advisory relationship to a Fortune 100 plan. This choice seemed obvious and so I decided to have both the corporate Retirement Group staffer and the institutional broker cover the meeting.

The meeting with the $500 million prospect was brief. First the corporate staffer gave a short speech extolling the firm's trust services and then quickly ended by saying he had prepared a booklet describing the services in detail and pushed the booklet across the table to Tom, the business manager we were attempting to sign up with us. The impression I got was that the corporate guy was indeed a staffer and had no idea what trust service work really was. I'm sure Tom got the same message. That phase of the presentation then ended and it was the broker's turn. *"Tom, have you thought about transitional services?"* asked the institutional broker whose expertise and experience he told me was crucial to winning and managing this large block of business. At this, Tom's hand went up, as if to stop that discussion in its tracks, and said: *"We give our people a very fine retirement; what they decide to do with it is up to them."* This was followed by silence. I then addressed the broker and suggested: *"George, why don't you tell Tom about our asset management capabilities."* George then looked across to Tom and asked: *"Tom, would you like to hear about our asset management capabilities?"* Tom answered *"Nooooo."* George then addressed me and said: *"Tom doesn't want to hear about our asset management capabilities."* End of meeting to win $500 million in assets using a top-tier firm's top people. Not only are they inept on product knowledge, they can't sell. If some very high-value retirement plan sponsor at a corporation in this area had called New York area headquarters for direction on a local contacts to manage a plan for them, that individual would have been directed to the gentlemen I had at this meeting.

I couldn't believe what I was seeing and hearing: the corporate talent plus big broker written up in the media and broker of record on the Fortune 100 advisory service laying an egg on a $500 million opportunity. I would learn later that even getting such a meeting was a once in a lifetime event for many brokers, and I had done it in months, and now it had totally blown up on me by the very people who were supposed to be top experts. I would also hear later that big broker got his book of business given to him, and as far as the Fortune 100 deal went, I was told that a friend at headquarters had asked him to be broker of record on a headquarters project for which he had done nothing. So it's all about smoke and mirrors to coax the skittish clients into opening an account. And the retirement plan magazine that had profiled this broker and his team? Another smoke and mirrors job to sell magazines.

I wrote Tom a letter thanking him for meeting with us but also apologizing for the poor performance. I then went back to the retirement plan magazine, not understanding yet how the system works, made a list of the biggest retirement broker teams in the firm nationally, and began a national discovery process. I finally settled on a much larger broker from another state, who told me among other things not to worry about the corporate guy, that when you got into his league, the corporate people go away. I met with this gentleman, was satisfied he could sell, and set up a number of meetings for him. On the day of the repeat meeting with Tom, the $500 million pension guy, I warned my new broker that although everything we had worked on thus far was 401(k), the meeting with Tom was about pension – defined-benefit rather than defined-contribution.

The meeting began with Tom pontificating for about 10 minutes on what was wrong with their present relationship and finally concluding with the thought that he should work with a regional bank well known in the area. My new broker then started in selling Tom on the benefits of a 401(k) plan. Obviously, game over.

This meeting was briefer than the first, and when I called Tom some weeks later for a third meeting, finally with the "right" people, he said no. I couldn't blame him because of the previous meetings, but it turned out my third pick was the right group. But then I had a new problem, getting paid. Later I won a $70 million project with this latest group, but my commission wound up being around $10,000 a year for three years for $70 million in assets, hardly worth the effort.

Getting paid by your partners is a big problem on Wall Street, because once you bring the broker in, it is his relationship, and your contribution in finding the client is no longer valued -- you have given up all leverage. I had similar results with other broker teams and even brokerage firm management, who transferred partner shares on my projects to suit their strategic interests in keeping larger brokers satisfied. I finally concluded that partnership is not possible with this Wall Street crowd, which explained to me why in all of my years I had been unable to find a good broker.

A German friend of mine once described the term "Potemkin Village" to me citing the story of Russian minister Grigory Potemkin erecting facades along his monarch Catherine the Great's route to impress her with his gains of a new "developed" territory. I came to understand in my new career I was living in a Potemkin Village, with wall-to-wall modern-day Potemkins.

I walked into the break room one afternoon and encountered a medium sized broker and just blurted out: *"There is no correlation between ability and assets under management."* The broker didn't say much; he sort of just grunted and left. Several days later as I walking toward my cubicle I heard my name being bellowed out across the entire room which would have included about 25 cubicles and maybe 10 adjoining offices: *"Pappanoooooo. No correlationnnnnnnnnn."* I looked across to see that the bellower was the broker I had encountered in the break room several days earlier. He had finally gotten it – there is no correlation between ability and assets under management. I think he had reached a new milestone that day.

Educating Brokers on Product

Because so much time is spent prospecting for new assets -- which is what the brokerage firms want brokers to do, like selling more cars -- the product education component was a constant activity that was brought to the brokerage office by staff people and lunch sessions hosted by various financial product aggregators such as mutual fund managers. There would be a lunch session almost every day and they were very popular because you didn't have to bring or buy your lunch, you just attended the session. And it seemed that the sessions worked because the mutual fund companies kept coming back and most of the brokers kept buying.

In a number of cases, the mutual fund company would bring in one of their top analysts and your attendance would be rewarded with, in some cases, stunning and insightful economic analyses. In any case, the brokerage firm is a treasure trove of educational opportunity on a wide variety of products. But therein lay the weakness: Presentation was really about packaged products to be sold and not discussion of individual companies or broad investment methodologies; these you would have to research on your own.

The products that were being promoted generally have two dimensions, both of which are daunting: the moving parts of the product itself, and the application of the product to a widely varied audience of clients of whom, in many cases, not enough was known for making a good fit. Take long-term care contracts as an example. Such contracts have numerous conditions that need to be studied and in some cases tailored to specific circumstances. For an advisor to become expert enough on both the product and the client is often too time-consuming a task, and in many cases, a specialist is brought in to do the detail application work. The specialist had little interest in the client and was driven only to make a sale, so the client would not necessarily be well served by an arrangement that included only product expertise rather than expertise in securing a proper fit. This is not discovery, it is subterfuge. I knew of many cases where clients had purchased products they thought they understood, but with the passage of time forgot how the product worked as well as the nature of the benefits, and the advisor was of little help because he wasn't much more knowledgeable himself. I say this not to condemn the Wall

Street culture, because for one thing many of these products are very useful and for another conveying their operation to a client who needs the product but is incapable or unmotivated to understand it is an almost impossible job. In addition, distributing such products through commission salespeople is probably a recipe for failure.

During my tenure at a major brokerage firm, I had arranged a meeting with a Fortune 100 company retirement committee. During the course of the meeting, one of the leaders said they had engaged a prominent national firm to offer education to their 401(k) plan participants, but cut off the engagement because the advisors from the firm simply viewed the engagement as an opportunity to sell variable annuities. This is called rollover business, in which 401(k) plan participants are encouraged to engage in tax-free rollovers of their 401(k) plan assets into positions outside of the plan and under the management of the outside advisor. In other words the advisors weren't educating, they were gathering assets.

This practice can have unfortunate consequences, but in the case of variable annuities one benefit is that they hold their value during periods of market upset, to be explained in another section of this book. So this company's complaints were well founded -- sales were trumping education -- but the outcome for the participants was not necessarily negative. Where it could turn negative is when a participant changes advisors and the new advisor prompts the sale of a depressed variable annuity, which is a frequent practice. In order to gain a new client, an advisor must exhibit a level of expertise greater than the existing advisor, and variable annuities offered such opportunities. The reason is that variable annuities have both very positive and very negative characteristics, and a case either way can be made, making variable annuities candidates for sales initiatives in both their acquisition and disposition. Most variable annuities are cashed in prematurely, which produces losses for their owners.

Building Credibility

Aside from packaged products, brokerage firms also encourage their brokers to work for designations that would add prestige and the appearance of expertise and trust-worthiness to their identities. For example, you could take a course and pass an exam and put the initials CFP after your name – Certified Financial Planner. Another designation that can be earned by about a 20-hour course is Accredited Investment Fiduciary – AIF. Perhaps the top designation is CFA, Certified Financial Analyst. Earning this designation is more difficult that earning a PhD in Economics from Harvard and is an entre to the field of security analysis, wherein work the analysts who make reports on the squawk box.

Many mutual fund managers today are CFAs, which speaks volumes for their accomplishment and brings the financial services industry closer in-line with the medical profession in preparing practitioners who really do know what they are doing. Sadly, however, there is one key difference between medicine and security analysis, and that is that medicine is backward looking -- the doctor is discovering a condition that exists now and will apply a remedy that has already been proven. The security analyst with a CFA designation will be very knowledgeable on what has happened so far, but will have no extraordinary power to forecast the future, and advising clients on where to put their money is all about the future.

As pointed out elsewhere, Burton Malkiel, PhD (Princeton) gave fundamental analysis no more credibility than technical analysis because the past doesn't forecast the future – the future is random. In my opinion, the study of economics, into which the CFA delves extensively, is the crucial prerequisite, and I would rather have a Harvard PhD in Economics than a CFA if only because the first does not require demonstrated mastery at picking stocks to be thought useful, whereas the latter does.

Picking stocks is a crap shoot, even in the best of times, and the best preparation is the ability to think ahead 10 or 20 years. Remember the example of ImClone, with Waksal, Stewart, and Bacanovic, all focused on tomorrow when five years later they could have cashed in. They didn't think that far ahead. There can be successful trading, but the success comes, as was enunciated by John Maynard Keynes, not by watching the stocks, but by watching the people watching the stocks – people behavior is not so random as stock prices. This is why the CFA, as prestigious and all-encompassing as it is, is not much help when it comes to managing assets. Nevertheless its cachet persists.

But Wall Street being Wall Street there is a reason for promoting CFA – CFA training so thoroughly educates its graduates on corporate and market operation that they are able to conjure detailed and elaborate analyses of investment theses with which their listeners can do nothing but agree. This brings in assets because investors, particularly the un-initiated, confuse a command of history with command of the future or a command of investment practice. And let me state unequivocally, *the stocks you pick are not nearly as important as what you do with them after you buy them. The genesis of investment success is inside your head and not inside the workings of a particular corporate entity.* It is wisdom and judgment that counts. It is the tenacity to stay the course when the squawk box is telling you to sell that brings about what the investor is looking for – long-term wealth creation.

After two years at my second brokerage firm, I had again failed to bring in the requisite level of assets and was facing dismissal. I had a number of sizeable 401(k) plan prospects, some quite close to closing, but none in the bag. The office manager was intrigued with my business and gave me a few more weeks but told me that rules required him to cut me off. He was an exceedingly effective manager I thought and had been very sympathetic to my case. During this period I was trying to close a very large 401(k) plan with a combined stock option management opportunity. What I didn't know was that the 401(k) plan was already with the firm, but being managed at the corporate Retirement Group (RG) level without an advisor. I was hoping to get the advisory role with the advisory fees.

My contact at this company left and I was talking with her boss, filling him in on the status of the project. Later that day, I received a call from the corporate retirement group, telling me that the client had called them and objected to my prospecting effort because I was not local to him, although the client had emailed me his home phone and office contact information. It didn't make any difference, I was told; when a client calls and objects, the personal advisory dimension of the relationship becomes theirs. I then stammered and said I was working with an institutional level broker who was very local to the client. *"Maybe that will work. We'll have to see,"* I was told. In the meantime I was out, and pretty much out of work. I immediately called my very local institutional level broker, whom I was trying to partner with, and filled him in. The result was I went on his payroll. I moved from Cleveland, Ohio, to Fairfield, Connecticut, which I wanted to do anyway because I was from Connecticut originally.

Not long after my move and because of my earlier work with the head of the corporate retirement group, the large 401(k) plan was awarded to the broker I was working with because of his partnership with me. I had the connection to the assets but was too small to be given the $325 million plan whereas my new partner was large enough but had no connection to the asset pool. The partnership worked for both of us and for the office manager who saw his office revenue go up. I was credited with a $325 million 401(k) plan and became a poster at the next inspirational meeting.

The reason I was given the plan by RG (Retirement Group) is illustrative of the asset gathering culture. Earlier I had prospected a very large company and gotten a meeting to present 401(k) participant education. I had become jaded on a broker I was sharing a $9million 401(k) plan with and decided to bring in the largest retirement broker in the firm for this new engagement. I never spoke to the broker himself so concluded that I would play a very peripheral role. I then took that broker team off the case. The next morning my email in-box contained a brief note from not the office manager, but the area manager—I "would honor my original commitment" to the big broker team. I looked at the distribution of this email and saw it included some of the biggest names at the firm. The big broker evidently had friends in very high places.

I was then resigned to working with this team on my project. Needless to say, I was marginalized during our meeting that was also attended by the head of RG, a very fine gentleman and an excellent presenter. The big team laid an egg at the presentation with a very poor performance that was only kept afloat by the occasional contribution of the RG guy, who as I said, was excellent.

After the meeting I was making my way out through the lobby and encountered the big team with the RG guy waiting for their car. As I walked through, I congratulated the team on the fine performance they had turned in, with all sincerity. It was not the expected response and the RG guy rewarded me at the next opportunity which was the $325 million plan. Also, when I got the partnership on the big plan, my partner on the $9 million plan, the guy who tried to sell Tom a 401(k) plan to solve his pension problem, yeah, that guy, cut-off my share of the $9million plan.

Our agreement on the $325 million plan with my new partner was to split 50/50, but revenue to me was very small because plans of that size pay very small fees. Then the first bump. In January it was time to renegotiate the splits, and my partner on it reduced my share to 30%. When I objected, my new partner said he would give me 40% but I would have to share in expenses, which would be extensive: He described the executives of the company whose 401(k) plan we were managing ordering very expensive bottles of wine over very expensive dinners he felt necessary to host in order to grow the relationship. I settled for the 30% since the cash flow from the plan was so small anyway. I had no choice; it was my partner's relationship, not mine, though I had brought it in.

Then my new partner left the firm. I was excited. I told my wife, my ship had finally come in, I was likely to get the whole revenue stream and our near-term cash flow problems were over. Wrong. The next bump came when the partner of the departing broker, one of the gentlemen who had paid my salary while waiting for the plan to come in, wanted a share in the plan. *"What for?"* I thundered. And he replied, *"Who do you think paid for you to come here?"* And then he accused the departing broker of milking the business by buying first-class airfare, five-star hotel rooms, and expensive dinners to entertain the new clients. He felt ripped off by his partner and he wanted the plan to pay himself back. No such luck. He didn't get any part of the plan and my share remained at 30%. The 70% share was given to, you guessed it, the largest broker in the office, who didn't even do 401(k) business. This was a further example of not an office manager dealing with his managerial responsibility by giving larger business to veteran brokers, but an area manager. This was the area manager who didn't want to lose one of the largest brokers in his area and so rewarded him as an incentive to stay. I left the firm.

A point that needs to be made about this episode is that although the cash flow from this plan was small, about $110,000 a year I was told, there was a catfight for it because whoever got the plan could then state, truthfully, that he was managing a $325 million relationship. Because prospects use assets under management as an indicator of success, as Bernie Madoff did, managing a $325 million account is a real plum. And because it was a 401(k) plan, the broker of record could use the client to claim both assets under management and expertise in managing 401(k) plans. This was true even though the client wasn't relying on the brokers for expertise; the plan throughout this period, continued to be managed from retirement group headquarters.

For the client, nothing had really changed. My partner had been named broker of record and that got him the advisory fee cash flow and the opportunity to present himself as the expert over meals at five-star restaurants, much to the consternation of his other partners, as I learned.

I was reminded of the episode of the other broker-trainee stealing my question intended to be a softball for the high muketymuck at our training session.

So I seem to have a history of blowing off ominous signals that I should pay more attention to. I probably should have left the industry after the question-stealing incident while I was in training, but I was intrigued with this new and venal world. I cite the following essay by Sam Lipsyte, *"A Monopoly on Cheating."*

A Monopoly on Cheating
By SAM LIPSYTE

I HATE cheats. They cut the line and snatch the bargain. They sweet-talk the customer service rep into bending the rules. They count cards and win the raffle with some sneaky ticket placement. They are the 100th caller every time. They trick you on mileage or square footage and bribe their way up the organ transplant list. They pump and dump their stocks, their families, their friends. They get ahead and they win. We lose. Then they explain ever so condescendingly that it's not a zero-sum game.

I never cheated much as a child, not on tests or papers, not at Go Fish or poker or even board games like Sorry or Risk. It's been the same since. I pay my taxes, under-claim expenses, give mistaken change back to the cashier. I don't lie on applications. I'd probably fill out my own death warrant with civic-minded meticulousness.

I'm not bragging. I find this part of me repellent. I'm not noble or good. I'm adult enough to know that the victories of cheats don't feel hollow to them. They live happy lives. They don't think they are cheats. They consider themselves warriors of life. The fact is, I don't cheat because I'm scared of getting caught, and I will be caught, because my fear will give me away.

You have to hand it to cheats. They have drive and nerve, though their ends tend toward the nefarious. Many great fortunes, from those of the robber barons to those of the robber geeks, bear some taint, an original murk, land wheedled here, software appropriated there. The upright schmoes just stood around, bewildered, fleeced.

We often claim otherwise, but cheating helped build the wealth of this country. That and murder, slavery and outright theft, of course, but the subject here is cheating. Our capitalist system has always harbored cheats, catapulted them through loopholes into riches and glory. The country has paid dearly for it. Predatory loan, anyone?

Still, I was raised to believe that America was the one place you didn't have to cheat. Hard work alone would deliver you. I think I learned this from a filmstrip at school. Boy, was that filmstrip wrong, ..."

After leaving this company, I went to work for an independent firm and was credited with a $10 million 401(k) plan and a $70 million endowment, but my commission on these two projects was only about $15,000 a year for 3 years. So I left the industry.

The asset management fee on this $70 million endowment is about $200,000 a year or an annual fee of about .285% of which I receive about $10,000 a year for 3 years. That's the finder's fee. The remaining $190,000 is for managing the engagement, which means quarterly meetings and creating the investment portfolio, which is a duplicate of portfolios already created. So I fit into a very thin segment of Wall Street wannabes, not the 90% who wash out because they don't gather enough assets, but a thinner subset who can't get paid on the assets they do gather. At any rate it became very clear to me why I had never been able to find a good broker, they are very, very few in number and very difficult to discern in the vast field of financial advisory obfuscation.

Meritocracy: The Changed Face of Wall Street

There's an interesting and perhaps prophetic story about a chance meeting in which a very sophisticated investor was explaining the growing failure of Wall Street to benefit Main Street.

According to the narrative, Wall Street was at one time populated by "blue bloods," or people from families with a long history of wealth and wealth management. In those times, the sons were sent to prestigious Ivy League colleges where they earned "gentlemanly grades"(Cs mostly) and then upon graduation, were brought into the "white shoe" firm to learn the business of wealth management. The sons were inevitably of mediocre intellect but brought up with a sense of Noblesse Oblige, and they plied their trade very evenly and took plenty of time off to spend with their families, and of course became very prominent in their communities for chairing various committees and taking an active role in various charities. Generally they set a tone of quiet sobriety, personal restraint, honesty and reliability.

Then society shifted toward meritocracy and the polite society was shunted aside by the "A" students who came mostly from lower middle-class families striving to get their sons and daughters into a better life. Many of the next generation became so fixed on success that not much else mattered. Those that felt particularly oppressed by their earlier poverty entered Wall Street as a way to cover over their wounds with wealth, and it worked. Soon, the titans of Wall Street could claim a-rags-to-riches rise entirely due to their own grit, sacrifice and focus. They had beaten the blue bloods at their own game. In one case, one of these titans, who left with over $100 million before his firm crashed, said in an interview he had been intimidated at Harvard until he saw he had outscored those he perceived to be his betters, and he said *"...after that, there was no looking back."* This story was pretty much validated in my experience.

Many of the most successful brokers I met had come from lower and lower-middle class backgrounds and saw Wall Street as a way out of the poor neighborhoods of their youth. I noted that that much of their success was displayed in their cars and clothes. This runs in stark contrast to when I was a youth, when successful people drove gray Buicks, eschewing the easily afforded but too ostentatious Cadillac -- Cadillacs were for the Nouveau Riche.

When I was a broker working at a major firm and began to run into conflicts with large brokers -- and the conflict was always the same, they wanted access to what I had found -- I once got a dressing down from a top manager, who was doing it in a nice way. At one point I said: *"You know, these brokers get a coupla bucks in their pockets and then they think they are somebody."* The conversation turned cold; he didn't want to hear it. He didn't want to hear that advisory relationships are Potemkin Villages where what the client sees is often far different from the reality. But it is the Potemkin Village effect that succeeds. It's when brokers think they are somebody that they are able to reel in those assets from a public that responds to confidence in a sea of doubt.

What do successful stock brokers have? Money and clients is the answer. Even if they are unable to exercise any control over their client's assets in a totally random market, they are validated by the devotion of their clients and the outsized paychecks they realize from them.

The theory of Capitalism is that wealth is only possible through great accomplishment, but those in the real world know this panegyric breaks down under analysis. Wealth often also goes to those not particularly accomplished, but rather focused on gaining the reward without the bothersome effort to earn it. My observation is that the Wall Street community is the best example of this phenomenon, many being Potemkin people to go along with the village. They look good on the outside, but once you walk in and dig a little deeper, even on the subject of investment, response will be pretty thin and mostly clichés and platitudes. My theory is that investment is all about character, something not very prevalent in Wall Street culture.

In an earlier era, the blue bloods were somebody, with cultures built up over generations, each being trained to understand who they were and what their mission was. With the new meritocracy from the Ivy League, this sense of self is missing and in the financial services business this is a game ender, as we have seen – the advisor must be somebody. So lacking a family pedigree or tradition, the next option is buying the apparent pedigree, with cars, clothes, watches, etc. It must work, because it is universal.

The brokers I saw trying the hardest were inevitably ostentatious in their life styles: the best cars, clothes that were obviously very expensive, and French cuffs with cuff-links were pretty standard with the larger brokers. And the people who pursued this occupation were changed by the money it produced for them. What may have at one time been sensitivity to second-class citizens, ultimately gave way to jovial and somewhat loud acting out, fielding all questions with flip one-liners, finding the silver lining in every investment idea. And this transformation is aided by the brokerage firms, who see these individuals as their ticket to success, and treat them like thoroughbreds in a race.

In the pecking order of a brokerage firm, the top management is king and the top brokers are the generals, but in reality it is the generals (big brokers) who rule; the managers are in reality the valets to the big brokers. The result is that when Mom and Pop open an account at a brokerage firm, they will size up the broker by dress, office size, assets under management, respect commanded in the office and all other imaginable visual signals, but the one thing not on the table for discussion, is a serious discussion of investment method, and if the subject does come up, it will be managed with a well-rehearsed "investment philosophy," or "value proposition."

We aren't back in the days of the blue bloods, who have largely disappeared; we are in the modern age of meritocracy, faced with buying products we need but don't understand -- and don't want to understand -- from people we don't trust. The Madoff case is a vivid example.

According to an article in *The New York Times*, Madoff developed a cult following:

"....with eager and sophisticated investors who could not contemplate that a man of his stature and track record could possibly be a fraud. Mr. Picard called the Mets owners sophisticated investors who should have known better but were "simply in too deep" to act on any warnings."

So in the above case even sophisticated investors preferred to look at the man rather than the product, and apparently got "in too deep," to exercise judgment. To this can be added that whereas in medicine, a result of a doctor's judgment will at some point manifest itself, this is not the case with investments. These will fluctuate, sometimes wildly, and there is a rational-sounding explanation for any eventuality, like "market correction," "flight to safety," "profit taking," "program trading," "liquidity preference," and many others designed to stop any unpleasant exploratory conversation.

There is one more episode worth relating that helps illustrate the Wall Street culture found in the professional investment world. I used to take a bus to work, which got me to the office very early. So I began using the gym in the office's building rather than the one where I lived. I would work out for about an hour, cool off upstairs in my cubicle and, after an hour or so, go back to the gym, shower, shave and dress for the day.

One morning I was in the break room, in my gym clothes getting a cup of tea, when a large broker walked in and commented on my dress. *"It's 7:30 and we don't open until 9:00,"* I countered. He replied with, *"Sometimes clients come in for early meetings."* I thought to myself, here is a big broker whose tenuous hold on his clients might be threatened by a client seeing someone in gym clothes early in the morning. I got further clarification. The office manager had decreed sometime earlier that Fridays would be dress down days to business casual and this large broker had objected.

One day, in a general meeting the big broker had an opportunity to describe bringing in a big account. He started by thanking everybody for their fine decorum during the prospective client's visit. The prospect was taken on a tour of the office and then he and the broker adjourned to the broker's very large and finely appointed office. The prospect was reassured enough to open up a $30 million relationship. The broker attributed the sale to the very professional decorum in the office, which pretty much meant how people were dressed. So there you have it – the winning of a big client with decorum.

Finding a good broker is not a new problem. Witness an episode of Benjamin Franklin in 1761. First it must be noted, that Franklin is not well understood by the general public, because he was an older and non-military man at the time of the American Revolution and so played a more peripheral role in those events central to our nation's military history – Franklin's career was largely behind him by then, though he did play a pivotal role in getting France in to help us.

In 1758 while traveling in Scotland on behalf of the "province" of Pennsylvania, Franklin was awarded an honorary doctorate of laws by St. Andrew's University with the following announcement:

"The ingenuous and worthy Benj. Franklin has not only been recommended to us for his knowledge of the law, the rectitude of his morals and sweetness of his life and conversation, but hath also by his ingenuous inventions and successful experiments, with which he hath enriched the science of natural philosophy and more especially of electricity which heretofore was little known, acquired so much praise throughout the world as to deserve the greatest honours in the Republic of Letters."

From that time, Franklin was often addressed as "Dr. Franklin." In addition, he had by this time become a coveted and highly esteemed member of London's Royal Society, which comprised many of the day's leading physicists. Franklin's inclusion owed to his experiments and technical papers on electricity leading to his invention of the lightning rod. These honors serve to call attention to Franklin's superior intellect, which had been on display from his youth. He escaped his family in Boston to strike out on his own, established a successful printing business, started a newspaper, an almanac, and a philosophical society in Philadelphia, founded what is today the University of Pennsylvania -- Pennsylvania's contribution to the Ivy League -- and came to the notice of the Royal Society of London from papers he had written. Franklin, by all measures, was an extraordinarily gifted individual.

In 1761, while in London, Franklin was made custodian of

£30,000, which was Pennsylvania's share of a parliamentary grant to the colonies for expenses connected to recent wars between England and France. Franklin was then confronted with the contemporary problem of what to do with a block of assets. Franklin's friends in London, and you can be sure these were well-placed friends, recommended a stock broker named John Rice, known for his "care and circumspection." Soon after, Franklin gave Rice £27,000 of the grant, which was then deployed in *"...stocks chosen for their stability and long term promise."* No too long after, the Pennsylvania Assembly decided they needed the money and asked Franklin to liquidate their holdings. That occurred just as England and France were undertaking new hostilities, dragging the market down. By the time all the positions were closed, the account was shown to have suffered a loss of £4,000. But John Rice, as it turned out, had to give up "care and circumspection" to cover some of his losses from customer accounts and was discovered to be somewhat of a fraud. He fled to France, which being at War with England, would be a good place for him to hide from his English creditors. But the hostilities ended as quickly as they had begun and France complied with an English extradition request -- Rice soon found himself back in England again. He was jailed, later tried, and hanged for financial chicanery. Thus ended Franklin's early experience with stock brokers.

The point of relating this episode is to illustrate a perennial problem – the difficulty if not the impossibility of finding asset management that can be described as "caring and circumspect." Nobody could have been in a better position to have succeeded in this endeavor that Dr. Franklin, and yet this great intellect and man-of-the-world with access to very prominent and knowledgeable friends, was clueless in securing good financial advice. It seems matching clients with financial advisors has not advanced since Franklin's day.

The point of this book is to separate Wall Street culture from investment – they are not synonymous and possibly even in opposition. Retail investors can't discriminate between good and bad advice and so Wall Street has no incentive to offer good advice. It is assets under management (AUM) that matter; the profession reduces to an assets game. You will probably do better by staying away from investment professionals.

Burton Malkiel in his oft quoted book points out that analysis of past stock performance is a very poor guide to future prospects. This means that the average person should be more than capable of selecting a portfolio of stocks just from everyday exposure in daily life. It's true, that small emerging and perhaps promising companies will be missed in the early stages, but few make it out of the starting blocks, and they are not needed to meet ambitious investment goals.

The best performance among non-professionals, or even portfolios served by professionals, is the long-term holding of stocks in well-known companies purchased over time using Dollar-Cost-Averaging (explained in Chapter 10). And if you still feel intimidated, just follow Malkiel's prescription and buy the S&P 500 index, but over time with dollar-cost-averaging. And you can do this in just a few hours a year. If you do this, you will not only beat most of Wall Street, you will have an asset pool to finance a retirement. While I agree with Burton Malkiel about the S&P 500, my prescription is to buy the 30 discrete common stocks that make up the Dow 30 so you can capture the dividends and stock splits as well, or even better select 15 or 20 stocks from 100 of the greatest global companies.

POSTSCRIPT:

The following is an interview from *Der Spiegel*, the German news magazine, with Daniel Kahneman, Nobel prize-winning psychologist who has focused on investor behavior.

SPIEGEL: Experts, for example, have gathered a lot of experience in their respective fields and, for this reason, are convinced that they have very good intuition about their particular field. Shouldn't we be able to rely on that?

Kahneman: It depends on the field. In the stock market, for example, the predictions of experts are practically worthless. Anyone who wants to invest money is better off choosing index funds, which simply follow a certain stock index without any intervention of gifted stock pickers. Year after year, they (index funds) perform better than 80 percent of the investment funds managed by highly paid specialists. Nevertheless, intuitively, we want to invest our money with somebody who appears to understand, even though the statistical evidence is plain that they are very unlikely to do so. Of course, there are fields in which expertise exists. This depends on two things: whether the domain is inherently predictable, and whether the expert has had sufficient experience to learn the regularities. The world of stock is inherently unpredictable.

SPIEGEL: So, all the experts' complex analyses and calculations are worthless and no better than simply betting on the index?

Kahneman: The experts are even worse because they're expensive.

SPIEGEL: So it's all about selling snake oil?

Kahneman: It's more complicated because the person who sells snake oil knows that there is no magic, whereas many people on Wall Street seem to believe that they understand. That's the illusion of validity …

SPIEGEL: … which earns them millions in bonuses.

Kahneman: There is no need to be cynical. You may be cynical about the whole banking system, but not about the individuals. Many believe they are building real value.

SPIEGEL: How did Wall Street respond to your book?

Kahneman: Oh, some people were really mad; others were quite interested and positive. It was on Wall Street, I heard, that somebody gave a thousand copies of my book to investors. But, of course, many professionals still don't believe me. Or, to be more precise, they believe me in general, but they don't apply that to themselves. They feel that they can trust their own judgment, and they feel comfortable with that.

In an April 22, 2012 article on Goldman Sachs written by Susanne Craig and edited by Andrew Ross Sorkin, *The New York Times* reported that the firm had been fined $22 million by regulators for providing favored clients with research that deviated from research published for their other clients. Apparently Massachusetts fined the firm $10 million in 2011 for the same practice. Also, as reported in the same article, *"The trading huddles grew out of a 2003 settlement with regulators in which several Wall Street firms, including Goldman, agreed to pay a $1.4 billion settlement to resolve accusations that they had been issuing overly optimistic stock research to win more lucrative investment banking business.*

Ferdinand Pecora was part of the Kennedy team under FDR to clean-up the market after the 1929 market crash and aggressively pursued "sweetheart" deals that involved high government officials and highly-placed justices. Pecora's work, perhaps more than that of any other individual, resulted in new regulations that brought about real change, like successful passage of the Glass-Steagall Act that separated commercial banking and investment banking. Pecora also uncovered the practice of setting up shadow corporations to unload debt onto, making the "host" corporation look better. Pecora's book: *Wall Street Under Oath: The Story of Modern Money Changers*, is available at Amazon for $550. A cheaper read is: *The Hellhound of Wall Street: How Ferdinand Pecora's investigation of the Great Crash Forever Changed American Finance* by Michael Perino. At Amazon for $11.18.

THE HELLHOUND
of WALL STREET

HOW FERDINAND PECORA'S
INVESTIGATION OF THE GREAT CRASH
FOREVER CHANGED AMERICAN FINANCE

MICHAEL PERINO

Volatility Index   Ben Aronson 2010
Oil on panel, 24 x 24 inches   *Private Collection*

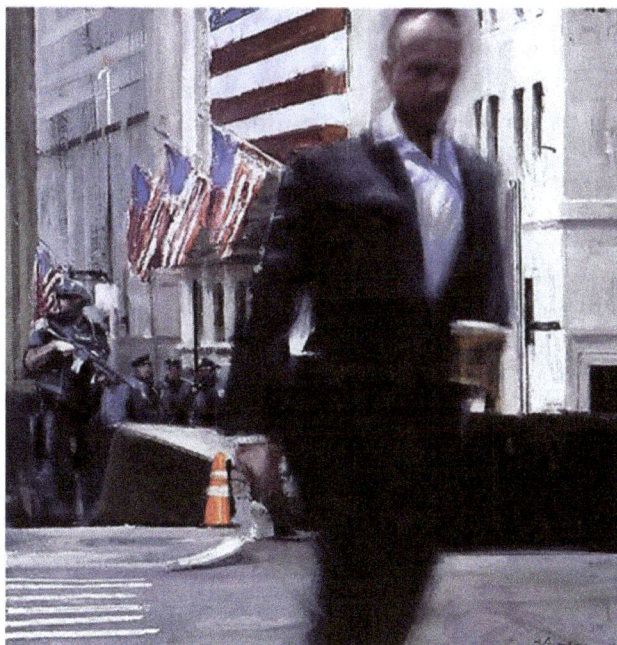

Chapter 6

You, the Investor

Libenter homines id quod volunt credunt.
Men freely believe in whatever they want.
Gaius Julius Caesar, from the Commentaries on the Gallic War.

In the last chapter we beat up on the unbridled venality of Wall Street actors, but just as in the disposition of used cars, not even the most venal used car salesman has as much larceny in his heart as the very nice young couple trading their car in: *"We hate to part with it."* Or how about the family man, having put off buying life insurance suddenly getting a warning from his doctor, goes home and "innocently" calls up a life insurance company. Of course incoming calls are red-flags to life insurers – they know better. As one insurance agent once told me, life insurance isn't bought, it's sold: If somebody is buying, there's a reason.

So while the venality of Wall Street is certainly something to be aware of, in many cases it is matched, if not exceeded, by the venality of its clients. So we have to come to an examination of investors, who as we all know are those well-meaning innocent people just trying to get through life and maybe put away a little bit for their retirements -- like the Madoff investors, all innocent as babies in a crib. But what we find is not a great deal of difference between investors and their Wall Street benefactors, all looking for the big hit that will take them, if not to Nirvana, then at least to someplace where they won't have to worry, and maybe not even have to work, but in all cases up and out of the ranks of the unwashed. Well, as a famous phrase goes, *"It takes two to tango,"* and the Wall Street tango has plenty of partners on both sides of the advisory divide.

Investment Lifestyle

What we will find after examining the investor side of the relationship is that it is difficult to separate investment from life. Intemperate people look for intemperate actors and get intemperate investment results and temperate people will look for temperate actors and perhaps get temperate results. That is the beauty of investment; it is really not a set syllabus of facts and procedures but rather a state of mind, an outgrowth of the entire individual that has traditionally been given the catch-word "wisdom" (or lack thereof). Wealth comes, but at its own pace; it cannot be hurried. Some people understand this and some don't.

At one point in my life I was filling out forms to open a brokerage account and came to the question of experience – they wanted to know how much investment experience I had. I had just graduated from business school with a Master's in business and was insulted by the question – I had a degree, what use is experience?

Now many years later I understand: The best investor may be illiterate and the worst a Harvard PhD in Economics. *Investment is all about character and vision and making mistakes and putting those mistakes to work to make a better life for yourself,* in other words all things learned from the time you took your first breath, and very little having to do with anything learned even in a prestigious school. Why? Because in school you learn by listening, recording, and regurgitating. In life, you don't get the lecture, you just get the problem and have to figure it out for yourself and if you don't get a good result, you try something different. You have no choice. After doing this a gazillion times you learn that life is a matter of keeping the needle somewhere between being a total skeptic, which doesn't get you anywhere, and total romantic, which takes you usually to some pretty painful places. But many people never learn that lesson.

What Investors Look Like

The newspaper *USA Today* used to run an investment challenge, annually it seems, and once a year would publish the results. I only read one article on this, the one publishing the results for that one-year period I happened to be reading about. The winner was a gas station attendant in Reno, Nevada. I was incredulous. I would have though some Finance major from Harvard or some obvious luminary in the investment world would have won. A Reno gas station attendant? It didn't compute.

That was then and this is now – it computes. The gift of playing the market that Burton Malkiel discusses in his book, *A Random Walk Down Wall Street,* is as random as lightning strikes, and it doesn't prefer hedge fund managers over gas station attendants.

An inordinate feel for the market exists but it cannot be isolated or identified. Of course, all intrepid investors claim to have it and when challenged by growing losses seize upon some heroic storyline of persistence eventually paying off for the most stalwart of actors, but for many it is a storyline that does not come true. Is it ego? Could George Soros have become the wealthy trader that he did without blowing through a lot of pain? Probably not. At what point do you discover you don't have it. First, if you are not a professional that devotes all your waking hours to trading; you are not a player and need to give it up. If you are like the 99% of humanity needing to save for retirement, trading is not for you. But this book is for you.

One other story is worth repeating because it directly challenges, or appears to challenge, the above rule of being a professional and involves one of my heroes – John Maynard Keynes. Keynes was a very interesting character. An Economics graduate of Kings College Cambridge, he worked in his youth at the British equivalent of the Treasury office. There developed a run on Spanish pesetas and he was instructed by his superiors to unload all of the Crown's holdings in pesetas. He disobeyed direct orders and instead bought all the pesetas he could and cornered enough of the market to make a huge windfall for the Crown. Of course he had to be fired, which was done, and from then on, at least for a while, he would slip into the building through a side door to resume his regular post.

The classic story of Keynes has him lounging in his bed in the morning studying the financial section of the newspaper. He would place his bets on the information he gleaned and then would go to the office. His family and friends gave him money to invest and at one point, he lost it all. Nevertheless, he had the temerity to ask for more money. He got it and eventually he did very well for all of them. It looks like Keynes was a dilettante dabbling in the market but primarily he was an economist and secondly his work was in the currency markets, so he was a professional.

When You Think You Know People

I was once visiting a very good friend in another state, and the purpose and pinnacle of the visit was to be a stop at a lounge to meet his new paramour. The evening arrived and with great anticipation my friend and I arrived at the lounge, really more of a cocktail lounge connected to a hotel, and were seated. Finally the big moment arrived and the woman came over, took our order and left. At that point my friend with great anticipation asked: *"Pat. What do you think? Isn't she great!"* I was in fact appalled. She looked old enough to be his mother, but not wishing to pop the balloon, I enthusiastically agreed that he had lucked out and happened upon a real find. He was elated with my approval.

The next morning as I was shaving with the bathroom door open, my friend suddenly burst in on me in a rage demanding that I keep my hands off his girl. *"Don't even think about it,"* he yelled in a rage. I couldn't believe it. I had never seen him so angry nor had I ever tried to insinuate myself into any of his relationships. I was stunned. *"Jim,"* I said *"She's your girl. I wouldn't dream of going after her. I am very happy for you."* Mollified he left and I just exhaled in that way you do when recovering from a shock. Of course, at that moment I realized that although we were close friends, the sameness was an illusion; we inhabited very different worlds apparently.

I tell this because it is a story of disconnects between two individuals who were good friends, friends who thought alike. The story is about choice. Choices cannot be made in partnership with others. You can listen to others, read newsletters, watch investment shows, and read blogs, but when you pull the trigger the choice is yours alone. It is your money, your decision, and yours to live with, and what other people think of it is what they think of it from criteria you are not privy to. If you make an investment because you have heard a lot of chatter about it, it may not be the right thing to do. It is what the Madoff investors did – just give it to Bernie because that is what everybody said to do. But there was no question that the Madoff investors thought they were getting a level of expertise not available to the general public. They just lived in a different world from Bernie and didn't know it.

Of course, much of humanity is venal and regards investment as an opportunity to hit the ball out of the park. This usually happens after a few speculative blow-ups in the wake of romantic tilting at windmills. After a few of these, things get desperate, and more study is devoted to the task, but with the same results. Einstein it is thought once to have said that the definition of insanity is doing the same thing again and again while expecting a different result. Nevertheless in investment this happens regularly because intemperate investors don't know they are doing the same thing over again – different stock, different bet.

Need Engenders Empowerment

But the big Achilles Heel is an investor's financial urgency driving a sense of control over events out of desperation that is not acknowledged. This unrecognized desperation leads to desperate investments that will inevitably go sour. For some reason need gives rise to a sense of empowerment over our environment to relieve that need.

Maybe it's a vestige from our origins in the jungle or on the savannah. Coming upon a lion kill and extracting what the lion couldn't is very empowering and takes the actor's mind off the possibility that maybe the lion will come back. Fast forward a million years or so, and you have the desperate investor coming upon a sleepy stock ready for extraction. Guess what? In the market, the lion is never very far away. Successful traders make their profits on the vestigial sense of empowerment that comes with need felt by counterparties to their trades. It is called "the greater fool theory."

Successful investment is for temperate investors, usually those who have learned temperance the hard way though perhaps in measured bites. Remember that when you win in investment, you don't learn much; it's when you lose that you really learn. But temperance is not only about money; it permeates your entire life. You can't be an intemperate person in one aspect of your life and a temperate person in another. Usually it's all one or the other – it's your style or your personality.

I speak from experience. For most of my life I was an intemperate actor and have reaped the expected results – great pain and great joy. I have won big in investment and lost my shirt. And one thing I have learned is that the market is the boss; it decides what the outcome will be. Think about George Soros, who made about 1£ billion on a bet against the British Pound Sterling, Later, Soros lost about $2 billion in the 1998 Russian debt crisis and lost $700 million in the 1999 tech bubble. Apparently reacting to the tech bubble loss, he bet big in anticipation of a rise then lost nearly $3 billion when the market crashed. Not to pick on George, because he can afford it -- he is reportedly the seventh richest American -- but it is a view that many intemperate people adopt, because they fail to understand the differences between themselves and George Soros. There is only one George Soros and there is only one you. My friend's cocktail waitress love interest was beautiful to him and a disaster to me and we were both oblivious to the other's thoughts, although good friends. What is good for someone else is not necessarily good for you because you are you. Investment is a lonely business.

In investment you must learn that the market, the aggregate actions of millions of people totally disconnected, drives events and all you can do is try to gain a long-term perspective supported by the conviction that well-financed and well-managed companies delivering needed goods or services will prosper at a rate greater than inflation. Given this starting point, the most successful investors are likely to be the most passive investors, those who just look at the great corporations, ones that are household words and invest in them with little thought to what others think.

That Illusive Quality Called Wisdom

I had a friend who grew up in what I considered a quite bizarre environment with a very aggressive and driven father forcing the son into a work regimen beyond his comfort zone. Apparently the son had inherited more of the genes of his mother, who was a total couch potato. The parents divorced and when the mother died she left everything to her son, a big block of Phillip Morris stock, which later became Altria and has since been spun off again. The stock has been tremendous. The son stopped working and for the last twenty years has divided his time between a northeastern home and an western home, with annual vacations to Belize. He is now a total couch potato when he's not traveling between residences and the beach.

When I was a stockbroker, I asked him if he wanted any help and he got very hostile. He said Phillip Morris had taken care of his mother and it would take care of him – case closed. Now keep in mind that Wall Street considers his investment method very dangerous because he has all his eggs in one basket, but, what a basket – Philip Morris. And I presume those shares were accumulated over time with a varied cost basis across many shares.

I am reminded of another episode in my stock broker career that bears on investment character. One day an experienced broker called me into his office and offered me a walk-in client who was given to him because he was broker-of-the-day. He was trying to help out a struggling new broker and God knows I needed all the help I could get. The client turned out to be an elderly black gentleman who wanted to sell some Union Pacific Railroad stock (UNP). He had stock certificates that he had accumulated as a lifetime employee and now needed to sell some to bury a close relative. I opened up an account for him, deposited his certificates and sold a few to meet his cash requirements. He was a very kindly old gentleman.

Several months later I came upon a report from our research department that had a "Sell" rating on Union Pacific. I thought this would be a good opportunity for me to ingratiate myself with my new client and show I was thinking about him. Accordingly I called him up, described the research report and offered to mail him a copy. I will never forget his response. He didn't speak it, he growled it – "*Don't touch that stock.*" I got off the phone as quickly as I could reassuring him he was in total control. Here was a man with an 8ᵗʰ grade education who knew more about investing than his stock broker with a Master's degree in business. Since then I have been very grateful I had that experience and grateful the client didn't listen to me.

Union Pacific had taken care of him throughout his life and was now taking care of him and his family needs in retirement; he had no reason to question the power of Union Pacific to keep on giving. Indeed, at the time (1995) the stock was trading around $25 a share and today the stock is around $125 a share, but that is just part of the story – the stock had split 2 for 1 since then. Yes, from $25 to $125 and twice as many shares. The recent split history is: 2 for 1 (1977), 2 for 1 (1980), 2 for 1 (1991) and 2 for 1 (2008). Yeah, a "Sell" rating from our research department: how useful, I wonder if it was with high or low volatility?

These two personal examples are now, of course, part of my experience and play a role in my investment outlook. They also profile successful investors who succeed through a commitment to a hard and fast rule: Don't mess with success in a process you don't understand. The market is its own thing and cannot be gamed very often, but that doesn't stop the more intrepid from interpreting gains as expertise.

So you have the two extremes. There are passive investors who don't pretend to know anything and just cling tenaciously to something that has worked for them -- in one case worked for their parent as well over a lifetime. At the other extreme of the investor spectrum is the George Soros wannabe who thinks the market can be predicted through inordinate talent and vision, and, like a bull rider, thinks they can ride out the eight seconds frequently enough to make a killing. Maybe, but usually only for a very few who spend most of their waking hours doing research and have the battle scars to prove it.

Perhaps there is no greater example of the danger of hubris than that of the Greek mythic story of Icarus. His father Daedalus fashioned wings for him out of feathers and attached them to the son's body with wax. Daedalus warned his son not to fly too close to the sun, nor too close to the sea, but to follow Daedalus's own temperate path of flight. In other words, keep the needle between skeptic and romantic. But Icarus became giddy with his newly found power and decided the laws of physics didn't apply to him. You know the rest of the story: the laws of physics mattered, and when Icarus flew too close to the sun, the wax melted -- the youth fell fatally into the sea.

I'll reference another expert, Dr. Thomas Harris who wrote *I'm Okay, You're Okay*. Harris takes up what he calls "Transactional Analysis" by describing our behaviors as being from our "Child," our "Parent" or our "Adult." According to Harris, when we are children we act petulantly to get what we want and those behaviors are learned and stored. Our parents become exasperated and act out violently towards us and these behaviors although not our own are also learned and stored. As we mature we learn that our child's emotional behaviors are not appropriate but sometimes cannot be stopped from arising, particularly when we want something. We also come to view our parent's emotional outbursts as inappropriate, although when angered, they escape and we use those as well. Harris wished to make us aware of these components in our personalities and drive us to cultivate the rational "Adult" response to life's challenges – the use of reason.

We all have components of the "Child," which will drive us to make rash investments. And we all have components of the "Parent," which will cause us to beat ourselves up when those investments go sour and we miss the lesson. That is all to be expected, but, listen to Daedalus: Use reason. It is the "Adult" in us that allows us to truly recalibrate, and, as Einstein would point out, not do the same thing over again expecting a different result. It is the "Adult" in us we are looking for when we invest.

We need to be a bit romantic to be open to new things and to the possibilities in life, but our optimism must be measured by our "Adult;" otherwise we will learn too late the best rule that has been around since chickens were domesticated, namely don't put all your eggs into one basket. The "Child" in you will put all the eggs in one basket and the "Parent" in you will be too skeptical to even gather the eggs. Obviously you need something in between.

In investment, don't be entirely a childish romantic; you will go broke on speculative new issues. Don't be a severe skeptic of everything new; you will lose your money to inflation in bonds. Be an adult, able to feel both the joy of childishness and the scolding of an angry parent and able to keep the needle in the middle. Be a Daedalus and an adult get to your destination.

We have pointed out that inattentive investors succeed, but Madoff investors were inattentive and they lost big. Were the Madoff investors childish in putting all their eggs in one basket? I think so. They could have been skeptics and put all their money in bonds and I'm sure many skeptical friends haunted by their "Parents" pointed that out to them. They could have been "Adults" and wondered about the wisdom of putting all their money with someone they only knew socially on the advice of non-professionals, all decisions made without scrutiny. How much scrutiny did the Union Pacific gentleman give to his stock? None, I would guess. How much scrutiny did my friend give to his solitary position in Phillip Morris? None, I would guess. Both of these gentlemen it seems were operating from their "Child" (desperate grasping – don't take my toy away) and then reacting with an angry "Parent" response at the mere questioning of the toy.

The "Adult" thing to do is to understand it is crucial to build an estate to send your kids to college and provide for your own retirement and that this task is manageable. You must believe in it with childish enthusiasm, but you must have a skeptical "Parent" ready to scold you when you start veering off into unfamiliar territory with the family farm. Most important, you must have a well-developed "Adult" within you to choose a process that is rational, and to learn when the process doesn't work but must be changed. You have to have the "Adult" discipline to stick to a rational process even when it looks hopeless in the early years. Remember, the market is volatile and the only way to profit from it reliably is to apply compartmentalization – to make order out of chaos. This takes time and the kind of "character" most people don't have.

The drive for a shortcut to riches is as old as civilization itself. An example from the Middle Ages is the practice called alchemy. The objective was to turn base materials into gold and thus eliminate the need for bothersome mining. Of course it never worked but there were multiple claims of success. Wall Street is today's alchemy machine drawing in multitudes with multiple claims of success conveniently failing to point out the losses in between.

A Brief Detour Into Problem Gambling

William R. Eadington, University of Nevada, has served as an Academic Visitor to the London School of Economics, as a Visiting Professor at the Center for Addiction Studies, Harvard Medical School, and as a Visiting Lecturer at the Kennedy School of Government, Harvard University. He also is on the faculty of the Centre for the Study of Gambling and Commercial Gaming at the University of Salford (U.K.). In 2008, he was awarded a Doctor of Business Administration honoris causa by the University of Macau. Obviously Dr. Eadington is a leading source for understanding gambling behavior, something investors should be aware of. In 1993 Eadington compiled into a book about 40 scholarly papers from around the world on studies conducted to understand and treat gambling addiction.

In general the papers report a high correlation with age, finding that as people grow older, *"The individual becomes more accepting of her or his fate...older people are less concerned with ego...and thus have more stable self-concepts...older people have less need to experiment for self-identity..."* This quote is from work performed by Erik Erikson a German-born American psychologist known for his theory on social development captured in his eight stages of development.

At the earlier end of the development spectrum, Dr. Erikson posits that adolescents are seeking their identity in behaviors that can lead to gambling. This is the fifth stage. Later stages see adults concerned with power which is strongly correlated with problem gambling.

Irving Goffman, an influential American sociologist, wrote that "self-presentation" drives much behavior including gambling, which is a way those seeking to present themselves as "successful" or "big-shots," can play out that role, which of course leads to braggadocio at the water-cooler. So self-esteem is a big component and given further support by the finding that desperation or feelings of helplessness often lead to gambling.

While the foregoing may help explain why some people are driven to gambling it says little about why they continue in the face of losses. Richard J. Rosenthal, a Co-Director of the UCLA Gambling Studies Program found that problem gamblers have a highly-developed capacity for self-deception and may have grown up in households where there was little emotional support and high emphasis placed on status and over-valuing of money, often a gambling family.

Julian I. Taber, a retired clinical psychologist who specialized in the treatment of addictions was one of the first mental health professionals to work with pathological gamblers. Dr. Tabor makes the statement that, *"Chronic addiction people see what they want to see and hear what they want to hear."* In a particularly nasty exploitation of such people, what are called "fruit machines" in one study, which are more typically called slot machines, are fitted with "nudge" and "hold" buttons giving the player the sense that they have some control over the outcome.

Other similar studies found that players, when interviewed, made statements that implied not only a level of control but preferences for some machines over others. I happened to be in Las Vegas at The World of Concrete Show, having nothing to do with gambling, and observed technicians working on a "fruit machine." When asked about gaming the machine they said the machine keeps 15%, everything else is random. Then his confederate scolded him for disclosing such information to a patron, and they walked away. They need not have worried, I never caught that disease, but I would put it in a book!

What this has to do with investing in stocks is the insidious role played by a misplaced sense of control over random processes. To be sure, stock market players do potentially have greater control than "fruit machine" players, but a hazard may be that more control doesn't mean control, it means more control, which means no control.

When the Time-Warner/AOL merger was first announced in 2001 I decided to get in on the action. I investigated how the merger was playing on the London Stock Exchange, six hours ahead of New York and saw that the new combined issue was up 20%. I got in pretty heavy with this information. At the end of the day I was chagrined to find my position had sunk 20%, what happened to this sure thing? The New York market decided that AOL, already trading at a very high earnings multiple (Perhaps a $3million company trading for $100 billion) or perhaps a P/E well over 100, had merged with a company trading at perhaps a P/E of 20. The combined P/E for the new issue had to come down, you couldn't have Time-Warner trading at say a P/E of 100, so the combined new issue saw the AOL P/E reduced down closer to earth. It made perfect sense when you thought about it and a very good lesson for those trying to game the market – people like me. As King Frederick The Great would have observed, it made me more circumspect.

I heard a funny story the other day that fits here. We have a neighbor with a little yappy dog named Coco. And although Coco knows us very well, and we have even fed Coco steak remains brought home from restaurant meals, it is to no avail: When Coco sees anybody, including us, she starts her vigorous barking. Her owners are always embarrassed and yell at Coco to get her to stop but with no effect. The other night when we heard Coco starting up, my wife remembered something she had heard recently: She said that when dogs hear people yelling at them, they think the people are barking and it encourages them to bark even louder. Think of the market as a barking dog and the futility of investing in the market thinking it will do what you want it to.

But on the other hand, the market works for you. The very simple truth is that the market works at twice or three times the speed of inflation and that's more than you need to meet your savings goals. The element that must be tamed is not the market, it's you. So beware of Wall Street but beware of yourself as well. You are the constant in your life that will determine the outcome.

Conference   Ben Aronson   2008
Oil on panel, 30 x 30 inches   Private Collection

Chapter 7

Companies

The Jamestown settlement in what later became the state of Virginia was the English response to Spain's successful exploitation for gold and silver in the New World. The English were exceedingly jealous of Spain's success and set about their own exploration ventures with the Virginia Company leading the way.

Martin Frobisher, who was partially financed by Queen Elizabeth, brought back what he thought was gold but turned out to be fool's gold, and that seems to have put a stop to any further investment from the English monarchy. The result was the formation of joint-stock companies like the Virginia Company, to pool wealth sufficiently for mounting a large venture. Investors who found themselves pressed by financial challenges could sell their shares to other fellow investors or new ones. Naturally the worth of those shares rose and fell with news coming back from the New World. The Jamestown venture was a bust, so the company re-formed and made a second "subscription" for a new venture, one that would feature families and not the vagabond men and dissolute adventurers who had staffed the original. The United States is a testament to the success of that second attempt.

If the internet had been around in 1620, and the New and Old Worlds wired, shares in the new Plymouth Colony venture would have gyrated wildly. In sequence there would have been news of starvation and death, then encouraging fishing, trapping and agriculture, then developing hostilities with the Indians, then religious battles after the Massachusetts Bay Colony was established challenging the Separatist theology of the Plymouth settlement and then news about forming such new colonies as Rhode Island and Connecticut, with very promising new trading venues.

Such a train of news events would have caused a pattern of alternating panic and euphoria. As it was, there was no internet and no quick news and so people hung onto their shares as long as they had no other pressing financial needs. Persons who did hang on to their shares did very well, because the new world was very successful, even spawning a sub-category of landed gentry on this side of the pond who were able to cite their provenance to the *Mayflower*, the ship that brought the settlers. Today tracing lineage to the *Mayflower* is a prestigious family link, and generally means money. In 1620 *Mayflower* meant poverty.

The Nature of Corporations

The reason for the *Mayflower* family prestige is not due so much to the success of those first Mayflower families, but to the downstream success that kept building and building, eventually leading to companies like IBM, General Foods, Procter & Gamble, General Electric, Exxon Mobil, and so on, and then going global. The success was so generally recognized that when President Jimmy Carter was ending his visit to Israel in the early 1970s, Golda Meir, then Prime Minister of Israel, beseeched him to send Israel his generals. Puzzled, Carter asked what generals she had in mind. *"General Motors, General Electric, General Foods,"* was the reported reply.

The commercial "Generals" Golda was after are indeed symbols of America's strength and prosperity. But it wasn't always so apparent and in some cases the ride has been rocky. The rockiness of the ride however varies dramatically among stock market investors. Some check the stock daily to see how they are doing, so they get a wild ride. Others don't check at all, merely relying on their faith that the company they selected is solid and growing and that the daily fluctuations are only so much noise created by the unseemly behavior of the unwashed; what they see and experience is a smooth ride.

This latter attitude may be snobbish, but it works, and it works because companies are a team of people united by a common corporate culture whose survival depends on constant improvement and refinement of their products in the face of competitors, economic swings, wars, droughts, floods, material shortages, commodity markets, changing technologies, changing fashions and so on. Companies exist in a constantly evolving landscape that requires constant intervention to keep them alive. Companies that survive do so because the employees are coming to work every day getting done what needs to get done.

Once a company has weathered a few storms, it seems to develop a personality like Hobbes' Leviathan, directed by a group of people working in concert to thrive in a hostile and ever-changing world. But, you must stay invested in the company to get the benefit, often with blinders on. To highlight the organic quality of a corporation, I cite a quote by William

Hester, CFA, I found at www.hussmanfunds.com:

"The shares of companies deleted from the S&P 500 have consistently outperformed those that took their place. Since the beginning of 1998, the median annualized return of all stocks deleted from the index and held from their exit date through March 15 of this year was 15.4 percent. The median annualized return of all stocks that were added to the index was 2.9 percent."

This very interesting quote may explain why index funds may not be the panacea their merchants claim them to be. If there had been index funds in 1620 along with the Internet, the Plymouth Plantation stock, I'm sure, would have been removed from the index.

Benjamin Graham, whose ground breaking book, *Security Analysis*, written with David Dodd, is also known for a well-publicized quote: *"The investor's chief problem and even worst enemy is likely to be himself."* And to this, I would add that most investors err not in what they buy, but in what they sell.

Buying decisions may often prove shortsighted, but in most cases the problem goes away when it is ignored. This is not to say that you shouldn't sell stocks that are manifestly suffering long-term or what looks like structural and permanent decline, but -- borrowing an expression once used by former President Bill Clinton -- any jackass can burn a barn down; it's in the building of the barn that the talent lies. Similarly, I would point out, any jackass can sell a stock; the talent is in the holding, and looking beyond the near-term noise to the long term. And so the first point, and it is an important point, is that stock price is a momentary aggregate measure of the relationship of supply to demand on such a small proportion of the stock outstanding that it is essentially a meaningless measure of anything other than the transient sentiment of a few shareholders. Many shares that are not in play would never be sold at current prices

-- what does that tell you about valuation? Capitalization is arrived at by multiplying the number of outstanding shares by share price. But only a very few shares are in play at the current price, so how can that possibly represent the total capitalization of the company? It is an absurd concept.

Stock traded on the various exchanges are issued by companies ranging from huge multi-national enterprises down to small firms struggling to advance a fledgling idea not yet proven a mainstream product. The larger companies typically trade on the New York Stock Exchange (NYSE), sometimes called "The Big Board." Smaller early-stage companies seem to congregate at the NASDAQ (National Association of Securities Dealers Automated Quotations). From an investor's point of view, the chief difference between the two populations is that the NYSE menu lists companies that are well established, slow growing, and pay dividends. Dividends are distributions companies make from profits not needed to grow and run the business. Many NYSE investors place great importance on dividends in making their investment decisions. NASDAQ investors usually have no interest in dividends, looking only for the promise of capital gain in stock splits and stock price appreciation.

You might think that the two disparate investing populations, with such disparate behaviors, might lead to very different market behaviors, but they are not so different, perhaps because many investors trade on both exchanges as they seek to diversify a portfolio that offers some growth but with volatility tamped down. Naturally, NASDAQ investors seeking only stock price appreciation are more apt to trade more frequently than NYSE investors waiting for their dividend checks. In addition to NYSE and NASDAQ, there are other exchanges and most investors simply enter a buy or sell order and really don't care on what exchange the trade is made.

Taxonomy of Commerce

Some years ago, a business consultancy named the Boston Consulting Group (BCG) developed a matrix that characterized companies by growth rate and market share, making the point that these two characteristics, which created a 4-box matrix, pretty much describe the basic challenge a business faces as it grows.

The BCG matrix traces the growth of a company from a beginning "Question Mark," to the break-out position of a "Star," then eventually a "Cash Cow," as investment needs decline and excess profits are re-routed to dividend distributions, and then the eventual decline back to a size too small to matter, called simply "Dogs." The next stage is death as has happened to so many brands that were household words in their day and are now not even remembered. Do you recall Ipana toothpaste? How about Packard automobiles, once the Lexus of its day. Other brands that have left center-stage or the stage altogether are: Dreft detergent, Lava soap, the super-charged Studebaker Golden Hawk, Bazooka bubble-gum, Lionel electric trains, Columbia bicycles, Rheingold beer with the Miss Rheingold campaign, Robert Hall clothing stores and many others. At one time radio broadcasts were sponsored by Perfect Circle piston rings, which are rings that surround the piston in a car engine that were at the time subject to high wear and required frequent replacement, or frequent enough to prompt retail advertising. These and other businesses went through the BCG stages and then left the stage of history.

Look at the illustration on the next page, you will see the BCG matrix from www.krikor.info. The arrow shows the typical route through the matrix from start-up to exit. The vertical coordinate is growth rate. New companies are usually started to exploit a fast growing market and so growth rates within a market are a characteristic almost all entrepreneurs look at very carefully before starting their business ventures. The horizontal coordinate is market share which often determines market power, which translates into pricing power and profitability.

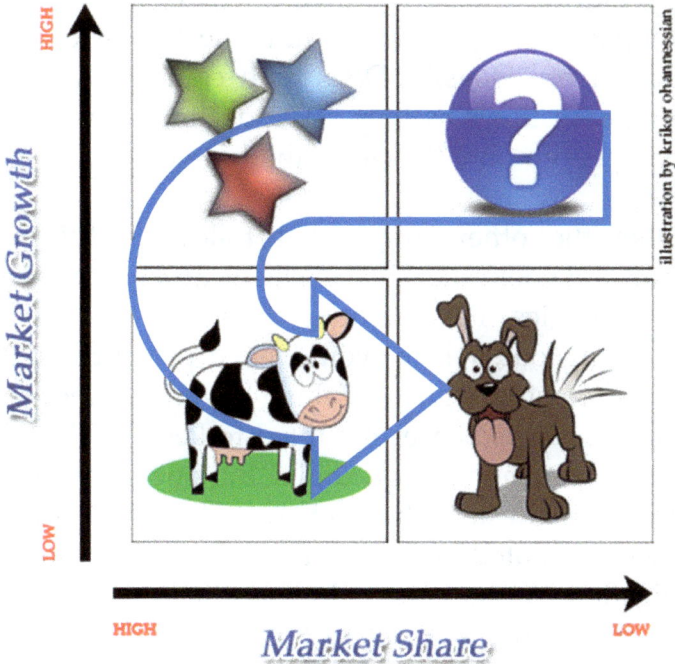

A startup company usually starts in the upper right "Question Mark" quadrant with little market share in a fast growing market. "Question Mark" refers to the uncertain future new entrants have as they battle with competitors for survival.

The "Question Marks" that do survive then move to the left, building market share to become "Stars." "Stars" obviously is a good place to be. Companies here command major market share in a fast-growing market but at the expense of heavy marketing and development costs to stay ahead of competition. After market growth slows and most of the competitors have either exited or been acquired, money needed to remain competitive can be redirected to dividend distribution to shareholders, thus transforming the company into a "Cash Cow."

"Cash Cow" businesses are in stable markets that allow them to spin off cash. Eventually almost all "Star" products, like Ipana toothpaste and Packard automobiles, shrink as markets fade or marketing investment is withdrawn causing the companies to go into a slow decline and earning the designation of "Dogs." "Dogs" are companies that spin off declining cash flows as they serve declining markets that one day may just go out. "Dogs" is the last stop before exiting the stage.

Unlike the other stages that follow pretty much of a standard playbook, the "Dogs" stage can has known a variety of exit strategies. For example, there was a case of a large retailer going out, which would have presented the investor with a depressing sight of falling revenues and profits and rising red ink as expenses mounted to keep the business alive. Stock price was in the single digits. But one investor decided to add up the real estate the firm owned on which their failing stores were situated and came up with a value far surpassing capitalization by stock price. In this situation, you can merely buy up the shares and sell the real estate. This would be an important lesson in learning the limitation stock price has on valuation.

Other than the BCG matrix, a way to view the life-cycle of a business is shown in the accompanying graphic on the following page; a more literal interpretation. The beginning stage, "Introduction," requires a lot of investment cash to grow the business so the company is in negative cash flow and hence not profitable, offering only promise or a question mark. If the company succeeds in establishing itself as a viable business and beating out its competition, it becomes appropriately enough, a "Star," As it enters the "Growth" stage. As the business goes mainstream, investment inflow for growth declines and cash then begins to flow out to the investors in the form of dividends, hence the designation "Maturity." After a time, the business gets old and is no longer as profitable. Alternative businesses take hold, sometimes within the same company, and when it is decided to harvest rather than grow or maintain a business, the business enters a stage of "Decline," and becomes a "Dog.".

"Question Mark" replaced at some point the term "Problem Child" which was the term *du jour* back in the 1980s for new businesses with uncertain futures in fast-growing markets. Of course, it was an apt name since you never know how a child is going to turn out, a star or otherwise. More baffling is how man's best friend came to stand for declining businesses.

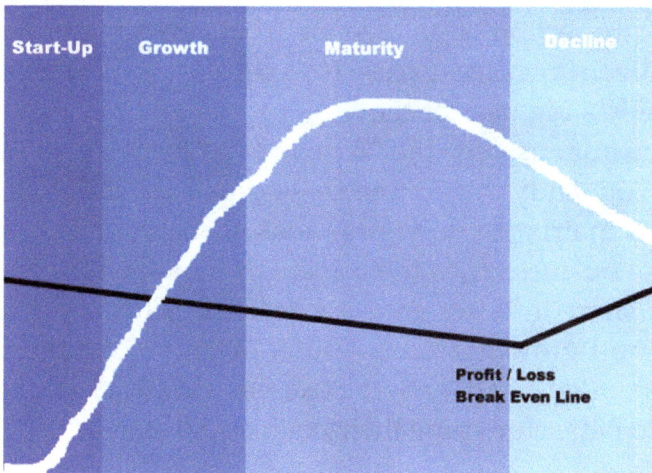

Life-Cycle of a Business

The BCG matrix and the life-cycle of a business chart apply to single products that may be the totality of a company, for example a start-up venture like the new fast-food chain Chipotle, or a single product within a larger corporate setting, like a new toothpaste from Procter & Gamble, or a brand within a field of brands like Oldsmobile within the GM lineup of automobile brands. Long before you contemplate investment candidates, company management has done much the same analysis deciding what to invest in. So while a company like GE may generally be categorized as a "Cash Cow," it has a stable of products in all life-cycle stages.

The successful company is constantly reinventing itself, knowing that today's "Star" is tomorrow's "Dog." And perhaps no company is easier to point to as an example of reinvention that General Electric. GE began life during the days of Thomas Edison, making light bulbs that he had invented. Then GE began making heavy equipment for power generating plants, like large transformers. Later GE got into the locomotive business and when these began their maturation, GE came up with appliances that eventually morphed into electric coffee pots, frying pans and even electric blankets. Today, GE derives a large proportion of its revenue from financing but is still well diversified across industries. It would not be surprising to learn that GE is a big user of the BCG matrix and has even refined it for its custom use, see the GE matrix below.

As you study the GE matrix you will see the evolution from the BCG matrix for very good reason. GE wishes to focus only on those businesses, to the upper left, in which they have major market share in faster growing markets. That gives GE pricing power and growth, which results in profits. So the GE matrix has expanded the two left boxes of the BCG matrix into six boxes to better fine-tune their business strategies.

Business Position - Strength

		High	Medium	Low
Market Attractiveness	**High**	Invest for Growth	Invest selectively for growth	Protect Develop selectively building upon strengths
	Medium	Invest. The organization is selective in choice of product/ service	Protect. Develop and build selectively for revenue generation	Harvest
	Low	Protect Develop for revenue generation	Harvest or Divest	Divest

The use of this matrix has helped to spawn a culture at GE known as the "GE Way," which pushes constructive decision making down and out to the farthest reaches of the company, making GE a very nimble player in the global competitive marketplace.

The use of the BCG matrix highlights not only successful corporate investment behavior, but also may be used to very good advantage by individual investors in laying out their personal portfolios. This is in addition to the portfolio diversification use of a style-box matrix developed by Morningstar described later.

GE's refinement and use of the BCG matrix allows GE to stay focused on "Star" businesses and abandon product areas that are "Dogs." Such a BCG matrix may be used by any investors as a guide to industries and companies that might make good investments. If GE is in a product area you can be sure it is profitable. For example, I would have thought the home appliance business had pretty much had the profits squeezed very thin on account of competition, but because GE is still in the home appliance business I surmise the sector is still profitable. Thus the sector should be a good place to look for non-GE home appliance manufacturer investment candidates.

The Centrality of Family and Employment

When considering the safety of common stock investment and then choices within that market, remember that all companies have staffs committed to improving what they do. It could be product development, manufacturing, delivery, marketing, advertising, packaging, or management. Every individual in a company is tasked with making improvements. This is true also of their competitors. And this collective energy devoted to competition will result in a field of competitors that will eventually shake out into a more or less fixed landscape where each player has developed unique attributes for competing in the same market with different competitive advantages. Remember, it is the rare product that has only upside and no downside.

A purpose of competition is to exploit whatever advantage exists and this is what occurs in an free market where every player is striving for monopoly. In such a field, it is impossible to tell which companies will thrive, which will survive, and which will die, and none of it will in any way be made clearer by media-delivered punditry. This is because investment horizons are far longer than even the most far-sighted pundits can imagine, and remember, punditry depends upon short-term validation, the kind of validation that is more a bet than an investment. The real money to be made is from investing in an organization that has in the past demonstrated an ability to not so much negotiate change, although this is important, as to produce change. The ability to produce change is one of the marks of a great company.

Think of the early days of the Ford Motor Company, where Henry Ford insisted on developing a homogenously cast V-8 block against all sentiment at the time. It couldn't be done, Henry was told. Henry then took a team of his engineers, separated them from the rest of the organization into an isolated building and refused to cave in to their negativity. The engineers found a solution, and in 1932, Ford Motor Company introduced a better, cheaper, homogenously cast V-8 engine for the mass market.

Up to that time, V-8 engines were produced from several castings bolted together, a scheme that was expensive and not as strong as a homogenous casting. For this reason, most 8-cylinder engines were inline and required long engine housings, giving cars of the '20s and '30s a very long hood. Auto companies changed that by casting V-8 blocks in two pieces and bolting them together. The result was a luxury car with V-8 power and the stylish new look of a shorter hood. Ford gave the public new style but still with eight cylinders yet made for a fraction of the price. Incidentally, The Beach Boys created a song about this car - "My Little Deuce Coupe" - "deuce" comes from the "2" in 1932.

This example of corporate leadership is also seen in Apple's developments under the leadership of Steve Jobs. American corporate history is riddled with such tales. For one such spellbinding story, read "*The Soul of a New Machine*," by Tracy Kidder.

At Ford, the team that developed the homogenous casting was composed of Ray Laird, Emil Zoerlein, and Carl Schultz, and later Charles Sorensen, who refined the design and as a result became known as "Cast Iron Charlie." In the case of Ford, the development was organic in the sense that Henry was only the catalyst -- the team made it happen and, of course, would make similar advances again and again. In fact, not long afterward, Sorensen's vision, energy, and autonomy led Ford's Willow Run factory to reduce the roll-out period of wartime B24 Liberator bombers from one day to one hour.

This is the type of information that is not readily discernible from an annual report, but may be gleaned from reading the newspaper, and is not only valuable, but central to selecting companies for investment. Investing in stocks is investing in people and how people are organized and managed to work in concert toward a common goal. I recall a time as a young worker recently out of college. I was reading the annual report of a company I was working for at the time and being completely baffled by what I read. The company was nothing like what was described in the annual report and the pictures in the report were amazing. I was in the art department and had no idea we had such pictures. The company went belly up a few years later. Good ad agency; lousy management.

Market Structures

The interplay of competing entities in moving markets gives rise to the concept of market structures. Everybody has heard the term monopoly and understands that it describes a player that has nearly 100% market share and it usually, but not always, means a large market. Church & Dwight is probably a company you have never heard of until you learn that their flagship product is Arm & Hammer baking soda, which enjoys a near monopoly in a niche market. Microsoft is a near monopoly in a mega-market. But monopoly is only one of multiple possible market structures. Markets can be sliced and diced in many ways, but ways identifying discrete market structures are: number of competitors, relative strength of buyers and sellers, product differentiation, company differentiation, degree of cooperation among competitors, and relative strength of the various competitors. All of these characteristics are incorporated into four basic market structures:

1. Perfect competition – many buyers and sellers. (bottled water)
2. Oligopoly – several major competitors that have some pricing power. (McDonalds, Burger King)
3. Monopoly – single seller with great pricing power. (Microsoft)
4. Monopsony – single buyer with buyer pricing power. (NASA)

There are many derivatives of this structure, but almost all incorporate the above four classifications. The derivatives are useful; for example there is the category "monopolistic competition" in which there are multiple competitors whose product differentiation earn them a low-competition business in market niches. An example is Marlboro cigarettes -- although there are many cigarette brands, it would be difficult to get a Marlboro smoker to switch.

Market structures are a useful way to analyze a company's investment potential, but apply mainly to the "Cash Cow" category, which is static enough to maintain a classification in one of the market structures described. The other three life-cycles, "Question Mark," "Star," and "Dog" seem to be too transient to really fit into a market structure. If a "Question Mark" doesn't advance to "Star" it generally gets swallowed up by a competitor or goes out of business.

As mentioned earlier, exit strategies for mature companies can vary dramatically, making "Dogs" difficult to classify. Usually businesses get bought up before getting to the "Dog" stage, giving those companies that survive to the "Dog" stage a negative bias. If they are businesses within a business, for example "Plymouth" in the Chrysler lineup of cars, they are simply shut down and go out of existence. But if the "Dog" is a discrete company, it often is past the attractive acquisition stage and is going through a slow death.

A notable recent case of a "Dog" going out is Bethlehem Steel. It is difficult to classify Bethlehem Steel as a "Dog," because at one time it was perhaps America's flagship steel maker, although not the largest, but still the largest U.S. wartime contractor during WWII.

Bethlehem Steel appears to have been overtaken by labor unions, technology, and global trade and was not nimble enough to respond, perhaps owing to the immense investment in infrastructure needed to make steel. I had the privilege of calling on Bethlehem as a younger salesman, and found it to be a very impressive organization largely free of any bias in its purchasing and eager to gain exposure to new products. The problem that I saw was a ruinous labor union and an enormous investment in process infrastructure that could not be abandoned.

Later in my life I had the good fortune of attending one of America's great graduate business schools. One of our classes was on pricing theory taught by a well-known thought leader on the subject, Alfred Oxenfeldt. One day Professor Oxenfeldt was making the point that setting a price for a product was unrelated to the cost of producing the product. One of the students in our class, perhaps a cost accountant, objected. Professor Oxenfeldt was, besides being a noted expert on pricing, was also a person not to be trifled with.

"Look Tom," he said, *"if you paid $10,000 for a piece of coal and had found a diamond at no cost, would you assign a higher selling price to the piece of coal or to the diamond?"* Tom retreated, as would we all. Price is set by the market and it is the mission of every business to produce product at a sufficiently low cost to realize a profit at market prices. When a company can no longer do that, it moves from "Cash Cow" to "Dog"" and then out.

An Early Lesson in the Death Throes of an Iconic Corporation

One of my most educational experiences occurred soon after I graduated from college in 1966. I worked for Remington-Rand in their Office Machines Division. Because I had no previous corporate experience, I was in no position to judge what was happening, but looking back on it now, the experience was almost out of Alice in Wonderland. On my first day I went to my boss to find out what I should be doing and learned that I had no function other than to be a threat to him, hired by his bosses who were hoping to fire him if I worked out. Soon I began to see that his bosses, who had hired me, were perceived unkindly by the entire engineering department. I could understand why. I had absolutely no work to do, but when I went to one of the gentleman who had hired me, to ask permission to take an afternoon off to take my wife to the airport, I got a blistering reprimand for planning a worktime absence without getting advance clearance.

The most memorable experience, however, had to do with the survival of the company. One day I was at a meeting when strategy was being discussed on how to counter IBM's recent introduction of the Selectric typewriter. The Selectric was a revolutionary new idea that used a set of interchangeable "balls" to strike the imprint on the paper. Up until this introduction by IBM, all typewriters used a moving carriage that passed the paper back and forth past a "basket" of individual type keys, which were activated by typing on the keyboard. By eliminating the moving carriage, IBM had revolutionized typing by not only reducing the amount of desktop space a typewriter required, but also by offering a variety of typefaces, and sizes, by merely substituting one ball for another. This was revolutionary and an instant hit with the secretaries of the period.

After listening to the discussion on how to respond to the Selectric challenge, I concluded that the best strategy would be to simply come out with our own interchangeable ball machine. But I kept those thoughts to myself in the meeting, because that was my place and I had already been warned about my attitude. After the meeting, in a quiet aside, I asked the gentleman who had hired me, the one who had earlier given me that blistering reprimand, why we just didn't copy IBM.

His eyes narrowed to a slit, and soon fire began coming out of them, and then he thundered: *"We had the ball back in 1923 and it wasn't a good idea then and it isn't a good idea now. What are you going to do for accountants, give them a 30-inch wide machine that weighs over 50 pounds?"* I managed to stammer out, "Nnnnno . . . .no . . . sssss . . . I . . . rrr," and went scurrying back to my desk.

Sometime after this episode there was another equally telling incident perhaps with the same group. Remington-Rand made a line of adding machines whose market was being threatened by the advent of electronics and they had completed design of our first "electronic" calculator. At the meeting, a working model was displayed in the middle of the conference table, plugged into an electrical outlet and with a bright nixie tube display. The output was pretty much limited to addition, subtraction, division and multiplication. It was clearly a pretty anemic attempt at going electronic, and it was a departure from the existing models mostly in appearance and the change to an electric key board.

Just as the meeting was getting underway an engineer caught everybody's attention by displaying a hand-held Bowman calculator from Japan that he was carrying in his shirt pocket. He held it aloft and said: *"Look what I bought over the weekend at Caldor. It's Japanese."* Caldor was a local discount store so he had evidently gotten it pretty cheaply. He went on: *"This thing can add, subtract, divide, multiply and even do functions."* The room went silent, as if the oxygen had gone missing. Then a marketing guy asked: *"Does it print out a paper tape?"* Chastened, the engineer admitted it didn't. Then another marketing guy shouted out: *"Who would buy anything made in Japan anyway?"* The entire room broke up into laughter, and the Bowman calculator was forgotten. This was 1967, just before the Japanese tsunami hit the U.S. calculator market. Amazingly, there was absolutely no interest in investigating this Japanese innovation, and these were the top executives.

Japan was devastated by WWII and to keep the economy going flooded the U.S market with junk that caused the label "Made in Japan" an object of derision. But the exports kept getting better and 20 years later were challenging not only U.S. manufacturing, but U.S. technology as well. Meanwhile Remington-Rand and this sector of the U.S. economy were asleep. What is even more surprising is that Remington-Rand was also a computer company, but if anything the office machines division and the Univac division were rivals rather than partners.

Sometime later, the typewriter project, the new Remington-Rand Model 26 that was going to eat IBM's lunch, was behind schedule; the Director of Engineering was demoted to Grounds Manager, and the Manager of Engineering, the guy who roughed me up, was put in charge of the library. As economist Schumpeter pointed out, it is hard to stop creative destruction in a free market, and it turned out, accountants liked the new

Selectric so much, that they switched to using 8½" x 11" paper. Moreover, soon after, everyone who needed a calculator carried a Bowman in their shirt pocket and got along just fine without a paper tape.

Remington-Rand was out of business a few years later. They had gone from iconic office typewriter supplier to a footnote in history and it happened before my very eyes -- I had witnessed the bureaucratic and arrogant behavior that led to the demise. For me, it was an affirmation that business really is a fast-moving and exciting field. It is a field that demands the successful and collegial orchestration of multiple players to cooperate in the face of competitive challenge to find revolutionary new ways, which is always healthy if you have your eye on the ball; and if you don't, you're out.

After Remington-Rand, I worked for Dresser Industries, Industrial Valve & Instrument Division, and found an atmosphere 180 degrees removed from that of Remington-Rand. At Dresser it was all about ideas and performance. The entire culture was devoted to getting things done, and in a collegial setting. I had gotten into trouble at Remington-Rand by visiting the marketing department to talk about how unorganized the product literature was and the opportunity being missed in building a recognizable corporate identity that would help position Remington-Rand as a major player in the office machine market. The first gentleman I met with at Remington-Rand was very enthusiastic and suggested I see the head of the marketing department. Several days later when I met with that gentleman, after laying out my argument, complete with examples from Remington-Rand and Olivetti, an Italian firm that was then the best example of corporate identity marketing, the manager asked: *"Does Jack know you're down here?"* Long story short, this interview led to my being demoted, with another blistering lecture on how Engineering does not talk to Marketing, *"We are enemies,"* I was told. This was before he was made head librarian.

I confronted a similar issue at Dresser. The product packaging didn't look anything like that represented in the product catalog. This is the same problem because such a disconnect fails to use all available means for building corporate recognition. So, I went down to Marketing, again -- I'm a hard learner -- and met with the person in charge of the catalog to discuss the issue. He was all in favor of coordinating, and since I liked the catalog graphics better than the packaging graphics, I redesigned the packaging to match that of the catalog. I was not demoted or lectured to; instead I was given all the support I needed to finish the work. The difference between these two companies will eventually show up in stock price, but long before that happens, a thoughtful investor will try to identify the Remington-Rands and Dressers of the world, avoiding the first and investing in the latter. Also remember, no matter how bad a company is, it is possible to put out a glowing annual report on it.

The Useful Role of Competition

Using market structure discussed above, it would be logical to investigate monopolies for investment possibilities, but the lack of competition in monopolies is not always an advantage to the monopolist; it can give rise to the kind of virus found at Remington-Rand. In these cases, corporate culture is the real driver. Church & Dwight is an example of a near monopoly company that seems to keep reinventing itself in order to keep pace with life, and since there are few outside influences, one must default to internal culture to explain their survival.

Coca-Cola is another story of great longevity pretty much built on a single product. While arch rival PepsiCo has kept pace, it has done so largely by branching into other products. Recent market share estimates put Coca-Cola at 42% and Pepsi-Cola at 30%. The difference is culture. At Coca-Cola, Coke is king. But perhaps Coke is successful because Pepsi is standing in the wings. This makes a good case for investment and may trump the uncertainties of more unfettered monopolies. Also, Coca-Cola depends on a robust Cola market, and Pepsi and the other competitors help maintain that market. Without Pepsi, Coke might have greater pricing power, but it also might be less successful, so there are trade-offs in near-monopolistic markets.

Other examples of similar market structures are McDonald's and Burger King, and in days gone by, Ford, GM, and Chrysler. Other examples are Staples, Office Depot, and Office Max, Land's End and L.L. Bean, Home Depot and Lowe's, AT&T and Verizon, and the interesting story of Colgate and Crest.

Although Colgate has been the perennial global leader, Crest led the U.S. market until Colgate introduced Colgate Total and raced ahead in this country. But Crest, a Procter & Gamble brand, fought back by introducing an array of oral care products, sort of enveloping Colgate, a strategy that after 10 years won back supremacy in the U.S. market for Crest. For investors, this is a sign that Procter & Gamble is alive and well, as is Colgate Palmolive, both good investment candidates, made stronger by competition.

The examples just cited are of oligopolies, where several major competitors pretty much carve up the marketplace leaving the crumbs, or niche markets, to much smaller niche players. Most markets are made up of multiple players with the largest market share typically going to the pioneer, if the pioneer was sufficiently capitalized to grow as fast as the market. Sometimes a better capitalized later entrant takes over a market founded by a pioneer. Often, niche players come in later to pick off the crumbs, which may be small but can be very profitable.

The first fall-out occurs soon after the market is discovered as too many entrants attempt to survive on too few customers and some fail or get bought out. This winnowing process not only eliminates the weak, but further differentiates the strong from the weak and may serve to further refine what is called the product bundle. This is the product with all of the attendant experiences the buyer will have in both purchasing and using the product. The product bundle may be highly differentiated by multiple players in the early stage but gradually will get consolidated into a major product bundle with several much smaller niche product bundles. For example, Hertz was for a long time the major auto rental company, and then Avis began setting up their counters at airports figuring people arriving by plane would need a car to complete their trip. Avis succeeded with a different product bundle – location. For a long time Zippo owned the cigarette lighter market. Then BIC introduced the disposable lighter and turned the market upside down with a replacement product. Sam Walton figured out that it was the retailers and not the manufacturers who had the customers; his vision changed retailing.

Iconic Corporations

A characteristic of markets not very well described by the monopoly/oligopoly mix is the level of differentiation between players. For example, in the automobile market BMW also makes motorcycles, a characteristic shared by few others in the auto market.

In baby food, Beech-Nut is a family owned business, Gerber is owned by Nestle, and then there is Heinz. A recent survey reported that combined, Heinz and Beech-Nut control 25% - 30% of the market, whereas Gerber controls 70% of the market. This presents a challenge to Beech-Nut, which as a family-owned business must fight off much larger rivals for shelf space. You can be sure that Heinz has already given thought to a Beech-Nut acquisition as a way to gain power in the wholesale food industry. But the real driver may be babies. When it comes to shopping for value, parents may make an exception in the case of their babies and buy on reputation rather than price. It would be hard to beat Gerber in that category -- their slogan at one time was and perhaps still is: "Babies are our only business." Buying Gerber is a cheap way for parents to say they care.

Some companies, like Gerber, are able to beat out the competition and emerge, if not the undisputed market leader, the prestige leader, which carries pricing power. Some of those brands that come to mind are Michelin when it comes to tires – they also put out respected travel guides. Another prestige leader is also French: Schlumberger, an oil exploration services company. Others in this category are: Hellman's for mayonnaise, Heinz for ketchup, Pendleton for clothing, Maytag for washing machines, Intel, Nokia, Gillette, Apple, Marlboro, American Express, Nike, KFC, Caterpillar, Budweiser, 3M and Johnson & Johnson to name a few. These are companies that have survived brutal competition to become market icons, which gives them pricing power. But this position of prestige doesn't just happen, and the ingredients for their success will probably not be evident in the annual report. Over many years cultures have grown up inside these companies that can begin a decline at any time, though currently show no signs of ebbing.

But if a former market leader does go into decline, all is not lost. Witness Xerox. This company went through a tumultuous period of transition -- for itself and for American industry in general – owing to global competition and rapid technological change. The tumult forced many companies, including Xerox, to dismantle aging bureaucracies, cut costs, and streamline manufacturing processes.

Xerox was flirting with bankruptcy in the early 1980s with just a fraction of the copier market it had once commanded — much of it lost to Japanese competitors. "We are in the proverbial soup," the CEO of Xerox told a New York Times reporter in 1984. Through revamped product lines and a broad and sometimes painful restructuring, including thousands of layoffs, Xerox was on the rebound by 1990. These events were captured in a book *Prophets in the Dark: How Xerox Reinvented Itself and Beat Back the Japanese* (1992). The rebound incidentally was credited to copying Japanese management methods forced on to them by the competition they encountered in the market. Such is the value of competition.

An early insight into the role of competition took place in the Roman republic around 150 BC. The Romans had beaten the Carthaginians in a war that almost took the republic down and some Romans were agitating for complete destruction of Carthage, but the counter argument was that Rome needed the competition provided by Carthage to keep the republic focused and strong. That argument lost and Carthage was destroyed. The Roman republic then went into decline and eventually disappeared as mercantilism, militarism, and bribery replaced Senate debate; many Romans evidently felt the decline owed to Carthage no longer being around as a threat to help refine Roman society.

There are purer market players that operate in competitive markets but because they produce such highly differentiated product bundles they are quasi-monopolies. Examples are BMW, Gucci, Rolls Royce, John Deere, IBM, Microsoft, Starbucks, Clorox, Disney, Google, Amazon, Ebay, L'Oreal, Louis Vuitton, and Tiffany. It's worthwhile to provide a few quotes from these companies that address maintaining leadership.

A quote from Dr. Uwe Ellinghaus, Director of Brand Steering at BMW:

"To quote our CEO, Dr. Norbert Reithofer, 'in the future, premium will be defined by sustainability.' At BMW, we follow a holistic approach to sustainability that includes clean production sites, HR initiatives, social and cultural commitments, as well as the development of alternative and environmentally friendly solutions. These measures are consistently being extended and examined, and will continue to be essential to brand-building in the future."

Patrizio DiMarco, CEO of Gucci.

"The world's leading brands are rightly judged today not just on the quality of their products and services, but also on the way they act in the community and towards the environment. In 2004, Gucci took a leadership position in the industry by voluntarily initiating the certification process for Corporate Social Responsibility (SA8000) across its supply chains. In the same year, Gucci established a partnership with UNICEF, which in the last six years has generated more than US $8 million for its projects supporting disadvantaged children and women in sub-Saharan Africa. These initiatives are very much part of our values system and they are of increasing concern to our customers as they make purchasing decisions."

The Oldest Corporations

However, perhaps the most reliable way to evaluate companies for investment is to look at longevity, because as we have seen given time, complacency, sloppiness or plain old self-centeredness at the top are ever-present threats to corporate culture and sooner or later bring down almost all companies. From the perspective of longevity, the Japanese trump all other nations and also have the oldest continuously operated company, a family that for 46 generations, beginning in 718, has operated a continuously running hotel.

One of the oldest professions is brewing. In fact, there are theories that homo sapien sapien gave up a much easier hunter-gatherer lifestyle for what proved to be a not so sedentary life in order to brew, raising our consciousness on just how important beer is to our species. This puts Germany, after Japan, as the country with more of the longest running companies; breweries there began as early as 1040 with the start of Weihenstephan. Unfortunately most of those 10 or so oldest continuously running breweries are family affairs and not public companies. One that is public has bought up a number of the older breweries, and that is Inbev (BUD), which acquired Anheuser-Busch several years ago. They seem to have acquired around 60 brands, which they break down into global brands (Stella Artois, Becks, and Budweiser), multi-country brands (Leffe and Hoegaarden) and local champions, which are too numerous to list here but include some very old breweries (Lowenbrau (1383) and St. Pauli Girl (17th century)).

One American company you can invest in that has been in continuous operation since 1792 is CIGNA (CI), offering a product that is very much in the news these days: health insurance. Over the past 10 years, CIGNA stock price has almost been a surrogate for the S&P 500.

Another very old company is Dixon Ticonderoga making such basic products as pencils. Today it is a privately owned company whose principal shareholder is Fila-Fabrica Italiana Lapis ed Affini S.p.A., located in Milan, Italy. Apparently a case of ownership that secures a strong personal future by removing the distraction of the stock market, much as Warren Buffet has done with his "poor man's hedge fund" Berkshire Hathaway.

Berkshire's Corporate Reporting or Non-Reporting

Berkshire CEOs don't have the distraction of stock price because all the companies in the Berkshire group trade as a group. Another aspect of public ownership is the onerous reporting requirements imposed by the regulatory bodies that oversee the stock exchanges and set reporting rules. Investors are then led to believe what they read in annual reports and quarterly 10K reports. It should come as no surprise that those reports, that even if accurate, are a poor guide to future promise, and are prepared with the intent of highlighting good news and hiding bad news.

The watchdog agency given power to set reporting standards, the Financial Accounting Standards Board (FASB), like every other government agency with the possible exception of the FDA, is subject to agency capture by the people they are supposed to be regulating. One example is the emerging use of "pro forma" figures, which essentially means, figures that should have happened but didn't. These figures are nevertheless fed to investors who are contemplating the investment worthiness of a company. It should be noted that the Securities and Exchange Commission looks for fraudulent use of *pro forma* figures used in public reporting. It is worthwhile to spend a paragraph on annual reporting requirements.

It's no surprise that a company likes its stock price high so that, for one thing, it can issue stock as a financing measure and thus get a pretty good return for giving up a piece of owner-ship. The company is also concerned with diluting the stock of existing stockholders by issuing more stock, and high stock price tamps this down. Theoretically there is no dilution because the cash from issuing the stock is now at the company, so they have merely traded one asset, stock, for another asset, cash. But to get that stock price high, annual reports are juiced up as much as possible.

Companies are required by law to issue three quarterly reports and one annual report, and one use of the reports is to attract investors. In the Securities Act of 1933, Congress accepted and then delegated reporting oversight to the SEC. The SEC appropriately enough decided that accounting standards must be issued so that all reports followed an easily recognizable standard, so the Financial Accounting Standards Board (FASB) came into existence to do that job. FASB creates rules that, if adopted by the industry (generally accepted), will become Generally Accepted Accounting Principles (GAAP).

There were holes in this process that were tolerated for a long time, up until the Enron debacle. What happened at Enron was the re-location of depressing debt, which might otherwise have discouraged investment, onto "off balance-sheet" entities that absorbed that debt and did not have to appear in the annual report, except perhaps as a footnote. How's that for varnish? The result was that many trusting people and entities lost big money when it came to light that rather than being a tremendous wealth creator as evidenced by the annual report complete with auditor's endorsement on the fairness of the report, and meeting GAAP, the company was in reality worse than broke, in fact, in deep debt.

In response, Congress passed the Sarbanes-Oxley Act of 2002 establishing the Public Company Accounting Oversight Board (PCAOB) whose mission it is to scrutinize company reports and plug the holes. But wait, there are still holes. A recent "rebuke" of a very prominent company found the firm relying too heavily on management input for gauging the health of the company. One way to look at this is that the accounting firm is just doing good client management. The point is, there are still holes. Many companies (but not all) make liberal use of varnish in reporting to make a profitable story in order to reel in investors, lenders, and other sources of profit. That is why annual reports should be taken with a grain of salt.

I began studying for the CFA designation, and much of the financial accounting section dealt with the most probable areas of abuse as well as how to spot them. But I make no pretense: I am not a trained CPA and view serious annual report scrutiny by non-CPAs as amateurish in light of the sophisticated chicanery used in reporting financial results.

Corporate Governance

It is also important to place CEO and Board of Directors chicanery into perspective. It's not unheard of for solid businesses, particularly very old businesses, to go through a period of poor management with tolerant or passive boards giving free reign to a CEO who is clearly "off the reservation." If it is a solid business, it will survive, if for no other reason than that the company has great depth in management and employees who are able to function effectively, particularly in decentralized corporate structures, and the business has customers. One only has to recall Imperial Rome surviving, even thriving, for hundreds of years despite a parade of emperors who clearly were lunatics. How did this happen? The answer is a well-entrenched administrative class that made the whole thing work and work well.

Closer to home is the observation by Warren Buffett and Charlie Munger that a ham sandwich could run Coca-Cola. So be cautious about businesses where a CEO is going to be the savior, and at the same time don't be overly alarmed by a CEO getting caught in a scandal. Look at the business, which means looking at the customers – do they need the product. In the following paragraphs I offer some examples.

Perhaps the oldest American company to offer an investor's view into long-term management is DuPont, founded in 1802. DuPont was incorporated in 1915 and was probably listed on the NYSE at that time. So in the case of DuPont, we have a listing with almost 100 years of history. The following is a quote about DuPont from a website that would interest investors looking for solid companies –

http://best.berkeley.edu/~pps/pps/imagemenu.html

Here is the quote:

"The DuPont that has emerged from the company's transformation of the 1990s has often been described by people inside and outside the company as "the new DuPont."This characterization is only partly appropriate, because while DuPont has changed, there are many things that remain the same. The core competency in science and technology, the commitment to safety, the concern for people, the feeling of community, the emphasis on personal and corporate integrity, the future focus, and indeed the willingness to change -- these are not "new" characteristics; they are the constant forces in

DuPont culture. However, in many ways DuPont is new and different. Jobs are less structured. People on production lines plan and implement process improvements. People from DuPont manufacturing sites meet with their counterparts at customer plants to find out how to do a better job. DuPont people with ideas for new products and businesses are encouraged to commercialize these businesses, and then run them. What has always set DuPont apart is the quality of the people, people committed to making life easier and better for everybody, proud to be a part of an enterprise making "better things for better living. "That was true in 1802. And it is just as true today.

To learn more about DuPont visit their DuPont Heritage page: http://www2.dupont.com/Heritage/en_US/index.html

One other company that like DuPont has been more or less intact throughout its long history is John Wiley & Sons, a publisher of books. Founded in 1807, they cite the following reasons for investors to take a look. From the Wiley website. *Reasons to invest in us:*

- *Consistent long-term performance*
- *Solid financial characteristics, including strong free cash flow, strong balance sheet, and solid earnings growth*
- *Strong growth drivers including growing investment in global R&D, education, and professional development.*
- *Emphasis on businesses that generate predictable revenues, earnings, and cash flow*
- *Proven track record with acquisitions*
- *High barriers to entry*
- *Solid growth opportunities in delivering workflow solutions enabling technologies around must-have content*
- *Ability to capitalize on significant global opportunities, particularly as the shift to knowledge-based economies continues*

- *Diverse product portfolio*
- *Veteran leadership team and independent Board of Directors distinguished by their longstanding commitment to effective governance, and the integrity of reported financial results*
- *Performance-driven, collaborative culture that has established Wiley as "the place to be" for authors, customers, employees, and partners*

As proof of good management, the stock has risen about four times more than the S&P 500. But Wiley is entering a new challenge, the growing influence of Amazon in book distribution and electronic books. Amazon is becoming a vertically integrated behemoth linking the reader directly with the author. Their presence in the market will be a challenge for Wiley that either kills them off or makes them stronger.

For a look at other long-lived companies, visit Wikipedia's list of oldest companies, and be surprised by what you find. http://en.wikipedia.org/wiki/List_of_oldest_companies

On the list you will find a running record of companies along with their start dates. No end dates are given; companies no longer operating are coded by color. What, one might reflect on, is the fundamental difference between the survivors and the expired? I think you have to go back to Burton Malkiel's perception that stock price reflects news and news is random. This means uncontrolled change, or change impossible to forecast.

Companies will be buffeted by both external change and the internal changes that must take place to survive, if not thrive, in a changing world. Some companies cannot change -- witness Remington Rand -- but other companies will occupy a range from managing change quite well -- perhaps Macy's department store -- to being agents of change, perhaps such as IBM, or 3M, even Starbucks. Some companies succeed by only changing the way they make or deliver the same product, like Coca-Cola, Kentucky Fried Chicken, Marlboro, and a few others. The trick here is brand management, to maintain supremacy against the daily assault of competition. There is always change.

But what probably is the common thread among great companies is an internal culture that succeeds in decentralizing a devotion to excellence, right down to the driver delivering the product or the third-party retailer handing the product to his customer with the bravado that comes from knowing satisfaction will not be an issue. Bad news about companies always depresses the stock price but that's because people don't understand that the bad news for a good company is an opportunity to plug another hole that got overlooked. The best companies will never be totally immune from bad news, because companies are living organisms that constantly change and are changed by events, but the good ones have healthy growth and prune away what doesn't add value.

One of the greatest companies of all time is Procter & Gamble. P&G has been able to weave devotion to customers into the cultural fabric at the company. Recently a very successful P&G CEO died and his obituary described his speaking at a recent P&G meeting of company leaders, with the aid of a breathing device, and urging them to think in the long term: *"We don't want to think in quarters or even years but in terms of decades and centuries."*

The Role of Prestige

I learned in business school that prestige has nothing to do with money, but is all about character. A case study described in our class about buyer behavior was a cocktail party attended by a wealthy entrepreneur, a wealthy Wall Street trader, a non-wealthy novelist, a non-wealthy pastor, a philanthropist, and a variety of working Americans like doctors, lawyers, etc. Among this group, the prestige leaders were likely to be the pastor, the novelist, and the philanthropist. Prestige it seems, is more about doing good than doing well.

Not studied in business school, but by my own observation having worked at a number of companies, is that what employees crave the most is not money, but prestige. Employees of prestigious companies communicate a pride and are quick to tell you who they work for. I recall one company I worked for that was far ahead of its competitors in prestige and had extraordinary pricing power, sometimes succeeding at twice the price of competition. I observed a new employee in some correspondence referencing the company name in every other sentence. But I have observed this behavior among all employees I have encountered, at trade shows for example, working for companies that are prestige leaders in their market; always the prominence of who they work for is evident in their encounters. And how many times have I heard: "Oh. I came over from Goldman." (Goldman Sachs). Obviously this is a demonstration of decentralizing devotion and it is done simply by managing a corporate effort in such a way that the company gains a reputation for quality that leads to prestige. If the corporate character that creates prestige can be maintained, the company should survive, if not thrive, indefinitely.

There was an attempt to package quality measures in a program called "Six Sigma." This was a brainchild of Motorola that in 1986 developed a strategy to reduce manufacturing defects to a statistical level called six sigma or 99.99966% free of defects which works out to 3.4 defects per million. Naturally in order to achieve this, quality thinking had to envelop the entire organization; you can't have a rigorous standard of performance for just one department. Accordingly companies either were or were not six sigma. This would seem to be a good place to start looking for investment candidates, but then, a *"funny thing happened on the way to the forum,"* as a rather dated expression goes. According to an article in Fortune magazine, of 58 companies that adopted Six Sigma, 91% have trailed the S&P 500. Evidently, while enveloping the entire culture, it really only is beneficial in repetitive activities such as manufacturing and may not have a similar effect in say, marketing activities. At any rate, there is enough evidence to warrant using adoption of Six Sigma as only one measure of investment promise.

Contingent Pension Liabilities

One corporation hazard increasingly talked about is "contingent liabilities" in the form of underfunded pension plans. After WWII, many companies, particularly larger companies, were concerned with attracting and keeping talented employees in a tight labor market. This was also a society that was strongly tied to recent military activity and pensions were initially developed for the military. Accordingly, companies began offering pensions to attract employee applications and then hand-cuff those who were hired to long-term employment. At that time, retirement age was set at 65 with the expectation that most employees could look forward to perhaps ten years of retirement before expiring. Contributions made by employers during a boom period of U.S. industrialization in a post-war consumer spending boom made pension plans sustainable. But as the U.S. economy began to decline in the wake of global trade and cheaper overseas labor, and as medical innovation and new focus on health led to great advances in longevity that replaced 10-year retirements with 30-year retirements, many pensions became underfunded.

Two notable examples are Nortel where the pension became underfunded and Lucent where the pension fund was apparently raided during a business downturn. Investors would have justifiably been impressed with the technical output of these two companies, but the shadow the pension obligations casts over operations makes them both questionable investment candidates.

Lucent was merged with a French company Alcatel and Nortel dumped their U.S. pension liability onto American taxpayers in the form of the Pension Benefit Guaranty Corporation (PBGC). That may sound like a corporation but is in reality a U.S. government entity. One would have to wonder about the managements of such companies that allowed pension plans to become a source of operating funds, or a deficit that it was then able to escape by handing it to American taxpayers, who are largely not covered by pensions. So in examining annual reports, be sure to check the footnotes, where such unpleasant disclosures are normally buried.

I must add a note about pensions at this point. Pensions were sustainable at an earlier time when longevity was much shorter and the U.S. economy was expanding with a strong export dimension that brought wealth into the country. At that time actuarial calculations did not make provision for either a slackening economy or greater longevity driven in part by the rise of modern medicine that can keep people collecting pension checks for a far longer period than originally thought. Eventually something had to give, and so most companies switched to 401(k) plans to take the place of pensions.

401(k), the Pension Antidote

Pensions are generically called "defined benefit" plans because they promise an outcome, a specified income for life. 401(k) plans are "defined contribution" plans because they don't define the outcome but only the process, regular deferrals invested for a retirement of undefined magnitude. One promises a result and the other promises a process – the opportunity to contribute to your own retirement fund.

It is fashionable to criticize companies for making this change, suggesting that pensions and 401(k) plans operate in two different markets. This concept is of course absurd. Pensions and 401(k) plans are invested in the same market, the stock and bond market. In reality pensions will perform no better that 401(k) plans. In fact they will perform worse, because they are more conservatively invested to provide cash for prior retirees. So where does the perception of safety in a pension come from? It comes from some people starting their pensions before they were closed and so are now entitled to the benefit such pensions guaranteed whether the pension funds are there or not. This doesn't make pensions safer; it just means someone is going to have to give something up to finance a benefit stream for someone else. In economic speak, this is an externality, a benefit for a few at the expense of the many, and primarily the many from the following generation. Such a system robs the kids to pay the parents.

In reality, a 401(k) plan should substantially outperform a pension because it can be much more aggressively invested over a longer term and cash-flow out is tailored to individual requirements.

In managing the assets in a pension plan, the first calculation the plan advisor makes is the liquidity (cash) needed to pay all current pensioners. That fraction of the overall asset base must then be invested in bonds and near cash assets that have very little return. The balance of the assets may then be invested in S&P 500 equivalents and other assets permitted in the plan document.

When the plan is new, the near-cash fraction is small because there are few retirees at the start, but as time passes, the retiree pool grows and requires a greater fraction of assets in near-cash positions to give those retirees an income; that puts a drag on overall return for everybody. At some point, return is no longer adequate to cover cash-flow out and the pension plan fails. Actually a pension plan becomes underfunded long before as pension calculations look out over a longer horizon. The core concept is that a growing retiree pool forces a growing investment shift to low-return assets in order to provide ready cash, and the higher return needed to sustain the pension is cut-off -- that means cut-off for all the younger members in the plan.

A 401(k) plan covers one individual only and therefore

better matches return with need. And on Day One of the retirement phase, the plan only begins a draw down, which can take many years. That allows the plan to seek higher returns over much of the retirement phase of the plan. The outcome is not guaranteed as in a pension plan, but at the same time, the guarantees of a pension plan are really not guaranteed either, only a forecast guaranteed on faulty data.

The faulty data was not only in missing increasing longevity but also the declining return forecasts owing to moving assets from stocks to bonds. Recently the State of Rhode Island found itself facing bankruptcy over public employee pension plans that were using 8.25% as a return calculation. Apparently the calculation assumed the asset base would be more fully invested, but it can't be because there are too many current or approaching retirees.

The S&P 500 total returns for the past few years are as follows: 2007 (5.49%), 2008 (-37.00%), 2009 (26.46%), 2010 (15.06%), 2011 (2.11), and 2012 (16.00%). To get a better view of price return and total return over different periods, you may use a calculator at: http://dqydj.net/sp-500-return-calculator/

The 25-year average total return on the S&P 500 as of 2012 was 9.72%. Returns on AAA-rated corporate bonds were: 2007 (5.56%), 2008 (5.63%), 2009 (5.31%) and 2010 (4.94%). Yield on 3-year Treasuries over the same period were 2007 (4.35%), 2008 (2.24%), 2009 (1.43%) and 2010 (1.11%). As you can see, the S&P 500 even with the upset of 2008 is able to deliver return over the long term. For example, look at the average S&P 500 annual total return over discrete periods backwards from 2010: All data (9.87%), 5-year (2.29%), 10-year (1.41%), 15-year (6.76%), 20-year (9.14%) and 25-year (9.72%). If an asset pool needs liquidity to satisfy current pensioners, you can't at the same time get the returns needed for future pensioners. Only an individually tailored plan can get maximum return matched to overall need, as in a 401(k) plan.

Pension plans are inflexible. Contributions into a pension

plan are regular fixed amounts that use dollar-cost-averaging to purchase a variable number of shares, that may be many when the market is down and few when the market is up. Accordingly, during a dis-investment phase, the cash out should be metered by a percentage of the asset base, causing the cash out to vary depending on whether the market is up or down. But this is never the case, so that when the market is down and the asset base is down, a much larger percentage is taken out, cutting off the possibility for a full recovery for the overall asset base when the market recovers. And since there will be ups and downs in the market, the failure to meter the cash out by proportion means that in periods of market upset, there can be dramatic draw down of the asset base. Individual 401(k) plans allow for some flexibility, allowing for withdrawals that more closely match market performance, but pension plans don't have this flexibility.

Getting back to the companies that undergird the performance of the S&P 500, in surveying the corporate landscape for investment candidates you are more than likely to come up against the conundrum of headline-grabbing CEO and the evolution of long-term corporate competitiveness. There is an old Chinese proverb: "The grass grows thin under a large tree." This applies to outsized CEOs grabbing all the oxygen in a company with the result that over time the company below him atrophies and doesn't do well after his/her exit.

The Corporate Marketing Mix
An example of a company succeeding through generations of leadership is Procter & Gamble (PG), one of America's greatest success stories. I have never read a story about the CEO of this company, except the obituary cited above, although stories about the CEOs of many other U.S. companies are the stuff of Wall Street media ad nauseam. My take on the P&G magic is that it is highly decentralized but also customer-

focused. It seems that every employee is inculcated with the core idea that understanding and finding new ways to satisfy customers are the keys to the future. In other words the customer is King and the employees serving those customers come next, not the CEO. Many companies claim to be doing this, but P&G has really been doing it since 1837.

Also P&G has the highest stewardship grades from GMI – Governance Metrics International. GMI rated P&G a 10.0 in 2007 the highest rating it issues (see Chapter 9).

The P&G story also raises another dimension of brand management – brand creation. What is unique to great companies is their understanding that it is the brand and not the product that counts -- products come and go. And most great companies are great because they have nurtured their brands through difficult times. But in the case of P&G, they have not only nurtured P&G brands but also created a number of brands that many people are unaware are owned by P&G. Examples are: Crest, Olay, Pert, Ivory, Cheer, Downy, Joy, Dawn, and Tide, to name a few. Some of these may have been acquisitions, but what sets P&G apart from most other great companies is its ability to create successful new brands. This ability is an outgrowth of understanding that what makes a business is not products, but customers preferring a favorite brand.

Another dimension of company research that bears attention is market structure as it pertains to barriers to entry, already mentioned in a negative way. At one time Bethlehem Steel was an excellent investment candidate because it had a huge plant and equipment infrastructure that discouraged competitors. However the business changed and that same infrastructure became a liability. But plant and equipment is only one type of infrastructure; another is brand management. Coca-Cola and Marlboro cigarettes are brands that have close competitors, but they are almost impossible to unseat because they have very skillfully managed their brands.

Sometimes the barrier to entry is the cost of change. Microsoft, for example, is almost unassailable because of the pain and cost of learning new software. Who wants to learn a new word processing program? Nobody I know. Another example is what in marketing is called "place." McDonald's is everywhere. Who could overnight put up a gazillion hamburger shops to compete with McDonald's? Nobody. Distribution is a big barrier to entry.

In 1953 a marketing man named Neil Borden coined the term "Marketing Mix" which came to be thought of as the four Ps: "Price," "Product," "Place," and "Promotion." It was thought that managing these four dimensions of a product bundle was the best predictor of success. "Price" means pricing power; the production efficiency to realize a profit with low price but also sell at higher profit margins than competitors.

"Price" also refers to pricing strategies that succeed in competitive markets. For example, pharmaceutical companies regularly price differently for different markets.

"Product" refers to all those dimensions that may be strategic to successful marketing and leads to the concept of "Product Bundle." In other words, how the product is packaged, how people learn to use it, and how the product is stored are not direct attributes of the product itself but will drive buying behavior, so they count as part of the "Product."

"Place" we have already described with the ubiquitous presence of McDonald's restaurants, but may also be seen in Dunkin' Donuts' successful beating off of the Krispy Kreme challenge. Krispy Kreme has 669 stores to Dunkin' Donuts' 9,760 stores. The key concept here is that you may have the greatest product but if it is not at a place where customers can buy it, it won't succeed. The flip side is that a lackluster product can succeed if it is well distributed.

"Promotion" means building the brand. It takes a lot of money to build a brand and it is perhaps the most decisive factor in investment, because it is almost impossible to unseat a well-built brand. Where brands fail, they usually do it to themselves.

One interesting case of brand management concerns Stolichnaya vodka, a Russian product and a brand leader in the U.S. at one time known affectionately as Stoli. In 1983, the Russians shot down Korean Air Lines flight 007, a passenger plane, for overflying a sensitive area in their Pacific military zone. The plane apparently did overfly the area but inadvertently. In any case, there was an immediate backlash against Russia in the U.S. and Stolichnaya immediately cancelled all advertising and pulled all their ads, which were a staple of the Sunday *New York Times* magazine. Normally every Sunday, in the first few pages, was a full-page bleed, 4-color ad showing the glamour of drinking Stoli. When the ads stopped, nobody missed them. Then, after a suitable period the ads began appearing again. Today, Stoli is still a mark of quality when it comes to vodka. This is a good example of "Promotion" in the marketing mix, undoubtedly executed by the brand manager at a well-heeled Madison Avenue firm, or by a very marketing savvy Russian.

Thinking about the "4 Ps" as barriers to entry -- or as moats around companies as Warren Buffett apparently once said -- each "P" has a particular strength in building a defensible position that may vary from product to product. For example, thinking about product or the product bundle and McDonald's, there is little doubt that any business could replicate a McDonald's hamburger. But McDonald's dominates by depending on "Place," although "Price" plays a role as does "Promotion" with all the McDonald's characters.

Procter & Gamble focuses on coming up with products that are clearly superior (Dawn being used to clean birds after the Exxon Valdez spill) and then promoting them vigorously. This wins P&G a lot of space at the grocery store ("Place") and then "Price" plays a greater role, allowing P&G to maintain a good profit margin and pay shareholders a 3.2% dividend. So P&G is difficult to unseat on three of the 4 Ps. P&G is definitely an investment candidate.

Apple is a company that seems to be all product, with products that come out first and trump the competition. Price, place and promotion seem to play little part in Apple's success. In a way, Apple is the anti-McDonald's, but it works. At one time Remington-Rand may have been a company like Apple complete with a Univac advanced computer division. But the loss of the "Product" initiative to IBM took away all of the advantage, and there was no "Promotion," "Place," or "Price" to fall back on.

Looking at investment candidates through the lens of the "4 Ps" may be a good way to do an initial winnowing of a starting population of candidates. Of course, you can save yourself all the effort and just pick at random 15 or 20 companies from 100 of the world's greatest corporations, or from the S&P 500.

A Business is Defined by Customers not Products

Another useful exercise is looking at companies through the eyes of their customers. Remember a business is defined by customers, not products. Product positioning might be a fine and fun exercise from inside the company, but it is the customers who will decide what the positioning is – prestige leader or market flop.

So looking at companies in which you are about to invest through the eyes of their customers can be a very insightful exercise. Take Ford, for example. What would Ford customers do if Ford suddenly disappeared? They would buy Chevrolets, Chryslers, Hyundais, Hondas, Toyotas, Nissans, BMWs, etc. And eventually they might wind up preferring their new ride to the old. So what does Ford have? Ford has "Place" and little else. Of course, Ford also has Congress that wants to keep the U.S. in the automobile game and will put it on life-support if needed. And this is not to be scoffed at as an investment thesis. But on the other hand, the investor may not make it to the other side with Ford.

Another example of investing in customers is Marlboro, a product of Altria in the U.S. and Philip Morris Company (PM) in the international market. Some investors may not wish to invest in tobacco but this does not materially affect the investment thesis – Marlboro is a very carefully nurtured iconic brand around the world.

What would happen if Marlboro disappeared? Would the result be as easy to bear as a Ford failure? I don't think so. I think Marlboro smokers not only like the taste of Marlboros, but they also derive a lot of identity from being Marlboro smokers, more identity that Ford drivers get from driving a Ford. This is because the folks at Marlboro have very carefully cultivated the brand even negotiating the contrary waters of government mandates against tobacco advertising, the considerable public relations effort to kill off smoking, and the taxes that have ratcheted up the price beyond what may be thought of as "affordable."

I was at the service desk at a local store of a major grocery chain and while waiting to be served, scrutinized the cigarette display. Marlboro had about 75% of the shelf space and when I asked the clerk what the best-selling brand was, she said without thinking about it: "Marlboro Lights." In my view -- and I am not a smoker, in fact I am worse than that, I am a reformed smoker who resents people lighting up in public spaces where I can smell it -- but I feel Altria is an excellent investment candidate for steering their iconic brand to the position of largest selling cigarette brand in the world. Marlboro smokers will not take lightly to losing their brand. So Altria has "Product," "Place," "Promotion," and "Price." "Price" for Marlboro does not seem to matter, a very envious position to be in.

Back in the 1980s when I was selling Continuous Emissions Monitors (CEMs), I visited the then Philip Morris power plant at Park 500 in Chester, Va., to meet with its power plant manager. When I entered the reception area I was amused to find a sign that said: "Thank you for smoking." I had long ago given up smoking so I didn't light up. I spent an hour or so with the manager touring the exhaust system of the power plant and then took this gentleman to lunch.

During our plant tour he didn't smoke. When we arrived at the restaurant the hostess asked the standard question: *"Smoking or non-smoking?" "Smoking"* my guest answered. *"Oh. I didn't realize you smoked,"* I said. *"I don't,"* the gentleman responded, *"But we support smoking."* After we had sat down and ordered lunch, he told me that Philip Morris regularly sent employees to many seminars and whenever a seminar began with the injunction that there would be no smoking, the Philip Morris people got up and walked out. This is an example of a company nurturing the brand at all levels right down to the power plant manager.

Focusing on brands is a good way to find good consumer goods and services stocks but misses the industrial sector that also has iconic, though less well-known, brands. Some brands are household words like CAT standing for Caterpillar, but two less well known industrial market leaders are: Cummins (CMI), a diesel engine builder since 1919, and Peterbilt trucks by Paccar (PCAR), the iconic long-haul truck-builder since 1939. Illinois Tool Works (ITW) is a company that since 1912 has acquired industrial companies and then gives them resources to succeed while leaving them alone to go at it.

In oil exploration field services, the French firm Schlumberger (SLB) has been leading the pack since 1926. Today Schlumberger is the largest global oil exploration field services provider with over 110,000 employees in 80 countries. All of these companies have competitors in the wings, ready to take over, but at the same time, by their prestige they attract the best of the best and that gives them a continuing edge, generation after generation.

In researching companies, look at their customers and

consider what they would do if suddenly denied their favorite brand. Would they just adopt an alternate and grow to like it, perhaps even better than the original? Or would they mount a counter charge and bring forth the same brand from another supplier? You get a sense of this when you see generic substitutes in packaging that mimics the look of the brand leader, or counterfeit luxury items exported from China.

Considering great companies with a culture of excellence that survive over generations no better example arises than the wine maker, Lafite Rothschild, which has been Number 1 since 1855. In that year, for the Exposition Universelle de Paris, Emperor Napoleon III decided to impose a quality grading system on wines from the Bordeaux region. Unlike other wines areas, except California, major wines of Bordeaux are entirely in-house creations; wineries there do not buy grapes from else-where for blending. The Bordeaux wine-producing properties are vertically integrated and are called "Chateaux."

In 1855, complying with Napoleon III's directive to classify wine for the exposition, third-party wine merchants placed each of the major chateaux in one of five quality ranks based on the chateau's reputation and trading price, which was felt captured that sometimes indefinable characteristic called quality. Amazingly, the four chateaux named "first growths" in 1855 have retained their ranks ever since, with some adjustments within the trailing three of the four, but the top-ranked chateau has never been challenged for first place: Chateau Lafite Rothschild. This chateau has been first since 1855. How is that for inter-generational maintenance of quality? And for something so dependent for outcome on nature.

Now comes the boring part. This statement is sure to attract a great deal of criticism if it ever gets out in France, and perhaps among some aficionados here in America. Chateau Mouton Rothschild, a cousin perhaps, sometime in 1973 as I recall reading, feeling stung by carrying a second-growth classification, demanded, and got, a re-classification to first growth. As far as I know, this is the only case of upending the work of 1855. But who cares? Lafite Rothschild is still Number 1 and Mouton is a wannabe.

I once bought a bottle of Lafite for my wife, and she has been a wine snob ever since. Every time we try a new, what promises to be "great" wine, she takes a sip, and invariably pronounces the familiar phrase: "*It's not Lafite.*" In this respect Lafite is the benchmark for wine. What other benchmark companies can you think of? Those are the ones you are looking for.

The reason for this discussion on company taxonomy is to drive home the point that you should invest in companies because they are great companies in great businesses and that to rely on Wall Street chatter and transient stock price charts or annual reports on performance is a false trail that will eat up valuable time and propel you on a wrong path. It is just not possible to follow the stock market and to research great companies -- the two activities are antithetical and mutually exclusive. To succeed in investment the stock market must be set aside and the mind focused on such questions as: What is a great business? Which companies are best positioned to dominate a great business? Which companies have consistently reinvented themselves to serve changing markets? Which companies are the prestige leaders? Which are the companies we cannot imagine being without? Which companies have the most devoted customers? These are the questions you should be asking, not the likes of "What did XYZ company closed at today?"

A good way to study companies is to just visit the "Investor" section of corporate websites and study the FAQs section. There you will find the commonly asked questions by investors, with answers from the company. This is where you will get information to stimulate a more detailed search. Remember, the function of research is to make you comfortable with the stocks you buy and hold through market upset.

As an alternative, the reader can just dispense with all of the company scrutiny discussed in this chapter and simply buy the common stocks of the companies making up the Dow 30. The long-term result from doing only this will probably outperform the result from any and all of the research devoted to companies outside of the Dow 30.

So why would I write a book like this? The answer is to show the beginning investor that in investment it is not effort that is important, but rather judgment, patience, and stamina. Success is not in the selection so much as in the behavior of the investor after the selection is made. In short, selection is not trivial, but the companies you want to invest in are out in plain sight – no research required. If you want to do research, look at the constituents of the S&P 500 or the S&P Dow-Jones High Quality Rankings Index or the 100 greatest global corporations. The most prominent corporations fought their way to the position they have by defeating weaker rivals and having attained dominance they have pricing power, making them more profitable. Why wouldn't you want to invest in the strongest most profitable companies?

Investment isn't difficult; it's easy; it just uses a part of your brain you are not used to using. Also remember that as soon as you buy the stock of a company you are catapulted into the position of owner. Sometimes I hear people grousing about all the money the oil companies are making in high gasoline prices people have to pay. Whenever such comments are directed to me I just tell people to just go buy the stock if they feel that way – don't be victims, be owners. You too can charge others high prices for gasoline, just go out and buy Exxon-Mobil, you too can own Main Street America.

POSTSCRIPT:

There was an interesting article in the July 26, 2013 *New York Times* by Mona El-Naggar about Toyota's charitable work with a New York City area food bank. Toyota had decided that it could supply something more valuable than money, expertise. At first the food service workers were skeptical that automotive engineers could make a difference in delivering food service to the poor. But Toyota sent in engineers and the results were as follows, according to the article: *"... cut down the wait time for dinner to 18 minutes from as long as 90. At a food pantry on Staten Island, they reduced the time people spent filling their bags to 6 minutes from 11. And at a warehouse in Bushwick, Brooklyn, where volunteers were packing boxes of supplies for victims of Hurricane Sandy, a dose of kaizen cut the time it took to pack one box to 11 seconds from 3 minutes."*

"Kaizen" is a Japanese word for process improvement, something that successful companies know something about.

Floor Traders   *Ben Aronson 2010*
Oil on panel, 26 x 24 inches   Private Collection

Chapter 8

Off the Beaten Path

The central thesis of this book is that the necessary and routine job of putting savings to work to provide a future retirement is not complicated even though it has the reputation for being akin to brain surgery and requiring a highly trained specialist. This obfuscation has one objective, to get your money for doing something that you can do better on your own. You are not going to beat a meat and potatoes diet with the fanciest soufflés, aspics, compotes, essences, infusions, etc. Meat and potatoes gets the job done and often with better results.

So it is with investing. Plain old common stocks are hard to beat, but as with all hyperbole, especially hyperbole coming out of the investment world, there will be the sense that you are missing something important. Instead, you are not, but just to protect you from the braggart who made one killing after a long string of losses, and can't wait to tell you about his off-the-beaten-path investment success, I try to offer, as Paul Harvey used to say, the rest of the story. Sticking to the common stocks of the Dow 30 is the best thing you can do, but there are other things. Here they are.

PTPs and LLCs

The companies we have discussed up to now are called "C" corporations or those corporations fitting the standard model of CEO, Board of Directors, and shareholders, where profits are taxed at the corporate level and then taxed again at the shareholder level in the case of dividend distributions. There are corporate structures that avoid taxation at the corporate level and you should know about them. They are known as Publicly Traded Partnerships and Limited Liability Corporations (LLCs). Trusts also are "Pass-Through" tax entities but will not be examined in detail because they generally exploit a "wasting" asset , which is an asset with a finite life expected to be exhausted at some point -- like a gold mine.

Partnerships and LLCs are for living assets that are expected to increase with time offering an opportunity for growth. Publicly Traded Partnerships may look like a "C" corporation from the outside but there are nomenclature differences. A "C" corporation has a board, a CEO, and various officers responsible for the many dimensions of a business. A Publicly Traded Partnership (PTP) has people assigned to similar functions but they all have the status of "General Partners," and they get paid a management fee plus a percentage of the profit after the "Limited Partners" (Unit holders) have been paid their share. The Unit holders are the investors, people like you. But there are PTPs that offer both General Partner and Limited Partner shares.

The reason for existence of Partnerships and LLCs is multifold but generally engineered by Congress to channel money where it wouldn't ordinarily flow. The channeling is done by avoiding tax on profit at the corporate level and taxing only once at the shareholder (Unit holder) level. In general, Congress is giving smaller private businesses in selected industries access to the public capital markets, and in the case of Business Development Companies (BDCs), access to more sophisticated management input than is typically available in a small business. For example, providing seed capital is a crucial activity but high risk. By allowing partnership entities to make a business of seed capitalization free of corporate tax there arose entities called Business Development Companies that support emerging businesses with management as well as money.

In order to gain the tax-free status at the corporate level, the Partnership or LLC is required to distribute 90% of what otherwise would be taxable income in a taxable business. Let's say a partnership realizes $10 million in revenue. Against that revenue, the partnership will charge expenses to operate the business including salaries, capital purchases, depreciation and losses that might result in a net taxable income of $1million. In order avoid paying tax on that net income, the partnership must distribute at least $900,000 to the limited partners.

The requirement to distribute 90% or more of otherwise "taxable" income translates into high yield for investors, usually anywhere from about 4% up to 14% and perhaps higher. Since these securities are mainly purchased for their yield, like bonds, you would expect to see less volatility in their daily pricing, though this is not the case for some reason. But since they have low retained earnings, they must borrow for capital projects and so are sensitive to interest rates.

Taxes and Liability in the PTP and LLC Landscape

Unlike a C-corporation, a partnership is not a taxable entity unto itself but rather a collection of partners of which you may be one if you are a Unit holder (fractional owner). Then all partners, whether managing "General Partners" or investing "Limited Partners," are fully exposed to the financial outcomes of the entity including gains or losses and are responsible for reporting and paying income tax. Usually quarterly distributions are made and they come from income, gains, deductions, losses and credits. As you might imagine, such a variety of sources of distributions will give rise to a complex tax accounting at your level as "Limited Partner," And produce a distribution that may well be in excess of 90% of profit.

The PTP typically makes distributions, which for tax purposes are characterized as "Return of Capital." These reduce "Cost Basis" and are not taxed. If you paid $30/unit and received a $4 distribution, your new cost-basis is $26. When you sell at perhaps $32/unit you will owe capital gains tax on $6/unit.

But the distributions are not merely or only profit from operations, but rather the adjusted income after all deductions for operating costs, losses, depreciation, etc. This is called "Distributable Income." At the end of the year, and usually well after tax day, you will receive a K-1 -- a tax statement – that breaks down distributions into profit and various sources of deductions. "Cost Basis" will be increased by profit and reduced by deductions. When the shares are sold, tax will be paid or if the cost basis goes to zero, all subsequent distributions will be taxed in the year they are received.

There is quite a large loophole in the tax code involving the taxation of capital gains, which is the spread between acquisition or "Coat Basis" and the gain on disposition, and this is the "Step Up" provision. When an heir inherits stocks, the cost basis is stepped-up to the trading price at time of death of the person leaving the bequest. Say your rich uncle leaves you 1400 shares of XYZ which he originally bought 100 years ago at $2/share, and at the time of his death the stock was trading at $30, and owing to stock-splits and dividend re-investment had become 1400 shares from originally100 shares. Your uncle's cost basis was $2/share for 100 shares ($200) but *your* cost basis is $30 for 1400 shares ($42,000). So if you sell the stock at $31, you will only pay capital gains tax on $1/share or $1400 and not on the gain from the original $200 investment. That difference is $43,400 - $200 = $43,200 that will never be taxed. That is a very powerful argument for keeping assets destined for heirs out of tax-deferred accounts, where step-up does not apply. A note of warning is needed: tax-deferred accounts are beyond the reach of creditors, taxable accounts are not.

Doctors routinely use life insurance for this reason because it too is beyond the reach of creditors. Doctors whose incomes can be quite high and are subject to malpractice suits are limited in the amount they can defer into retirement accounts, so the only option for them is life insurance.

The complex tax accounting for PTPs can be illustrated with an example derived from the National Association of Publicly Traded Partnerships website shown [ON THE FOLLOWING PAGE]. For tax reasons alone PTPs are sometimes shunned as too much work, but for the persistent there may be rewards. Nevertheless, PTPs and LLCs as a class perform no better than plain old common stocks that have no special tax accounting rules, thus calling into question the value of avoiding double taxation on dividends from common stock by buying into partnerships. But the tax accounting on the following page needs to be covered to understand how these partnership investments work.

Event	Cash Flow	Cost Basis	Tax Basis – Ordinary Income	Tax Basis – Capital Gains
Year 1: 1,000 units purchased @ $30.00.	($30,000)	$30,000		
Investor receives total cash distributions of $2.50/unit reducing Cost Basis by $2500. Investor is allocated $2.00/unit in income and $1.50/unit in depreciation increasing Cost Basis by $500.	$2,500			$2000 - $1500 = $500
Tax on Year 1		$28,000		Tax $500
Year 2: All units sold @ $32.00 Gain per unit: $32.00 - $28.00 = $4.00	$32,000	$28,000		
Tax on Year 2			Tax $1500	Tax $2500

Okay, what's going on here? Cost basis 1,000 units is $30/unit. Annual distributions are $2.50 /unit. Since distributions are a "Return of Capital," they go to reduce cost basis, in this case to $27.50. But the distribution is characterized as $2.00 Income (increases Cost Basis by $2.00) and Depreciation (reduces Cost Basis by $1.50) so the final cost basis at the end of the first year is $28.00.

Depreciation is the lost value due to aging of assets, which is a real loss but not be realized until the asset is disposed of for a lot less money than it took to buy it. But the tax rules allow owners of such assets to get the tax benefit of this loss in annual increments. Although the loss is recognized there is no cash associated with it. It is a paper loss but one that reduces taxable profit and so produces an internal cash-flow which increases profit.

In the second year the shares are sold for $32/unit for an apparent profit of $2/unit over the original cost. But for tax purposes the Cost Basis has been reduced downward to

$28/unit, adding to the tax bill. So the unit holder must pay tax on $4/unit of gain. Keep in mind that of the $2.50 distribution in the prior year, tax was paid on only 50¢ of that distribution.

Now is the time to pay for that untaxed $2.00/unit of that prior year distribution at the Capital Gains rate. The remaining $1500 from the $4000 gain is paid at the investor's default Ordinary Income tax rate.

If the position is held for many years one could assume that Cost Basis will go to zero and at that point all further distributions will be taxed in the year they are received. At some point, the asset may pass to an heir and in a step-up valuation, cost basis will be reset to the valuation on date of death. This is one reason you may not want to hold PTPs in a tax-deferred IRA account if you are not subject to attachment by creditors.

The $64,000 question is: Who keeps track of the various Cost Bases with additions and subtractions over the years, particularly with Dollar-Cost-Averaging? This is a nightmare tax accounting issue that can be avoided in an IRA, particularly a Roth IRA. There is no tax accounting in a Roth IRA. But wait, there is a very large fly in the ointment.

To understand these complex tax issues, tax policy must be dealt with. Number one, the Federal government does not want tax-sheltered organizations like Publicly Traded Partnerships, competing with tax-paying organizations. One example is prison industries, where license plates and office furniture are manufactured in prisons to give the inmates something to do. Since license plates are not sold by private industry, their manufacture by prison industries is not a problem. But office furniture is a robust and competitive commercial market engaged in by tax paying organizations both at the manufacturing and distribution levels. Accordingly, while office furniture is manufactured in prisons it is only used to supply state agencies, so the disruption to commerce is very limited and strictly guarded. The Federal government wants tax-paying industry to succeed in a big way and frowns on any tax-sheltered challenge to that.

But tax-sheltered organizations are always looking for ways to raise money and, as an example, a university might operate an upscale eatery that draws in a robust non-university trade. The Federal government allows school cafeterias to shelter their income but not upscale eateries with significant non-university income. This would compete with local restaurants on a tax-sheltered basis and is therefore not allowed. If a university had such a business and attempted to claim the income as part of their tax-sheltered status, the deduction would be classified as Unrelated Business Taxable Income (UBTI) and be taxed at the corporate rate.

What does this have to do with tax-deferred accounts? Deferring taxes, of course. Tax-deferred accounts are intended to give investors a way to save for retirement by tax-deferred passive investing in for-profit corporations while not being part of the corporation. As a partner in a PTP, you are in a profit-seeking entity and therefore engaged in an activity not strictly related to passive investment for retirement savings. Accordingly, that fraction of the distribution that is gains is disallowed as UBTI, Unrelated Business Taxable Income. There is a $1,000 per account exclusion however, which is generally felt to be generous enough to eliminate concern over UBTI in a retirement account. So if you want to save yourself some headache, use individual IRA accounts, but be careful, because most institutions charge $50 per year to custody IRA accounts.

There is also another wrinkle, the custodian, and not you, is responsible for paying the tax which presumably includes identifying the tax liability and filing a form 990. Many custodians don't want the liability and extra work and so simply will not allow accounts they are trustees for to hold PTPs. But for the intrepid investor not afraid of the above referenced language you can download form 990 and see it is not all that scary. The real heavy lifting is done by the PTP in preparing the K-1. A lot really hinges on how much of the distribution is profit. The portion that exceeds $1,000 per year in UBTI per account is immediately taxed at ordinary income tax rates, but it does get added to cost basis thus reducing tax on capital gain upon sale.

In order to expand ownership of their units, Kinder Morgan invented I-units (Institutional Units) that pay out distributions in the form of units. So instead of getting cash that must be characterized by "Depreciation" or "Return of Capital," the unit holder in (KMR) just receives more units and this allows those securities to be held in tax-deferred accounts without incurring UBTI. But again it must be pointed out, there is no step-up valuation in tax-deferred accounts.

An example is called for. An investment of $10,000 is made to buy 400 units at $25 each of XYZ, a Publicly Traded Partnership (PTP). The first quarterly distribution is two shares. After the distribution, the unit holder owns 402 shares at a Cost Basis of $10,000 or $24.88 each. But, it won't take long for the Cost Basis to go to zero at this rate. This means that when you sell, you will pay capital gains tax on the difference between the Cost Basis and the sale price and that means paying tax twice on your original investment as far as I can tell.

In the above example, if the original $10,000 was after-tax cash (cash that had already been taxed) it will be taxed again upon sale of your position if the Cost Basis went to zero, but in the meantime, you will have received quarterly distributions that included offsetting profit that would have been all free of tax.

At the time of sale, the difference between cost basis and sale price is segmented into two discrete taxable proceeds: Capital Gains and Depreciation "Recapture." Capital Gains are taxed at the more favorable capital gains rate. Depreciation is taxed at the higher Ordinary Income rates. In the above example, Depreciation was $1,500 or $1.50/unit. So the difference between the gain on sale and Depreciation is Capital Gain.

Retirees like PTPs because they obtain a tax-free income and only "pay the Piper" upon sale, and if the assets are passed onto heirs rather than sold, the step-up takes care of the tax problem, unless of course, the PTPs are held inside an IRA, 401(k) or other tax-deferred account.

General Partner Shares

Partnerships require management, as in a "C" corporation, and that role is undertaken by the General Partners (GP) who are typically remunerated at the rate of 2% until they break through a threshold of return for Limited Partners (unit holders), at which point GPs begin a remuneration rise though a schedule of participation percentages that reaches 50% at its maximum, and obviously for doing a very good job. This is called Incentive Distribution Rights – IDR. So seeing the GPs in your PTP investment obtaining a 50% payout is a good thing for you. For one thing, you have already been paid your share of 98% of the take up to the profit threshold.

The following MLPs offer GP shares: Crosstex Energy Inc. (XTXI), Energy Transfer Equity, L.P. (ETE), Alliance GP, L.P. (AHGP), Atlas Pipeline (ATLS), Kinder Morgan (KMI), Oneok, Inc. (OKE), and Targa Resources Corp. (TRGP). There may be others I have missed and the list is constantly changing.

By visiting the website of the National Association of Publicly Traded Partnerships you can find a pretty exhaustive list of PTPs and you will no doubt be impressed by both the breadth of offerings in multiple business sectors, and by the many ways that PTPs can be held -- in open-end funds, closed-end funds, exchange-traded funds and index funds -- all with much simpler tax accounting. But just a random sampling of discrete issues checked for dividend yield found that yields like $8\frac{1}{2}\%$ and 9% are not unusual. There is a list at the end of the chapter though it may be outdated.

MLP & LLC Flavors

At this point it may be useful to look at some of the business sectors, because once beyond the tax issues the differences in PTPs is quite pronounced. They include real estate, asset management, tankers, pipelines, coal, timber, and others. Perhaps the largest segment is pipelines.

At one time major refiners may have owned a network of pipelines that transported their refined product to other transporters, but now almost all pipelines are owned and operated by pipeline companies that are organized as PTPs. These entities are known as Master Limited Partnerships (MLPs) and specifically in the energy sector they fall under the umbrella term "Energy MLPs." These are further segmented by the phase of the industry in which they operate: for exploration (upstream) or for distribution (downstream). Pipelines began as "Midstream" assets in that they occupied a role midway between exploration and distribution. But today MLPs can be found in both "upstream" businesses of exploration and refining, and "downstream" businesses distributing product, particularly in propane.

The choice between upstream, midstream, and downstream is a one of risk. Upstream means exploration and refining, both activities that will be highly affected by crude-oil pricing, which is very volatile. For those wishing to sit out crude oil volatility, midstream pipelines are a good choice because as mere transporters of petroleum and gas, they are largely insulated from gyrations in market pricing. Downstream distribution MLPs are again affected by market pricing, but energy is a largely inelastic commodity so price spikes will result merely in a somewhat muted slack in demand.

There is an aspect of ownership to be considered and that is what happens to the price of the product during its period of storage. With petroleum products you can expect change, and given the quantities involved, some very big money changes. To manage these changes, providers and users can lock in contracts, called forwards, that guarantee a price when they are ready to deliver, or take delivery, say, in the case of an airline purchasing jet fuel. Some years back while most airlines got caught in steep fuel price hikes, Southwest had ownership of fuel futures at prices set before the spike and thus saved themselves considerable operating cost, but that fuel they had locked in for future delivery did need to be stored.

There is a cost to storage in foregone revenue (time value of money), the maintenance of the storage facilities, and of course the accounting as well and perhaps insurance. Accordingly, you would expect to pay a higher price going forward, but locking in $3/gal for delivery in six months for a fuel available at the forward spot price of $2.50/gal is questionable. In six months if the spot price goes to $4/gal owing to tightening supply the buyer of the forward has saved himself $1/gal perhaps for a million gallons or more. As time passes and the tightening supply becomes more visible, forward purchases ramp up to lock in supply for forward price rises, thus putting a strain on storage facilities. This is called a "Contango" market and is typical for non-perishable commodities that have fluctuating supply/demand relationships. Deep Contango markets benefit MLPs that take custody and have the storage capacity to exploit the windfall. MLPs well positioned for Contango markets are: Enbridge Energy Partners, LP (EEP), Plains All American Pipeline, LP (PAA), Sunoco Logistics Partners, LP (SXL), TEPPCO Partners, LP (TPP). Buckeye Partners, LP (BPL), Kinder Morgan Energy Partners, LP (KMP), Magellan Midstream Partners, LP (MMP) and Valero LP (VL).

A good place to start examining energy MLPs is with *An Investor Guide to Energy MLPs* prepared by a team at Merrill Lynch led by Gabe Moreen. This document may still be available on the internet at: http://www.naptp.org/News/Weeklyupdates/MLMLPGuide.pdf.

Another worthwhile and free document available on the internet is from *Master Limited Partnership Primer* by SteelPath at
www. http://steelpath.com/wp-content/uploads/MLP-Primer.pdf

And another primer by Wachovia at:
http://www.naptp.org/documentlinks/05Wacovia.pdf

PTPs operate in markets having high infrastructure demands that produce high incomes and also high depreciation that together result in high distribution to unit-holders who are the "Limited Partners." "Master Limited Partnerships" generally fall into five sectors. They have different names but share similar organizational structures and tax treatment. The five are:

- REITs (Real Estate Investment Trusts)
- MLPs (Master Limited Partnerships, mostly petroleum pipelines)
- BDCs (Business Development Companies)
- Tankers
- Miscellaneous, forests, farms, amusement parks, etc.

PTPs are listed by market sector at the end of this chapter. The list is drawn from the National Association of Publicly Traded Partnerships' website.

REITs (Real Estate Investment Trusts)
REITs are organizations that either own (Equity REITs) or finance (mortgage mREITs) real estate. Mortgage REITs are often called "mREITs." A subcategory is called "Agency mREITs" which are mREITs restricting their activity to mortgages guaranteed by Fannie Mae, Freddie Mac or Ginnie Mae.
The core competency of mREITs is borrowing low and

lending high. In a finance course I took in graduate school, the professor taught that as long as cost of capital (COC) was below project return, access to capital was unlimited. This of course caused a ripple of comment in the class but the concept makes sense as long as the return is guaranteed. In many cases there is a hiccup in the returns and the firm goes belly up. So one rule of investment is to keep leverage manageable or have a balanced capital structure, 50/50 debt to equity.

But mREITs make money on the spread and are by definition highly leveraged. This is scary but in the case Agency mREITs may be sustainable because they fund mortgages that are guaranteed by Freddie, Fannie or Ginnie. Theoretically these Agency mREITs are safe but in being safe offer a somewhat lower return, though at a 14.30% dividend (January 2012), Annaly Capital Management (NLY) makes a compelling Agency mREIT case. Other standout Agency mREITs are Anworth Mortgage Asset Corp. (ANH) 13.40% dividend, American Capital Agency Corp. (AGNC) 19.90% dividend, Hatteras Financial Corp. (HTS) 13.70% dividend, and CYS Investments (CYS) 15.00% dividend.

For more on this sector, you can visit mREIT.com. The point to note is that mREITs are on the supply side of mortgage interest rates and will ride the interest roller coaster. In a high-interest rate environment they should do very well because they lock in high rates that will see their loan portfolio rise in value with declining rates. But expertise in managing the spread is the core issue that trumps everything else.

Equity REITs are on the other side of the mortgage interest divide and thrive in lower interest rate environments. But Equity REITs also have one other core characteristic, hard assets (real estate) that is depreciated. Depreciation is an income tax shelter the federal government allows companies to use in order to replenish their factors of production. Say a company earns $1million in profit and must give up $300,000 in income tax. That tax can be reduced by taking a depreciation charge of say $100,000 for the aging of manufacturing or building infrastructure. The tax is then calculated on $900,000 instead of $1million resulting in a tax bill of $270,000, saving the company $30,000. That $30,000 can then be saved to replenish plant and equipment as it ages and fails. But the $30,000 is also cash to the company.

Equity REITs all have lots of hard-assets in the form of various types of real estate, and they are further defined by the type of real estate they operate in, such as shopping centers, apartment buildings, office buildings, industrial buildings, hotels and so on. There are even timber REITs.

Like Master Limited Partnerships, Equity REITs are free of taxation as long as they distribute 90% of profit. But "profit" does not include depreciation and so Equity REITs have access to a lot more cash flow than is communicated by a "profit" figure. This being so, REITs often distribute more than the federally mandated 90%; depreciation is where that money comes from.

A key issue in deciding among REITs sectors is occupancy. Hotel occupancy is the most profitable but also most fickle owing to such variables as fluctuating demand, travel issues like weather, and changing demographic patterns. Hotels also operate in competitive environments. For example, a hotel may be doing well until the new Grand Bonanza opens up down the street. Of course hotel REITs are well diversified owning many properties and they are expert in location and tracking demand.

Hotels earn very high per-square-foot revenue but of course the lease period is one night. Office space earns lower revenue per square foot but locks in lease commitments for 10 years and longer, allowing office REITs to weather storms. You could say if office REITs get a sniffle, hotels get pneumonia. But these are the dimensions to be thought about when investing in REITS.

Office REITs are more stable than hotel ones because tenants are locked into 5- or 10-year lease terms that are difficult or impossible to break. Office REITs can also be defined by locality and even types of space. A building can be pure office or something called "flex-space," which may allow some light manufacturing. Currency can also be a factor. Some office REIT do business strictly in the U.S. while others also operate in several offshore markets, a trait that makes them more targeted currency diversifiers.

For Office REITs, look for iconic office buildings that are likely to house tenants that would probably be the last affected in a downturn. SL Green Realty Corp(SLG) is a REIT well known for focusing on the Manhattan office space market, but there are other REITs that own landmark buildings such as the Empire State Building that will probably be the last to suffer in a downturn. But a recent article in *The New York Times* reporting on the Empire Building going public in a REIT structure pointed out that the building was only two-thirds occupied and that a major source of revenue was $60 million annually from visitors to its observation levels. Visitors -- the most short-lived occupant of all -- it turns out deliver the highest revenue.

There are shopping mall REITs, which, of course, are challenged by competing malls -- the newest mall in any given area traditionally cannibalizes pre-existing malls. But shopping mall REITs have a unique dimension; profit-sharing with the retail tenants. Leases may contain fixed space rentals plus a percentage of profit over a negotiated minimum. This is sometimes done to act as a shock absorber for retail businesses that experience volatility in their month-to-month revenue.

Then there are specialty REITs such as a high-tech space REIT called Digital Realty (DLR) and other sub-sub-sector REITs. To explore the REIT world you can go to several internet sites and get very comprehensive information on each REIT. But a word of caution in your investigation and investment. Be prepared for the outsized shouting of the REIT flavor of the day, which you will hopefully dismiss in your search for enduring value. Second, always use dollar-cost-averaging to build a position in any REIT you decide upon.

One REIT that has been prominent for years is Vornado (VNO). Recently I happened to be calling on several major architect/engineering firms located in the Penn Plaza complex behind Madison Square Garden in Manhattan. While waiting to get cleared through security I noticed how well managed the place was. It was clean, the security staff were well dressed, well groomed, and anxious to help. I wasn't thinking investment until I got in the elevator and went to push the button for my floor when I noticed the Vornado nameplate on the control panel. I considered that office tenants have very long and inescapable leases, and what could be better that owning a piece of Penn Plaza. Since I already knew about Vornado (VNO), I determined add them to my REIT investment list.

For a more complete treatment on the subject you may want to pick up *Investing in REITs* by Ralph L. Block, Bloomberg Press, New York. Block goes into an array of segmentation criteria such as ability to develop giving the particular REIT a leg up on creating rather than buying properties. But the key segmenting variable is good management, which comes about from highly skilled and knowledgeable management and then management depth, circumventing a crisis when the top executive retires. To save the reader some research, I'll list a few of those REITs that are generally acknowledged to have demonstrated expertise over multiple boom-and-bear cycles:

- Kimco – retail, nationwide USA
- Vornado – office, New York City, Washington DC
- ProLogis – industrial, global
- AMB Property Corp. – industrial, global
- Weingarten – retail, southwest USA
- Developers Diversifies Realty – retail, nationwide USA
- Simon Property Group – retail, nationwide USA

- Tanger Outlet Centers – discount shopping centers, nationwide USA
- S.L. Green – office, New York City

Business Development Companies (BDC)

Business Development Companies (BDCs) are financing organizations that typically make secured loans to enterprises not served by banks or other more traditional financing channels.

In many cases it may be early-stage financing, giving the BDC investor an opportunity only afforded accredited investors for getting in on the ground floor of a rising star. In general, BDC investment is very challenging in that the entity must be able to discriminate between stars in the making and busts in the making at a time when it may be very difficult to tell the difference. The BDC management must be very discerning, and as you might expect, the field is small.

BDC investing will naturally be more volatile, but dollar-cost-averaging into a position will tame volatility and in the meantime will provide a steady dividend income stream while offering good diversification to all other positions and probably outperformance relative to other portfolio components. A list of BDCs is presented in Chapter 4.

Before leaving the subject of BDCs I'll mention that one BDC offers an interesting mix: Blackstone Group with its acquisition of Hilton Hotels, which owns the iconic Waldorf-Astoria. As stated, hotels make excellent money per square foot although they are vulnerable to economic swings, but this does not apply to a global iconic hotel like the Waldorf.

Shortly after he was elected President, Richard Nixon wanted to book the Grand Ballroom at the Waldorf for his daughter Tricia's wedding reception. He learned that the room was already reserved for that day for another wedding reception and so called the mother of the other bride to ask her to reschedule. The report I read had Nixon introducing himself as the President of the United States requesting the woman to make way for his daughter's wedding reception. *"Are you crazy,"* the woman responded, blowing right past the fact that he had recently won the U.S. Presidency, *"Do you know what it takes to get that room booked?"* Nixon apparently was the one who did the rescheduling. The Waldorf will probably be a good investment for the rest of your natural life and certainly increasing the attractiveness of Blackstone Group (BX) with its already legendary investor CEO Steve Schwarzman.

Tankers

Tankers are a special case. First, the obvious issue, losing a tanker at sea, as was pointed out to me, is a non-issue thanks to Lloyds of London. When a tanker goes down Lloyds comes in and covers the loss. Tankers like other partnership sectors are further defined by dry bulk vs. liquid tankers with the liquids being petroleum, chemicals and sometimes gases, like LNG (liquefied natural gas).

There are also tanker fleets that carry petroleum that have mostly double-hulled ships that prevent spills when running aground, avoiding the fate of the Exxon Valdez in creating an environmental disaster. Some tanker fleets are ahead of others in making those costly investments. Another defining factor of tanker fleets is whether they can navigate the Panama Canal. Ships today are being built larger than ever but the downside is that they are too big to fit through the Panama Canal, requiring much longer journeys.

But as you might imagine, each fleet has its own markets and routes that are optimized to keep the fleet working full time, and that is the rub with investing in tankers -- keeping them working. To the investor in tankers, and this makes tankers an interesting and uncorrelated asset class, stock price is driven by demand that may vary globally from port to port. I was told by a graduate of King's Point merchant marine academy that the Greeks are masters of this game, keeping their ships just beyond the horizon until freight rates rise, at which point they magically appear, steaming into port to pick up their pre-assigned and negotiated cargoes.

This is not the first time the Greeks have used this technique. They used it in the Trojan War around 1300BC, when they sailed just beyond the Trojan horizon and waited. When they got the signal that the wooden horse they had left behind had been hauled into the city, they sailed back to rush the opened walls. So the Greeks have had plenty of practice at keeping out of sight when it counts.

Like all other partnership investments, tanker yields are high and dollar-cost-averaging takes out the volatility. Naturally nobody is in the tanker business unless they know what they are doing, but the Greeks have been at this a long time, since 700BC or earlier.

Royalty Trusts

Finally we come to royalty trusts that sound like they are something everybody should be into but can't because membership is limited. Nothing could be further from the truth; if there is any "royalty" to royalty trusts, it is strictly for promotional purposes. Royalties are payments made for the right to control the declining flow of value from a wasting asset, which is an asset that is used up, such as a gold mine. Like all mines, a gold mine requires substantial investment to locate and exploit. The first pay-off is big as the larger gold deposits are exploited, but over time, most of the gold is gone and the ratio of cost to value grows to the point where the mine is no longer profitable – it is a wasting asset. Royalty trusts are by and large wasting assets that provide a cash flow of uncertain term, perhaps years, perhaps only a few years. While there are forecasts for the life of the trust, there are plenty of ways to invest in commodities without taking on the added risk of investing in a soon-to-be-exhausted asset.

MLPs and LLCs are Uncorrelated to the Broader Market

When contemplating investments in MLPs in their various flavors note that they have two key characteristics making them excellent portfolio constituents: outsize dividends and low-correlation to market swings. But the correlation can be very tricky. For example, tanker stocks move on capacity. If global trade ramps up and there aren't enough tankers to move the goods, freight rates rise and tanker stocks go up. When this happens there will soon be a global glut in tankers as every marine economy builds to cash in on the opportunity. When this happens, excuse the pun, your tanker stocks will go into the tank. The prominent tanker operators are known, focus on capacity, and are keenly aware of where we are in the oversupply/ undersupply cycle.

The same goes for other MLP flavors, they all have their individual catalysts that make them good portfolio actors, but focus on what those catalysts are and invest accordingly. Hotel REITs are the richest just thinking in terms of income per square foot of space, but when the economy tanks, they will suffer much more quickly that their Office REIT cousins.

The asset classes discussed next do not suffer the same tax and tax reporting disadvantages of PTPs and so this is the point at which you can ask yourself if you really want the tax reporting headache of PTPs. You can ignore this asset class, get plenty of diversification in common stocks and certainly realize all of your investment goals. You don't need PTPs to succeed and the whole point in presenting them here is to save you the bother of having to learn enough about them to reject them as a necessary asset class for a well-balanced portfolio. You don't need them.

Utilities, Power Generation, Gas, Water and Cable

Another sector that doesn't easily fall into any of the capitalization or growth rate investment segmenting variables are utilities, which may be power generation, gas, or water utilities. These typically offer dividend yields though not as high as those of partnerships, still they offer the stability that comes from operating in a pretty non-competitive environment with an inelastic product. Utilities offer one other unique channel, the opportunity to invest in currencies, because utilities make all, or most, of their revenue in the home currency.

Over the years I have invested in British, German, South Korean, Japanese, Brazilian, and Egyptian power generation utilities, to name a few. International investing can be risky because you don't have the day-to-day understanding of the entity you are investing in, but since power generation utilities are monopolies there is a dampening of company risk -- although country risk remains. Such risk can be an issue in developing countries, but sticking to the more developed countries should offer all the currency diversification anyone could hope for without undue country risk. Again, dollar-cost-averaging is the way in.

Utilities generally break down into three sectors: power, gas, and water. Cable may also be thought of as a kind of utility. Utilities are controlled by the government, the PUC (Public Utilities Commission) in the case of power, but report profits and pay dividends as other companies do. There has been deregulation in the power industry but what remains are generally sober and well-managed companies largely without competition and delivering a needed service, although some do occasionally get into trouble.

What sets utilities apart, particularly power generation utilities, is that they operate between two giant threats that can at any time do devastating damage: the huge cost of fuel that must be burned as economically as possible to stay profitable and the huge potential for explosions if the boilers are not well managed -- remember Three-Mile Island? There is little room for foolishness at a power utility and this sober culture permeates throughout the organization making them sober and well managed investment candidates. I used to call on utilities as a sales engineer and one that stood out for me was the Southern Company (SO). I visited the headquarters of the various divisions and many of the plants and was always impressed with the culture of devotion and care I found at all Southern Company facilities.

In the general scheme of Wall Street, utilities are considered "non-cyclical" companies because power demand is not highly elastic to the general business climate. Utilities are low-volatility, low Beta (explained in Chapter 8). Any portfolio would be well served by holding some utility stocks. Some may be better than others and the ones I have found to be particularly good are Southern Company (SO) Beta 0.35, Pennsylvania Power & Light (PPL) Beta 0.49, Duke Power (DUK) Beta 0.44, First Energy (FE) Beta 0.53 and Dominion Energy (D) Beta 0.55. There are others, of course, but this is a good starting point for the beginning investor. Also, as mentioned in the section on global investing, overseas utilities provide a good opportunity to diversify into other currencies. Germany is noted for two very fine utilities: Eon and RWE. Spain's Iberdrola is a global leader in renewable energy. South Korea's Kepco is majority-owned by the government.

When it comes to power generation bets, one has a choice between fossil, wind, solar, hydro, and nuclear. For the most part, access to those technologies will be through your local utility, except perhaps in the case of hydro, which will be restricted to areas with large rivers and locations for dams. Utilities are further defined by how much power they generate with renewable sources and nuclear. But a very cursory examination will get you that information so you can place your bets according to your views and forecasts.

Although this is a book that scorns "betting" and talks-up "investing," I use the phrase "place your bets" because it is a good term for investing and a bad term for betting. In the real world, a bettor bets because he or she has visibility into the result and wishes to profit from that visibility by placing a wager – a bet. The term has come to be synonymous with risk, but in fact in most bets the risk is only 50% and the wager is attended by a good bit of knowledge and visibility. In investment, risk can be 90% or more if you factor in the investor, and attended by very little knowledge and no visibility.

One crucial advantage investing has over betting is that the investor has total control over the term of the investment whereas the bettor is locked into a fixed term that may be as short as a few minutes. This would appear to be a huge advantage to investment, but most investors throw away this advantage at the first sign of a downturn and wind up converting a reasonable risk into a certain loss.

The aim of this book is to instruct the reader on the level of risk and how to reduce that risk by process. Nevertheless, the term "bet," while it does not capture the process of investing, does capture the risk of investing, and so I use that term. Risk is a major concern and the way to manage risk is by diversification and remaining focused on the objective: You invest for long-term gain and not for any other reason and certainly not as an experiment.

Water utilities are also global but offer an opportunity like no other: exposure to a vital but declining resource. Today water has to be one of the soundest bets you can make and a good global play on water is the French company Veolia, stock symbol VE; it had a dividend yield of 4% the last time I looked. My feeling is that Veolia should be in any portfolio with a 20-year or greater horizon. Of course, once again, dollar-cost-average your way into your position, particularly since VE has a high Beta (1.79 the last time I looked). Incidentally, note that a Beta of 1.79 is not a reflection of the company but rather a reflection of investors in the company.

Before leaving the subject of utilities, I'll mention a company that is not a utility, but sure to be a major player if the world moves to nuclear power: a French firm called Areva. France produces 80% of its power with 59 identical nuclear power plants, giving Areva a leg up on nuclear power issues. Areva shares may be purchased in the United States on the OTC market under the symbol (ARVCF).

Infrastructure

There is a growing global movement toward private contractors taking on the work and services formerly done by government, and nowhere is this more apparent than in the growing global network of infrastructure and toll road operators. Several global toll road operators have come to the United States and acquired ownership of domestic toll roads. Some of the more prominent toll road operators are Abertis, Cintra, Brisa, APRR and Macquarie. Although it is possible for maintenance costs to rise faster than tolls, eventually the balance is restored and in the meantime the toll road operator has a monopoly on one of the most reliable sources of revenue one can imagine, rush-hour traffic. But be careful of toll roads in centrally managed economies like that in China. During a period when rail was overextended, the Chinese authorities authorized trucks carrying rail cargo to use the toll roads without charge. Although this may be a small matter, be aware that in totalitarian countries like China and Russia, what looks like a compelling investment case may not be if the government is using the monopoly as a personal ATM machine. Gazprom in Russia is one example. Perhaps the world's largest gas supplier, Gazprom is a great investment thesis and a bad investment.

Gold in Times of Trouble

Gold has risen from around $200 per ounce in the mid-1970s to around $1,600 today. Nevertheless while gold seems very high, things could get worse, so starting a dollar-cost-averaging position in gold is a good diversification move. But keep in mind as you look at that rise in gold price, that gold is really not a great investment Vehicle. In the case of Starbucks discussed later, due to stock splits 10 shares grew to 320 shares. This will not happen with gold – that makes gold look like a waste of time. The 40-year rise of gold from $200 to $1,600 works out to an annual compounding rate of about 5.34% -- and remember, commodities don't split or pay dividends. However, gold is a good counter-cyclical for a balanced portfolio.

Counter-Cyclical Stocks

Counter-cyclical stocks are hard to find but generally are ones that people flock to, or at least default to, in hard times. McDonald's has already been mentioned but there are other fast-food retailers like Wendy's (WEN), Burger King (BKC), Chipotle (CMG), Jack in the Box (JBX), and Sonic (SONC). There is also an interesting global fast-food stock, Yum Brands (YUM), which owns a stable of fast-food brands and is international, namely KFC, Pizza Hut, Taco Bell, Long John Silver's and A&W. These are all good counter-cyclical stocks and offer a choice between U.S.-only currency and global currency.

Other counter-cyclicals are retailers Wal-Mart (WMT), Family Dollar (FDO), Dollar General (DG), Dollar Tree Stores (DLTR), Tuesday Morning (TUES), Price Smart Inc. (PSMT), 99 Cents Only Stores (NDN), and several others. Wal-Mart offers a Roth DRIP (explained in Chapter 11).

Stock Exchange Stocks

A small group of stocks offer an interesting position on cyclicality: stock exchange stocks. When markets tank, stock exchanges are overwhelmed by traders stampeding for the exits, making the market makers busier than ever.

Three stock exchange stocks make an interesting counter-cyclical component for their longevity, because in my view, upon the arrival of Armageddon, which everyone wants to diversify against, stock exchanges will be the last companies standing as they execute orders for the global population of investors wishing to liquidate their positions and get cash to buy their way out of whatever predicament they are in. Shown below are the three candidates, all U.S.-based but operating internationally.

	CAPITALIZATION	P/E	YIELD
NYX	$6.57B	12.25	4.70%
ICE	$9.81B	18.79	----
NDAQ	$3.87B	11.05	2.30%

- NYX is NYSE Euronext which operates the NYSE (The Big Board) and 5 European exchanges in London, Paris, Amsterdam, Brussels and Lisbon. In addition to operating stock exchanges, NYX sells technology to Europe and Asia. Headquartered in New York City.
- ICE is the Intercontinental Exchange Inc., which operates OTC exchanges and exchanges for emissions trading in 70 countries. Headquartered in Atlanta.
- NDAQ is the NASDAQ OMX sells technology to 70 exchanges in 50 countries. Headquartered in New York.

When we talk about cyclical stocks we are speaking of stocks that exhibit elasticity to economic cycles – they go up when cheap access to money drives growth and recede when an overheated economy implodes. But the elasticity is different among the cyclicals -- for example luxury goods suppliers like Hermes or Louis Vuitton are much more elastic than say Michelin. In good times all three will prosper but in bad times there will be people who have to drive to shop, look for a job, attend funerals, and so on. So Michelin (MGDDF) could be thought of as a semi-cyclical. There are other tire stocks that are also semi-cyclical in that spending on tires can be postponed, but not indefinitely. So within the cyclical universe, a good portfolio will contain both highly elastic and somewhat inelastic cyclicals providing according to Modern Portfolio Theory, a smoothing effect as the effect of gainers offsets the effect of losers.

Diversification with MLPs and LLCs

However, I must again caution that the entire idea of stock selection is overblown. Once you elect to construct a portfolio of 15-20 stocks and you select from 100 of the world's greatest corporations, or the S&P 500 or the Dow 30, it really doesn't matter which stocks you pick or how well diversified, the end result will be determined by your discipline in setting a process and sticking to that process.

The weakness of such a narrowing to the common stock of major corporations is that you miss the diversification and high-yield from the universe of PTPs and utilities described in this chapter. Accordingly, you might want to reserve several positions for an mREIT, a BDC, and perhaps a utility or two, or even a tanker stock if you are of a nautical turn of mind. But in such cases be aware that while common stocks move in understandable response to the business cycle, many PTPs move in response to factors that are unique to their world -- their gyrations will be more difficult to understand and therefore digest. That is what makes PTPs excellent diversifiers, and if you are a totally passive investor PTPs may be fine, but if you look forward to studying every quarterly statement, PTPs may be a challenge as you try to decide whether a fall in price is due to some cyclical rotation or real decline in company fundamentals.

A note on dividend yield is also timely. Stock yield is the reciprocal of P/E (Price/Earnings ratio), a major investment segmenting variable. As a rule-of-thumb, companies are purchased at a price determined by some multiple of expected earnings. For a cash-cow a multiple of 15 times earnings is a good starting point. This translates into a P/E of 15. On a share of stock if the price is $15 per share and the P/E is 15 then the company reports as profit $1 per share. This is a P/E ratio of 15/1 or simply 15. The reciprocal is 1/15 or 6.66%. This is what the company earns in profit which may be thought of as the earnings ratio. Because of the volatility of stock price, P/E figures are also somewhat volatile rising with the rise in stock price and falling as stock price collapses. The term yield in connection with stock may mean the earnings yield per share but usually means dividend yield, which is how much per share is distributed to the stockholder. Here also the yield figure is tied to stock price and could be written as D/P or dividend over price = dividend yield. Usually dividend paying companies payout no more than 50% of profit as dividend distribution so the dividend yield would be expected to be about half the yield calculated from earnings. Some investors might search for stock candidates by looking for dividend yield but be aware that the dividend yield number will fluctuate with stock price and what looks like a very attractive yield might in fact be nothing more than stock price in a trough. As the stock price declines the very stable yield will loom larger in relation to stock price. For this reason I use 5-year average dividend yield figures.

On the following pages is a list of PTPs drawn from the website of National Association of Publicly Traded Partnerships **www.naptp.org**

Natural Resources: Oil and Gas Products

Pipelines and Other Midstream Operations, Compressing, Refining

American
Midstream Partners, LP	AMID
Atlas Pipeline Partners, L.P.	APL
Blueknight Energy Partners, L.P.	BKEP

Boardwalk Pipeline Partners, LP	BWP
Buckeye Partners, L.P.	BPL
Calumet Specialty Products Partners, L.P.	CLMT
Central Energy Partners, L.P.	ENGY.PK
Cheniere Energy Partners, L.P.	CQP
Chesapeake Midstream Partners, L.P.	CHKM
Compressco Partners, L.P.	GSJK
Copano Energy, L.L.C.	CPNO
Crosstex Energy, L.P.	XTEX
Crestwood Midstream Partners LP	CMLP
DCP Midstream Partners, LP	DPM
Eagle Rock Energy Partners, L.P.	EROC
El Paso Pipeline Partners, L.P.	EPB
Enbridge Energy Partners, L.P.	EEP
Energy Transfer Partners, L.P. (also has propane operations)	ETP
Energy Transfer Equity, L.P.	ETE
Enterprise Products Partners L.P.	EPD
Exterran Partners, L.P.	EXLP
Genesis Energy, L.P.	GEL
Holly Energy Partners, L.P.	HEP
Inergy Midstream, L.P.	NRGM
Kinder Morgan Energy Partners, L.P.	KMP
Magellan Midstream Partners, L.P.	MMP
MarkWest Energy Partners,	MWE

L.P.	
Niska Gas Storage Partners LLC	NKA
NuStar Energy L.P.	NS
NuStar GP Holdings, LLC	NSH
Oiltanking Partners, L.P.	OILT
ONEOK Partners, L.P.	OKS
PAA Natural Gas Storage, L.P.	PNG
Plains All American Pipeline, L.P.	PAA
Quicksilver Gas Services LP	KGS
Regency Energy Partners LP	RGP
Rose Rock Midstream, L.P.	RRMS
Spectra Energy Partners, LP	SEP
Sunoco Logistics Partners L.P.	SXL
Targa Resources Partners LP	NGLS
TC PipeLines, LP	TCP
Tesoro Logistics LP	TLLP
TransMontaigne Partners L.P.	TLP
Western Gas Partners, LP	WES
Williams Partners L.P.	WPZ

Exploration and Production

Atlas Energy, L.P.	ATLS
BreitBurn Energy Partners L.P.	BBEP
Constellation Energy Partners LLC	CEP
Dorchester Minerals, L.P.	DMLP
EV Energy Partners, L.P.	EVEP
Legacy Reserves LP	LGCY
Linn Energy, LLC	LINE

LRR Energy, L.P.	LRE
Memorial Production Partners LP	MEMP
Mid-Con Energy Partners LP	MCEP
Pioneer Southwest Energy Partners, L.P.	PSE
QR Energy, LP	QRE
Vanguard Natural Resources, LLC	VNR

Propane and Refined Fuel Distribution

AmeriGas Partners L.P	APU
Ferrellgas Partners, L.P.	FGP
Global Partners LP	GLP
Inergy, L.P.	NRGY
NGL Energy Partners LP	NGL
Star Gas Partners, L.P.	SGU
Suburban Propane Partners, L.P.	SPH

Marine Transportation

Capital Product Partners L.P. [1]	CPLP
Golar LNG Partners LP [1]	GMLP
Martin Midstream Partners L.P.	MMLP
Navios Maritime Partners L.P. [1]	NMM
Teekay LNG Partners L.P.	TGP
Teekay Offshore Partners L.P. (Not an MLP organized as a C Corp)	TOO

Natural Resources – Coal, Other Minerals, Timber

Alliance Resource Partners, L.P.	ARLP
Alliance Holdings GP, L.P.	AHGP

CVR Partners, LP	UAN
Natural Resource Partners L.P.	NRP
Oxford Resource Partners LP	OXF
Penn Virginia Resource Partners, L.P.	PVR
Pope Resources	POPE
Rhino Resource Partners LP	RNO
Terra Nitrogen Company, L.P.	TNH
Real Estate Properties	
New England Realty Associates, L.P.	NEN
NTS Realty Holdings, L.P.	NLP
W.P. Carey & Co. LLC	WPC

Real Estate – Mortgage Securities

American First Tax Exempt Investors	ATAX
Ellington Financial LLC	EFC
Municipal Mortgage and Equity, LLC	MMAB.PK

Investment / Financial Management

Alliance Bernstein Holding L.P.	AB
Apollo Global Management, LLC	APO
The Blackstone Group L.P.	BX
Compass Diversified Holdings LLC	CODI
Fortress Investment Group LLC	FIG

Icahn Enterprises, L.P.	IEP
KKR & Co, L.P.	KKR
KKR Financial Holdings LLC	KFN
Lazard, Ltd.	LAZ
Och-Ziff Capital Management Group LLC	OZM

Other Businesses

Brookfield Infrastructure Partners L.P.	BIP
Cedar Fair, L.P.	FUN
ML Macadamia Orchards, L.P.	NNUT
StoneMor Partners L.P.	STON

Oil and Gas Royalty Trusts in PTP Form

Although these entities are treated as partnerships for tax purposes and are publicly traded, they are royalty trusts rather than MLPs, operating simply as vehicles for passing through cash from royalty interests in oil and gas produced by active energy companies.

ECT Marcellus Trust I	ECT
Chesapeake Granite Wash Trust	CHKR
SandRidge Mississippian Tr I	SDT
SandRidge Permian Trust	PER

Commodity Funds

Over 40 publicly traded partnerships are commodity fund PTPs. Rather than companies that operate active businesses, they are simply investment funds. These partnerships are not considered MLPs and are not included on this list. If you would like a list of the PTP commodity funds that we know about

Open-End MLP Funds

Center Coast MLP Focus Fund	CCCAX CCCCX, CCCNX
Cushing® MLP Premier Fund	CSHAX, CSHCX, CSHZX
Famco MLP & Energy Income Fund	INFIX
Famco MLP & Energy Infrastructure Fund	MLPPX
MainGate MLP Fund	AMLPX
SteelPath MLP Alpha Fund	MLPAX, MLPOX
SteelPath MLP Income Fund	MLPDX, MLPZX
SteelPath MLP Select 40 Fund	MLPFX, MLPTX
Tortoise MLP & Pipeline Fund	TORTX, TORIX

Note: The various ticker symbols for each fund are for different classes of shares.

Closed-End MLP Funds

ClearBridge Energy MLP Fund	CEM
ClearBridge Energy MLP Opportunity Fund	EMO
Cushing MLP Total Return Fund	SRV
Energy Income and Growth Fund	FEN
Fiduciary/Claymore MLP Opportunity Fund	FMO
Kayne Anderson Energy Development Company	KED

Kayne Anderson Energy Total Return Fund	KYE
Kayne Anderson Midstream / Energy Fund	KMF
Kayne Anderson MLP Investment Company	KYN
MLP & Strategic Equity Fund	MTP
Nuveen Energy MLP Total Return Fund	JMF
Salient MLP & Energy Infrastructure Fund	SMF
Tortoise Capital Resources Corp.	TTO
Tortoise Energy Capital Corp.	TYY
Tortoise Energy Infrastructure Corp.	TYG
Tortoise MLP Fund, Inc.	NTG
Tortoise North American Energy Corp.	TYN

MLP Exchange-Traded Funds

Alerian MLP ETF	AMLP
Credit Suisse Cushing® 30 MLP Index ETN	MLPN
J.P. Morgan - Alerian MLP Index ETN	AMJ
Morgan Stanley Cushing MLP High Income ETN	MLPY
UBS E-TRACS Alerian MLP Infrastructure ETN	MLPI
UBS E-TRACS 1x Leveraged Long Alerian MLP Infrastructure Index ETN	MLPS
UBS E-TRACS 2x Leveraged Long Alerian MLP Infrastructure Index ETN	MLPL

E-TRACS Alerian Natural Gas MLP Index	MLPG
UBS E-TRACS Wells Fargo MLP Index	MLPW

MLP Indexes

Alerian MLP Index	AMZ (Price Return), AMZX (Total Return)
Alerian MLP Infrastructure Index	AMZ I (Price Return), AMZIX (Total Return)
Alerian Large Cap Index	ALCI (Price Return), ACLIX (Total Return)
Alerian Coal Index	ACI (Price Return), ACIX (Total Return)
Alerian E&P Index	AEPI (Price Return), AEPIX (Total Return)
Alerian Natural Gas Index	ANGI (Price Return), ANGIX (Total Return)
Alerian Petroleum Transportation Index	APTI (Price Return), APTIX (Total Return)
Citigroup ® MLP Index	CITIMLP (Price Return), CITIMLPT(Total Return)
Cushing® 30 MLP Index	MLPX (Price Return), MLPXTR(Total Return)
S&P MLP Index	SPMLP (Price Return), SPMLPT (Total Return)
Tortoise MLP Index	TMLP (Price Return), TMLPT (Total Return)
Wells Fargo Securities, LLC MLP Index	WMLP (Price Return), WMLPT (Total Return)

Suits   *Ben Aronson 2011*
Oil on panel, 30 x 30 inches   *Alpha Gallery*

Chapter 9
Corporation Governance

When Christopher Columbus first conceived of a project to bring back goods from the Indies free of all handling and transportation costs required by overland caravans by the alternate method of using ships traveling westward, he immediately ran up against the problem facing any entrepreneur: how to raise capital.

Raising Capital

Today we have capital raising organizations in our society as anxious to capitalize entrepreneurs as the entrepreneurs are wishing to be capitalized, but in Columbus' day these organizations did not exist. So although most of the world focuses on Columbus's exploits as a marine navigator, his exploits as a capital formation navigator are more noteworthy but neglected. So what may be the first recorded need for capital formation may be found in the life of Cristoforo Colombo of Genova, then a city state, and perhaps the most visionary entrepreneur of his time.

Of course, the first recorded need for capital formation should have been during classical Roman times but if it happened it apparently wasn't recorded. Perhaps the largest public project in Rome was the Coliseum erected by Vespasian about 72AD and paid for by the sack of the Jerusalem temple, which supplied the capital. So the earliest sign of capital formation is perhaps the construction of the first and second temples in Jerusalem. We do know that King Joash of Judah asked the people to deposit money into a receptacle placed near the Temple precinct for the accumulation of capital to restore the first temple. That may be the first recorded raising of capital from the public to finance a greater and larger public good.

Columbus was ultimately financed by the Spanish Monarchy. Other monarchies lacked the necessary wealth and so perhaps prompting the first private capital raising as in England and Holland, perennial rivals in trade. Once capital goes private, then the need for capital law arises to protect various parties to the process, and here England was slightly ahead of Holland in creating the East India Trading Company in 1601. A year later the Dutch East India Trading Company (Vereenigde Oost-Indische Compagnie, VOC) was created and issued stock, which was a first. These first companies were quasi-governmental entities, the Crown contributing power to trade, wage war, imprison and execute in return for a piece of the action. Over the next 400 years, corporation law would evolve to separate the state from the corporation, and create entities whose function however remains the same: create wealth for the state and its people.

Corporate Governance Laws

Of course the central issue of corporation law is money, how it is accounted for, invested, collected and distributed. This immediately raises the question – who is going to do it? And it is the "who" question with which much corporate law is concerned. The parties to the process are as follows:

- Owners
- Managers
- Employees
- Customers
- Creditors
- Suppliers
- Governing agency

In defining the various roles of the players the guiding principle has always been and needs to be optimal wealth creation. However, a conflict is immediately apparent between those providing the capital and those investing the capital. How do the owners know that the funds are actually being invested and invested responsibly? Also, how do they reap the rewards of their investment? In what proportion? This continues to be an unresolved (as far as the owners are concerned) issue as they see management thumbing their noses at them while enriching themselves with the proceeds. This comes about owing to the public nature of ownership through shares of stock that are held by an inattentive public in no way capable of exercising any kind of oversight over their investment interests.

Recognizing this gap, state and not federal corporation law calls for an owner-elected Board of Directors to act in the interest of the owners. In the United States these laws are generally written at the state level and intended to attract revenue to the state issuing the incorporation. Thus far the state of Delaware has won out with the most liberal and lowest-burden landscape in which to incorporate, giving Directors a large measure of autonomy. At the same time, the *Delaware Journal of Corporate Law* is a respected publication and has a website, www.djcl.com, which is an excellent resource for studying corporate law: its articles are available free to the public.

As in general law, the federal government takes on several core tasks and leaves everything else to the states. Federal law includes securities laws, employment laws, environmental laws, food and drug regulation, intellectual property laws, and laws regulating foreign trade. All other laws defining or regulating what a corporation is and does is left to the states. Federal law covers one other issue of incorporation, where a company may incorporate relative to its business address or business footprint. Federal law allows a corporation to incorporate in any of the 50 states, without regard to its business geography and so there are 50 models of corporate governance.

More than half of U.S. corporations are incorporated in the state of Delaware owing to a perceived landscape friendly to business, for example, granting a great deal of autonomy to board members, who are charged with the task of deciding in which state the company should be incorporated.

In Delaware, as in all of the U.S., what is regarded as corporation law is two sets of laws: Articles of Incorporation regulating external relationships and Articles of Association regulating internal relationships. External issues are what product or service the corporation provides and the capitalization of the enterprise by outside stockholders. Internal issues are those affecting governance, such as procedures for board meetings. The most important rules are those defining the relationship between the Board of Directors and the owners (shareholders). The core concept is that the Board of Directors has a right to manage the corporation for the benefit of the owners. Regulation of the board is contained in the Articles of

Association and states specifically the number of "directors" (or "governors," "regents," "trustees," etc.), how they are chosen and when they are to meet.

Although there are variations, most larger U.S. corporations follow a standard model of the top management selecting Board of Director candidates to be voted on by shareholders. Most shareholders just go along, not being owners in a proprietary sense but just owning the stock as an investment. This results in boards and hence CEOs being largely immune from shareholder action.

Wealth Shift

During the Great Depression, two Harvard scholars linked the financial crisis to failure to hold boards accountable. One of the scholars, Adolf Berle, warned that the disengagement of owner oversight on the corporations they owned as shareholders would lead to a wealth shift away from them to the boards and CEOs, who are the owner's subordinates. This has certainly occurred where boards approve runaway compensation for the CEOs they are supposed to be supervising. But since the CEO may have a lot to do with their appointment, they are just repaying the favor. Directors, incidentally, usually serve on multiple boards and may be paid $100,000 per board seat.

In the case of Christopher Columbus, the Spanish Monarchy was the majority owner of the enterprise, and Columbus the minority owner. No directors were needed because the owners were directly involved in the person of Columbus. But as corporations grew and shares were sold, the divide between ownership and management began to widen until finally the need for owner's representatives close to the action was needed. There also arose another dimension to this relationship, which still looms very large today: the incapacity of owners to add value to the stewardship of their investments. Just the need for expertise forces owners to look outside of themselves for stewards who can better look after their interests. This would become particularly true for high-tech or research-intensive enterprises like computer chip and pharmaceutical companies.

This situation morphed into the extreme condition of executive arrogance that persists to this day, but began in the post-war era of the '50s. There is a proliferation of toothless boards whose members just go along with whatever program the CEO lays out, including his or her own salary. This state of affairs hit a speed-bump in 2002 with the Sarbanes-Oxley Act, which simply made executives and corporate boards personally, financially, and criminally responsible for bad outcomes that could have been avoided by good stewardship. This, of course, raises the question of what good stewardship is and how it is defined and judged.

The Meaning of "Fiduciary."

I had the good fortune of being required to earn a designation, described in another section of this book, under the general category of making salespeople more credible. The designation required of me was AIF, Accredited Investment Fiduciary. It took about a week of study using a Power-Point like module provided by the AIF accrediting organization. The module was designed to prepare candidates to act as a fiduciary for endowments and retirement plans regulated by ERISA (Employee Retirement Income Security Act) and the U.S. Department of Labor (DOL). Without the training, even the well-intentioned might fail to do a good job, and in the investment arena, this can be tricky. But the lesson is that fiduciary grades are given out not on performance but on process. One must show that a process is in place to make stewardship or investment decisions without influence other than the welfare of the beneficiary or owner. For example, investment decisions must be outsourced to one or more parties that have passed a rigorous screening for expertise, which is evidenced by investment process and recordkeeping that is audited by outside auditors.

Much of the AIF curriculum has to do with recognizing potential conflicts of interest and implementing processes to defeat them. The typical process is the hiring of disinterested third-parties that are demonstrated to be expert and free of outside influence. Now here comes the core concept: If such a process was followed and audited, and the result was disappointment and loss, there are no grounds for a lawsuit or prosecution. A fiduciary process was in place but led to a bad result. Too bad, or bad luck. On the other hand, if the assets were given to a trustee's brother-in-law without bothering to inquire into his expertise and his stewardship grades, and he provided a big win, the trustees, all of the trustees, are subject to lawsuit and prosecution, providing the plan is under the jurisdiction of either ERISA or the U.S. Department of Labor (as nearly all plans are, because you cannot obtain favorable tax treatment without operating an ERISA and DOL plan). What fiduciary stewardship means is taking actions that do two things:

- Determine the presence of expertise in a custodial role requiring expertise
- Eliminate encroachment of interests other than those of the beneficiary

At one time in this country there was a sentiment for business expressed as: "What's good for GM is good for America." That sentiment has gone the way of the phone booth, of course, as this country shifted gears from concentrating on the general good to concentrating on the private good of individuals. This all blew up in the late 1990s when it was learned that such stalwart companies as Enron had "cooked the books." That prompted passage of Sarbanes-Oxley. What Sarbanes-Oxley did was impose fiduciary process on corporate boards and made executives and board members financially and criminally responsible. So we are now living in an era when managers, executives, and board member must be held financially and criminally responsible. This may sound good to some; others may see a "red-flag."

The problem is the same as described earlier in managing ERISA- and DOL-regulated assets: how to inspire those closest to the assets to work on behalf of those who own the assets but are distant from them. In the case of Christopher Columbus, he was on his series of voyages personally looking after his own interests plus those of the Spanish monarchy. Henry Ford was the top manager at Ford and so looked out for his own interests. But in a way the Ford story is a poster child for the problem. Henry was the enabling component of an auto company carrying his name. He was the chief engineer, and had earned prominence through his auto racing activity. The only thing Henry lacked to make a successful auto company was money and his backers knew that. The Ford Motor Company as we know it today was Henry's third or perhaps fourth attempt to start a Ford Motor Company. The earlier attempts saw the owners cutting Henry out after the company was established and Henry, although strictly a technical person, quickly caught on. On his final attempt Henry made sure he was a prominent owner regardless of where the money came from, and he acted as follows. He put out a rumor that he was retiring, apparently due to poor health; as he suspected it would, the stock price collapsed, and he secretly bought as much as he could through a third-party. He thus came out a major owner in the end, beating the financiers at their own game.

The case of Columbus and Ford are unique in that there was no separation between ownership and management, but that is not the case with most investment candidates where the lines between ownership and management are so far apart they aren't even on the same table. What can be said with certainty is that in the U.S model, ownership and management are two different profit centers with conflicting objectives – more for the shareholders means less for the CEO.

The U.S. Model

Looking at the global picture two characteristics stand out: 1)insistence of U.S. managers that the American style of combined management and board composition is the fiduciary model for rectitude in management of company affairs, and 2), U. S. managers' insistence that foreign models have huge fiduciary holes. This is all stated with a straight face even while defending the idea of combining the position of Chairman of the Board (owner's representative) and chief executive officer (Management) into the single office of Chairman & CEO.

This is justified by custom – it works, is the argument. Of course, but works for whom is the question. Judging by the outlandish salaries American CEOs receive, works for the CEO is the clear answer. But from a fiduciary grades perspective, combining the role of Chairman and CEO into one person not only falls short of fiduciary rigor, it is antithetical to it. And for one reason it should be ended is that today owners are stockholders and are in no position to exercise any kind of stewardship role over their investments. Investors need an independent Board whose members have an arm's length relationship to the day-to-day operation of the firm.

It might be well to look at some of the foreign models to see what all the complaining is about. After examining them I am sure that you will, like me, find more comfort in foreign holdings.

Corporate Governance in Germany

German corporations have a junior board ((Vorstand) and a senior board a (Aufischtsrat). The junior board has day-to-day operational oversight on product development, manufacturing, finance, marketing, etc. The senior board appoints members to the junior board, approves financial statements, decides on major financial initiatives and mergers and decides on the payment of dividends. No internal managers are allowed on the senior board. In addition, the junior board must have one-third of its members drawn from labor in companies of 500 or more employees and that number goes up to one-half for companies with over 2,000 employees. Also German junior boards almost always include a banking representative, which theoretically increases the availability of debt financing -- for example, Deutsche Bank at one time owned around 12% of Daimler Chrysler. Of course, in all of this, the CEO is separate and subject to the oversight of a two-tiered oversight model that looks after the interests of not only owners but all stakeholders as well.

I have had the opportunity to work directly for two German companies as well as in concert with several others and in the course of that work made a number of trips to Germany for consultation and training. My observation about German industry is that corporate Germany is an integral part of the country that may be thought of as Germany, Inc. And the close bidirectional co-existence I believe, leads to an empowerment of a workforce that is constantly innovating and produces what was up until very recently the world's largest exporter. I don't mean largest per-capita exporter, I mean little Germany being largest global exporter.

On one trip I came upon a machine that converted ordinary kraft paper into a cushioning material, which of course is far cheaper that the unruly and expensive plastic "peanuts" relied upon in the United States for packaging. I was astounded at the simple and novel nature of the product and its total absence in our country. On another trip, I learned that company employees were picked up by a company bus every morning and dropped off every afternoon after work. During another trip I witnessed high school boys entering the manufacturing plant en masse and learned they were apprentices preparing for a career in manufacturing. On my first trip to Germany I brought back information on a highway product that had been successful on German highways for years but was entirely unknown to the U.S. market, though there was much greater need for it here. On my last trip, I had the opportunity to have lunch at the Bayer facility in Leverkusen, a suburb of Cologne, and would have to rate the dining room as a 5-star eatery, though it was a company cafeteria. So my admiration for German corporate governance is borne out of hands-on experience. My greatest regret is currency union in the Euro, taking the German Deutschemark off the table as an investment vehicle.

The German formula of including labor on the boards of corporations seems to be unique to Germany and is perhaps the reason you doesn't see crippling labor strikes in Germany as you do in France and the United States, the recent Lufthansa strike aside. But management remuneration is also more balanced as evidenced by the merger of Daimler-Benz and Chrysler Corporation in 1997. At the public announcement of the merger in Detroit, a reporter asked Juergen Schrempp, Daimler-Benz CEO and driving force behind the merger, about the lopsided remuneration between him and his counterpart at Chrysler, CEO Bob Eaton, who was perhaps making five times or more of Schrempp's pay package. Schrempp's answer was that he was not exactly poor.

Another event that illustrates differing governance styles between Germany and the U.S. has to do with NYSE listing. Some years ago Daimler was turned down by NYSE for incomplete disclosure in reporting as in annual reports. It seems that Daimler did not fully disclose all assets. There seemed to be no question that liabilities were adequately disclosed but not assets. No listing on the NYSE without full disclosure Daimler was told. This was cited, with a straight face, as a product of the "superiority" of U.S. governance. All this while Enron was perfectly fine disclosing liabilities with footnotes alluding to subsidiaries. This level of disclosure was okay at NYSE. Even when Enron was delisted, the reason given by NYSE was bankruptcy and the price of the stock - $1. Nothing about disclosure.

Americans like to have it both ways, loading up annual reports with sleight-of-hand and obfuscations, papering those over with purchased endorsements by top auditing firms and then parading around the world as paragons of public virtue. Where are Moliere and Daumier when you need them? I guess our modern world is unable to produce such restorative characters.

Later, German workers learned that their American counterparts at Chrysler were being paid four times as much as the German workers for cars that they regarded as junk. Such disparate governance and outcomes played out in many other ways, eventually sinking the personal relationships needed to make the Chrysler-Daimler merger work.

But the central issue was apparently culture. Daimler-Benz operated a company meant to benefit the owners, all the stakeholders, and the German state and to be a point of pride for Germany. Chrysler was operated to benefit top management and the unions.

When the merger with Daimler was announced, key Chrysler executives left for Ford or GM and there was apparently no depth to the management team to fill the vacuum. The failure to fill-in may be due to the culture of top managers working strictly for themselves and not developing back-up to be stewards of the ownership interest.

So here is a case where although the CEO and top managers were making the kind of money needed to "align their interests with those of the corporation they were stewards of," in the end their interests were not aligned at all despite the pay. My take on this is that when you separate pay and performance, you get performance for long range pay. When you combine pay with performance you get pay. All that matters at that point, is the paycheck, how big is it, and when is it coming. Of course, performance goes missing.

Another interesting study in corporate governance is Japan. First, I must relate that there is a movement for integrating the reporting requirements of listed corporations into a global standard. This is very slow moving as each country struggles with the cost of complying with existing home country regulations and then add the extra cost of complying with the new global regulations.

But in my examination of these new reporting standards, I read that relative to their U.S. counterparts, Japanese companies understate earnings owing to more rigorous characterization. Consequently, P/Es of Japanese companies were prone to be higher than those of similarly priced U.S. corporations. A U.S. company may have a P/E of say 15, that is, stock price 15 times what the stock might earn in profit. The reciprocal is yield at 1/15 = 0.66 or 6.6%. Identical performance of a Japanese company may only show a yield of say 0.50 or 5%, thus a P/E of 20 due to a Japanese more stringent recognition of "profit."

Corporate Governance in Japan

The Japanese model, like the German, is also quite different from the U.S. model, but unlike the German, puts an emphasis on insiders, who know the business intimately and may be relied upon for more useful contribution. Toyota explained their position this way:

"With respect to our system regarding directors, we believe that it is important to elect individuals that comprehend and engage in Toyota's strengths, including commitment to manufacturing, with an emphasis on frontline operations and problem solving based on the actual situation on the site (genchi genbutsu).Toyota will consider the appointment of outside directors should there be suitable individuals."

The reason this insider culture works in Japan is for the same reason it doesn't work at Chrysler as illustrated in the case above. The insiders in Japan have a more holistic view of their roles. It's not all "me, me, me," as at Chrysler, but more "we, we, we." It is this orientation and not structure that I regard as the essential glue which makes Japanese corporate governance effective. At the end of this chapter is an illustration of the Toyota governance model.

Corporate Governance in the UK
The British experience I read is much like the U.S. model. In the early '90s the Cadbury committee made a number of recommendations for improving board composition and mission. One provision they made was that annual reports to stockholders must contain a statement of compliance with Cadbury recommendations and other recommendations for fiduciary vigor proposed by Sir Derek Higg, a former investment banker. Together the prescription was called the Code and the regulation to declare compliance as "comply or explain," meaning that the report must either comply with the Code or explain why the report would not do so.

A survey found that of the 350 largest British corporations there was a 45% failure to disclose how outside directors were chosen, 21% failure to have a financial professional on the audit committee, and 21% failure of the audit committee to review internal audits. This is obviously a mixed bag but at least one can separate the compliers from the explainers and make investment decisions accordingly.

A failure to have a financial professional on the audit committee looks to me like a breathless lapse in stewardship. The fundamental idea behind fiduciary measures is to assume larceny on the part of the steward and then lay down rules to prevent that from happening. This is how the U.S. government was framed by our founders – larceny was assumed and provided for. This is one model and perhaps the default model.

It comes down to the difference between democracy and monarchy, but monarchy, particularly when it comes to building and preserving capital, may not be the villain it is cracked up to be -- witness the monarchy that is Sweden, a model of propriety and fair dealing. The Swedish model on corporate propriety on the following page.

Corporate Governance in Sweden

In Sweden, the Wallenberg family, referred to by some as the royal family of Swedish business, has dominated that country's financial and industrial companies for 100 years. Through the holding company Investor AB and a family foundation, the Wallenbergs own positions in AstraZeneca, Ericsson, GAMBRO, and SAS (Scandinavian Airlines System), and hold board seats on one-third of the companies in the OMX Stockholm 30 Index.

The Wallenbergs are dedicated to the preservation of Swedish influence over these multinational corporations. Jacob Wallenberg, chairman of Investor AB, stated:"

"We have a vested interest in Sweden having as many skilled people as possible in society, and one of the most important ways of generating that is by having head offices of businesses [located in the country] because normally they demand the highest-quality services. So we will always fight to have head offices in Sweden."

When all is said and done, this statement and state of affairs does not make me uncomfortable about investing in Swedish companies. I am not uncomfortable since the Wallenbergs as owners seem to pretty well run industry inside the country. I get the impression that shareholders along with the Swedish state are well looked after. I also note that the Wallenbergs take a back seat to the State; it is about the Sweden and not them.

While on the subject of investing in Sweden, I refer you to a

10-year chart on Swedish Kroner (SEK) per U.S. Dollar (USD). Go to **www.xe.com** and enter from USD to SEK and you will see that over a 10-year period, with some hiccups, the SEK has strengthened against the USD from around 9 per USD to 6.8 per USD or about a 25% gain, signaling a healthy demand for Swedish Kroner by U.S. Dollar holders. I am invested in Sweden in a position in AtlasCopco, a global powerhouse in industrial tools and machinery particularly air-compressors.

Corporate Governance in Holland
The Dutch have a two-tiered system similar to the German model, but the senior board is selected with management input, which of course begs the question why a two-tiered model is needed. In another dimension of Dutch stewardship, the Dutch and the Brits have gotten together, finally, after beating each other up for over 500 years, and shared listing on several issues, notably Royal Dutch Shell and Unilever. These companies must meet regulation of both countries and are listed in both countries as home companies.

Corporate Governance in South Korea
South Korea is an interesting case, somewhat like the Japanese model. Up until the end of WWII, Japan industry was managed by leading families organized in large conglomerates known as Zaibatsu. Under the direction of General Douglas McArthur, the Zaibatsu were broken up into smaller units called Keiretsu. The theory was that Zaibatsu drove policy to attack the United States at Pearl Harbor and needed to be downsized. It should be noted at this point that when Truman fired McArthur and McArthur left Japan, the entire route of his motorcade was lined with Japanese people showing up to pay their respects to the departing leader. This certainly illustrates the unique and respectful character of the Japanese people.
The South Koreans have adopted the Japanese model of Zaibatsu with large conglomerates known as Chaebol. You will

immediately recognize Samsung, which operates in insurance, construction, shipbuilding, textiles, consulting, electronics and a number of other industries. Other major Chaebol are Hyundai Group, LG Group, and SK Group. Given this lineup, investing in Korean companies would mean taking on a much smaller fraction of company risk in the overall risk landscape since the Chaebol are so diversified.

I spent some time in Saudi Arabia earlier in my career and fell in with a group of South Koreans who were prominent in the Riyadh construction boom of the '80s. One day as we were relaxing by the pool on a Friday, I asked one of the South Koreans I was closest to, what the differences were between the Chinese, Vietnamese, Japanese, and South Koreans. He practically jumped out of his chair and urged me not to mention the Japanese; they are very aggressive, he said, and should not even be talked about. He then went on to say that the Koreans were originally Chinese and then broke away many centuries ago and formed their own society. The Vietnamese were not worth discussing. Such was my introduction to Asian culture.

The Chaebol like the Japanese and Swedish models are mainly family-run affairs with professional management. The upside to this arrangement is vigorous assertion of owner interests which bodes well for investors. The downside is that with family influence there is a tendency to put some businesses on life support only because they have sentimental value. However, the Asian financial crisis of 1997 brought in the International Monetary Fund (IMF) for a bailout, and conditions of the assistance included measures to disaggregate some of the family influence at least as far as allowing failing businesses to fail. Another requirement was to expand foreign ownership, which translates into South Korean investment candidates for Americans.

Corporate Governance in India

In 1997 I happened to be in Mumbai (Bombay), India, coincidentally during the 50th anniversary of India's independence from Britain. I picked up the paper one day and the headline read something to the effect that India's infrastructure had been in a constant state of decay over the 50-year period of independence. In other words, India had Britain to thank for its infrastructure and, left on their own, the Indians couldn't maintain it. At least it was an honest appraisal and on the front page of a major daily newspaper and in English.

On the previous evening my in-country rep, Patok, had taken me on a brief tour of the city of Mumbai, and we finished up on a bay that was ringed with lights. *"We call this the Queen's necklace,"* Patok told me proudly. I answered that he *"...was no doubt referring to Queen Victoria. "Yes. Yes. Queen Victoria,"* agreed Patok. *"Well, Queen Victoria was the Empress of India. Why don't you call it the Empress' necklace?"* I asked. *"No. No. Queen Victoria was the Empress of India in England, not here,"* stated Patok with finality, *"This is the Queen's necklace."* Such was my introduction to Indian culture. Evidently they loved the British but at arm's length. Nevertheless, after 50 years, British influence is apparent everywhere in India.

It didn't take me long to learn why the infrastructure was deteriorating – corruption. I was in the country selling combustion-gas monitoring systems for power plants and other major combustion sources like refineries and steel mills. Early in my stay I was taken to an environmental ministry where I found myself ascending unlit stairs in an office building to a fourth floor, which showed all the evidence of no maintenance for 50 years. On the 4th floor I was shown into a cavernous dimly lit room populated by about 70 desks or so with people pecking away on old Remington typewriters with fans listlessly rotating overhead to keep the warm air moving. Files were folders tied on three sides with ribbons and stacked on the floor up against the walls. I guessed each employee had his or her wall section for filing. It was so dark I couldn't understand how all this typing could be going on and the whole scene looked like something out of a Rudyard Kipling story.

After about 15 minutes Patok and I were shown into the Director's office, which was air conditioned, very comfortably furnished, brightly illuminated and computerized. I felt like I had been transported to another planet. My rep made the introduction and then passed the initiative to me, which prompted me to go into my regular speech about measuring combustion gas constituents as an enabling step in controlling emissions for clean air environmental initiatives. The Director had not the slightest interest in the environment or clean air -- what he wanted to know was if there was some sale that could be made in the public interest that would allow him to profit personally. Finally it was decided that measuring SO_2 (sulfur dioxide), a precursor to acid rain, was a worthy goal and that my rep would get the systems assembled and cut the Director in on the profit while the Director mandated their use. This is India, the world's largest Democracy – largest Kleptocracy is a better description.

The challenge in building an SO_2 monitor for India was that the cost had to come in so low that proper gas sample drying was not possible. I provided a design with very cheap and inefficient separation of water from gas resulting in much loss of gas sample in the condensate. This would produce very inaccurate sample gas measurements. I presume the apparatus was built and sold but lost contact with the players. In any case, it would have been a very small step in the right direction had it been implemented. Patok and I then traveled north and met with Indian engineers in the Gujarat region where the refineries and chemical companies are located and I found the engineers there, like the Polish and the Israelis, extraordinarily astute and demanding. I left India with a great respect for their intellect but put off by their corruption.

In 1991 as a reform measure for Indian business, which had

followed a communist-inspired model and largely failed to produce much value, measures were instituted that led to the Corporate Governance Code of 1998. The code has been revised since and superseded by Clause 49, which requires a majority of board directors to be non-executive, that is to say, outsiders. Audit committees are required to have two or three members as outsiders. And as a sop to their British heritage, annual reports are required to carry a statement of compliance to Clause 49 – comply or explain. I don't know what the rate on compliance is but in aggregate 45% of all equity listed on the Indian exchange is in the hands of families and insiders. Here again, however, you can be sure that very sophisticated owners know how to sniff out corruption working against them, making Indian companies seem to be owner-centered, but not always with good results for investors.

Two Indian companies have stood out in the IT arena: Satyam Computer and Infosys. Satyam, which employs 53,000, has survived a massive fraud that prompted top government intervention that fired the old board and put a new board into place. Now new rules require outside auditing of corporate financials.

The other company, Infosys, has been a model of rectitude and has actively participated in raising fiduciary standards for Indian-listed companies. So perhaps the Satyam episode has plugged the hole on governance. The old board members had no idea what was going on and they seem not to have profited. They were evidently fired for incompetence rather than larceny. And this illustrates the problem with relying on formulas like "outside" or "independent" overseers: Without competence it is just a worthless veneer. Having management whose interests truly are aligned with owner and corporate interests brings about the best results, but may be difficult to impossible to discern from the outside as an investor.

Infosys was in the news recently on account of whistle-blowing by an American employee. The problem was visa infractions by Infosys apparently owing to a bottleneck for obtaining as many American visas for Indian-born employees needed to staff their U.S. operations. I was attracted to the story when I saw it regarded Infosys but blew it off when I understood the problem stemmed from the failure of the U.S. State Department to manage the legitimate demands of industry globalization. Here the poor stewardship grades goes to the U.S. State Department and not Infosys, which had a legitimate need for visas to staff their U.S. operations and was forced to circumvent the system in order to get them.

Totalitarian States

Two other economies are on the investment radar of most investors – Russia and China -- but owing to corporate governance issues in these totalitarian states, I view them as non-starters. Totalitarian means that the government serves itself first, so investors always come in second, if at all. This was driven home for me upon learning that in Moscow government officials' cars are fitted with flashing blue lights that allow them to require other drivers to pull over and let them by. I must assume dividend distributions are given the same blue-light treatment. So even though Gazprom is a wonderful story, I stay away.

Executive Compensation in the United States

When I first went to work in American industry (Remington-Rand in 1966) the term CEO was not used as I recall – a company had a President. And the Presidents of the various corporations were not celebrities as they are these days, and they made a lot less money. Today, the top office is CEO and not Chairman & CEO if you are lucky, with an astronomical pay package to go with the job. Below is a quote from an article entitled "Making Sense of Executive Compensation," in the *Delaware Journal on Corporate Law*, volume 36, number 1, 2011:

"The organizational structure of the publicly held corporation, however, prevents firms from implementing these solutions [offered in the journal article]. Therefore, regulatory intervention is necessary to promote adoption of optimal mixed payment schedules to remunerate managers. The article argues that the Dodd-Frank Act fails to meet this goal and [the journal article] puts forward measures that are better tailored to promote efficient compensation structures."

U.S. Organized Labor in Corporate Governance

Before launching into my thoughts on U.S. corporate governance, I'll relate an episode out of *Snowball*, a fine book on the life of Warren Buffet. Buffett and Charlie Munger, the legendary investment team, purchased the *Buffalo Evening News*. The thesis was that newspapers are a crucial service to the community and therefore an enduring investment. During their early years of ownership the *Buffalo Evening News* was crippled by labor strikes and ruinous competition by a competing paper that cared more for market share than profits and operated at a loss, as did the *Buffalo Evening News* in response. Finally the competitor folded; the *Buffalo Evening News* became the only paper serving the area and, of course, became immensely profitable. The employees -- and loyal employees they were -- who suffered through the thin times then wanted profit-sharing. Buffett said no -- spoils go to owners who are the risk-takers and the financiers. The managers and employees were paid throughout; their reward was steady employment. Of course, in Germany, they would also get half the representatives on the supervisory board, which brings me to another story of corporate governance -- that of Stella D'Oro.

Stella D'Oro had been a robust cookie bakery business that traced its roots to New York City in 1922 with an Italian immigrant cookie maker who married another Italian immigrant cookie maker. The company was started around

1930. The descendants sold the business in 1992 to Nabisco for $100 million. In 2006 Stella D'Oro was sold to a private equity firm for $17.5 million; apparently the business was suffering. The new owner, a private equity firm tried to get concessions from their labor union. This precipitated a strike and the private equity firm shut the business down. In 2009 Lance, Inc. bought the company and relocated it to Ashland, Ohio and began operating the company non-union. The labor union back in New York complained to the National Labor Relations Board, which ruled that the private equity firm had not sufficiently disclosed operating revenues to justify the requested labor concessions and in the end the new owners had to pay several months' wages to the now un-employed workers who "won" their case.

There are several lessons to be drawn from the Stella D'Oro story. First, the fact that the Stella D'Oro product has endured from 1930 to the present speaks to the longevity of basic products, such as cookies, when they are well conceived, well crafted and well managed. Second, the family did an excellent job of building the brand. If they realized $100 million in the sale you can extrapolate that a non-growth product like cookies would perhaps garner a Price/Earnings (P/E) ratio of 10, indicating a probable annual earnings stream of $10 million – a very nice business. Of course Nabisco may have paid a very large premium on the expectation that their distribution would dramatically ramp up Stella D'Oro sales. Apparently, however, the acquisition did not work. Maybe Nabisco didn't have the family touch or other factors were at work. In any case, it is a testament that a blue-chip buyout does not guarantee success. Today, Lance owns Stella D'Oro and we'll see where the brand goes from here. In any case we know the brand is capable of producing wealth for owners, managers, and employees alike, but unless they work in concert it's a no-go.

Another lesson is the self-defeating action of organized labor. I learned of the Stella D'Oro case from a person who lived where the factory was located and he described a union effort that was totally out of control because it thought it had the owners cornered. As with the automobile unions, they don't just want to work at the company, they want a say in running it for their benefit. The modern U.S. labor union movement was born in the confrontation of the 1932 sit-down strike at General Motors, and remains confrontational rather than cooperative to this day. As in 1932 at GM, the labor-management struggle wasn't about money; it was about power. The nickname for GM at the time of the strike was "Generous Motors," because wages and benefits outstripped prevailing ones, a necessity to assure GM of the large and willing work force it needed.

In recent action at Boeing in Seattle, the unions brought a successful action to prevent Boeing from relocating a portion of manufacturing to Atlanta, which would have been a footprint for Boeing in the non-union manufacturing world. It appeared to some to be overreach on the part of the unions and the courts. But the real blowback from that case and so many similar cases of union overreach with court approval is the loss of manufacturing to other countries. Just look around you if you are over 50.

One thing unions and courts cannot do is create manu-facturing, that is the role of capital, and increasingly capital in the United States is moving away from manufacturing. If you examine the new industries that have arisen in the wake of the 1932 strike, you will note that for the most part, they are union-proof. That is the new unspoken mantra of capital: "What can we create that will be union-proof?" Well, fast-food franchises, big-box stores staffed with "Associates," and software enter-prises are three that stand out, and of course the service industry. But very little if any big manufacturing has sprung up since 1932 that is not either mechanized or outsourced. In contrast, Germany is the one bright light in the Western world that has both kept its manufacturing and has been the least affected by the financial Tsunami of 2008.

The Difference Between Capital and Labor

But getting back to Warren Buffett, Charlie Munger and the *Buffalo Evening News*, the point that Buffett makes or implies to the employees is that there is a divide between owners and managers and employees. Owners put capital at risk in a studied attempt to make a profit, and as a byproduct produce jobs and goods and services that otherwise would not exist. Employees take risks, to be sure, but they don't create jobs and without capital they are dead in the water. After customers, capital is the enabling component always operating in a competitive market environment and must therefore have the knowledge beforehand on what that profit is going to be, taking into consideration all costs, including wages. Wages therefore, are a fixed cost and not a function of profitability – wages are due regardless of profit. And it is upon expected profit that investment is made. If the expected profit is thought to be a reliable figure, investments will be made. In the U.S. expected profit from manufacturing cannot be relied upon., therefore, no investment.

The Limits of Management

On the flip side, however, there are arguments that can be made when owners, and CEOs for that matter, lay outsize claim to success through their ownership or unique abilities. Long before an owner's capital or a CEO's management can do any good, there must be an enabling infrastructure made up of a population with the education and initiative to staff the business and then buy its products. There must be transportation infrastructure to allow staff to get to work and get the product to distribution points. There must be gas stations to fuel the transportation infrastructure. There must be vehicles to serve the transportation needs. There must be public order to allow a merchant to stock the product and get paid for distributing it. There must be infrastructure to use the product – you can't have a baseball glove without a bat and a ball and a place to play. Without enabling infrastructure you don't have a business to manage or a place to put capital. Or as related in *Snowball* when the wealthy were feeling entitled, Buffett would say *"If they thought they did it all themselves, reincarnate them as one of five children of a scared, starving mother in Mali and see how rich and successful they would be after being sent to work as a slave on a cocoa plantation in Cote d'Ivoire."* Then on the subject of CEO contribution to company success: *"…a ham sandwich could run Coca-Cola."* And there were times when Munger and Buffett would have preferred that a ham sandwich was running Coca-Cola. So the point is to have perspective; capital must invest with expectation of profit, managers and employees must work for predictable wages, and government must provide an infrastructure to make it all work.

Of course, there are contentious positions that really don't contribute to winning cooperative sentiment among owners, managers, and employees to make a company successful, but they arise when one of the three become imbalanced. My observation is that only in the United State do those forces get out of proportion, particularly when it comes to executive pay and union demands, and in either case, management or union power can often trump that of owners in what might only be described as screwy state of affairs. The most successful and enduring companies work to balance the interests of these disparate populations all of which are crucial to the process.

Cooking the Books

The need for balancing may be seen in the Enron case, where CEO & Chairman Kenneth Lay essentially used the company as a vehicle for his own enrichment, even going so far as encouraging employees to buy the stock while he was unloading it in what may have been a case of insider trading – he saw the fall coming from the inside. The debacle at Enron also took down its auditors, Arthur Andersen, one of the Big 5 or Big 6 at the time, who after stating their "opinion" on the fairness of the reported results, began to shred documents.

Today what used to be the Big Seven or Big Eight is now the Big Four, whose opinion you will undoubtedly see on most annual Reports: Deloitte Touche Tohmatsu, Pricewaterhouse Coopers, Ernst & Young, and KPMG.

The accounting in the annual report is prepared by the company's accounting department and includes at least three statements: Income Statement or Profit & Loss Statement; Balance Sheet; and Statement of Changes in Financial Position. Given the tremendous range of operations in a large company just reporting the activity is a departmental job. Then there is always the temptation to massage the figures with an eye on earnings because earning "surprises" to the upside or "misses" to the downside will propel stock price and many corporate cultures dictate that stock price is pre-eminent even if measures needed to propel stock price are deleterious to the long run performance of the company. This may in part be due to executive compensation tied to stock price and the use of stock warrants in remuneration. A warrant is "exercised" or cashed when the stock price reaches an established level. Where warrants are used in remuneration, they often dwarf the salary component of the remuneration formula, driving short-term management initiatives such as seen at Enron.

One way numbers are massaged is described elsewhere in this book as "pro forma" accounting. This is when bad results are explained away by a non-recurring negative event being removed, the results being reported as "pro forma." In any case, to give the investing public a sense of security an auditor's opinion appears in the rear of the annual report, stating that the financial statements contained in the report comply with Generally Accepted Accounting Principles (GAAP) and fairly represent the state of the company's finances. Up until Sarbanes-Oxley, the opinion could be pretty loose and apparently was, no doubt in part because the auditing firm was hired by the firm being audited, which on the face of it would never pass fiduciary principles. At Enron, Ken Lay hired Arthur Andersen.

It was the Enron episode that prompted Sarbanes-Oxley. This new law added rigor to the auditing process as well as made board members and executives, and the auditors, financially and criminally responsible for fair reporting.

Fiduciary Rigor: The Board and the CEO

Sarbanes-Oxley left alone the separation of CEO and Chairman of the Board, and this remains a contentious issue. About 95% of British companies listed on the London Stock Exchange separate the two roles. In the United States, about 30% split the roles but the number is growing. Recently the following companies have moved to separate the two roles: Boeing, Dell, Walt Disney, MCI, and Oracle. Look for this list to grow.

The obvious argument is that if the CEO is also the Chairman, who has the power to look after the interests of the owners? The answer is nobody. Also there is the issue of continuity. If the two roles are combined and the CEO leaves, who picks up the slack to select a new CEO? In short, there are arguments for separating the roles and no arguments against except removing any restraint to a CEO's freedom of action including setting CEO pay and incentives. The grotesque pay packages going to CEOs today I believe has part of its origin in the work of Gerry Spence, an attorney, who may have taken his cue from union successes in replacing market outcomes with negotiated outcomes.

One principle in negotiation is the concept of power. For example, a child will not prevail against a parent in any argument unless the parent yields. Courtrooms go a long way to establish the negotiating power of the judge. It is generally accepted that for fair negotiations to proceed, the power of the two negotiators must be nearly equal. When the United Auto Workers (UAW) negotiates with an auto company an imbalanced negotiation exists, because the same union covers all the auto makers and is in a much more powerful position than any single auto maker. The result is that Chrysler workers (negotiating through the UAW with Chrysler) make four times as much as Daimler-Benz workers even though workers interests are represented on the Daimler-Benz Board. Each auto company should only have to negotiate with a union made up of that company's workers. Similarly, when a company requires new employees to sign employment contracts or non-compete contracts, there is an imbalance of power that makes any negotiation meaningless. If the prospective employee wants the job, he or she will sign.

When Gerry Spence won a suit against a company for a client and it came time to set a damage amount, Spence asked the jury to judge that if a little girl had flipped over on her tricycle because of a crack in the sidewalk, what should the owner of the sidewalk have to pay? What about a sum equal to the girl's weekly allowance, Spence suggested. The jury agreed this sounded reasonable and made the settlement of one week's allowance (income) for the company. This turned out to be a breathtaking settlement, which of course was shared by Spence. The rest of America found the settlement dizzying, and I believe CEOs took note. In any event, with the example of the labor unions and then Spence an upward spiral of remuneration was started that changed the center of gravity from owners whose interests were tied to long-term market performance to those closest to the money whose interests were the enrichment of themselves and their cohorts and as soon as possible. Earnings surprises were inevitably cited as the result of brilliant initiatives by the CEOs and earnings misses the result of structural market conditions or cleaning up someone else's mistakes. The concept is that boards in this atmosphere have important functions in looking after the owners and the corporation – at present and long after the CEO is gone. Some of these mission objectives are:

- Representing the interests of owners.
- Setting corporate strategy.
- Establishing succession planning.
- Recruiting board members.
- Forming an independent Audit Committee to audit corporate finances.
- Forming and staffing a Compensation Committee.
- Acting as a governance body exercising oversight of CEO actions.
- Setting capital structure parameters.
- Declaring dividend distributions.

It's difficult for me to envision a CEO who would have an interest in performing all of these functions (as he or she would if functioning as a Chairman), let alone the time. But the core concept is that CEOs will inevitably value their own contributions higher than those of the owners' contribution of capital and will compensate themselves accordingly. CEOs will inevitably see themselves as the enabling ingredient of success. This raises what economists call, the problem of "Agency," that is, Can CEOs fairly represent the interests of owners?

A number of third-party organizations have weighed in on these governance issues:

- The Corporate Library
- Governance Metrics International (GMI)
- Institutional Shareholder Services (ISS)

These organizations publish ratings on companies. As in the Enron case with Arthur Andersen auditing, there have been misses. An example is a company rated in the upper 35% of all rated companies and in the upper 8% of peer companies. The company was later discovered to have falsified financial statements overstating earnings by $1.4 billion. The company's subterfuge and crime reinforce the point that structure does not trump culture. Presence of an independent board alone does not guarantee success. It is a culture devoted to fair dealing, or as in the case of Toyota a culture of "Us" and not "Me." Nevertheless the need for outside rating remains.

Board Members Who Think Alike

One other aspect to boards needing attention is their propensity to fall into "Groupthink." This is a condition perhaps first noted in the run-up to the failed Bay of Pigs invasion of Cuba by the U.S. government back in the '60s. A committee tasked with evaluating the project ultimately reached consensus on a bad premise, that given the chance most Cubans would rise up and overthrow Fidel Castro. That's not the way it played out, and absence of any contrary thinking on the committee led to a consensus-building now known as "Groupthink," or when consensus-building trumps critical thinking and debate.

A good corporate example of Groupthink is the Merrill Lynch case. An independent board selected an insider as the next CEO despite that gentleman's penchant for risk taking in his former Merrill roles and that may have led to big losses. Merrill had a $470 million loss in the junk bond division when he was a senior banker there. The same man was CFO when Merrill got hit with big losses from the collapse of Long Term Capital Management. During the run-up to the mortgage securitization collapse he raised Merrill's exposure from $1 billion to $40 billion and when a trader objected to this extraordinary exposure he was over-ruled and apparently fired.

The CEO then brought in two like-minded lieutenants and it was off to the races.

Where was the board in all of this? When the CEO saw the

big hiccup coming that would overwhelm Merrill, he took initiatives to sell Merrill to a big bank. When this came to the attention of the board members, they fired him. One of the fault lines was the traditional "Mother Merrill" culture of taking care of its own and always citing the fact that of all the Wall Street houses, only Merrill had remained Merrill since its 1913 founding by Charlie Merrill. The CEO was apparently contemptuous of this Merrill "culture," considering it cronyism. In the end, Merrill was acquired by Bank of America and at what many consider an outlandish price. It turns out that the CEO had it right on the exit strategy before the board did. In fact, the acquisition by BOA seems have been driven more by the Federal Reserve than by the Merrill board.

The core issue of this case is one that is raised in another section of this book, and that is the role meritocracy plays in the investment world. In an earlier era in U.S. society, there was an establishment made up of actors who were more entitled than deserving but by that very entitlement were better stewards and not driven to "make a name for themselves" -- they were more focused on finding good process. This all got upended in the '60s and was replaced by a meritocracy that saw lower middle-class kids going to Harvard and coming out ready to "knock the cover off the ball." The Merrill Lynch CEO was this phenomenon on steroids. He was a minority kid from the south who through merit got a seat at the Harvard Graduate School of Business and felt intimidated until his first grades came out and he saw he was at or near the top. From that point on, as he said: *"There was no looking back."* He then made a meteoric rise to the top, of course fueled by merit which eventually brought him into contact with mortgage backed securities. These proved his undoing, if you call an undoing walking away from a mess with upwards of $100 million.

But it is for these CEOs of the world that a Board of Directors exists. One reason the CEO may have been given free reign is that although he was certainly interested in his own remuneration, his drive seems to have been fueled by the need to succeed by benefitting the stockholders of Merrill. This is what he was hired to do. In contrast, his successor seems not to have had such an orientation, preferring to focus on furnishing his office. In both cases the board seems to have slept through the action.

The CEO's job is to create value with the resources at his or her disposal. The board's job is to see if that is actually happening. In the case of Merrill Lynch all the focus has been on the failure of the CEOs and no spotlight has ever been shined on the board. It is perhaps this emphasis on CEO performance to the exclusion of any board initiative that drives the lopsided American corporate governance culture. In the United States, the Board of Directors often simply doesn't count for very much and doesn't do very much.

When I was a stockbroker, I and my fellows were constantly barraged with the prescription to diversify client assets, putting a portion into bonds. I was a stock guy and although I passed all the firm's benchmarks for fixed-income product knowledge, I wasn't interested in fixed-income -- I wanted to make money. Finally I came to the sentiment that investors needed at least two people managing their assets: a stock person for growth and a fixed-income person for conservation. For example, I was friendly with a broker who had become a broker in the '60s and he told me one day he had never shorted a stock in all those years since: "I can't think that way," he said. To my mind it comes down to direction of thinking. CEOs and Board of Directors need to be thinking about the same thing but in different ways. I would say in the case of Merrill Lynch the CEO was doing his job and the Board of Directors wasn't, or not very well.

Many of the financial institutions that failed in 2008 had independent boards and from an outsider would seem to have the kind of governance in place that would head off any activity that could lead to collapse. Citigroup, one of the worst hit banks, had 18 persons on the board of which 16 were outsiders. This drives home the point that what looks good does not necessarily work, and that new criteria for effective corporate governance need to be used. However, one cannot challenge the idea of a Chairman independent from the CEO. That's a no brainer.

One of the central issues is motivating the CEO. In the '60s, the role of CEO was much less high profile -- a more collaborative atmosphere prevailed. Gradually business schools began to attract attention and an MBA from a name school became a key component of a CEO's resume. Then CEOs became high profile, which of course meant that they had to be "gunslinger" types whom the board hired to "knock the cover off the ball." This eventually led to very high-profile CEOs who essentially operated solo or with a proven team brought over from their former companies. When it was learned that there were some bumps in that scenario the fix turned out to be aligning CEO interests with the fortunes of the companies they were managing. That was brought about by higher pay, much higher pay as well as stock options. The theory was that if the CEOs knew they were going to cash in, they were much more inspired to give it their all. My view is that what the stock option incentive and high pay really do is take the CEOs' eye off the management function and re-direct their attention to the self-enrichment function.

In looking for investment candidates, corporate governance is a key parameter. What I look for is evidence of both a targeted holistic societal good and value creation – and on the part of both the board and the CEO. If I read that a CEO is measured in his outlook, I feel more comfortable. "Knocking the cover off the ball" is fun to watch, but then you need a new ball. In my view, the best metric is a Board of Directors that represents the interests of the owners; separating Chairman of the Board from CEO is only the first step.

Much of the information presented above and the ratings

and illustrations below are drawn from a paper in the Harvard Business Review library entitled: *Models of Corporate Governance: Who's the Fairest of Them all?* prepared in January 2008 by the Stanford Graduate School of Business. The source for ratings is cited as Bloomberg. The Toyota illustration is from the Toyota 2006 annual report and the Hewlett-Packard stakeholder table is from Hewlett-Packard.

As seems clear, it is difficult to discern good governance from examining governance structures, and good governance is an analog measure that may vary over time to various shades of gray. Additionally, because we have seen good governance structures don't necessarily lead to good governance outcomes, it is really culture that is the most important variable. So it may be easier to merely look at the outcomes, and just investing in the Dow 30 may be all the looking you need to get investment with good governance.

GMI Metrics

On the following pages are exhibits relating to corporate governance. First is a 2007 table of ratings -- by country alphabetically -- for 36 international corporations published by Governance Metrics International (GMI).The GMI ratings are 0 to 10 with 10 being the highest. Their website states: *"Our flagship service, GMI Analyst, is a comprehensive web-based platform providing research, ratings, real-time updates, robust search functionality and analytical tools to help clients assess issuer risk. The research platform provides:*

- *ESG ratings, research and real-time updates on about 5,500 companies worldwide based on 120 carefully selected risk factors (ESG KeyMetrics™)*

- *AGR® ratings, research and real-time updates on about 18,000 companies worldwide based on more than 50 discrete risk factors*

- *Environmental performance data from Trucost, the world's leading provider of comparative data on corporate environmental impacts, including Greenhouse Gases (GHGs), water, waste, pollutants and natural resource dependency.*

- *Unique data on litigation and financial-distress risk*
- *Daily and weekly updates, quarterly ratings reviews and event-driven analysis*
- *Robust search functionality, screening and analytical tools, including WatchLists, Portfolio Analysis, Alerts, Industry Browser, peer-group analysis and historical data on AGR risk"*

Governance Metrics International: Ratings on International Corporations (2007)

Company	GMI Rating	Country
BHP Billiton	9.5	Australia
InBev	4.5	Belgium
Banco Bradesco	3.5	Brazil
Royal Bank of Canada	10.0	Canada
PetroChina	1.5	China
Dansk Bank Group	7.0	Denmark
Nokia	9.0	Finland
Michelin	3.0	France
BMW Group	7.0	Germany
Infosys	7.5	India
ENI	8.0	Italy
Sony	7.0	Japan
Toyota Motor Corp.	4.5	Japan
Kuala Lumpur Kepong	5.0	Malaysia
Aegon	7.0	Netherlands
Heineken Holdings	1.5	Netherlands
Norsk Hydro	6.5	Norway
Gazprom	4.5	Russia
Flextronics International	7.5	Singapore
Posco	5.5	South Korea
Samsung Electronics	4.0	South Korea

Banco Santander	7.5	Spain
Ericsson	6.5	Sweden
UBS	6.0	Switzerland
Hon Hai Precision Ind.	4.5	Taiwan
Bangkok Bank	6.0	Thailand
Turkcell Iletisim Hizmetleri	6.0	Turkey
BP	8.5	United Kingdom
HSBC	8.0	United Kingdom
Royal Dutch Shell	8.0	UK/Netherlands
Unilever	10.0	UK/Netherlands
General Electric	8.5	United States
Johnson&Johnson	9.0	United States
Microsoft	8.0	United States
Procter & Gamble	10.0	United States
Washington Post	7.0	United States

GMI also flags companies where the CEO makes more than three times the median pay for the other named executive officers (NEOs). In the words of GMI:

"If a large pay differential is justified by the relative value of the executives' contributions, it suggests that the company in question has a "weak bench" and may struggle with internal succession planning if the CEO needs to be replaced. On the other hand, if the other named executive officers are in fact near- equal partners with the CEO, the latter is being overpaid for his or her work. This overpayment is both a misuse of shareholder resources and a potential source of poor morale in the executive team."

As of August 2012 the companies listed were among those companies cited for Internal Pay Equity issues.

Company Name	Ticker
Lorillard Inc.	LO

Deere & Company	DE
Avery Dennison Corp.	AVY
CBS Corporation	CBS
The Hain Celestial Group	HAIN
Tupperware Brands Corp.	TUP
Johnson Controls, Inc.	JCI
Big Lots, Inc.	BIG
Pitney Bowes Inc.	PBI
Rock-Tenn Company	RKT

On the next page is a diagram of Toyota's corporate governance infrastructure.

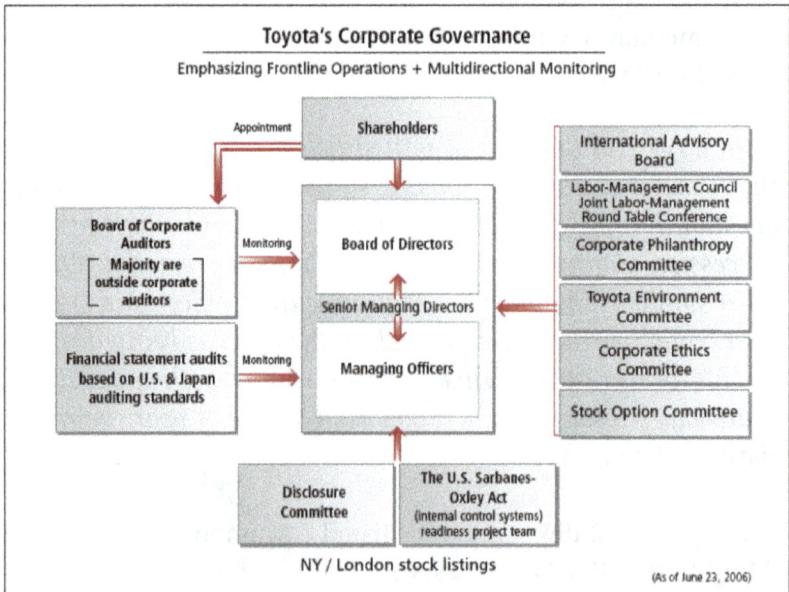

Hewlett Packard's statement of overall societal economic impacts from their 2006 "Global Citizenship Report."

Group	HP's direct economic impacts (on relevant group)	HP's indirect economic impacts (through relevant group)
Suppliers	HP spent approximately $50 billion in 2006 in its supply chain on products, materials, components and services.	Our supply chain spending in turn creates jobs in supplier companies. These companies and their workers pay taxes and support local economies. Suppliers also pay taxes to governments and pay dividends to their investors.
Employees	Compensation and benefits are a significant proportion of HP's overall expenses. We also invest in training and development ($306 million in 2006), which increases employees' skills and competencies and expands their opportunities.	Employees' private spending generates economic activity and taxes, and supports their local communities.
Customers	Customers paid HP $91.7 billion in 2006 in exchange for our products and services.	Equipment and services we sell to customers improve their productivity, which may increase their economic contribution to society through greater employment, more purchases from their suppliers and more taxes.
Local, regional and national communities	Philanthropic investments ($46.3 million in 2006), support of non-governmental organizations, and employee giving and volunteering support communities directly.	HP social investments and taxes in turn support further economic activity.

| | Local, state and national governments benefit from taxes paid by HP. | |
| Investors | Owners of HP stock receive dividends and may benefit from growth in the value of their shares. | Investors may pay taxes on stock gains when they sell their shares. |

POSTSCRIPT:

On September 21st, 2011 *The New York Times* published an article by Quentin Hardy and Nick Wingfield titled "Ouster of Hewlett-Packard C.E.O. Is Expected," and a second article "Voting to Hire a Chief Without Meeting Him," by James B. Stewart. The two articles and several follow-on articles describe a board that in some ways appears to be dysfunctional but grappling with the challenging problem of finding a CEO who can provide a vision for the company and then execute on that vision. The board eventually settled on an insider, a board member, Meg Whitman, former CEO of ebay.

From another *New York Times* article of September 22nd by Quentin Hardy and Nick Wingfield titled "Meg Whitman Is Named Hewlett-Packard Chief," came the following quote: *"Although Ms. Whitman lacks experience running a complex technology company that sells to consumers as well as corporate customers, the company's board considers her communications skills and understanding of customers to be her strongest qualifications for the job, according to a person with knowledge of discussions among directors, but who is not authorized to speak for the board."* As a postscript, the CEO whose firing prompted the new search was given a $13 million exit check.

Reporting another revealing episode regarding boards and CEOs, *The New York Times* published on April 26th, 2012 an article written by Clifford Krauss titled *"Trouble With the Top Man."* It concerned the roller-coaster ride of the CEO of Chesapeake Energy, Aubrey K. McClendon. McClendon gyrated between exceptional prescience in acquiring energy assets and personal excess as evidenced by his purchasing an NBA team as well as a $12 million map collection and by his borrowing $846 million in order to participate alongside his company in drilling ventures. It all went south with the collapse of natural gas prices.

What looked like an out of control CEO prompted analysts to call for separation of the roles of the company's Board Chairman and CEO. This is not surprising given a quote from the article: *"Chesapeake tried to give him a financial lift with a $75 million bonus and by agreeing to buy his personal map collection. After a shareholder lawsuit, Mr. McClendon agreed to buy back the maps."*

Despite the nonsense, the core issue is McClendon's ability to acquire energy assets, which is exactly what he is paid to do and what he was doing. The question is whether McClendon could function at the same level with a Board overseeing what he was doing. Chesapeake is the largest natural gas producer after Exxon-Mobil and according to one analyst, as of April 2012, Chesapeake was the most undervalued energy asset on the market. To get a good sense of this investment thesis, compare the stock price movement of Chesapeake (CHK) with Exxon-Mobil (XOM) and the S&P 500 since 2001.

Exxon-Mobil incidentally combines the role of Chairman and CEO but reserves the right at the Board level to separate those two functions. What I like about Exxon-Mobil is that they seem to have been able to institutionalize performance like Mr. McClendon's but without the antics.

Woman by a Window   *Ben Aronson 2008*
Oil on panel, 24 x 24 inches   *Collection of the Artist*

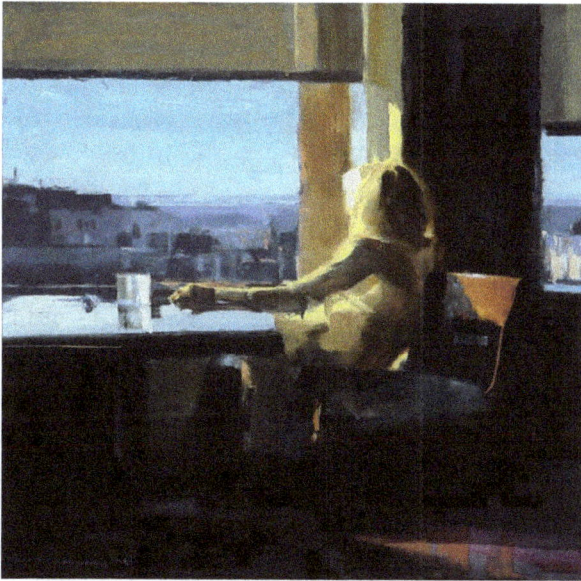

Chapter 10
How to Invest in Companies

The herding of humanity to a common view operates like a fish weir. In a weir, channeling structures are inserted into the river bed in a series of lines. At the entrance to the weir, there are open exits reassuring those fish entering the weir that they are free to leave at any time. But as the fish proceed down the weir, the channeling structures get closer together and offer fewer exits. At the end of the weir, the fish finds itself in a net with no exit.

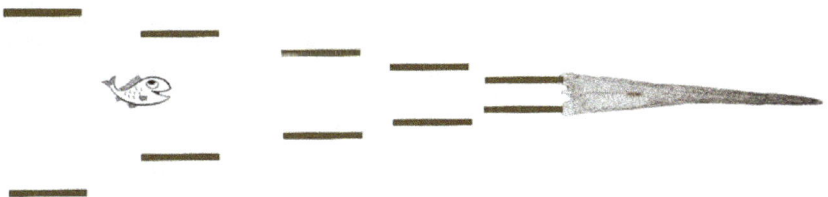

fish weir

That happens to people in a society, but the net is invisible; it is a net of conformity. This works well in social structures, but does not work at all in investing. The cornerstone of investment is true freedom of thought. The best investor when it comes to investment is likely to be the loner.

The weir phenomenon was perhaps best explained as "Groupthink," which is what happens when a committee convenes to discuss an issue or a project. Ultimately all committees come to a unified view, which is called "Groupthink." Contrary views are discouraged, pretty much as occurs in juries deliberating trial evidence. Everyone wants to go home and so the independent thinkers are browbeaten into conforming to the majority view. This happens in society at large with perhaps more subtlety but the same result, cutting off independent thinking, but the victims never realize they are victims.

One of the first things the beginning investor will notice about the investment culture is the tremendous amount of information that is not merely available, but broadcast relentlessly in all manner of media: radio, television, magazines, newspapers, newsletters, and every imaginable channel. And the more engaged an investor becomes in scrutinizing this cornucopia of information the larger the cornucopia is discovered to be – it keeps getting larger.

The neophyte only has ready access to the more readily broadcast material, but this is an industry that thrives on the appearance of exclusivity, so the non-neophyte is bombarded with an even greater array of information "...that is only available to a select few." So to enter the world of investment is to enter a world of information processing on an unparalleled scale. It is also the entry point to the Wall Street weir to land you in the Wall Street net.

The impact this maelstrom of information has on the beginning investor particularly, but also on all investors, is that it imparts a sense that successful investment requires digestion of a significant fraction of the information broadcast. Counter to the fish-weir effect, I propose a general rule: Less is more.

Forget the noise; focus on what interests you. And don't ever think that painstaking research is ever going to reduce the amount of information needed to make an informed decision. Consider also the cost in time to gather that information. Investment in companies will always be a gamble no matter how much you know about the company and the industry it operates in. So discard the broader "investment world," and create your own investment world made up of those issues you have an affinity for. And remember that investing is making a bet on a process and not merely a discreet outcome of a process but outcomes playing out over more cycles than anyone can envision. You must have vision certainly, but more important you must also have a process, commitment, and faith.

This is worth repeating, you can never acquire enough information to make a truly informed decision. For one thing, the time you have taken to acquire the information will have made you unavailable for more fruitful consideration of the information you have — think more about less might be a good rule. Second, the fortunes of companies do not rise and fall at the rate of information flow. Companies are multi-component human agglomerations whose trajectory, up, down or sideways, is determined by multiple human acts made up of both positive and negative force inside and outside the company that creates a long-term vector impossible to discern on a day-to-day basis.

The market and all that information infecting the atmosphere caters to that population seeking to profit, if only minimally, but quickly, in bets associated with some piece of arcane information. This information generally has high emotional content, which by experience is shown to move its associated stock in the direction of the bet, thus procuring that quick but temporary profit.

What is the beginning investor to make of this culture? If an investor is not engaging a stockbroker what is supposed to happen is the investor will subscribe to a variety of print media, including perhaps a newsletter with access to privileged information, and then the investor is supposed to tune in to morning and evening financial news programs and go online to see what various pundits are saying. Or instead this cacophonous nonsense can be turned off, and the investor can then get down to the business of investing.

Stock Price Changes

In order to turn off the noise, you must understand the relationship of news to stock price – news is the driver. As you might imagine, news is a constant stream, and not only real news, but opinion that may be news to some or many. All of it drives sentiment to buy or sell and this drives stock price. You might conclude very rationally that such daily sound bites don't really say too much about the essence of a company and for the most part this is the case. When there is significant news, it is usually disseminated in a press release, but not surprisingly, by that time, the news is out already. And even press release news while having high momentary interest will not dramatically affect the trajectory of a company. So one method of investment research is to forget news and just focus on company fundamentals that will be both qualitative and quantitative. Is the company likely to prosper in the future and how profitable is it? Is it in a growing business? In other words, apply the Boston Consulting Group matrix to you investment candidates and look at market structure.

This might be a good approach for an investment, but not for an investment advisor, or the investment advisory media that must earn a living by stimulating change. For these two groups, each sound bite offers an opportunity to gain a new client, to get a client to make a trade or buy a newsletter or a magazine or a newspaper. And because quick profits may occasionally be made, and the profits can be tied to information, there exists this turbulent sea of hyperbole upon which financial advisors venture in search of clients and quick profits. The profits, of course, are quickly put at risk again to gain more profits. At the end of the day, or year, or life, the profits often are quite thin and certainly throughout, very uncertain. And as the profits get thinner, then choppier seas must be negotiated in search of even greater profits, to make up for the losses. I once had a client ask me when he would know if he had profits, and I told him his first signal would be when he detected whether his spouse was going to bury him in mahogany or pine. He was very disappointed but on Wall Street that is the way it is for clients.

There is another aspect to news merging into opinion. Essentially, Wall Street culture is opinion citing news as support for a position. Naturally by the time the news hits the airwaves, the people closest to the news, those expecting it, for example, have already acted on the information. That is why sometimes Wall Street is called the perfect market; it reacts very quickly. Of course, analysts and pundits who just recite the news really can't attract much of a following; they must anticipate the news to make their forecasts actionable. Of course, news is hard to anticipate, but analysts and pundits must work at that intersection of news and incipient news and once the news is identified, it naturally has to be built up to add to value of the punditry. That is where the frantic nature of Wall Street media comes from. Get in on the action before it's too late and remember where you heard it from, or read it from; hot..hot..hot.

Beyond that is the space of most of newsletters, forecasting the next big thing, but in plenty of time to get in early. The problem here is each newsletter might carry a dozen forecasts, some of which might lead to some profit, but which ones? And the ones that don't take off as promised may take a dramatic downturn. In the meantime, the newsletter has been studied taking away valuable time from the process of thinking about what companies you want to be invested in, and why.

Supply and Demand in the Stock Market.
It may be useful to take a brief detour to examine the mechanics of stock price movements. In classical economic thinking, price is arrived at by reconciling supply with demand, which are forces in opposition to each other. As price moves higher, more of a good or service is supplied but less is demanded. As price moves lower, suddenly demand picks up but supply slows as the profit incentive dampens enthusiasm for producing greater supply in the face of thinning profits.

The above description is a classical definition of supply and demand but from a demand perspective. All the demanders have to do is decide whether to buy one more of what is being offered at the new higher price. Providers don't have that luxury. They must decide whether to invest in a factor of production that will reduce cost but for the next 100,000 units. So unlike demanders that think in units of 1, suppliers must think in units of 100,000 or more.

A good illustration of this relationship may be seen in Marlboro cigarette smokers who will continue to smoke Marlboros regardless of the price, but one cigarette at a time. However, Marlboro the maker of the cigarettes must decide whether to spend $10,000,000, for example, on an additional cigarette rolling machine for demand they can only anticipate. For the company, demand/supply is a stepped affair and not a smooth line.

In the stock market by contrast, both supply and demand are released of all constraints and are allowed to move up and down freely. So given the freedom to move, it is stock price that reconciles supply and demand. If more buyers than sellers show up to trade XYZ common stock, the price will rise to attract more sellers, possibly even the sellers who just bought a few minutes ago hoping for a quick rise based on the hot tip of the day. If suddenly bad news is broadcast about XYZ, perhaps failing to get FDA approval for a new drug, buyers disappear leaving sellers with the option to either hold their shares for another day, or offering them at a lower price. Price will then decline until enough new buyers come in to match sellers. At this point, the stock price has settled at a new lower price – until the next news event with attendant flurry of buyer/seller activity. So the stock market has smooth lines for both demand and supply, allowing some to call it a "perfect" market. The stock market demand/supply curve is shown below.

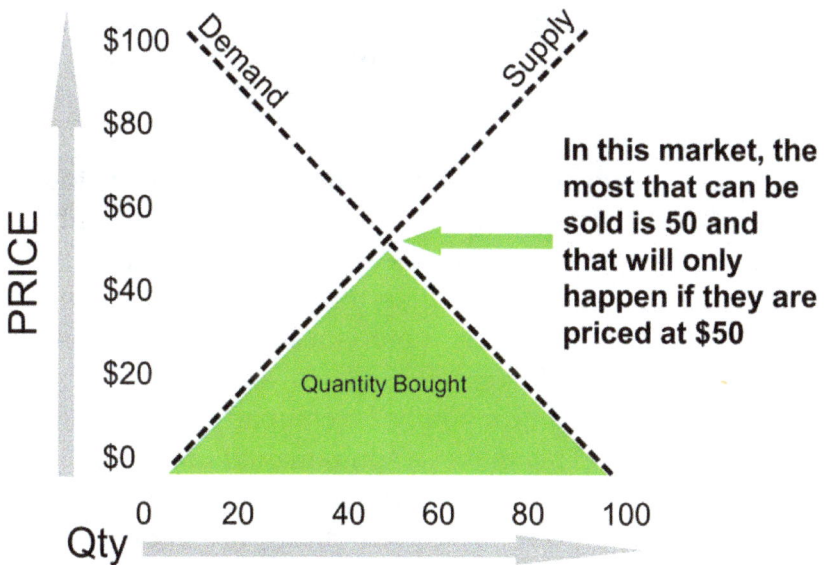

As shown in the chart, in perfectly free demand/supply markets everything is perfectly linear (perfect linearity being rare in most markets). Classical economics teaches that at the intersection of $50 the market clears as supply and demand are both satisfied. Additional buyers will not be found unless price is reduced and additional suppliers will not be found unless price is increased. Since price cannot be both increased and reduced simultaneously, markets clear and everybody is satisfied.

As stated, this idealized relationship found in the stock

market is rare because supply and demand are seldom completely free to act upon price alone. So companies seek out those demand/supply relationships that give them pricing power, like a monopoly on a good or service that is required for survival. This is called "Rent-Seeking" and all companies seek to accomplish it. The few that do, only enjoy it briefly because "me-too" players come in like sharks feasting on a whale carcass, and the party is spoiled. But the point of this little exercise is to demonstrate that there is one market totally free to act on price alone and that is the stock market.

So while companies struggle with trying to get the most out of investments already made and planning new investments in uncertain markets, their fortunes are sticky but their stock price is free of all stickiness and is free to move freely, into outer space even, as too many buyers come in to feast on too few mobile shares, other shares being locked up in untraded portfolios. The quantity of shares available for sale are a subset of all shares created to capitalize the company and while the quantity may be in millions there is a limit to how many are available for trade. Buyers for shares are also limited but limited by the appetite for a specific company's shares and the number of buyers. This makes a fundamental imbalance in that demand can quickly outstrip supply. And since buyers do not look at total capitalization when bidding up stocks, it is not unheard of for stock prices to be bid up into unrealistic corporate valuations. The limitation to this out of balance result is (1) investor sentiment on the "right" price and (2) short-sellers looking for overpriced stocks to short. One metric available with stock quotes is "Short Interest" or that amount of money taking a short position on the stock. This highlights the futility of trying to assess a corporation's earning power by looking at its stock price, yet this is what most people do, having been taught to do it by their Wall Street mentors.

Brokers Prospecting for Assets to Manage

Turning off Wall Street is going to be very hard to do, somewhat like the lone elevator rider sticking to his assertion that the elevator really is going up when the other five riders maintain, against reality, that it is going down. Most riders change their mind when confronted with the solidarity of the many, and abandon their common sense. But in this instance, remember the function of information flow is to enrich the information providers not the receivers. If the receivers could reliably be enriched by information flow, there wouldn't be any information flow because the information would be hoarded. In fact, it is the information that is not flowing that has value, and because it has value, it is proscribed as insider information and not to be shared unless it can be publicly broadcast to the general investing public. But material information will eventually get out, though only after those closest to the information have profited, in the short term, from it. And it is this characteristic that produces that culture we call Wall Street – actionable information received prior to the opening bell.

There is also a lot of program trading and proprietary trading or "prop" trading as the Wall Street lingo has it, and occasionally the program trading prompts out of control swings that forces the exchange to suspend all trading until order can be restored. This highlights the frantic nature of Wall Street trading that seeks to profit from price swings rather than value creation.

Jean-Jacques Rousseau, an 18th century French philosopher, concluded that it was every woman's ambition to inspire love. I don't know about that, but I do know that it is every broker's ambition to inspire trust that they, among the few, have access to near-insider information with which to enrich their clients.

For the savvy investor, this is a distraction, first because information is not reliable until its effect has been assessed and then it is too late, and second, at best, only a fraction of such tips work out. There will be winners and losers and in the meantime; the serious contemplation of good investment candidates will be foregone.

Don't be disappointed if you missed a fast moving investment opportunity, the kind of opportunity that produces Wall Street chatter. Eventually your fortunes will be determined by not your short-term profits, but what you have amassed over the long-term, and I will state unequivocally, the less attention you give to day-to-day market movements, the greater the likelihood you will amass the nest egg you need and envision for yourself.

Before leaving the subject of trashing the media's contribution to investment, I wish to share an episode in the early journalistic career of Gail Collins, columnist for *The New York Times*, and one whom I read regularly. In an editorial on a Presidential candidate, she wrote:

"Once, early in my journalistic career, I spent an unhappy season writing the stock market report for United Press International, and I remember trying to divert myself by beginning all my verbs with the same letter.("Stocks zigged and zagged today in mixed trading, but the Dow zoomed on a late-day rally. ...").

One take-away I have from this vignette is that stock market reporting evidently is the basement of journalism, where newbies are relegated while they get acclimated to their new profession. Such is the seriousness with which even the media regards stock market "reports."

The S&P 500 Standard

A term you will hear often is "market capitalization," which is a number arrived at by multiplying number of shares outstanding by their current stock price. All companies may then be thought of as large capitalization or large cap, mid-cap, small-cap, micro-cap, and nano-cap. And if you added them all up you would have total market capitalization of all companies listed on stock exchanges. Now if that money stayed put and there was no market action, much money would be held away from the market, in mattresses for example, for fear that an investment would be locked up for years with no way out. Market trading action, called "liquidity," eliminates that fear and thus the market attracts the maximum amount of money. So the frenetic pace of market trading is very useful in providing liquidity, allowing investors to have "buy" or "sell" orders filled within seconds on almost all issues. In fact, a requirement for listing on the NYSE or other exchanges is meeting "volume" thresholds. If a company issue of stock does not prompt sufficient volume, the stock will not be listed. So Wall Street culture is necessary to provide liquidity and does an excellent job of it, although that doesn't mean frenetic trading is necessary to build wealth from the market. As long as companies continue to survive in a competitive and hostile environment by growing their businesses they will create value and what daily market actors attempt to do is take that increment of created value off the table for themselves at the earliest opportunity.

When holdings are sold, the proceeds may be moved into bonds, making the bond market a banker, so to speak, to the stock market. And during periods of stock market upset, money will be withdrawn from the market, making total market capitalization of all markets smaller and, of course, taking with it, the paper value of your stock holdings. Patience is rewarded, however, and when the stock market calms down, that money held away will come flooding back into the stock market pushing up all stock prices as stock price rises to create enough sellers to satisfy demand of those wishing to get back into the stock market.

Just to introduce an overall perspective to investing in common stocks, Russell, a creator of stock market indices, has a Russell Global Index that purports to track every global common stock, of which I counted to be about 10,000. Incidentally "global" means all countries including the United States and "international" means all non-U.S. issues. The Russell Global Index has had a total return of about 10% per year over the last 10 years with an annual dividend yield of about 2.71%. You can think about that as an investor baseline – a widely diversified portfolio of common stocks will return about 10% per year of which about 2.71% will be in dividends. As explained in other sections of this book, the term "Total Return" includes dividends whereas the term "Return" used without qualifier is a price-return only.

The S&P 500 is the standard broad U.S. market index created in 1957 but tracked back to 1789. From 1926 to the end of 2008, the 25-year total return, including a dividend yield of about 2.25%, has fluctuated between 7.94% and 17.25%. That volatility reflects annual returns that have fluctuated between -- -35.03% and +53.99%. At the end of 2011, the 25-year total return was 9.28% Now you know what all the shouting is about, but none of the shouting changes the outcome. All the Wall Street shouting does is report this information as news. But it's not news; it's the immutable investment dimension of life.

Wall Street actors will have you believe they will expose you to the upside while protecting you from the downside, but think about this – What is the S&P 500? It is not some third-party aggregate action that Wall Street tracks for investor convenience; it *is* Wall Street. The S&P 500 is what Wall Street produces. The S&P 500 index is what stock brokers actually got for their clients. That is what the record is and means. It is what happened on Wall Street.

As has been mentioned and will be mentioned again, Burton Malkiel, author of *A Random Walk Down Wall Street*, points out in his book that investors can bypass the Wall Street nonsense and just buy the S&P 500 index. I think this is good advice but feel that the Dow 30, another broad-based U.S.

equity index is more selective and may give a better result. Buying the discrete stocks included in the Dow 30 would be an even better option because there would be no fees and nothing getting in the way of stock splits and dividends.

Below, you have a graph showing the Price return performance of the S&P 500 since 1789 (source: Wikipedia).

In the past 20 years or so there has been a trend among technical graduates from MIT and other top technical schools moving to Wall Street rather than into manufacturing. These quantitative types have then applied their studies to stock market securities rather than figuring out how to make a new product or machine, and the results have ranged from the ridiculous to the sublime. At the ridiculous end is the pronouncement that the stock market is a perfect market and that stock price incorporates all that is known about a company at any given time and therefore the stock price is always, at all times, the correct price, leading to the rule that always is a good time to buy stock. This, of course, neglects 95% of other stockholders who have no interest in profiting or losing on day-to-day information and who probably don't know what the price is on any given day, or week, or month. The correct price? Utter nonsense. Stock price is mostly sentiment if even that.

Not All Gains Are Equal

On the sublime side of crunchkins working on Wall Street, in my opinion, comes the "Sharpe Ratio," named after William Sharpe, who as it turns out was a quantitative type from UCLA. Sharpe postulated that return can be characterized as low-risk or high-risk, and that low-risk return is the correct mantra. For example, I recall during the height of the tech-bubble in 1999, one could make as much money playing GE as Dr. Koop.com. Because GE having been a major U.S. business since 1892 could generally be considered a safer bet that Dr. Koop.com, which was an attempt to exploit all things dot com including a website supported by advertising revenue, it made more sense to play GE. The Dr. Koop.com thesis was that a website dispensing free health advice, such as smoking is bad for your health, would attract wide readership (visitors) who would then be exposed to advertising at the Dr.Koop.com website reaping huge revenues from the advertisers. Dr. Koop.com soon disappeared taking many investors dollars with it but not before turning in stellar profits for early players.

Profits in GE stock ownership were equally heady because it too was seen as a technology company, but it made a much safer investment in that tech bubble. Investors probably saw their investment cut in half instead of lost entirely as GE stock price resumed its old level after the tech bubble burst, while Dr. Koop.com stock price went to zero. In such a case, during the bubble, the Sharpe Ratio for GE gains would have been much higher than the Sharpe Ratio for Dr. Koop.com gains. The Sharpe Ratio is a measure of the quality of the gain as calculated by the amount of risk taken on to make those gains.

The Sharpe Ratio is calculated by finding the difference between the subject return and the return on a risk-free asset such as Treasury bonds and then dividing that difference in return by the volatility of the subject asset.

To illustrate, say that the return in both GE and Dr. Koop.com was 20%, a very nice return. Now look at the volatility called "Beta" of the two stocks as a percent deviation from an average price. GE would exhibit very little deviation around an average number because it is just not a fast moving stock – it is too big and too well known – so deviation around the average for GE might be 20%. Now look at the deviation around the average for Dr. Koop.com and you will see great volatility. There might be, for example, a news story on Dr. Koop.com prompting a flood of incoming money, followed by panic selling as unfavorable news on the issue is broadcast, followed by another in-wash as a Wall Street pundit predicts that Dr. Koop.com will hit $168 per share because it provides a fundamental service everyone can use. So in the case of GE volatility might be 20% whereas in the case of Dr. Koop.com volatility might be 50% or more. Now take those volatility numbers and divide them into the 20% return. For GE you have 20%/20% or a value of 1 and for Dr. Koop.com you have 20%/50% or a value of 0.4. So in this case the GE gain with a Sharpe Ratio of 1 is a dramatically better return that Dr. Koop.com with a Sharpe Ratio of 0.4, although the actual gains are equal.

This is an important point, that not all gains are equal although they may appear so, and that there was absolutely no advantage in putting money at greater risk for the same gain. This may also be further testimony against the silly notion that all stocks are correctly priced at all times. Also a word of disclosure: The detailed Sharpe Ratio calculation is more complicated. I have simplified it in the interests of communicating with non-MIT types like me. I like picking on MIT; it is so emblematic. I recall vividly Gov. George Corley Wallace of Alabama railing against those northeastern "Pointy-Heads" (PhDs), people from the northeastern academic community who did not sign on to the Governor's racist agenda. It was all politics. When racism didn't work anymore George Wallace changed his mantra.

Corporations are the Aggregate Personality of its People

Taking another look at the GE/Dr. Koop.com match-up, it is useful to think about management. After all, a company is a collection of people charged with making the best use of corporate resources, which are all things tangible and intangible that may be used to advance the fortunes of a company as a whole. Managing the effort of people who are managing the corporate assets is a job that takes not only vision and talent but also deeply rooted knowledge of the business and capabilities of its actors.

At GE, the process of developing an overall manager, a CEO, develops an infrastructure of management talent and know-how. The management infrastructure, not reported or even quantifiable in an annual report, is perhaps the most prominent part of the puzzle making up the company's future. But although it is not possible to gain much visibility into this infrastructure, knowing that such a management infrastructure process exists – as evidenced by long running success over many CEO tenures – is generally enough to guide investment decisions. One can only imagine that the management development of a hot start-up like Dr. Koop.com was pretty thin. Of course, great companies begin as such start-ups and in such cases the reporting made to acquire capital will focus on not only the product, but also the management talent.

As referred to earlier, companies are people organizations that spend their time trying to survive in a hostile environment by innovation. Innovation sounds as if it might be pretty easy to do, with the right people, but the problem with innovation is that it challenges the status quo. For example, in my post-college experience at Remington-Rand described in an earlier chapter, the market takeover of the office typewriter market by

IBM with the Selectric typewriter presented Remington-Rand with a challenge. How did Remington-Rand respond? They designed a new "same-old, same-old" typewriter. It seems they listened to themselves rather that the market. Also, I'm sure they couldn't admit to themselves that they had been bested by a rival.

Imagine the Remington-Rand executives convening a group to consider the IBM Selectric initiative and what to do about it. At Remington-Rand this was a recipe for groupthink: "Oh how great we are" became the mantra - in business since when? I'm sure the stock price didn't change much when Remington-Rand brought out the new Model 26, but the handwriting was clearly on the wall. The savviest investor could have pored over Remington-Rand annual reports ad infinitum but the real story was in the people – they couldn't react to outside change because they were too taken up with maintaining their internal positions.

It's probably not possible to get a sense of management culture out of an annual report unless you are looking for it. A more holistic approach is needed, which includes not only annual report study, but also examining how the company is responding to competitive challenges and broader technological challenges, like the replacement of office typewriters with PCs. The great companies are not so much responding to these challenges, as creating them. Indeed IBM had its brush with death when they got too committed to their mainframe computers in a world that was increasingly going PC. Then new management was brought in, presumably by the Board of Directors, and IBM changed course and recovered, building a business in which their old business forms a very small part.

You can imagine the pain that IBM must have endured in the transformation, and incidentally retraining thousands of loyal workers along the way. These are the companies you are looking for as investments, companies that can not only meet the challenge but also create the challenge. Apple is a supreme example, just cranking out product after product building its hegemony in the IT market. The question is: What is life at Apple like after Steve Jobs? Recently a major hedge fund manager with a large position in Microsoft called for the ouster of Steve Ballmer at Microsoft for the very reason discussed here: Steve's inability to see beyond incremental expansion of the present product lineup. As at Remington-Rand, incremental thinking won't get the job done that needs doing in a competitive world. The world is driven by the most intrepid actors.

An Example of Board Action

Looking at management and dramatic management changes is a good way to identify companies that may be poised for a growth spurt. Recently, for example, J.C. Penney (JCP) went on the outside to recruit a CEO from Apple, a decidedly higher tech business than a store retailing traditional J.C. Penney products. But the board of J.C. Penney decided that the prospective CEO had figured a way to sell Apple products in a "brick and mortar" setting, which is what J.C. Penney is, brick and mortar. This was a dramatic departure for the retailer and was expected to propel the fortunes of the company and the stock price – though one could not be sure in which direction. In the case of a dramatic move such as this, the stock market is a reliable gauge of the effectiveness of the move, as the collective intelligence of new investors bargain with existing investors in J.C. Penney to weigh in with their stock purchases or liquidations. In this case, the stock moved from $30 to about $35.50 before settling at about $34.20. So the market approved the move and rewarded the company with a 14% valuation increase.

The increase is what the market expects J.C. Penney to realize in profit growth going forward as a result of their changing the CEO to deal with the game-changing challenge of online purchasing. Here is an example of a board doing what they are supposed to do, assessing the needs of the company and taking action to address those needs even if it requires changing CEOs. Obviously where the CEO is also Chairman of the Board, this type of management change is more difficult.

The Survival of Iconic Brands

In considering corporations that have survived over many technological transformations, it is often difficult to see the market-winning skills in play. Sometimes the technological changes are more subtle. For example at Coca-Cola, the company has successfully responded to dramatic changes in packaging and distribution. Another major change felt by Coca-Cola has been the proliferation of alternative products, like juices, waters, high-energy drinks, and now coffees. Yet through it all, Coca-Cola remains ubiquitous.

The process at Coca-Cola (KO) doesn't receive much press, but you can be sure that a company that has maintained a winning position since 1886 has a process in place for developing not only management talent but employee infrastructure and as a company is not afraid to reinvent itself should the need arise. The objective is not Coca-Cola syrup, it is the Coca-Cola brand.

Sometimes a brand is taken on a wild ride but still survives owing to the staying power of the brand and the product it identifies. When Nabisco and Standard Brands merged, two outsized CEOs got into a wrangle over who was going to really take the helm. The company was later acquired by R.J. Reynolds, the tobacco company and the ensuing dustup eventually led to the takeover by essentially a hedge fund, KKR (Kohlberg, Kravis, Roberts). The private equity firm them sold off the pieces and what remained was sold to Philip Morris. Throughout all of this, Nabisco, has remained a flagship brand and is now owned by Kraft Foods. Ritz cracker, the flagship product goes back to 1934.

Another dimension to corporate survival is the environment

in which game-changing new directions are set. Is the new direction set because of eroding market share, and, if so, at what point is the change made, at death's door or as soon as new alternatives become visible? Remington-Rand was not quite at death's door when the type ball was rejected, but the trajectory of IBM was clear and the end-point although less clear was inexorable. IBM had a brush with death before bringing in Louis Gerstner as a direction changer.

Coca-Cola's greatest challenge was brought about by product innovation, namely playing with the original formula – they quickly backtracked. GE is wired for change, using a business matrix that identifies businesses seeming to be core competencies but are disposed of because they don't meet growth and profitability targets. You could say, at GE nothing is sacred but the brand. This is what you are looking for in investment candidates – devotion not to a product but to supremacy of the brand.

JC Penney: The Limitations of Research and Perhaps Thought

James Cash Penney began his retailing career in Wyoming in 1902 at the age of 27. JC Penney stores was incorporated in 1913 under the JC Penney name and grew dramatically seeing its headquarters moved to New York City to better facilitate purchasing, transportation and financing. A few years after Penney's death in 1971 the company reached $5 billion in sales and reached the limits of its expansion to 2,053 stores. Sam Walton began his career at JC Penney in 1940 before starting his meteoric rise in retailing as Wal-Mart. Today Wal-Mart is ranked 20 in the S&P 500. JC Penney is ranked 103. Nevertheless with 1200 retail locations in 50 states, Mexico, Puerto Rico and Chile, JCP is the largest US department store retailer.

Over the past 30 years, JCP has evolved from a wide product range Sears-like format to a greater concentration on apparel, selling off interests in cosmetics, drugstores, firearms and auto repair. The strategy seems to have worked as evidenced by a rise in stock price from around $11 in 2001 to $32 ten years later with about $6 per share in dividend distributions. A ten-year gain of $27 on an $11 share price works out to an annualized return of 13.2%. But perhaps more significant is that over that ten-year period, in 2007, the stock price reached a high of about $82. What happened?

Looking at a stock price chart from 1993 to 2013 you see that the last stock split was in 1993 and since then the stock price has been on a wild ride. Thinking it might be characteristic of department store retailing, I brought up charts for Macys and Kohls, thought to be JCP's direct competitors and saw similar charts. What happened apparently was department store retailing.

But the JCP story then began to appear to unravel. During a six-year period starting in 2005 the stock price declined from about $40 to $30 and then the former CEO Myron Ullman stepped down. In June 2011 it was announced that Ron Johnson from Apple would be the new CEO.

In a March 9, 2013 article, The New York Times reported on a suit against J.C. Penney and CEO Ron Johnson by Macys, brought on by J.C. Penney trespassing on Macys exclusive marketing arrangements with Martha Stewart. According to the article:" *J. C. Penney has been floundering – it recently reported a staggering $4.28 billion loss in sales for the year since Mr. Johnson became chief executive and announced the layoff of 2,200 workers this week. Its shares have dropped more than 60 percent. So the star-crossed Martha Stewart deal may not be its biggest problem.*" There have been calls for the board to act in firing Ron Johnson but as one hedge fund manager pointed out, there are only three possibilities: (1) a new CEO undoing Ron Johnson's work and returning JCP to its former mediocrity. (2) bringing in a new CEO to carry out Ron Johnson's program less well than Ron himself or (3) bring in a new CEO to try a new program for which JCP does not have a robust enough cash position to finance.

The compensation committee of the board is also being scrutinized by rating agencies finding fault with awarding the prior departing CEO an additional $10 million in compensation for several month's work in assuring a smooth transition and on top of stock options for targets not met.

So is JCP, around since 1913 and with a ranking in the upper quartile of the S&P 500 a good investment candidate? Vornado Realty, a REIT detailed in another part of this book, took a reported $250 million write-down to unload 10 million shares of JCP. Vornado may be assumed to be a very savvy investor and to take a loss must mean that they forecast even worse for JCP. There is even talk of bankruptcy. What is an investor to make of this?

With 1200 locations in 50 states and a highly recognized brand, I don't think JC Penney stores are going away although the public ownership of the stock may go away. My guess is that a group may take the company private in a Private Equity deal, turn it around and go public at some future date. This may be what Vornado sees and would rather sell at $15 than say $5 or even 5¢. As an investor, it is not the future of the company that hangs in the balance but the future of the stock.

Dollar-Cost-Averaging: Up and Down Aberrations

This book promotes the concept of passive investing into companies like JCP using Dollar-Cost-Averaging (DCA) and such a prescription will miss the outsize profits of Wall Street style opportunistic investment, but the core concept is that the "feast" offered by the JCP stock experience is first of all, uncertain and secondly, difficult to identify in the obfuscating world of Wall Street chatter. On the other hand, the investor's need for financing education, retirement and other urgent needs is a certainty, and it is far better to provide for certain needs by using certain solutions.

DCA through Troughs and Mountains

This episode with J.C. Penney stock also raises an important point about dollar-cost-averaging. In the Starbucks (SBUX) case discussed later, there was a stock price upset to the down side creating a stock-price trough or valley (chart of tracking stock price through time) through which dollar-cost-averaging would have resulted in an outsize accumulation of cheap shares – Good! An upset to the upside as in the case of J.C. Penney, however, would have resulted in a stock-price mountain in which dollar-cost-averaging would have accumulated a much smaller but still outsize fraction of expensive shares – Bad! Keep in mind that while this "good" episode for Starbucks (SBUX) dollar-cost-averagers was going on, the media and Wall Street was shouting "sell, sell, sell." Conversely, while the "bad" event was going on for JCP dollar-cost-averagers, the same Wall Street media machine was shouting: "buy, buy, buy." This topsy-turvy phenomenon is the reason the word "contrarian" has so much respect in the investment world. Contrarians do the opposite of what the Wall Street media machine is promoting. Warren Buffett, quoted elsewhere in this book, said: *"Be fearful when others are greedy and greedy when others are fearful."*

This criticism of dollar-cost-averaging not working for up-side upsets is justifiable, but over the life of a portfolio, having one or several positions experiencing this should not materially affect the overall result. What will affect the overall result is listening to and then acting on Wall Street punditry and that will have an investment result to the downside.

Dollar-Cost-Averaging, the Default Case

For the actual buying part of stock ownership, take a lesson from Bill Miller, Chief Investment Officer of Legg Mason, who once described his buying process as "munching" his way slowly into a position. Although Bill mentioned munching to give him time to focus and assess his position, the real way to munch is dollar-cost-averaging over a very long period, thus taking advantage of market lows. Dollar-cost-averaging, as illustrated above in the J.C. Penney case, is the practice of purchasing a fixed dollar amount of shares at regular intervals, like in a 401(k) plan taking bi-monthly deferrals to fund purchases. Both the regularity in time and the fixed amount of the purchases guarantees the greatest advantage being taken of the natural fluctuations that are characteristic of all stocks trading on public exchanges.

This staging of purchases has several corollary advantages. First, analyzing a stock position built over time by periodic purchases leads one to expect seeing something approaching a normal distribution in the prices of the stocks purchased over time, like a bell curve. That is, most shares purchased at medium prices would form the central hump while very cheap shares and very expensive shares would make up the two tails. Such a bell curve shape describes a totally random process. But dollar-cost-averaging is not random; it is stacked in your favor, so the curve that emerges is a hump of cheap shares to the left at the low price end of the curve, followed by a downward slope to the right to show a declining proportion of expensive shares, down to almost zero for the most expensive shares. Let's illustrate how this works. There are two ways to make periodic purchases of stocks: by a fixed share amount or by a fixed dollar amount. If I directed a trustee, for example, to buy one share of JCP every month, at the end of 3 years I would have 36 shares of JCP. As we have seen, JCP stock went on a wild ride and by buying 1 share every month, my account also went on a wild ride. On the other hand, if I directed the trustee to buy a fixed Dollar amount every month, say $30/month at the end of 3 years my investment would be 36 X $30 or $1080. Illustrated on the next page is the outcome in chart form.

Dollar-cost-averaging your way into a stock position will inevitably become a prominent component of your overall gain as your holding in this stock grows.

DCA Chart

	Early Period $10/share	Middle Period $80/share	Late Period $30/share	Average Share Price
1 share/month	12 shares X $10 = $120	12 shares X $80= $960	12 shares X $30 = $360	$1440/36 = $40/share
$30/month	36 shares X $10 = $360	4.5 shares X $80 = $360	12 shares X $30 = $360	$1080/52.5 = $20.57/share

Dollar-cost-averaging also refocuses the investor from concern over day-to-day volatility instead toward building a portfolio position in a well-considered stock that plays a diversifying role in a well-considered portfolio. In short, dollar-cost-averaging promotes long-term thinking, and long-term thinking leads to profit.

Remember that in portfolio management, unlike almost all other occupations, you are better served by doing less. This is both un-intuitive and a key problem of the investment industry today, what we call Wall Street.

The Wall Street hucksters, which are the media as well as the individual practitioners, can only gain revenue by promoting a constant churning of stock positions. The media sells papers and magazines, and the practitioners gain new accounts with the hot new stock. But this is not the foundation for sound investment and allowing yourself to be herded into frequent trading by the bandwagon effect will have a detrimental impact on your drive to build financial security.

In contrast, by its very nature, dollar-cost-averaging is a long-haul activity that is not driven by day-to-day stock price, but rather by thoughtful rumination about the long-term prospects of a business and a company serving that business. on the next page you will see that dollar-cost-averaging does not produce a "normal" distribution but rather an abnormal distribution in your favor.

Dollar-Cost-Averaging

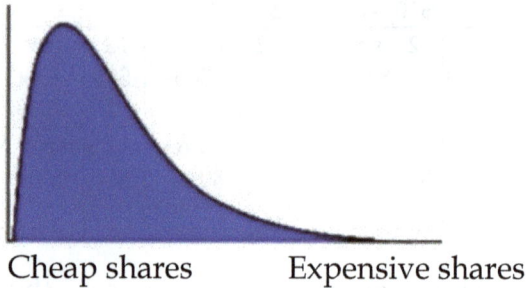

Cheap shares   Expensive shares

Notice that using the dollar-cost-averaging filter you sift out expensive shares and bias in cheaper shares, over time shares that you buy cheaply greatly outnumber shares you buy at a high price. Dollar-cost-averaging is also another way to diversify. The cornerstone of investment is diversification to spread your risk in a random process. Diversification is almost exclusively used to describe investment in multiple stocks but perhaps an even greater risk-dampening diversification move is to diversify over time rather than company or industry. For example, compare the risk of purchasing a portfolio of stocks at one time and purchasing the stock of just one company, say Procter & Gamble over a long period of time. If the market tanks, your entire diversified portfolio will be underwater, while your PG portfolio will be down but in all likelihood will have some portion in positive territory from cheaper shares acquired at an earlier time. Diversification by time is just as important as diversification by position.

But there is another reason to focus on dollar-cost-averaging, and that is orientation. If you purchase a block of stock, then all you have is one homogenous block to observe as it rises and falls on transient sentiment. You are afloat on a sea of doubt. With every rise comes salvation and with every fall comes agony. Too much agony and you pull the plug and lock in losses. When you dollar-cost-average you are building a position, and with every rise you take pride in your selection although this is accompanied by disappointment that your regular allocation buys so few shares and adds so little to your position. Later the stock falls but with it you see the opportunity for an outsized addition with which to grow your position. Now instead of being afloat in a sea of doubt, you are observing how wealth is created, over time, little by little. Market dips become sources of opportunity rather than prompters of doubt.

I argue that the benefit of 401(k) plan participation comes not so much from the tax treatment accorded non-Roth 401(k) plan contributions and withdrawals – a benefit I question – but from the power of dollar-cost-averaging. Keep in mind that through the darkest days of the 2008 market downturn, 401(k) plan participants continued to buy those bargain-basement shares, pretty much without realizing it.

Stock Selection the Overblown Parameter

Now that we have covered the issues of Wall Street culture, and are diversifying over the dimension of time, we turn to the subject of investing in stocks and bonds. The main thrust of this book is stock investing for capital gains as a means to stay ahead of inflation. Bonds do not fit this strategy, although it is possible to stay ahead of inflation with the very skillful use of bonds.

So we need now turn to the common stock of companies as an investment vehicle to stay ahead of inflation. Perhaps you can identify with a scenario where a buyer has just been convinced by a salesman's long and winding oration on the merits of a purchase.

The salesman's job was to give the buyer enough information to make the buyer confident in a purchase decision, but that level of confidence varies among different buyers with differing capacities to absorb technical information and digest it on the spot. In many cases, a buyer will simply throw up his or her hands and say "Okay. I'll bite." Of course this will not be the first time the buyer has used that phrase and in most cases, it has turned out okay, hence its continued use. This scenario describes most decision-making which takes place in the presence of uncertainty.

Very few decisions are open-and-shut cases. Instead, people bring the totality of their experiences, with all the biases and old-wives tales included, to bear on their decision-making. This is also the case with investing in the stock market, but with one glaring difference: congruence of objectives. A decision to purchase this or that car, for example, will put the salesman if not on your side of the table at least no more in opposition than off to the side. The salesman wants to make his commission but will want to satisfy the customer in the process. This is not the case with buying corporate stock; you are buying the stock from someone who wants to unload it because it is no longer attractive to them or they need to liquidate and selected their least favorite stock for liquidation. The question then is: Who is right, you or your seller? It will serve you well to regard the stock market as a battleground where you match wits with those of your opponent.

This means you need more information than what is contained in a salesman's oratory. But the principle remains the same – no matter how much information you obtain, and there is a steep cost to acquiring information, you will never reach that level of certainty to acquire the requisite confidence to call a decision "informed." The decision will always be a gamble.

What makes even the most studied stock purchase a gamble is the unknown, of which there are at least three: unknown stock, unknown future, and unknown you. But you have tools. You can buy stocks of companies that have a demonstrated track record of successful management and then use dollar-cost-averaging to tame the future and tame you, all while you accumulate a disproportionate number of cheap shares.

As the beginning investor struggles into investment mode, there will be an overwhelming focus on making the correct, or best buying decision. However, even this focus takes us off the mark. I would say that in company stock investing, more money is lost on the exit than the entry. Yes, entering stock purchase orders are mostly attended with doubt even when the stock has been researched to death, because at the end of the day, there is still great uncertainty – it is a gamble. Not so most sell orders. In such cases the seller feels great certainty that the position must be sold out – without question. Thus there is – to the investor – usually great doubt in opening a position and very little doubt in closing it. May I state unequivocally that this is 180 degrees wrong. Errors in opening a position can only be demonstrated with time and what that study of time will inevitably show is a chaotic line of ups and downs that may result in no gain after many months or even years. But the question is, what are you looking at? You are looking at transient investor sentiment on a tiny proportion of shares outstanding – you are looking at nothing.

If a stock is bad bet, then investor sentiment would cause the stock price to trace a generally downward sloping line. Why the annoying upswings in sentiment? Because there are multiple forces with multiple views; there are multiple buyers and sellers, and the only way to even out buyers with sellers, which must be done to fill all orders, is to adjust price – up to draw in more sellers, or down to attract more buyers . None of this has much to do with a company's performance, but much to do with demand for a company's stock, which is driven primarily by fleeting sentiment rather than any calculation on ability of a company to generate profits. Bad news brings out sellers but bad news is in no way more prone to accuracy than good news and we all know how accurate that is.

It is in the selling, not the buying, where real investment losses lie. Less time should be spent on researching a stock to buy and more time spent thinking about the consequences of selling. This will eventually lead to buying only stocks that are comfortably held during periods of volatility. But just acknowledging this fact is not enough; it must be felt, it must be instinctive, it must come from a view cultivated away from Wall Street and focused on people working inside corporations fully invested in what they are doing. One reason Remington-Rand may have gone down was the exit of more capable employees and managers seeing the writing on the wall for the inevitable slide into oblivion. This is a slow process as the more prescient find exits. As a stockholder, you must be prescient also and wonder: Are you holding a Remington-Rand or an IBM? How can you find out?

Fundamental vs. Technical Analysis

There are generally two accepted methods to evaluate the investment worthiness of company stock: fundamental analysis and technical analysis.

Fundamental Analysis

The first excludes transient buyer sentiment or demand and focuses on those dimensions that are likely to determine future success. Fundamental analysis parameters might be price/earnings ratio (P/E), PEG ratio, (P/E divided by growth rate), profitability, profitability trend (up/down), rate of growth, proportion of debt to assets, proportion of short-term debt to long-term debt, book value, receivables relative to payables, proportion of assets in cash or near-cash forms (liquidity), proportion of patents expiring if a research-driven company and status of patent applications, FDA approval status if a pharmaceutical company, and any and all information bearing on the near future earning power of the enterprise. Of course, all of these data points are in constant motion and not necessarily in one direction.

Many very well regarded investor sources talk up the value of fundamental analysis, but as does Burton Malkiel, I dismiss much of it while using the analogy of the flea. A flea can jump more than 50 times its length, an extraordinary feat. Fundamental analysis might lead to a very careful and thorough microscopic examination of the flea's anatomy but such study has never been able to explain the flea's jumping performance, even after 1,000 years of careful study. So looking at the anatomy of a stock may just be just as much of a distraction as studying the anatomy of a flea.

By studying the illustration below, the reader is invited to make a fundamental analysis of the flea and determine the origin of its unlikely ability to jump vast distances, well beyond what a human can do.

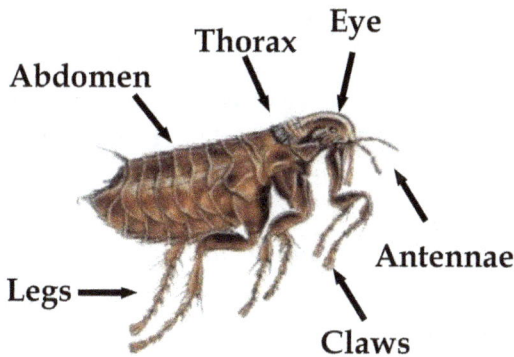

Technical Analysis

Technical analysis dismisses all fundamental information, and often awareness of the company identity itself, focusing only on stock price movement, and only on movement over the past few months at most. These stock studiers are often called "chartists" for their preoccupation of studying stock charts. And what are they looking for? Patterns, tell-tale patterns. Chartists will use such terms as double-bottom, head and shoulders, Bollinger bands, and saucers and spikes, to refer to patterns that have been demonstrated on occasion to forecast future movements. A key parameter chartists also use is relative volume.

Trading volume does not always lead to higher prices but

does indicate level of interest in the issue. So volume alone may not tell you very much, but increasing volume with price movement may be a good indicator of price direction. But in any case, chartists are typically shorter-term investors looking over a several month horizon at most.

Some investors fine-tune their trading on fundamental research by using technical analysis to time their purchases. Both fundamental analysis and technical analysis seem to have enough credibility to have a following, but not enough credibility for one to knock the other out of the box. In other words, results are mixed for both, or as my manager at a major brokerage once said: "*Nothing works very well.*"

This book is intended to build long-term wealth for education or retirement and as such, uses a horizon of 10-years or longer. Obviously technical analysis has little use in such an endeavor but even fundamental analysis is suspect. This point of view was espoused by Burton Malkiel in his investment "Bible," *A Random Walk Down Wall Street.* Malkiel points out that all fundamental analysis can do is point you toward the past; but where you need to look is toward the future, and there will be little help in doing that in fundamental analysis. In fact, Malkiel might have argued, fundamental analysis may be as much a distraction as technical analysis. This brings us nearer to the analytical method proposed by this book, but first a discussion about "top-down," "bottom-up" and sector analysis.

Top-Down and Bottom-Up Analysis

Almost all companies operate in markets populated with competitors who may be quite similar or quite distinct in product mix. Take, for example, McDonald's and Burger King. These two companies have almost 100% overlap in product mix, whereas Coca-Cola and PepsiCo overlap in only a few products. So the competitive landscape for each company is to some degree unique but also possesses some homogeneity.

Top-down analysis starts by looking at the broader market a company competes in and gradually drilling down to the company itself. So a top-down analysis of Coca-Cola would start by looking at the beverage industry in general, then look at PepsiCo and all other competitive beverage producers that encroach on Coca-Cola's market. For example, a gradual and global shift toward healthier fruit juices might suggest that Coca-Cola stock might be entering a downtrend unless Coca-Cola offers a line of beverages for the health-conscious, a market sub-segment of which you can bet the Coca-Cola management would be acutely aware. But in a top-down analysis, what will be missed are strategies internal to Coca-Cola in managing their competitiveness. Perhaps the formula for Coke doesn't need to change but the marketing strategy does, or the manufacturing process requires updating. Such things may be missed in a top-down analysis, which typically looks at external forces on a company, things like market share and pricing power.

Bottom-up analysis, as the name implies, focuses on forces internal to the enterprise. It asks questions such as the following. How competitive is the product mix and the product bundle? How effective is the management? Is the debt/equity ratio optimal and is it manageable through a market upset? Is there sufficient liquidity to meet expenses? Has the company demonstrated resilience to market forces? Is the company profitable and growing? Is the board made up of CEO cronies or outside advisors really capable and empowered to make change where needed? Answers to these questions would provide direction on investment worthiness. Moving from that granular look to a wider survey of the market sector and the broader market would be an example of bottom-up analysis.

To really be informed one would have to do a top-down analysis on a market sector and then do a bottom-up analysis on all the players, starting with those who have a large overlap in product mix and product bundle. Such a top-down and bottom-up analysis is much too much work, and in the end may not provide much direction, because the 100 or so parameters identified as pertinent, are all moving targets that will defy any kind of relational analysis.

Sometimes you will read a report on a company that will cite some promising aspect such as a product breakthrough, or strategic marketing partnership, or CEO change, and recommend a buy. No matter how long or how detailed that report, it omits other forces inside the company and many outside forces. It may be an interesting read, but that is all it is, a good read or for the thoughtful long-term investor, a useful data-point. The acid test of reports is how vital are they in the period following their distribution. The value of most brokerage research reports decay to zero in six months. Obviously for companies that have been in business for 25 years or more, such "reports," no matter how well researched, are fluff.

People who spend most of their waking hours scrutinizing companies for investment will start out reading a book like *Security Analysis*, by Graham and Dodd, and then purchase a position in a company over time, gradually drilling down from a cursory examination of all internal and external forces to a detailed examination. This is a quantity of information that will not be processed quickly, but rather take years to accumulate. Such investors also acquire their positions over years. There is no reason why the reader of this book cannot do the same. Pick out a few companies that are class leaders and start reading and investing, slowly but with growing confidence from long-term study.

Annual Reports

Publicly held corporations are required to file quarterly and annual reports. The purpose is to provide an unvarnished look at company operations for driving investment decisions in the case of investors, but also for the use of lenders, and all parties interested in taking a financial position in the company. As you might imagine, the people putting the annual report together are not interested in showing the unvarnished information and instead make liberal use of varnish to present as glowing a report as possible. This is supposed to be headed off by FASB, the Financial Accounting Standards Board enforcing GAAP rules (Generally Accepted Accounting Principles), but as in almost all regulatory cases, the regulatory organization winds up getting captured by the people they are regulating, and what you get as a result is a well varnished annual report.

Sophisticated investors know that annual reports are dressed up and are able to read between the lines to a degree, but piercing all the obfuscation is probably not going to happen except for the savviest of CPAs. To allay any investor doubt, the well-varnished report (which is all reports) will have a testimonial at the end by an "independent" auditor stating that the report has been examined and fairly represents the state of the company. The auditor is usually a prominent global firm, often one of the "big four." But whichever firm it is, it is paid by the company that it is auditing, and it is hard to imagine a company re-engaging a firm that offered a tepid view of the fairness of the report. Also, companies employ prestigious firms to give their annual reports added cachet. Enough said. When it comes to studying annual reports, consider them fiction and not an unbiased third-party assessment.

There are limits, however, to the amount of fiction that can be crammed into an annual report, so annual reports may be relied upon for some basic financial information. For example the data will show if the company is able to consistently grow revenue and earnings. The annual report will also discuss the general business climate and how the company is exploiting its assets to capitalize on the economic opportunities. Also, the annual report will give a full description of the business, with both product and geographical dispersion. The investor should also pay attention to the footnotes, which often contain the truth beneath the varnish, and also look for signs of under-funded pension costs that will ultimately drag the company down if not out.

As stated elsewhere, run away from "pro forma" items. This is a device undertaken for no other purpose than to lead investors astray. "Pro forma" sounds like it might mean a higher form or a more formal accounting. It is the opposite. It is what coulda, shouda, woulda happened, but didn't happen. It is a less formal, lower level of reporting that takes out non-recurring events like bad luck, that wasn't the fault of the company officers and therefore should not be counted – it is much like a child's game, where a miss is counted as a hit for a crying child who feels crushed by events. Forget the "pro forma;" look at what really happened. But keep in mind, the companies the beginning investor should be studying, such as GE, Caterpillar, Procter & Gamble, should not require information contained in an annual report for a go/no-go investment decision. Annual report study is for professionals able to wade through the nonsense on more obscure companies in consideration of major buys or even buy outs or in evaluating loan applications. Beginning investors need to focus on dollar-cost-averaging into perennial sector leading companies found by just being alert to the investment opportunities visible in every-day life.

Diversification

In general, companies may be viewed as either "cyclical," "non-cyclical," or "counter-cyclical," – or sometimes "semi-cyclical." When capital is cheap, the theory goes, companies are more apt to raise capital and invest that capital in growth. Since the largest companies are like ocean liners, not very maneuverable, among all companies they tend to grow the slowest even with quite revolutionary product development. This is because there is just too much inertia to move a revenue number that is already huge. Also, large companies are usually in strong cash position and aren't as vulnerable to changing interest rates. Small companies on the other hand, small-capitalization, and micro-capitalization companies, may see their revenue double or even triple in a year with a revolutionary new product. So during periods of easy money (quantitative easing in Fed-speak), smaller companies have access to capital to grow their businesses and they do so. Consequently small companies are usually thought of as in the "growth sector" or as being "cyclical," prospering or lagging with the economy. Other companies in a growth category would be ones that thrive on cheap money, by either borrowing that money to grow or making a product that thrives in a growth market, like luxury products such as boats.

Also affected by the cost of money are Publicly Traded Partnerships and LLCs, which distribute most of their earnings so must have access to cheap borrowed money for growth. When "quantitative easing" turns to "quantitative tightening," look for the growth sector to wind down as not only access to money is tightened, but also short-term investors sell out to look for more opportunistic placement of their money. As money tightens and becomes more expensive, opportunistic investors move to big companies that usually have a lot of cash on hand and can grow their businesses from internal resources. This is often called "flight to quality," and is accompanied by bidding up the stock prices of the target sector in response to supply and demand relationships.

Money has a limited number of places it can be stored: cash, near-cash, bonds, international sovereign bonds, real estate, art & collectibles, low-beta non-cyclical stocks, the broad market for stocks, international stocks, start-up stocks and that is about it. When interest rates are raised, look for the stock market to deflate as money moves into higher performing fixed-income securities. The same thing happens when real estate goes on a tear on the other hand, high interest rates and a sluggish real estate market directs money flows away from real estate to stocks and pumps up the stock market.

The cyclical in-and-out inhalation/exhalation of the availability of money has a parallel effect on market sectors defined by size or capital needs. Sectors include industrials, pharmaceuticals, transportation, banks, housing, and so forth, which may be made up of both large and small players. And there are other drivers than the cost of capital. If fuel prices rise, the transportation sector will be negatively impacted. If there is a grain shortage, food stocks will suffer, regardless of size. So in developing a portfolio of stocks, diversifying in various sectors keeps the drama down by spreading positions across diverse life-cycles, thus diluting whatever transient condition might crop up.

The Morningstar Style-Box Matrix

A very prominent organization serving the investment community is Morningstar, which offers research. It began by researching mutual funds but moved on to stocks as well. Morningstar is well known, perhaps best known, for its mutual fund matrix called "style boxes", which is like the BCG matrix. The Morningstar matrix is nine boxes that are differentiated somewhat differently than the BCG matrix but along the same lines: growth rate and capitalization size instead of market share (see the illustration).

Big Cap Value	Big Cap Blend	Big Cap Growth
Mid Cap Value	Mid Cap Blend	Mid Cap Growth
Small Cap Value	Small Cap Blend	Small Cap Growth

"Capitalization" or "Cap" is the total dollar amount invested in a particular company and may be calculated by multiplying the number of shares outstanding by the share price. Many internet financial pages will have summary pages that display this information. Just as an aside, to show that stock price has a life of its own, not infrequently a stock will be bid up in price without recognizing the implications for total market capitalization, and there have been cases where small cap stocks have been bid up nearly into large cap status, totally out of sync with reality.

The vertical axis of the Morningstar matrix is company size, or capitalization, and the horizontal axis is growth rate. So applying the BCG matrix to the Morningstar matrix, the lower right corner would be a "Question Mark" and the upper right corner would be a "Star," major market share in a fast growing market. The top left corner would be a "Cash Cow" as a dominant player in a static market able to spin off cash. The lower left corner is "Dog" territory, a declining company in a shrinking market. Some caution is in order in that this is not a direct overlap with the BCG matrix in that not all market structures will support big cap companies. It might be possible to have an entire and stable market made up of mid-cap or even small-cap companies.

The Morningstar matrix is not a perfect fit for the BCG matrix but it is a good attempt at segmentation along useful parameters. The reason for the disparity is that the Morningstar matrix was developed for mutual fund selection. As described in Chapter 4, a mutual fund is a professionally managed portfolio of stocks that may be all "Stars," "Question Marks," "Cash Cows," or "Dogs," or a blend of those components – thus the middle column, a blend of those characteristics in the left and right columns.

The middle column in the Morningstar matrix is side-to-side blending only, representing mutual funds that contain both slow-growing "value" stocks and fast-growing "growth" stocks. In the Morningstar Matrix , there is no vertical blending as in combining small-cap and large-cap stocks in the same fund. Size diversification is accomplished by selecting mutual-funds by capitalization: large, mid or small.

The value of the BCG and Morningstar matrices is that they can act as good diversification guides. As we have discussed, economic cycles attended by expanding and contracting interest rates will have quite different impacts on large and small capitalization companies and on the cyclical "growth" sector and non-cyclical "value" sector. The weakness of the matrices is that they may give the impression that they encompass the universe of stocks, but they don't. For example, utilities would occupy the center left box in the Morningstar matrix "Mid-Value" but utilities could react quite differently than other occupants of the same box. And the Morningstar matrix is of no value in looking for counter-cyclical stocks like McDonald's, Family Dollar, and Wal-Mart that thrive in bad times as more people shop in lower-cost stores and for lower-cost products.

When I was a stock broker or "Financial Advisor" my experience was that 90% or more of advisors put their clients into mutual funds. The standard practice is to use the Morningstar 9 style boxes as a guide and there were advisors I overheard saying their objective was to fill all 9 boxes. I have always felt that you could skip the center column as just a blend of the two outboard columns. But the core idea I think is good which is to diversify by parameters that are likely to provide diversification to many characteristics of the economic cycle which is more than just up and down interest rates. The big problem for the stock investor is how do you classify stocks to fit a Morningstar style box? Most if not all mutual funds prominently display their style-box position in all communication. This is not the case for individual stocks. Capitalization is easy, you can just look that up at Yahoo under "key statistics." The other diversifying parameter, growth rate is more challenging. In general you can use dividend yield. "Value" stocks distribute a dividend whereas "growth" stocks do not or may have perhaps a 1% dividend. So using capitalization and dividend yield, you too can fill the Morningstar style-boxes, but be aware, getting back to basics, it is very difficult to beat the S&P 500 and this means the box in the upper left corner.

Sector Analysis

In addition to stock market segmentation by BCG and Morningstar style-boxes and by "cyclical," "semi-cyclical," "non-cyclical," and "counter-cyclical" segmentation, companies also fall into other sectors that offer additional investment views and help develop diversification strategies, although each of the sectors has variability in elasticity to economic cycles within its ranks.

For example, "industrials," as opposed to "foods," is more cyclical, but within the "industrials" segment there is additional segmentation; defense stocks and construction stocks tend to move out of sync.

Defense stocks are driven by government spending on defense, which is mostly irrespective of general economic conditions and so is a good diversification move against the rest of the market. For example, General Dynamics (GD), a key defense contractor, is currently trading at a P/E of under 11 and paying a 2.7% dividend. Another defense stock is United Technologies (UTX) but only a portion of revenue is derived from Defense; it is trading at a P/E of around 18 and is currently paying a 2.20% dividend. Choosing between these two companies, I would prefer dollar-cost-averaging my way into General Dynamics as a diversification move against cyclical economic swings. Below is a sector analysis: drilling down into the consumer goods sector to coffee retailing.

SECTORS:

- Consumer Goods
  - Appliances
  - Beverages
    - Beer
    - Wine
    - Soft Drinks
    - Juices
    - Coffee & Tea
      - ❖ Starbucks (SBUX) – P/E 28, Dividend 1.29% - Wholesale & retail since 1971, 16,858 stores and sales in 50 countries – Revenue $11,190,000,000, profit 9.79%
      - ❖ Green Mountain Coffee Roasters (GMCR) – P/E 15, Dividend N/A – Wholesale & retail since 1981, supplier of Keurig single-cup brewing system – Revenue $1,910,000,000, profit 5.92%
      - ❖ Peets Coffee & Tea – P/E 41.35, Dividend N/A – Wholesale & retail since 1966 – Revenue $341,080,000, profit 5.85%
      - ❖ Caribou Coffee (CBOU) – 8.37, Dividend N/A – wholesale & retail, 534 stores, Since 1992, Revenue $289,220,000, profit 11.21%
      - ❖ Farmer Brothers Co. (FARM) – N/A, Dividend 2.70% - wholesale only since 1912 Revenue $451,670,000, profit (-11.73%)
      - ❖ Coffee Holding Company (JVA) – P/E 35.62, Dividend 0.60% - wholesale only since 1971 – Revenue $105,190,000, profit 3.10%
    - Water
    - Sports Drinks
    - Liquor
  - Electronic Equipment
  - Food

- o Housewares
- o Furniture
- o Apparel
- o Toys
- o Automobiles
- Conglomerate
- Technology
- Financial
- Services
- Healthcare
- Industrial Goods
- Utilities
- Basic Materials

As you can see, sector analysis is done in multiple levels and you may have to drill down several levels to get to a sector level whose constituents have enough overlap to act in concert to the economic cycle. Even in the above case of coffee, Starbucks relying mostly on single cup coffee sales will be less cyclical than Green Mountain relying in greater measure on sales of their Keurig coffeemaker which would be more cyclical.

Sector Rotation

There is a school of thought on Wall Street that gives credence to what is called "Sector Rotation." In this analytical technique, all common stocks are segmented by sector and then each sector is thought to move independently, up, down or sideways. Sector Rotation calls for rolling out of declining sectors and rolling into ascending sectors.

When I was a stockbroker I learned of a very successful broker in another office of our firm, who had refined Sector Rotation to a very high art – or science, depending on your view. He would be retiring before too long and so was heavily guarded by two lieutenants he had chosen to succeed him, gaining for them a nice book of built-in business, although they had nothing particular to offer on their own, which is why they heavily guarded him.

I listened to the broker go through an explanation of his method, which used an internet-based sector rotation service and in the course of showing me how he executed on the analysis, he cited gains that were clearly beyond what one might expect from the most diligent and inspired analysis. I was moved. I was offered no connection to his business and so drove back to my office full of new energy to employ this wonderful new tool in my prospecting for new clients. I was so affected that I reasoned that I would succeed in communicating my excitement and thus inspire the acquisition of many new clients. But later on the drive back to my office, doubts began creeping in. Then it hit me, if Sector Rotation was so great, why wasn't it more mainstream? By the time I got back to my office, I was totally deflated and merely went back to the phones with the same old story. Sector Rotation for me was just another Wall Street mirage.

The main objective on Wall Street is to get assets to manage and charge a management fee on. The various brokerage houses have very powerful computer platforms giving each broker incredible access to all sorts of sales ideas which have to have just enough credibility to work some of the time. There are portfolio analytics of all sorts and ways to slice and dice a portfolio by industry, by capitalization, by currency or whatever. Sector rotation is one such idea that proposes to slice and dice the market by sector and then doing data mining to prove some credibility. The paucity of solid scientific data leads brokers to see things that may or may not be there in order to come up with a sales theme. Often, the broker begins to believe very fervently in an idea not so much because the science is solid but more because he/she needs an idea. This is what appeared to have happened to the sector rotation gentleman, he had found something most brokers didn't use, so for him the magic of sector rotation is that he was one of the few that used it and it had some logic to it, why wouldn't some sectors be more cyclical than others? So he had an idea and logical chatter to go along with it and from this he had built a sizeable book of business.

His inspiring presentation to me was designed to bring him clients we could share. I would have something solid to sell and he would have more clients. It was perfect, except that by the time I got back to the office I no longer believed the magic. If sector rotation consistently outperformed the S&P 500, everybody would be using or know about it. Sector rotation would be part of broker training, it would be on the Series 7 exam. Sector rotation was none of these. Sector rotation just happened to be that broker's mantra that allowed him to offer a sales thesis with conviction that perhaps only he had and may have been shared by his two lieutenants. In brokerage house lingo, sector rotation was his value proposition.

The Power of Stock Splits

The interesting thing about coffee is that it represents both cyclical and non-cyclical stocks. Starbucks went through some dramatic management changes that saw the founder leave the company and then return when things were going south and succeed in once again establishing Starbucks as a global leader in coffee. So that stock price in the case of Starbucks was counter-cyclical as it played out its own drama. See chart below from 1991(source: Starbucks website).

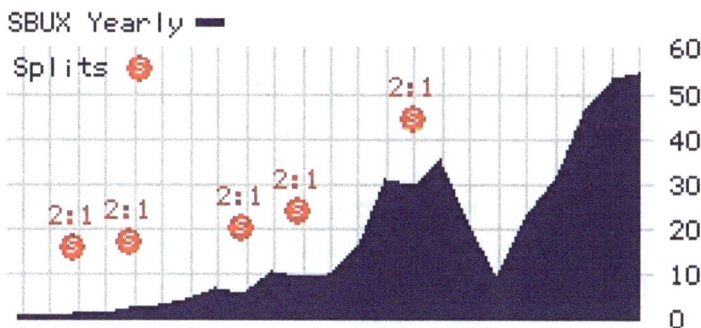

A note about charts is relevant here. Stock splits are shown on charts by reducing the line trace prior to the split – in half for a two-for-one split – making the rise in price look more dramatic than what appeared to earlier investors. The price rise was dramatic but not so visible as it is in a backward looking chart incorporating stock splits.

For this reason it is best to use interactive charts that compare the stock with, say, the S&P 500 index. Only then can you get a useful picture of the growth in stock appreciation and then only if you do the mathematical calculation of annualized return based on a starting and ending value.

There is another dimension to splits that needs to be discussed – the value of splits. Most companies want stock price to reflect success without being priced out of the market. Many investors will pass up a stock if it is too expensive. Typical NYSE stock price is around $45 per share or a range perhaps from $30 to $60. As share prices get bid up on account of increasing corporate performance, inflation, and investor confidence, the share price will eventually reach a stage considered to be out of the "sweet spot" for most investors and the stock will be split, often 2 for 1, that is one share of a $70 stock becomes two shares at $35 per share.

The value of the split lies in the fact that people buy shares of stock by individual stock price rather than by total company capitalization. In other words stock price has a life of its own and that being the case, you are better off with twice as many shares.

Starbucks; An Entrepreneur's Story

The Starbucks stock price began to slide in 2006 and went from $35/share down to about $10/ share over the next two years.

Howard Schultz, the apparent luminary of the company had left in 2000 but returned to restore the company's fortunes in 2008, which seems to be the point when stock price reversed and began its two-year recovery. The stock apparently rose 8% on the day he was named new CEO.

What Howard Shultz did to spur the recovery was to return the company to a customer-centric focus from a bureaucracy that had moved the company away from its roots. Reportedly Shultz received a standing ovation from a group of 4,000 composed largely of employees when he first returned. There seems to be no question that Shultz has the vision and energy to manage the Starbuck's business, but what happens after Shultz? What would have happened had Shultz not returned? I don't think there are answers to those questions, but I nevertheless like the stock because despite all of the troubles no competitor moved into the space vacated by Starbucks during its four-year slide and recovery. This seems to have been a case where the absence of competition almost killed the company off.

So is Starbucks a "cyclical, "semi-cyclical," "non-cyclical," or "counter-cyclical?" Well Starbucks is first of all, the cup of morning joe that everybody needs to kick-start the day. So in this respect, it is a "non-cyclical." But Starbucks coffee is expensive relative to a 7-Eleven store coffee, for example, so during tough times, one would expect some trade off. In this respect there should be some amount of cyclicality in SBUX.

Here's how I came to like Starbucks. As a young salesman in the '70s, I spent many days on the road driving from morning until evening, and each day usually began with a stop at a Greek diner to get a cup of coffee-to-go in that iconic blue and white paper cup with the Greek column motif. I think I probably got two or three cups of coffee-to-go per day in those days and if I had passengers, they did the same and usually at a Greek diner. Then along comes Starbucks but I was at a point in life where I didn't drink much coffee anymore and so I missed out on the coffee revolution brought about by the firm, which now included an inviting array of bakery items and at some pretty fancy prices.

One morning not too long ago, around 6 AM I had a passenger who wanted his morning joe and since I had been away from it, I had no clue where to get it. As we drove on in the darkness I saw lights up ahead in a strip mall, and I slowed, thinking maybe there would be a Greek diner. It was a Starbucks! The entire strip mall was in darkness except this one Starbucks shop, with lights burning brightly and half a dozen cars parked outside. My passenger got his coffee and seemed not at all put out by the price, just happy to get it. As I drove on, I got to thinking that Greek diners were becoming a thing of the past and I even noticed that the last one I had visited, the Silver Star, was almost empty. I asked the proprietor what happened to his business. He didn't really know. The market changed. People no longer have time for a leisurely breakfast while reading the paper, everything is on the go. Starbucks saw that and the proprietors at Greek diners didn't.

The country changed. The idea of stopping at a Greek diner for a couple of eggs over easy with home fries and coffee has been replaced by a Starbucks latte to go with a pastry. And the most astounding thing about this is that only Starbucks is doing it. Do I need an annual report to decide if Starbucks is a good investment? I don't think so. What I am investing in is not Starbucks, but the propensity of the U.S. adult population to start their day with their morning joe, even before they get to where they're going for a cheaper cup – they have to have it now. And if they are not in a hurry, Starbucks offers a place to meet and read the paper or catch up on some paperwork. Howard Shultz figured out what people wanted and gave it to them.

But getting back to the purpose of sector segmentation, you can see that drilling down through market sectors does several things. First, it is a good way to start thinking about diversification. Second, it is a top-down style of analysis that invites you to consider a rank of companies before focusing on any single one as an investment candidate. You will not be able to devote much analysis to each one so picking your candidate early from among the field will allow you to build a case not so much for investing in the company as holding it through bad times as well as good.

Witness Starbucks' wild ride. How many people got disgusted with Starbucks when the stock price began its two-year slide and bailed out with a loss sure of what they were doing? What were the Wall Street pundits saying about Starbucks stock? How badly were dollar-cost-averaging investors hurt by the downturn? Notice that the stock had split 2 for 1 five times before the downturn, so say you began with 10 shares in 1991. The first split left you with 20, the second split with 40, the third split with 80, the fourth split with 160 and after the fifth split you would wind up owning 320 shares from your original 10 shares. If that is not impressive enough, consider the dollar-cost-averaging investor who kept on buying during the four-year slide and recovery – there were a lot of cheap shares there. So the Wall Street view would have been to get in, get out and then get in again. Please reflect for a moment on the differences in wealth accumulation between following the Wall Street pundits shouting "sell" and the dollar-cost-averaging investor who stayed the course the whole time because he or she thought 1) that coffee wasn't going away anytime soon, and 2) that Starbucks does coffee better than anybody else from 5:30 AM to 9:30 PM at 17,000 retail outlets in 50 countries. Or think about the dollar-cost-averaging investor who never bothered to look at their statements – they just kept on investing. Also think about this: How difficult would it be to switch a Starbucks coffee drinker to say 7-Eleven, Dunkin Donuts or McDonald's? It won't happen. Starbucks, like 7-Eleven, Dunkin Donuts and McDonald's, has established its market of devoted customers. Very simply, what would have happened, did happen to devoted dollar-cost-averaging Starbucks investors; They wound up with a big chunk of change with no more effort than ignoring the Wall Street chatter.

The Coffee Sector and Diversification

Looking beyond Starbucks at the other coffee stocks, Caribou comes closest to the Starbucks business model but is not serious competition, which may not be a good thing for Starbucks. It may have been precisely the lack of direct competition that temporarily sunk Starbucks and could be its future undoing – Shultz can't go on forever.

Green Mountain looks like an interesting company first of all in growing a business in the already crowded specialty coffee business but also then in rolling out the Keurig single-cup coffee brewer that uses competing coffees in its K-cups, which is becoming ubiquitous in corporate offices as well as homes and now even hotel rooms. The Keurig seems to be building a lock on how coffee is brewed at home, at work and now, while traveling. Another differentiator for Green Mountain is the impressive depth of its management team. Starbucks has Howard and Green Mountain has a team with very targeted resumes that include experience at perhaps the world's greatest marketer of consumer goods: Procter & Gamble.

But Green Mountain and Starbucks are sufficiently different to offer diversification within the coffee space. Of course, they will probably move in lockstep in response to market risk, but as has already been seen they will move quite differently in response to company risk. And because Starbucks is international and Green Mountain is mainly domestic, they will move differently in response to country and currency risk. So the two companies look like good investment candidates for companies that will have low-elasticity to almost any source of market upset, even famine and war.

Shown below are other common diversification parameters.

- Beta (volatility)
- Capitalization

- rate-of-growth
- sector
- cyclicality
- competition (market structure, monopoly or perfect competition)
- organization (C-corp or Partnership)
- Currency

As has already been alluded to, another diversifying variable is the source of risk. Most people think only of company risk: Will a company flourish or fail? But there is also market risk – that the whole market will decline. And there is currency risk, tied to country risk. For example, a national recession or inflation or even public disorder will prompt reaction in currency valuations. And there is weather risk – a prolonged drought can mean high grain prices affecting food stocks and water stocks or storms can wreak economic havoc to a locality. There might also be other risk factors that can be included in thoughts about adequately diversifying. These risks are often hedged with investments in other asset classes, such as commodities and bonds.

One may think of almost any company, particularly a coffee company, as being invested indirectly in the commodity markets and so reflecting the commodity markets themselves. This, of course, is very true of the petroleum companies, and together with companies that are vertically integrated like paper companies that own forests.

When Henry Ford began offering the station wagon with a partially wooden body, he bought a forest of hardwoods in northern Michigan to supply his factories. Companies sometimes integrate vertically as a growth strategy.

Commodities

Some commodities can be thought about as diversifiers or hedges against multiple upsets. Gold has long been considered the ultimate store of value, attracting much investment during periods of uncertainty and strife. This brings into focus a key differentiator between commodities and corporations: gold is gold and you don't have to concern yourself with company risk. What you are hedging with commodities, particularly gold, is global risk. As the economy goes global, gold will become a globally driven store of value.

Commodities may be segmented as follows:
- Energy
  - Gasoline
  - Heating oil
  - Coal
  - Nuclear
- Precious Metals
  - Gold
  - Silver
  - Platinum
  - Palladium
- Base Metals
  - Copper
  - Aluminum
  - Zinc
  - Lead
  - Nickel
  - Tin
- Agricultural
  - Corn
  - Wheat
  - Soybeans
  - Cattle
  - Hogs
- Softs
  - Coffee
  - Cocoa

- o Sugar
- o Cotton
- Alternate Energy
- o Solar
- o Wind
- o Fuel Cell
- o Biofuels
- Strategic Rare Earths

Looking over the list, you can see that a portfolio of common stocks would include exposure to most of the commodities listed – sometimes directly as in an investment in Exxon Mobil, but sometimes indirectly as in Exide supplying lead-acid batteries since 1888. But if you feel that to realize a profit you have to jump the food chain, you can invest in mining companies like BHT Billiton, or the metal processors like Arcelor-Mittal Steel or Alcoa Aluminum. And getting ore to where it is processed usually involves ships and rail, which is another way to gain exposure to commodities.

The reason to invest in commodities is that, as has already been mentioned, they are pure plays and not filtered through management structures as is the case with Starbucks. Commodities move pretty much on demand for raw material, which earns them the designation, "Basic Materials." But most materials are cyclical and elastic to economic swings. Moreover, keep in mind that commodities don't produce dividends and stock splits and for that reason are generally not good long-term investments. Also commodities investors invariably find themselves glued to some media outlet to get out before disaster strikes. You can avoid the paranoia and just invest in the common stocks of the Dow 30.

Water has been mentioned at another place in this book as an inescapable commodity on a collision course with population and pollution, but there are also several others that fit into the urgent category. One is the nuclear power generation fuel uranium, which is mined by a company named Cameco and several others – though the recent events in Japan have clouded the nuclear power picture. On the other hand, the buildup of greenhouse gases and the collateral effects they are believed to be causing is an equally unhappy end predicted for non-nuclear fossil-fuel power generation. Given this crosscurrent of conflicting public opinion you can probably count on a vector somewhere between nuclear and fossil fuel but almost assuredly more of both. In such a conflict of public opinion, alternative energy sources are slow going, but also inexorable.

The wind market seems to be more or less made up of six major players, the large industrial conglomerates GE and Siemens, and the small but dedicated companies whose entire fortunes are dependent upon wind power: Vestas of Denmark, Gamesa of Spain, Suzion of India, and Goldwind of China.

Reading the Wall Street chatter will only confuse and lead to misconstruing the investment potential of this sub-sector. Siemens and GE are large enough and have enough overlap with other complementary business sectors to be in the game as long as they want. As already discussed, if GE is in the business, it is because it meets growth and profitability targets, so the smaller players can bask in a fast growing and profitable market being developed by the giants. Also, the smaller players are large enough to stay in the game, perhaps being acquired by the giants as an exit strategy. The table below gives the trend in market share for the more prominent players:

COMPANY	2006	2008	2011
Vestas (Denmark)	28%	19%	12%
Gamesa (Spain)	18%	11%	7%
GE Wind (USA)	15%	18%	10%
Suzion (India)	8%	7%	6%
Siemens (Germany)	7%	7%	5%
Goldwind (China)	3%	4%	10%

One of the takeaways of this table is the national character of the business. Europeans will buy from the Danes, the Spanish, or the Germans as a rule. And having spent time selling to the Germans, I can tell you the Germans will, in all likelihood, buy strictly German.

India will buy India and China will buy China. The United States will buy from all, being the open market landscape that we are. So in terms of investment potential in wind, I would select out GE and Siemens as having too small a wind component in their profiles to reflect the wind opportunity in their stock. Vestas, is a good candidate for being first of all a pioneer and a proven market leader in a brutal competition. Although the erosion of market share for Vestas is worrying, this is because the technology is not all that specialized, prompting a proliferation of new entrants. But the data to remain focused on is the growth in the overall market, the continuing profitability as evidenced by GE participation, and the eventual shaking out those fringe players that will either go out or be acquired. If this market follows historical precedent, in the end there will be two major global suppliers and two or three niche suppliers. Vestas, I suspect will survive in part because of national pride on the part of the Danes.

The opportunity here is a fast growing position in a non-cyclical segment, a very compelling case. Vestas is not listed on any U.S. exchange but is available as an ADR at BNY Mellon (VWDRY) (explained below).

A word of warning may be in order here. One might extrapolate from the above data that Goldwind is the best candidate. But as discussed elsewhere, China investments are subject to the whims of the Chinese leadership and what they may decide to do in the future is, well, inscrutable as the Chinese themselves. There are, of course, no absolutes, but there are plenty of investment candidates, so one doesn't need to go looking in totalitarian countries like China and Russia for investment candidates.

Offshore Companies

In looking to offshore companies for investment, you have some choices besides locating companies listing directly on the NYSE. One choice is mutual funds and index funds that hold or track offshore issuers, and another option are ADRs, American Depositary Receipts. That is not a misspelling; the word is "depositary." Companies that don't want to list in the United States may engage a U.S.-situated financial firm to "sponsor" ADRs by holding a block of the stock and then issuing shares of that block in U.S. dollars. There are four sponsoring financial firms as of this writing: Deutsche Bank, Citigroup, Bank of New York (BNY) Mellon, and JP Morgan.

There are various levels of ADR and some investigation may be merited, but you can short-cut this by just focusing on the better known companies, for example, Deutsche Bank sponsors ADRs for Akzo Nobel, Credit Suisse (trades on NYSE), Fiat Spa – the Italian automaker – and the German software giant Sap AG, just to name a few. Generally the shares trade in the United States at par with their home markets, but there can be variances.

To locate ADRs, just visit the websites of the firms listed above. Deutsche Bank offers, in addition to a stable of ADRs, access to a Direct Investment Plan (DRIP) whereby you can sign up online and then dollar-cost-average through their service that includes an election to reinvest dividends. There are fees for this service, however; it looks like 6 cents per share plus a $2.50 purchase fee, a $15.00 sales transaction fee, and a 2% dividend reinvestment fee. The minimum initial purchase is $250.00 so that the transaction would wind up costing, for 10 shares of a $25 stock: $250 + $15 + $2.50 + $0.36 = $267.86, or 7.14%, which seems a pretty expensive way to buy stock. Many DRIP plans (discussed in Chapter 10) are free with free dividend reinvestment. Some even offer discounts. Capital One ShareBuilder charges $12 for 12 program trades with free dividend reinvestment.

ADRs come in several flavors having to do with gaining access to the U.S. market for raising capital in return for meeting U.S. reporting and listing standards. A company may not wish to meet U.S. reporting standards because they are already reporting to the standards set by their home country, and find a second set of standards too burdensome. There has been underway a movement to unify various reporting standards around the world, but the effort seems to have gone nowhere.

The last time I looked, Japan had the most stringent reporting requirements. Also, many years ago a CPA who was preparing our company's reports told me in casual conversation that UK standards were more rigorous than American standards. In any case, at the lowest level, you have unsponsored ADRs, which may be issued by multiple banks. Sponsored ADRs come in several flavors as well, and again balancing the need for additional host country reporting with the need to raise capital in the host country. The lowest level are simply U.S. issues of foreign stocks by one of the above four listed issuers. Both the unsponsored and what are called "Level I" sponsored shares trade on the Over-the-Counter (OTC) market. Level II ADRs meet American reporting requirements and are then traded on major American exchanges, NYSE, etc. Level III ADRs are permitted to raise capital in the U.S. by issuing new shares. Also arguing in favor of Level II and Level III ADRs is that they must meet the listing requirements of the exchanges they are listed on, which may winnow out some shares you would rather not have access to. But my experience has been that ADRs, by and large, are issued for major offshore corporations, in all levels. Nevertheless, sponsored ADR shares are easier to locate and research.

It may be possible that I never encountered a questionable ADR because I always began my search from looking at a company thesis and from there drilling down and finding out it was only available as an ADR. This is case for Nestle, for example, a global powerhouse in food founded in Switzerland in 1866. The following is a partial list of Nestle brands: Gerber baby food, Poland Spring, S. Pellegrino and Perrier waters, Butterfinger, Crunch and KitKat candy bars, Maggi, Stouffers, Coffee-Mate, Dreyer's and Haagen Dazs ice creams, Carnation condensed milk, Lean Cuisine, Alpo pet food, Jenny Craig and, of course, the flagship brand, Nestle. Nestle is not listed on any major U.S. exchanges and trades in the U.S. as either an unsponsored ADR or a Level I ADR, and may be purchased in the Over The Counter (OTC) market trading under the symbol (NSRGY.PK). Nestle is an outstanding investment candidate and a visit to the investor section of their global website is well worth the time.

Examples of Level III ADRs trading on major exchanges are two good stocks: The British telephone company Vodafone (VOD) and the Brazilian oil company Petrobras (PBR).

As mentioned earlier, many ADRs trade in the Over-the-Counter market (OTC). Like the ADR system, the OTC also has a multiple tier system for identifying companies that provide more and less disclosure. Companies wishing full access to the U.S. markets, just for capital raising, are likely to be larger companies with sufficient trading volume to merit listing on one of the U.S. exchanges, typically the NYSE. But some major companies choose not to for some reason and Nestle is one. If companies don't intend to raise capital in the market, but just allow their shares to trade, they may see the additional NYSE reporting as a burden and prefer the OTC market. Then there are lower-tier OTC securities that simply don't do a very thorough or timely job of reporting, and simply use the OTC for convenience. One other characteristic of ADRs worth noting is that they are not always offered one-to-one, but may represent multiple shares of the underlying security.

The tiers at the OTC are as follows. QX is the highest tier and most likely used by companies not wishing to raise capital, therefore choosing not to undergo the extra work to meet NYSE or NASDAQ listing requirements. The next tier down is QB, which is made up of companies that provide full disclosure but don't meet the more rigorous requirements for QX listing. The last tier down is the Pink Sheets tier, composed of companies with a range of reporting deficiencies from quite minor to not providing any information at all.

OTC listings are also identifiable by their strange symbols, which may be five letters followed by a period and two more letters. The symbols are issued by the Financial Industry Regulatory Authority (FINRA), the watchdog financial services agency.

The fifth letter is more significant than the others and may mean, in the case of "Q," that a bankruptcy filing has been made. A foreign issue will have an "F" as the fifth character.

For example the symbol for an ordinary share of Nestle is NSRGF.PK. The letter "Y" in the fifth position means the issue is for an ADR, and so Nestle may also be listed as an ADR as NSRGY in the Pink Sheets tier. This is a clear case of one of the world's great companies simply not wishing to meet listing requirements and satisfied to be listed in the lowest tier of the U. S. OTC market. To further investigate the OTC, you can visit an excellent website: www.otcmarkets.com.

Stock Symbols

It might be useful to cover the subject of stock symbols very briefly. At one time brokerage offices had a machine that spit out a constant flow of market pricing information on a continuous paper tape. The machine was called a stock ticker and the tape containing the up-to-the-second action at the stock exchange was called ticker tape. The volume of such tape was so great that there arose the expression "ticker-tape parade." Returning U.S. heroes were driven up one of the major New York City avenues in a convertible and office workers would disgorge shredded ticker tape out the windows showering the returning hero in the laurel of that day – stock prices.

Ticker tape was replaced by electronic boards but the

moving stream of prices at the bottom of the screen is often still called a tape. In any case, to compress information down to its most compact form, symbols were decided upon to identify the stocks of companies, thus giving rise to the term "stock symbol," or "ticker symbol." The first major stock exchange was the New York Stock Exchange (NYSE) and so perhaps they got to pick first and listed all companies with one, two or three letters. Ford Motor Company is "F," Citigroup is "C." Most NYSE symbols are three letters but there are some two-letter symbols like "AA" for Alcoa Aluminum and "PG" for Procter & Gamble. Otherwise three-letter symbols usually mean a stock on the NYSE or perhaps the American Exchange known as the AMEX.

Four letter stock symbols usually denote the NASDAQ market and are generally younger and faster growing companies, but contain some large companies that began on the NASDAQ but over the years became more like cash cows, companies like Intel (INTC) and Google (GOOG).

Five letters usually denote an ADR, an off-shore company traded on the Over-The-Counter market. But some ADRs trade on the NYSE and carry three-letter symbols. In the end, however, which exchange the stock trades in hardly matters except that NYSE, AMEX, and NASDAQ do have thresholds that can act as a filter to keep out more speculative issues. There are also other exchanges and, of course, other major off-shore exchanges like the London Stock Exchange which is the third largest in the world but provides access to many global shares that are not available in the United States. Persons in our country wishing to purchase shares available in London but not New York may be able to do so cheaply at the U.S.-based Interactive Brokers. Otherwise these overseas issues not available in ADRs can be purchased by mainstream brokerage houses but usually in threshold levels of $10,000 or more and at perhaps $1,000 or more in commissions.

Investing for the Long Term

In this chapter we have discussed ways of looking at companies as investment candidates and the value of dollar-cost-averaging into a position to take advantage of the natural fluctuations that occur in markets due to country risk (interest rate movements), company risk, and the effects of competition. We have also examined sectors such as cyclical and non-cyclical sectors and then drilled down to look at coffee and wind power, both pretty non-cyclical but cyclical in the sense that coffee is really a non-essential and wind power is an alternative to a needed commodity – there is plenty of power without wind-power. Nevertheless they are both compelling investment candidates.

As you move into stock research mode, think about sectors and cyclicality and market structure. Water has already been mentioned as a looming case of global shortage. Veolia, a French company has a prominent global position on water. Another interesting sector is infrastructure, toll road operators and other infrastructure contractors. As families continue to struggle in two-earner households with little time, food preparation becomes a challenge. Who is recognizing and serving this sector. The population is aging, how is this going to play out?

Markets are not created but discovered. And when an entrepreneur discovers a new market, soon he is followed into the business by me-too entrants, and after a scuffle that may last a few years, the market settles down to the suppliers who are left after the dust settles. This leaves most businesses in a market populated by several or more competitors that are differentiated enough to define a customer base – Coke and Pepsi drinkers, if you will. This is market structure that reaches equilibrium, which is the case with most markets.

Market structure in a top/down analysis is a good way to get started putting together a portfolio. I have listed below investment candidates I like and why. Use this list or make up one of your own; begin to think about units inside a diversified portfolio and which unit has the strongest fundamental market position.

Dismiss all market chatter as being irrelevant and, of course, dollar-cost-average your way in. Of course, you can skip all of this research and just buy the Dow 30, a subset of the S&P 500, a subset of the 100 greatest global corporations, and get as good or better result. For all practical purposes, as long as companies are all staffed by Homo Sapien Sapien, it doesn't much matter which companies you pick.

What do you do if you can't dollar-cost-average because you have a lump of money to invest? This is a difficult question because DCA a is such a powerful force in harnessing the power of the market. If the market is in a down phase of the business cycle, just deploying a lump into a dozen or more positions seems to be a pretty safe thing to do, but if the market is closer to the top of the economic cycle the challenge becomes greater. In such a case diversification by position is still indicated but informed by a more opportunistic search for stocks going thru an out-of-favor phase that would represent bargain buying.

Below are stocks that at their lows might make very good bargains. If you are not sure they are at a low, compare the moving averages of their stock price, like say a 50-day moving average against a 200-day moving average. If the 50-day average is below the 200-day moving average, the stock may be a bargain at the price in consideration of its future promise. But be careful with this technique and use it only companies you are interested in due to their prominent position in the markets they serve.

• Procter & Gamble (PG) is a company that seems to shun the limelight and just concentrate on churning out winners, decade after decade. P&G has been a perennial leader in consumer goods marketing doing something few companies can do, creating new iconic brands as they go. This would be a non-cyclical stock. Dividend 3.20%.

• Illinois Tool Works (ITW) since 1912 has been acquiring manufacturing businesses but keeping them independently managed to be closer to the customer. This is a unique strategy among industrials and offers good exposure to a cyclical market. Also ITW offers a DRIP program. Dividend 1.80%

• Coca-Cola (KO) has been the real thing since 1892. I have been privileged to have traveled to many third-world countries all over the world, and wherever I have gone, in the remotest regions, the ubiquitous Coca-Cola sign is always present, sometimes dented and dusty, but always present. This is a good non-cyclical. Dividend 3.00%

• Johnson&Johnson (JNJ) There is no company quite like J&J, ubiquitous in medical supplies but also with a pharma and medical device dimension. This really is a company the world cannot do without. A non-cyclical with a dividend of 3.70%

• Schlumberger Ltd. (SLB) since 1912 has been a standout oil field services firm throughout its history. Schlumberger is the quality leader in a high-tech and evolving field. Dividend 1.20%

• Veolia (VE) created in 1853 as Compagnie Generale des Eaux (water) has been growing into the world's leading environmental and infrastructure management company. Invest in water, the globe's best non-cyclical. Dividend 4.00%

• LVMH Moet Hennessy Louis Vuitton (MC.PA) since 1854 has acquired almost every luxury brand there is that is not already owned by L'Oreal.

• L'Oreal (OR.PA) has been a leader in cosmetics since 1909.

Other brands are Lancome, Giorgio Armani, Helena Rubinstein and more. L'Oreal is the ultimate cyclical but with proven brands everybody wants. In fact, it is not so much the product that is wanted, but the brand. No dividend from these luxury goods stocks. They perhaps may be thought of as a class as small growth stocks occupying the bottom right cell of the Morningstar style-box matrix.

• Hermes (RMS.PA) Since 1837 a man can never go wrong by presenting the object of his desires with an Hermes scarf. No dividend.

• Beiersdorf (BEI.DE) Since 1882 Beiersdorf has been supplying Nivea skin products throughout the world. Since then its early years it has branched out but maintained corporate headquarters in Hamburg Germany. No dividend.

• AtlasCopco (ATLCY) is a Swedish firm supplying the global market for air compressors on construction projects. The stock has split twice, 3 for 1 and 2 for 1, and it distributes a 3% dividend.

• Burberry (BURBY.PK) The world's raincoat since 1856. No dividend.
• Starbucks (SBUX) In 1971 Starbucks set out to supply the world's morning Joe, and succeeded in about 50 countries. I couldn't believe somebody could make a business out of coffee until I found myself in unfamiliar territory one morning looking for a place to get a cup to go while I drove to my first meeting of the day. There it was, in a large strip-mall, the only open store in the mall with about half-a-dozen cars parked out in front around 6 AM. On another occasion in New York City, I witnessed 30 people patiently standing in line at a Starbucks while they could have gotten much quicker service, and cheaper, at a nearby diner. Dividend 1.50%

• Tiffany (TIF) since 1837 Tiffany has been the #1 destination for wedding gifts and heirloom gifts for all occasions. Mostly cyclical but people get married even in bad times. Dividend 1.60%.

• John Wiley (JWa) A publisher that has continually re-invented itself since 1807. Dividend 1.30%.

• Harley-Davidson (HOG) has been not everyone's cup of tea since 1903, but they keep churning hogs out and people, of all stripes, keep buying them. I once rode a Jap bike which was faster than most hogs, but I still got no respect. Definitely a cyclical play. Dividend 1.00%

• Kimberly-Clark (KMB) launched Kleenex in 1924 and has been a paper innovator ever since. A non-cyclical of the first order, or maybe even a counter-cyclical as people reach for a Kleenex to mop up their tears when times are bad. Dividend 4.30%.

• Intel (INTC) was co-founded by Robert Noyce who in 1957 introduced a campus-like atmosphere to technology development and manufacturing that allowed his employees to achieve their maximum potential. Dividend 3.60%.

• Avon (AVP) has been calling since 1886 and does it worldwide. Dividend 3.40%.

• Caterpillar (CAT) since 1925 Caterpillar has been the most prestigious name in heavy equipment for construction worldwide. A cyclical for sure. Dividend 1.60%.
• John Deere (DE) Since 1837 nothing has run quite like a Deere in agriculture and forestry worldwide. Dividend 1.50%.

• Colgate-Palmolive (CL) has been winning the toothpaste wars since 1896. Dividend 3.00%.

• HJ Heinz (HNZ) has been the #1 in fixin's for hot dogs and hamburgers since 1869. Also 56 other varieties and big in pickles, very big. Dividend 3.70%.

• General Electric (GE) has been on Charles Dow's industrial list since 1896. No other company quite like it; with its own derivative BCG matrix of business mapping, GE continually re-invents itself. Dividend 2.90%.

• Southern Company (SO) Of all the utilities I called on nationally as a sales engineer, this was a standout for corporate culture devoted to excellence. Dividend 4.70%.

• Jardine Matheson (JMHLY.PK) Began in 1832 sending tea to England. Based in Hong Kong and experts in the China trade. If you want to hitch your wagon to the China star, this is the way to do it. No dividend.

• PACCAR Inc. (PCAR) Since 1939, PACCAR has been choosing to build the best trucks and not the most trucks – by paying attention to what drivers wanted. Today it is the dream of most truckers to own a Peterbilt. Dividend 1.00%.

• DuPont (DD) Since 1802 DuPont has been committed to research for new products establishing the first research laboratories in the U.S. Dividend 3.10%.

• Kellogg Company (K) The older brother John employed his younger, good-for-nothing brother, Will, to make corn meal to be served to his patients at his sanatorium. One day Will forgot to package the drying meal and it dried out into, well, corn flakes. Will instantly saw the possibilities while his older brother couldn't get over his consternation at Will's ineptitude. They parted ways and Will went into the corn flake business. The rest is history. They are even eating corn flakes in India now. Right up to his death, John never acknowledged Will's success. Kellogg's, the world's leading producer of cereal. Dividend 3.00%.

• Cummins Inc. (CMI) Since 1919 Cummins has been committed to perfecting the diesel engine. In 1940, Cummins offered the industry's first 100,000-mile warranty, and it has been on top ever since. Dividend 1.00%.

• Anheuser-Busch InBev (BUD) There is no question that Anheuser-Busch gained supremacy in the U.S. market for beer, making them a successful takeover target by InBev, a Belgian brewing powerhouse since 1366. InBev has also bought up the world's most renowned beer brands, including one of my favorites, Lowenbrau. My backup is Stella for Stella Artois. Dividend 0.70%.

• Amazon.com (AMZN) Amazon's origins cannot be separated from its founder, Jeff Bezos, who persevered through much travail and financial panic to give birth to an idea, online shopping. Today, Amazon is a staple of online shopping.

• Parker Hannifin (PH) Since 1935 Parker Hannifin has sought to become the world's supplier of hydraulic systems to the transportation industry, making 58 acquisitions along the way. To those "in the know," like Charles Lindbergh, only Parker Hannifin will do. Dividend 1.40%.

• Unilever (UL) Beginning in the 1890s Unilever became the soapmaker and grocer to the world – somewhat the English equivalent of Procter&Gamble but with a food dimension. Unilever owns Lipton, which is globally the most recognized name in tea, even in China. Dividend 3.90%.

• 3M Co. (MMM) Like Intel, 3M Company has since 1902

grown by empowering its workers to innovate. This organic, ground-up process has propelled 3M into leadership positions in multiple business sectors with products such as Scotch Tape® and Post-it Notes®. This company is perhaps the most diversified company in the world, and like DuPont, innovation is in the gene pool. Dividend 2.40%.

• Michelin (ML.PA) Michelin has led tire innovation since 1888, including the radial tire (1946), eventually becoming the world's largest tire manufacturer. Michelin came to my attention in graduate business school, when studying for a case discussion on the company. I learned that when a boiler had to be replaced at one of their factories, they constructed a tunnel into the factory to prevent spies from infiltrating the plant for trade secrets. This certainly illustrated a company that both produced and protected value. The publication of the Michelin guide is a bonus. Traveling in Italy, my wife and I, came upon a hidden gem of a restaurant that was off the beaten path, but in the Michelin guide. No dividend.

• Boeing Co. (BA) The end of WWI saw the aviation market flooded with surplus airplanes, and while their competitors went out of business, Boeing began making furniture. Since then, Boeing has been an innovation leader, eventually, for a time, becoming the world's only global airliner builder. That ended with the rise of EADS, a French-British consortium, but Boeing keeps making the right decisions, like staying away from the supersonic detour, eventually realized and then dropped by EADS. Dividend 2.30%.

• Clorox Corp. (CLX) From 1913 up until the buyout by Procter & Gamble in 1957, Clorox concentrated on making Clorox brand bleach the undisputed quality leader. In 1969, P&G was forced by the FTC to divest Clorox, which then went on a hunt to remake itself into a P&G lite. This failed but left

Clorox with some decent brands, like Glad bags and Kingsford charcoal. Still, this is an interesting investment not so much for the management as for the unshakeable position of Clorox, perhaps won during WWII, when the company's management decided to sell less but full-strength product in response to wartime conservation policies, thus establishing it as the quality leader. No matter how bad the management, they can't seem to shake that Clorox brand. Dividend 3.20%.

• Nestle (NESN.VX) Nestle is a result of a fierce American-Swiss rivalry for condensed milk, baby food, and the use of condensed milk to make chocolate bars. Finally, in 1905 the companies merged and today have no direct competitors for a wide assortment of global brands and markets, all connected to food. No dividend.

• McDonald's (MCD) While not everybody's idea of a good meal, McDonald's has nevertheless forged an uncontested global business in the "quick-bite" sector. Recently, I opted to go to a competitor up the street off an interstate exit, and regretted my choice. McDonalds just seems to be able to do the same thing, over and over again, without losing their step. In China you can never find an open seat at a McDonalds. Dividend 3.30%.

• Eaton Corp. (ETN) Since 1916, Eaton has been an aggressive global aggregator of businesses that contribute to process management; important products are axles, valves and industrial controls. You don't hear too much about Eaton, because they are too busy doing good. Dividend 2.60%.

• United Parcel Service (UPS) Started in 1907, UPS adopted its familiar "Pullman" brown color in 1930 because of communicating a quality of "neat, dignified and professional." Today the company continues that tradition, but has integrated backwards toward the shipper end by offering a variety of services that expedite shipment and delivery. For example, the lobster that arrives at your door from Maine most likely was routed through the UPS lobster pound in Louisville. Lobster in, lobster out. Dividend 2.80%.

• Packaging Corporation of America (PKG) PCA has its origins in a straw and fiber company started in 1867. Since then, PCA has striven to become the quality leader in the use of corrugated fiber board. Nobody else quite does what PCA does. If you need a printed corrugated cardboard display, nobody does it better. Dividend 2.90%.

• Microsoft (MSFT) Bill Gates, while perhaps not overtly demonstrating any personal excellence, seems to have put together a company of enduring excellence. They make mistakes, but seem to have an ability to recover and they have successfully negotiated competition from the free generic rival, Linux. Microsoft is a company the world cannot do without. Dividend 2.50%.

• American Express (AXP) Ratings like 22nd most valuable brand in the world and one of the top 30 most admired companies in the world put Amex well ahead of their competition. In addition, Amex cards have the largest market share of U.S. credit card transactions. But while I have been a devoted user since 1975, I became a believer when I used an American Express traveler's check on a European train to pay a fare and got too much change back. When I objected, the conductor stated that American Express traveler's checks were better than cash and received a better rate of exchange. Dividend 1.60%.

• Southwest Airlines (LUV) Southwest was created in 1967, reportedly on the back of a cocktail napkin. Herb Kelleher and

Rollin King set out to establish a new aviation culture and model. Frightened by this attack on their turf, the big airlines fought back, keeping Southwest on the ground, for a time. Today Southwest is the nation's largest airline. What impressed me most, however, was when I read that at the height of one of the cyclical run-ups in petroleum prices, Southwest had purchased forwards on cheap fuel, a huge amount, keeping them flying through the crisis. Kelleher died but the airline seems to have retained his spirit. Dividend 0.50%.

• Costco, Marriott, Santander, Soc Gen, FIAT , Adobe, all are leaders and not going out of business anytime soon.

I hope by this list and my recommendation of the Dow 30 and other indices, that I have provided a reason not to go looking for "Undiscovered Gems." A gem is a company that has been discovered and found to dominate in a competitive market over a long period of change and appears to offer the greatest opportunity to dollar-cost-average over a very long period of time into a sizeable position, diversified by time and built up not only by market forces, but also by regular reinvestment of dividends. Additionally, all companies have their audiences; there is nothing undiscovered in the stock market.

POSTSCRIPT

On April 10, 2013 a New York Times article reported the ouster of the JC Penney CEO, Ron Johnson, by the board of directors. This plays out like a western movie. The aging sheriff (former CEO Ullman) is seen as too old to keep order so one of the more influential merchants, William A. Ackman ("...activist hedge-fund titan..." and board member) says that he knows of a gunslinger from the San Francisco area who can clean-up the town (read Paladin, "Have Gun, Will Travel"). Soon Johnson, sporting a Harvard MBA, blows into Plano TX "a star." He gets rid of the "dead- wood" in the Sheriff's office and brings in his own people. But they are from far away too and don't plan on staying long, just clean up the town and get out. But first it's time for a little partying down at the saloon to celebrate the arrival of order, complete with light show and ice sculptures. Then it's down to business. Well first thing is, the townspeople get roughed up by the newcomers. Many of them leave town. Things go from bad to worse and the leading merchants, including the alpha dog, decide to bring back the old sheriff. It ain't perfect but at least they can keep the town going for the moment while they find another gunslinger.

It is interesting to note that JC Penney, having been around for 100 years, doesn't have a bench of talent to draw from. For example at PG and GE, developing a management bench is in the DNA of the organization. It would be difficult to imagine any issue for the board having primacy over succession planning. That is a dimension that GMI ratings can help with as well as FAQs from corporate investor web pages.

Closing Bell   *Ben Aronson 2010*
Oil on panel, 11 x 14 inches   Collection of the Artist

Chapter 11
Risk Management

During one college summer an uncle of mine, my dear uncle Eddie, got me a job as a Mutuel Messenger at a thorough-bred horse racetrack. I soon fell in with the cashiers in our booth and began to get "trained" on handicapping horses.

One gentleman in particular took an interest in my education. As the summer wore on I learned that each cashier, and there were six of them, had a personal story of out-of-control gambling. Most were reformed gamblers and most of those wouldn't go near the *Daily Racing Form*, the rag that Warren Buffett wanted to buy and is the mainstay of the horse betting set. But by mid-summer, I was an avid reader.

My "professor" taught me to look at the condition of the track and match it up with the past performance of the horses under similar track conditions – some horses were good in the mud and others weren't. I was also taught to look at the purses as a sign of the quality of the racing history – a consistent winner of small purses was no match for an "out-of-the-money" horse in a big purse race. There was a lot to think about, and a lot to do in handicapping nine or so horses in nine or more races.

My job was to set up the pads of paper that were used to take down the payoff figures when the Pari-Mutuel office called in after each race. The pages would be distributed to all the cashiers so they would know what to pay on "Win" "Place" and "Show" tickets for the top three finishers. Since there were three horses in the money and they could be bet in any of three positions (Win, Place or Show) there were nine payoff figures. Each cashier was assigned a particular order so that you had "Win" cashiers, "Place" cashiers, and "Show" cashiers who would all be cashing tickets for all three finishers.

The pads were about 9"-square and contained a grid on which the various payoff figures would be written. Each pad had about five carbons so that the figures could be distributed to all the cashiers. There were about six pads. About 15 minutes after each race the phone would ring. The booth manager answered, wrote down the various payoffs, ripped the pages out of the pads, and distributed them to the cashiers. My job was to pick up all the carbons that had landed on the floor and insert them back into the pads for the next race. Meanwhile after another 15 minutes, the cashiers were finished paying the winners, and the booth manager collected all the turned-in winning tickets. He put them into a canvas bag and handed the bag to me to deliver to the Pari-Mutuel office. After that I was off until the next race, which might be another 20 minutes. For doing this for about six hours a day, five days a week, I was paid $130 a week. After graduating college four years later with a bachelor's degree, my starting salary was $100 a week and I worked like a dog. This was an early lesson in union work.

As the summer wore on and I got more engrossed in the

Daily Racing Form. I made my first bet -- $2 on Blackfly to win. Blackfly won and paid off $9. As Stan O'Neal , CEO of Merrill Lynch, said after getting his first top grades at Harvard: *"After that, there was no looking back."* The rest of the summer I bet frequently and just as frequently lost. At one point I got so engrossed in handicapping that I inserted the carbons upside down in the payoff pads. The call came in, the booth manager wrote down the results and then, as usual, ripped out the pages to distribute them and he instantly saw the problem I had caused. He also knew the cause of the problem. As he and I and the other cashiers saw those unmarked payoff sheets, carbons fluttering through the air in a frozen moment in time, we anticipated the explosion that was about to follow.

I won't bother to relate the very ugly scene but my ears were ringing and the last thing I heard was:"*....and if I even see your nose in a racing form even once more, you're out."* Well, that event added to my training but the best lesson came on the last race on the last day of the season. My "professor" who was packing up to go to Hialeah in Florida for the winter season, said to me: *"Paddy, you put $5 on this horse to win in the last race and you will be able to take your gal out for a show and dinner at the best club in town. This is a sure thing."* Five dollars was a lot of money in those days and I didn't do it. The horse didn't come in, the "professor" packed up for Hialeah, and I went back to school with a new rule for risk-management: Handicapping horses mostly doesn't work and there is no such thing as a sure thing.

Working Out the Bugs

In the late '90s, before I was a stockbroker, I got caught up in my old gambling ways when I began to hear chatter about the stock market and the evolution of online trading platforms like DLJ Direct. Because I had never been able to find a good broker, I decided to do it myself. It wasn't long before I abandoned the staid Blue Chip companies and began throwing money at the hot internet stocks that were in the forefront of day trader investor sentiment at the time: ICGE and CMGI. These were two companies that incubated internet companies, mainly start-ups. I then subscribed to a magazine called *Upside* and began to visit the website, *Raging Bull*. I devoted a great deal of time to researching these two sources and saw *Upside* go from a 50-page newsprint rag up to a 300-page glossy publication that looked more like a fashion magazine, and then back to a 50-page newsprint rag again. I followed the same trend with gambling instincts intact after a 25-year hiatus from the race track.

At the height of my fun, I took a ski trip to Chamonix in France, staying at a Relaix & Chateau property and then realized a lifelong dream of visiting Berlin and staying at the Adlon Hotel, all with outrageous winnings from the internet bubble. Of course I didn't see it as a bubble at the time. When I got to Berlin, I visited an internet café and logged on to see how my portfolio was doing. I was very heavy in CMGI at the time and I brought up a chart to look at my position and was flabbergasted to find my position had tanked, cut in half. I involuntarily and loudly emitted an expletive that I learned that day, is understood in all languages, and saw that all eyes were turned toward me. *"Sorry, sorry, sorry,"* I yelled out and went back to studying the chart on the screen. How could this happen, I thought. As I examined more closely, I saw that the stock had been split and instead of tanking, my position had twice as many shares and had gone up another $20,000. I closed down the computer and went strutting up the Kufurstendamm back to the Adlon for a drink – life was good.

Toward the end on 1999 in an effort to diversify away from CMGI and ICGE I studied *Upside* and *Raging Bull* and began to read about a start-up software company named SilverStream Software. I thought that this would follow the pattern set by the other internet stocks and began to move money heavily into this new position. It didn't do well. Then one day as volatility was ramping up, I brought up a chart on my SilverStream position and saw it lose $25,000 before my very eyes. I thought, there is something going on I don't understand and sold out of everything. I was out of the internet investment game. My total profit was about $150,000 at the height, and I wound up giving $75,000 back before getting out – the Gods had to be appeased, as John Maynard Keynes's mother declared when her son was wiped out for the first time and took a good chunk of her change with it. But still, I was ahead by $75,000.

But where I was really ahead was in having lived through that roller coaster, made the decisions I made, and in the end came out even.

Yes, the $75,000 only made up for years of losses with a little left over. I was able to start from scratch but much wiser in the way of the market. I cancelled my subscription to *Upside*, which by that time had become a newsprint rag again, and decided I needed a better way.

The Problem With "Risk Management"

In the aftermath of the mortgage meltdown that took major banks and put them on life support there has been much conversation about risk and risk management. It turns out the very banks that got caught up in the mortgage collapse had risk management in place, in some cases, risk management departments. One case has already been illustrated is the firing of Jeff Kronthal at Merrill Lynch when he was standing in the way of the train to riches. Kronthal raised the specter of risk but to people focused on wealth creation, risk has a different face. Kronthal was replaced with a more congenial face of risk and Merrill Lynch subsequently bought up as much CDO (Collateralized Debt Obligation) as they could manage; they then went down the proverbial tubes. According to this risk management model, $1 billion of mortgage-backed securities is good and $40 billion of mortgage-backed securities is bad – it's a matter of scale and diversification.

While Kronthal thought that scale was the way to play the game, using good risk-management procedures of scaling or limiting risk, a gentleman named John Paulson was, like the CEO at Merrill Lynch, blowing through risk-management controls, and shorting what Merrill was buying. Instead of going down, Paulson went up, reportedly to the tune of $1billion or more. Does Paulson have a risk management model? Perhaps. But his next big move was on a Chinese timber company that had some fraudulent characteristics and reportedly dealt Paulson a $340 - $500 million loss. This may have been a classic case of early wins setting the stage for the bravado needed to take on later losses. And as I write this I recall very clearly my own episodes of bravado.

Investment Objective vs. Risk Management
What is risk management? What is it that the CEO at the top of the heap at Merrill Lynch neglected and I possessed as a teenage Pari-Mutuel Messenger and later as an internet stock player? Cognition of loss. For one thing, at the top, the CEO wasn't on the front lines seeing the loss of upward momentum in real up-close terms. But there is another characteristic of vision enunciated by a gentleman investor who was first published in 1929: this was Justin Mamis and his book was *The Nature of Risk*. Mamis makes the very startling statement, at least for me, that the blindness attendant to many investment busts is a greed driven by envy. Envy is the driver. For example, the literature on the CEO's tenure at the top of Merrill Lynch makes reference to his wanting to beat the performance turned in by Goldman Sachs. It wasn't performance for its own sake, it was a need to throttle Goldman Sachs. This is certainly enough to take one's eye off what is going on and reorient the investor toward what the mission is – beating somebody else.

Classical risk-management takes note of this fact and separates decision-making into two, or more, centers of authority. It is axiomatic that everybody cannot think clearly at all times and when it comes to handling big money, a second set of eyes is a good idea. But a second set of eyes may get in the way of the mission (see Paulson above). In addition, individual investors may not have a second set of eyes and at the other end of the spectrum, decision by committee may not bring about a great deal of success as the group moves toward "Groupthink," or wishing to avoid that, may just triangulate to a point that everyone can live with, which is usually, nowhere.

Successful investment may be many things, but one thing it is for sure is the prudent and savvy decision making of a single individual who has mastered him or herself along with his or her demons, fears and aspirations. The successful individual investor is not blinded by a mission other than to read the signs as they are and make dispassionate decisions in an atmosphere of containment. By containment I mean a healthy respect for the vagaries of all information and, after achieving that respect, then creating a structure where one or several imprudent acts is not going to bring the whole house down. There will be imprudence, but it does not have to be fatal.

It's inevitable that in the course of stock research a condition will be uncovered that looks like a sure thing, and something that should be loaded up on. If the investor so smitten has a mission outside of just staying ahead of inflation, like hitting the cover off the ball, that investor has no protection, and is likely to not have receptors needed to process countervailing information, perhaps even shutting out information in a classic case of denial.

What is the mission? The best answer is: no mission and no end game other that reading the tea leaves and staying ahead of inflation. When someone takes on a mission the first act is to shut everything out and just focus on the mission. This is how great accomplishments happen. But in investment nothing can be shut out, all information is relevant and should be processed. So in investment you have the opposite of mission and so any thought of setting a target is a potential source of ruin.

In a lifelong career in sales I have been in an occupation that is riddled with the idea of hitting targets. I remember, many years ago, interviewing over the phone for a job as a salesman of corrugated shipping cartons. I was speaking to a recently appointed sales manager who was building up a new sales staff and was out for blood. He described typical corrugated carton salesmen hanging around tried and true customers and not taking on the challenge of finding new customers. I can still remember clearly his warning, if I was one of those: *"....and then if you think you are going in with a low price to win new business, think again. I will give you such a high price, it will make your head spin."* Not wishing to have my head spin like the key character in the movie *The Exorcist*, I continued my search elsewhere. But this was sales management in the old days along with quotas that had to be met, no matter what. I had one boss who told me that if a project was cancelled, it was my job to find another project to replace it. It was a "no excuses" world.

Process vs. Targets in Uncertain Regimes

One day I was in a sales management position and I was forced to confront this conventional wisdom that I had never really signed onto. As I thought about the problem of gaining sales through the efforts of others, I decided that quotas were really meaningless and if anything, should be used merely as a compass to adjust a process. I fixed upon the idea of establishing a process that would completely ignore any consideration of outcome. If a salesperson contacted so many prospects, statistics would pretty much determine the outcome. I felt that giving a salesperson a process to follow, and removing the pressure of results, would probably lead to greater productivity just by people enjoying what they were doing. I can't say that I got better results, but what I got was a process that could be examined and adjusted and gave me a degree of control that I wouldn't have if people just turned in results unconnected to any quantifiable effort.

There is also another factor, which is that while individual effort can certainly make a difference, the larger predictor is overall economic conditions. A star salesperson in a down market isn't going to do very well and a poor salesperson in an upmarket will turn in a serviceable result. The lesson is to focus on the process that brings about the result and not on a disconnected result. In investing, this means to put aside any thought of a target and develop a process that you think should work -- and if it doesn't work, change the process until you find one that does work.

There is a concept rampant in the investment world that risk equals profit. In another section of this book I raise the comparison of GE and Dr. Koop Dot Com, two stocks that offered approximately the same return over the years 1998 to the end of 1999. Today Dr. Koop Dot Com is gone and people who bought GE at the peak are perhaps just now starting to see some daylight in investments made at that time. The point is that the relationship between risk and return is much more complicated; there is risk and there is risk. The GE - Dr. Koop Dot Com match-up is the poster child for investment risk. GE is a company that has been at the forefront of reinventing itself since Thomas Edison patented the light bulb around 1880, thereby very soon launching the GE brand. From there, GE branched out in any direction that drew on core competencies in fast growing markets. The concept behind Dr. Koop Dot Com was that all companies with Dot Com after their name had stock prices that were rocketed into the stratosphere when they were first offered in the market as an IPO (Initial Public Offering) and what could be better than a company that married the dot com phenomenon with public health in the form of a highly revered figure like Dr. Koop.

The revenue was going to be from advertising to people visiting the Dr. Koop website to get helpful health information. It certainly sounds good but it crashed. For the beginning investor, however, the choice between GE and Dr. Kopp Dot Com is a simple one: a leading corporation since its founding over 100 years ago and a concept on deriving advertising revenue from a website. Perhaps the best way to judge the match-up is to think of customers and brand. How long will it take Dr. Koop Dot Com to build brand loyalty enjoyed by GE? GE has already beaten out whatever competition there was for its market, which was mostly Westinghouse. That fight is over. What fights will Dr. Koop Dot Com have to win to succeed? Not even that is known. It is also instructive to sort risk by classification. There is company risk, industry risk, market risk, country risk, global economy risk and so on to any number of sources of risk that may be identified. GE has much lower company risk that Dr. Koop Dot Com. The risk of an investment in GE is mainly risk other than company risk. The risk associated with Dr. Koop Dot Com is almost all conceivable sources of risk but mostly company risk.

One could argue that the appeal of Dr. Koop Dot Com was that it might have been catapulted into the stratosphere. If there is visibility into that outcome then some risk might be assigned to it, but without that visibility, there is absolutely no reward in the balance, only risk. This also brings into focus what it is that stocks must do to fulfill their promise. In the case of GE an investor may be only hoping to stay ahead of inflation by investing in a company that has been at the top of its game for over 100 years. What is the Dr. Koop Dot Com investor looking for? To hit the cover off the ball probably. That is what the Wall Street crowd is looking for.

What about Madoff investors, what were they looking for? In their case one may assume that they were after extraordinary returns without the research effort – just give it to Bernie. What about the migrant worker getting a liar loan on a house, what is he hoping for? He is hoping to flip the house for a profit that will dwarf his annual wages. In the cases of Dr. Koop Dot Com, house flippers, and Madoff investors there is absolutely no visibility of a reward, just an implied promise of one. These are cases that are all about mission but no process.

There is one other perspective that needs to be considered, the essence of the market. As Burton Malkiel observed, the market is random and cannot be gamed. At the opposite end of the spectrum is Wall Street that makes a business out of gaming the market, and survives doing it because of the total intimidation of the investing public. There are actors who beat the market but you will never hire them because first, even if you did find them they would be unrecognizable; second, they would not want any retail accounts; and third you would abandon them at the first volatility because you had no way to judge them in the first place. The winners on Wall Street are always identified after the fact and any anticipatory identification is just a guess. Where does that leave us? It leaves us with a market about which we know two things: (1) it is random day-to-day (2) over time it has grown between two and three times the rate of inflation. So given this state of affairs I would develop a process the core principle of which would be to not do the work myself but rather let the market do the work. The stock market is an inexorable wealth building machine whose daily gyrations are a distraction only for the people without a process to harness its power. Into that vacuum descends the carnival we know as Wall Street, which has little use to the investor other than liquidity.

A Risk-Management Model

So what is my prescription for risk management? Forget the mission. Forget all the nonsense spouted by Wall Street about planning your retirement (as in "How much will you need in retirement?"). Forget the very prudent-sounding idea of planning right down to the gnat's eyebrow what your expenses will be in retirement and making that your mission. It sounds good but it's a red-herring, a distraction. Instead, think about a process that will keep you invested in good stocks and keep you away from the bad idea of the day. Think about a process that will inure you from the braggart at the water cooler who never lost a nickel and just reeled in another mother lode. Think about a process that is as much on auto-pilot as you can make it; then leave it alone and let it work. If at the end of a year, you are unhappy with the results, revisit your assumptions, think about new assumptions, mull their validity, then reset for another year, and repeat. Your process, whatever it is, will be your Terra Firma through storms, droughts, crashes, bubbles, and whatever else life throws at you. That process will be the constant in your life which in the end will deliver you not only from Wall Street actors and the worst excesses of the market, but also from the most challenging component in the mix, your transient reactions to what is going on around you.

If you have a mission, you are toast; if you have a process, you are saved. That is risk management. That is the long and the short of it. And if you don't want to bother coming up with a process, just dollar-cost-average your way into the discrete common stocks that make up the Dow 30, reinvest all dividends, and get on with your life. If you want to be even more passive, selected the S&P 500 High-Quality index and several of the Russell indices, set-up a regular investment account and your future finances will have been given the best chance of succeeding. Either way, setting it and forgetting it, is how wealth is created.

Manhattan Sunrise, 6ᵗʰ & 55ᵗʰ   *Ben Aronson 2010*
Oil on panel, 60 x 31 inches   Tibor de Nagy Gallery

Chapter 12
ShareBuilder &
Direct Investment

Two very powerful wealth builders most investors ignore: rebalancing and dollar-cost-averaging.

Rebalancing was perhaps first espoused by Morningstar in

their prominent role as mutual fund advisors. Morningstar then developed what has come to be termed the Morningstar style-box matrix which is the 9-box matrix described earlier. Many advisors make a practice of deploying client assets in mutual funds that are benchmarked to each of the 9 boxes, in this way modern portfolio theory is carried out in practice. Since the center column is a blend of the left and right columns, a thorough allocation to MPT principles may also be accomplished by using just the 6 boxes that make up the left and right columns or using just the three boxes in the center column. Rebalancing is the act of restoring whatever balance is assigned to each box at the beginning of the year. If the allocation calls for equal balance in all 3, 6 or 9 boxes, those balances over a period of 12 months will grow at different rates and become imbalanced. Rebalancing is the act of reducing assets in faster growing boxes and allocating those proceeds to slower growing boxes until all boxes are at their original and intended weighting. This sounds like a bad idea because it "rewards" the laggards, but just as espoused by "Dow Theory" last year's laggards are likely to be this year's stars. So rebalancing is something I strongly recommend. I would not sell out positions to rebalance however, merely direct new flows into lagging positions.

What dollar-cost-averaging does is manage the two moving parts in the investor's world: the market and the investor. As has been described, dollar-cost-averaging is the regularly scheduled purchase of a fixed dollar amount, making the investment phase a mechanical process. It is investing on auto-pilot.

As pointed out earlier, the most powerful aspect of a 401(k) plan is not the tax treatment, which is controversial, but the dollar-cost-averaging feature of regular payroll deductions for pay deferrals into the 401(k) account. The participant never sees the deferrals – they are split off automatically from the paycheck and directed into the 401(k) plan without passing the scrutiny of the participant. So one moving part, the investor is circumvented. The second moving part, the market, is also circumvented, because the investments are made regardless of market position – the market is ignored. The blind or programmed aspect of deferrals (which is a kind of dollar-cost-averaging), along with voluntary and regular dollar-cost-averaging are perhaps the most powerful pillars of building wealth.

The Power of Automatic Deferrals

There is a story I must relate that bears on this. Companies are called the "sponsors" of 401(k) plans because they offer them and then take the action to make deferral contributions into the plan for the employee participants. In the capacity of sponsor, companies are alert to the potential for lawsuits if a 401(k) plan fails to provide adequate retirements. A major point in this potential flash-point is that 401(k) plans are "self-directed" meaning the participants make their own investment decisions, and because most employees are not investors they are clueless to make crucial decisions affecting their financial futures. The most intimidated employees have been known just to put their deferrals into a bond fund and then lag inflation. After 30 years of this, you can imagine the result, not enough to retire on and time to call in the attorneys.

To head off lawsuits arising from disgruntled retirees, companies offer education so they cannot be accused of not addressing the hazard of an all-bond retirement portfolio or any other investment outcome that could possibly be tied to poor choices. In fact education is one of the government-mandated components of 401(k) plan sponsorship.

When I was a broker, I had been working with a Fortune 500 company on the education problem and finally came up with what I thought was solution. It was a presentation that in a few slides explained the life cycle of companies and related it to the Morningstar matrix. It gave participants some insight into diversifying by size and elasticity to interest rates using a matrix they are familiar with, the Morningstar matrix. The person in charge of the effort was very impressed with the result but said that there was a problem; participants rarely changed their allocations once enrolled in the program, and for the initial allocation, they got professional help. I digested this, after all my effort, and concluded that not changing allocations, in fact not touching the plan at all, was a good thing. My listener, the plan sponsor, agreed. That is how I first encountered the idea that keeping the investor out of it was central to building wealth, a thought that echoes an earlier pronouncement by Benjamin Graham: *"The investor's chief problem - and even his worst enemy - is likely to be himself."*

Direct Investment

In addition to company sponsored 401(k) plans there are two other ways to make automatic deferrals and this is with, first, a company-sponsored Direct Stock Purchase Plans (DSPPs) and Direct Reinvestment Plan (called DRIPs) and, second, Capital One ShareBuilder.

Sometimes other acronyms are used for direct investment plans like DSPP and DRP, but the meaning is the same: bypassing Wall Street and buying stock directly from the issuing company. The sponsoring company in this case is the company you are investing in. The second-by-second re-pricing of stocks offered on the various exchanges is the result of unrestricted trading occurring in a free market and creating liquidity, which is a good thing. The problem arises when people assign importance to stock price movements as if such movements somehow signaled the health of the company. Unfortunately many people feel this way, creating a distraction that company managements must pay attention to. So some companies try to attract a more stable investing public by offering direct investment with automated, and often free, dividend re-investment. The theory is that doing so attracts long-haul investors who are not traders, with the result that volatility in stock price would be dampened. Whether volatility is dampened or not I cannot say, but the automated investment aspect of the plans plus avoiding or reducing trading costs is a boon to the investor.

Companies also sponsor DRIPS as a way to obtain capital. The more traditional methods of capital raising is for a company to engage a brokerage house to sell new shares to their existing clients. There are fees for this of course which can be bypassed by issuing shares directly to the public.

As in all financial services products, as soon as you descend below the top layer, you encounter a writhing sea of spaghetti of complexity, which is what puts so many people off, making them passive bystanders to their own financial health. So it is with direct investment. Stock ownership must be defined. When you buy stock you need three things, a stock, a market for that stock to trade in, and an agent who regularly trades in that market to make trades for you. Once a trade is made, your agent can simply hand you a certificate denoting your ownership.

Street Name

At one time it was common for investors to take custody of their own stock certificates, perhaps one of the driving forces behind the evolution of safe deposit boxes at banks. Any investor in those times might well have enjoyed a proliferation of colorful and beautifully engraved stock certificates, illustrating the nature of the business -- locomotives for railroad stocks, for example. The certificate would also be overprinted with the number of shares the certificate represented, so with each trade a certificate would be issued documenting the number of shares purchased.

The stock certificates were registered with the company, so if you lost it, it could be replaced, making the certificates a symbolic record as well as a negotiable security. But since certificates may be a negotiable security they must be accounted for, and losing a certificate will create a documentation headache. Perhaps for this reason, custody of stock certificates gave way to simply registering the securities at the brokerage firm that executed the trade. This became known as "Book Entry" or "Street Name" registration -- the issuing company showed your broker as the custodian of so many shares and your broker then kept a record of which clients owned which shares. The advantage of this method, which is the default method today, is that the certificates don't have to be produced to make a trade; everything is book-entry. Investors may still opt to possess certificates but it is quite inconvenient for all concerned. See stock certificate below.

When investors choose to invest directly with the issuing company, as in a DRIP or DSP, then "Direct Registration" may occur in which the ownership of the stock is book-entry at the issuing company or its transfer agent, i.e., Computershare, etc. These organizations are not stock brokers per se so the acquisition and sale of stock in direct plans does not take advantage of up-to-the-second market pricing. But direct investment is for the long-haul, so second-by-second market pricing in my opinion is really not an issue. As a matter of fact, since stock can gyrate up and down, a more staged buy trade may just as likely garner a lower price. So for the consistent investor this is a non-issue.

Direct Investment Operations

The way direct investment plans work is that you either sign up directly with the company or a transfer agent for the company. A transfer agent is a subcontractor to a corporation hired to account for stock transactions and manage customer contact on acquiring and disposing of shares. The investor will be required to use provided enrollment forms that usually include a transfer form. These forms can usually be downloaded.

The enrollment form documents your elections for automated monthly withdrawals and dividend reinvestment. The transfer form will be used for an initial purchase of shares.

As of today about 1,100 companies offer direct purchase plans but with a bewildering variety of conditions and fees. Once enrolled, the company or company's transfer agent then takes over and automatically executes investor elections documented on enrollment and transfer forms. The investor will then receive quarterly statements of activities.

Because of the fixed dollar amount and the automated nature of the withdrawals and stock purchases, this amounts to dollar-cost-averaging on auto-pilot. There is an added bonus: many of the companies also pay dividends, and you have the opportunity to have those dividends automatically reinvested in additional share or fractional share purchases at no charge. Although there are only 1,100 companies (out of perhaps 10,000 listed companies) offering DSP or DRIPs, those 1,100 allow you to construct a well-diversified portfolio and build wealth needed for retirement.

Most DRIP plans offer the investor the opportunity to have automated withdrawals made from their checking accounts, such withdrawals being as little as $25, debited monthly. They then mail out quarterly statements. Of course, the money they are debiting from a checking account has already been taxed, so the investment qualifies as after-tax dollars. What this means is that the DRIP plan you choose may either be a taxable plan, or a Roth IRA plan. The difference is that in a Roth IRA, capital gains will not be taxed, but the money is locked up for five years and may not be withdrawn without penalty (10%) before age 59½. Also, in a Roth IRA, there is no step-up valuation for heirs. Withdrawals from a taxable account will be taxed on gains, at the long-term capital gains rate if there are no withdrawals of gains within the first year. Withdrawal of gains within the first year are taxed at the significantly higher ordinary income tax rate. Tax deferred accounts that are not Roth IRAs are denied the long-term capital gains rate and all withdrawals, which means all contributions and gains, are taxed at ordinary income tax rates. It is, in my view for reasons discussed more fully in the chapter on taxes, a "no-brainer" to do a Roth IRA However, few DPPs and DRIPs offer them and as of this writing, the annual limit on IRA contributions is $5,000 for most investors and $6,000 for older investors.

The objective of this book is to inform the reader that Wall Street's culture of self-destructive trading behavior is counterproductive of one's investment health. Along the way I point out how to avoid self-destructive behavior and show the way toward a constructive investment life that will keep the investor's assets comfortably ahead of inflation. I counsel against making any decisions on transient information, such as performance for the past year, and look to fundamentals of market power and trends, and of threats affecting market power. Stock price has a life of its own; trying to anticipate stock price movements takes the investor away from more sound analysis of not only individual stock issues but also how to stage those investments.

We have also explored the frailty of man and how it is

better to remove decision-making as much as possible and resort instead to emotionless automated stratagems. We have discussed dollar-cost-averaging as being one of the most powerful tools for building wealth. But there is another very powerful tool and that is direct investment with dividend reinvestment, all done automatically once the account is opened and often, without fee. This is investment nirvana. Of course, there is a fee for holding an IRA account, usually about $45 a year per account, except for Capital One ShareBuilder which does not charge to custody IRA accounts.

Like all discussion of investment products, what starts out as the examination of a simple concept turns very quickly into one of a complicated stew of options. So it is with direct investment. I will not get into the minutia of the many types of plans available and the multiple ways of accessing them but point you instead to several books and heartily recommend their purchase.

- *Investing Without a Silver Spoon*, Fischer, Jeff, 1999, Motley Fool
- *Buying Stocks Without a Broker*, Carlson Charles B., 1992, McGraw Hill
- *All About DRIPs and DSPs*, Fisher, George, 2001, McGraw Hill

Direct stock purchase plans vary in how you access them, in some cases directly with the company and in other cases through a stock transfer agent like Computershare or Wells Fargo. The best way into a transfer agent is through the investor site of a stock you are interested in. If the company offers a DRIP, there will be a number to call, which may be at a transfer agent, but this greeting menu will get you to a live person -- at least that has been my experience. But calling Computershare directly got me nowhere.

Once you get through to a live person at a transfer agent,

that person should be able to tell you which companies it is agent for and that offer a Roth IRA DRIP (though they could not at Computershare). They can send you a kit for each company. Your research should also include fees. The same agent will have a fee structure for each company DRIP plan. Be sure to examine the fee schedule. You may find yourself preferring one company over another due to the fee schedule alone. This is okay. As long as the company is in a selection set, fees need to be a final screen.

If you go to the Computershare website you will be able to examine each of the individual company programs and download all the enrollment forms. If you have questions and need to speak to a Computershare representative be very cautious. I have found on many occasions that the person I am speaking with is not well trained and gave incorrect information or could provide no information. In one case, Computershare returned cashier's checks drawn against a Roth IRA account at Chase, stating that only personal checks are acceptable. This required moving Roth IRA funds into a regular checking account and then writing personal checks from there. IRA rules allow 60 days to make the transfer before it is considered a distribution, which, in the case of a Roth, might trigger a penalty if the person is under the age of 59½ or has held any Roth for under five years.

CapitalOne ShareBuilder

I had originally intended this chapter to focus on DRIPs but then I studied CapitalOne ShareBuilder more closely and decided as a result to close out my wife's Computershare DRIP accounts and move them to ShareBuilder. My wife and I then encountered a nightmare experience with Computershare. During the very difficult transition, ShareBuilder, with outstanding and easily accessed live support, kept us updated on the status of the transfer. Long story short, a January 2nd email to my wife stating that everything had been straightened out with Computershare was followed with about five or six further emails alternating between "good news" and "updates" that at one time required us to re-submit all paperwork. The new paperwork request was subsequently cancelled and on January 22nd my wife received the following message from ShareBuilder:

> *Hi Laura, I have some good news. I spoke with Computershare today, and was informed they were able to setup transfers for all the shares that you listed on your transfer form. They were able to use your social security number listed in order to look up the accounts for the other stock companies. We are setting everything up on our side so they can send the shares electronically to us. We should receive your securities within the next 5 business days. If you have any questions please let me know. Thanks and have a great day.*

> Capital One ShareBuilder Customer Service

Now to be clear. This is a cautionary tale but with limits. The problem arose mostly due to the IRA nature of the holdings. Non-IRA assets would probably not prompted much of the problem and many Computershare DRIPs are entirely free with free reinvestment of dividends and with some companies offering discounts through Computershare. So while ShareBuilder charges for trades Computershare does not.

The reason we moved my wife's accounts is that in addition to limited menu of Roth IRA stocks in Computershare, they also charge an IRA custodial fee of $45 on each of my wife's 7 accounts. At ShareBuilder there are no IRA custodial fees and you can put any security you want into a Roth, with some limitations on some PTPs and LLCs.

Make your own investigation. As an example, I put my wife into a Roth IRA direct stock plan with dividend reinvestment in Exxon Mobil which uses Computershare as a transfer agent. Computershare withdraws $50 a month from her checking account for stock purchases that, as far as I have been able to determine, are entirely without fee. You can visit the Computershare site – www.us.computershare.com and it will offer four lists of participating companies:

- All Plans
- Direct Stock Purchase Plans
- Dividend Reinvestment Plans
- No Purchase Fee Plans

Another accessible website for DRIPs is at Wells Fargo's www.shareowneronline.com. At this site you will have ready access to around 60 company direct investment plans. BNY Mellon seems to have sold their DRIP business to Computershare.

Direct Investment on the Web

Several web presences serving the DRIP community are well worth visiting. DRIP Central's website (**www.dripcentral.com**) lists all of the known DRIP administrators and Transfer Agents, 25 when I last looked.

Another site is Drip Wizard (www.dripwizard.com), which offers DRIP investors a screening utility by sector. Drip Advice (www.dripadvice.com) offers among other thing a page that lists all DRIP plans and another that lists lowest-cost DRIPs. There are also a variety of other resources online including First Share, which is a way to satisfy those DRIPs that are limited to existing shareholders. At www.firstshare.com you can acquire your first share for those DRIPs otherwise closed to non-shareholders. You may want to visit Amazon.com to check for any up to the minute book releases on the subject of DRIPs.

In the meantime, I am providing a list of DSP/DRIPs offering Roth IRA options that I found after a casual search, but this list may not be complete. In any event, in other parts of this book I have alluded to Burton Malkiel's prescription of just buying the S&P 500 index. In other words, Malkiel is saying that unless you possess an uncanny talent for timing stocks, which move randomly, save yourself a lot of bother and a lot of losses and just buy the index. I adjust this prescription to focus on a smaller and more selective index, the Dow 30. I advocate buying the discrete common stocks that make up the Dow 30 because you are then in a position to capture splits and dividends directly and without a fee. But, before you do that, max out your annual IRA limit by signing up for several of the Roth IRA DRIPs below, or even better point your mouse to CapitalOne ShareBuilder and open a Roth IRA account and max that out with selections from the Dow 30.

If you elect to use Computershare, pick any of the 12 stocks listed on the next page and sign up for auto investment at the rate of $400 per month in the aggregate, automatically debited from your checking account. That will get you $4800 a year in Roth IRA contributions, $200 below the current limit. Be aware that each Roth IRA DRIP account carries an annual fee of about $45 so you will want to narrow your beginning selection to a few and perhaps only 1.

- Altria (*NYSE: MO*) Roth IRA
- American Electric Power (*NYSE: AEP*) Roth IRA
- Aqua America *(NYSE: WTR*) Roth IRA
- AT&T (*NYSE: T*) Roth IRA
- Campbell Soup (*NYSE: CPB*) Roth IRA
- ExxonMobil (*NYSE: XOM*) Roth IRA
- Fannie Mae (*NYSE: FNM*)
- Ford Motor (*NYSE: F*) Roth IRA
- McDonald's (*NYSE: MCD*) Roth IRA
- Philip Morris (NYSE: PM) Roth IRA
- Verizon (*NYSE: VZ*) Roth IRA
- Wal-Mart Stores (*NYSE: WMT*) Roth IRA

On the next pages are listed companies offering DSPPs and DRIPS. While the programs generally follow established procedures, there are variations.

A list comes from http://noload.info/ and

www.dripwizard.com. It is presented as a guide and is certain
to be out of date as will be the data, so find the companies you
like and then investigate to see if they offer a DRIP. Another
way of finding DRIPs is to visit stock transfer agent sites like
Computershare and Wells Fargo.

COMPANY	SYMBOL	BUSINESS	YIELD	Roth IRA
Abbott Labs.	ABT	Pharma	4.00%	
AFLAC	AFL	Insurance	2.20%	
AGL Resources	ATG	Utility	4.60%	
Allegheny Technologies	ATI	Metals	1.10%	
Allstate	ALL	Insurance	2.60%	
Altria	MO	Consumer Goods	6.10%	Yes
Amcol International Corp.	ACO	Materials	2.20%	
American Electric Power	AEP	Utility	5.20%	Yes
American Express	AXP	Financial	1.60%	
American Water Works	AWK	Utility	3.20%	
A.O. Smith	AOS	Manufacturing	1.40%	
Aqua America	WTR	Utility	2.80%	Yes
Arrow Financial Corp.	AROW	Financial	4.20%	
AT&T	T	Telecom	4.90%	Yes
Atmos Energy	ATO	Utility	4.00%	
Bank of America	BAC	Financial	0.30%	
Bard, C.R.	BCR	Medical	0.80%	
Barnes Group, Inc.	B	Manufacturing	1.50%	
Black Hills Corp.	BKH	Utility	4.60%	
Bob Evans Farms	BOBE	Food	2.60%	
Borg-Warner	BWA	Auto Parts	0.00%	
BRE Properties	BRE	REIT	3.30%	
Campbell's Soup	CPB	Food	3.50%	Yes
Capstead Mortgage	CMO	REIT	12.00%	

Carpenter Technology	CRS	Metals	1.80%	
Caterpillar	CAT	Const. Equip.	1.70%	
Center Point Energy	CNP	Utility	5.00%	
CH Energy Group	CHG	Utility	4.50%	
Central VT Public Service	CV	Utility	4.00%	
Chevron Texaco	CVX	Petroleum	2.90%	
CMS Energy	CMS	Utility	4.40%	
The Coca-Cola Co.	KO	Beverage	2.90%	
Colgate-Palmolive Co.	CL	Consumer	3.00%	
Computer Associates	CA	Tech	0.70%	
CSX Corp	CSX	Railroad	1.40%	
Delta Airlines	DAL	Airline	0.00%	
Walt Disney Company	DIS	Entertainment	0.90%	
Dominion Resources	D	Utility	4.40%	
DTE Energy	DTE	Utility	4.60%	
Duke Energy	DUK	Utility	5.40%	
Duke Realty Investments	DRE	REIT	5.00%	
Eastern Co.	EML	Metal Prods.	1.90%	
Eastman Kodak	EK	Imaging	0.00%	
Entergy	ETR	Utility	4.70%	
Exxon Mobil	XOM	Petroleum	2.10%	Yes
Fannie Mae	FNMA	Financial Services	_	Yes
FedEx	FDX	Transportation	0.50%	
First Energy Corporation	FE	Utility	5.70%	
Ford Motor Co.	F	Automobile	0.00%	Yes
General Electric	GE	Industrial	2.80%	
General Growth Properties	GGP	REIT	0.00%	

Hawaiian Elec. Industries	HE	Utility	5.10%	
Health Care Property Inv.	HCP	REIT	5.10%	
Home Depot	HD	Retail	2.70%	
Home Properties	HME	REIT	4.40%	
IBM	IBM	Tech	1.60%	
Johnson Controls	JCI	Instruments	1.60%	
Johnson&Johnson	JNJ	Medical	3.70%	
JP Morgan Chase	JPM	Financial	0.40%	
Eli Lilly	LLY	Pharma	5.60%	
Lockheed Martin	LMT	Aerospace	3.70%	
Lowe's Company	LOW	Retail	1.60%	
Mattel	MAT	Toys	3.70%	
McDonalds	MCD	Food	3.20%	Yes
Merck	MRK	Pharma	4.70%	
Microsoft	MSFT	Tech	2.50%	
Monsanto	MON	Chemicals	1.70%	
Oklahoma Gas & Electric	OGE	Utility	3.10%	
Oneok	OKE	Energy MLP	3.20%	
J.C. Penney	JCP	Retail	2.20%	
Pfizer Inc.	PFE	Pharma	4.00%	
PG&E Corp	PCG	Utility	4.10%	
Phillip Morris	PM	Tobacco	3.40%	Yes
Piedmont Nat. Gas	PNY	Utility	3.90%	
Pinnacle West Capital	PNW	Utility	4.80%	
Popular	BPOP	Financial	0.00%	
Portland General	POR	Utility	4.40%	
Procter & Gamble	PG	Consumer	3.10%	
Public Service NM	PNM	Utility	3.40%	
Quanex Bldg. Prod.	NX	Manufacturing	0.80%	
Questar Corp.	STR	Energy	3.60%	
Regions Financial Corp.	RF	Financial	3.60%	
Scana Corporation	SCG	Utility	5.00%	
Schnitzer Steel Ind.	SCHN	Steel	0.10%	
Southern Company	SO	Utility	4.70%	

Southern Union Co.	SUG	Energy	2.20%	
Taubman Centers Inc.	TCO	REIT	3.30%	
Tenneco Inc.	TEN	Energy	0.00%	
Tyson Foods	TSN	Food	0.80%	
United Parcel Service	UPS	Transportation	2.80%	
Verizon	VZ	Telecom	4.40%	Yes
Wal-Mart	WMT	Retail	2.80%	Yes
Westar Energy	WR	Utility	4.90%	
Williams Companies, Inc.	WMB	MLP	1.70%	
Wisconsin Energy	WEC	Utility	3.50%	

I opened a Roth account at Capital One ShareBuilder, elected the premium service for $12/month, which provides 12 trades per month ($1 per trade), automatically debiting my checking account for the funds, and then selected 12 common stocks with an aggregate yield of about 4.7% for automatic monthly purchases (shown with yield). The companies selected for investment, as is the case with most companies, do not offer Roth IRA DRIPS:

Ambev (ABV) (0.30%)	Nestle (NSRGY) (3.0%)
Intel (INTC) (4.10%)	NYSE Euronext (NYX) (4.90%)
Illinois Tool Works (ITW) (2.50%)	Procter & Gamble (PG) (3.20%)
Johnson&Johnson (JNJ) (3.40%)	Royal Dutch Shell (RDSa) (4.70%)
Arcelor Mittal (MT) (3.90%)	Veolia Environnement (VE) (6.90%)
Annaly Capital (NLY) (12.50%)	Vodafone (VOD) (7.10%)

In addition, there is no custodial fee charged for the Roth IRA. So for $12 per month or for $144 per year, I will maintain an account that automatically purchases $2,880 a year or $20 per month per security. That works out to a fee 5% for the first year but will with time will decline to a much more manageable fee. At Computershare, and most brokerage houses I know of, there would be about a $45 annual custodial fee for each IRA.

Since the ShareBuilder accounts debit your checking account automatically, you must set up that communication between ShareBuilder and your checking account. That communication is bi-directional and you may also direct funds out of your ShareBuilder account into your checking account. But to do that penalty-free from an IRA, requires you to be over 59½ years old.

I was so impressed with the ShareBuilder service that I decided to open a second Roth account with the same fee structure, 12 trades per month for $12. My second portfolio is shown below with an aggregate yield of about 3%.

A.O. Smith (AOS) (1.30%)	Digital Realty (DLR) (4.60%)
Bank of Montreal (BMO) (4.20%)	Eaton (ETN) (3.00%)
Caterpillar (CAT) (2.50%)	McDonald's (MCD) (3.60%)
Cummins (CMI) (2.00%)	Royal Bank of Canada (RY) (4.20%)
DuPont (DD) (4.10%)	Union Pacific (UNP) (2.30%)
John Deere (DE) (2.20%)	Yum Brands (YUM) (1.80%)

IBM offers a DRIP with an initial setup fee of $10, an initial cash purchase fee of $5, ongoing automatic investment fee of $1, and a dividend reinvestment fee of 2% to a maximum of $3. For $2,400 at $200 monthly this works out to $10 + $5 + $12 + $12 = $39 plus a $45 annual fee from Computershare for Roth IRA custody if IBM has an IRA program, which they don't last time I looked. So that's a total of $89 a year or 3.7% ($89/$2400) which is considerably more expensive than ShareBuilder at $12 per stock.

I also have a small taxable (non-IRA) DRIP plan directly with Cincinnati Financial Corporation in which they withdraw $25 per month automatically from my checking account and together with dividend reinvestment there is absolutely no-charge. And they send not quarterly, but monthly statements. The first shares that were purchased for me were priced at $26.92. My most recent statement showed a share price of $44.51 and a quarterly dividend of $9.47. It is difficult for me to imagine a better set of circumstances, all of this wealth creation with no participation on my part apart from one-time enrollment that perhaps took me 15 minutes.

There are free DRIPs and some discount DRIPS, but alas, all without the Roth IRA option. Of course, in both cases, as the position builds value the fees become negligible.

The key point, however, is whether you use DRIPs or Capital One ShareBuilder, either is investment on autopilot, which captures splits, dividends, and stock price appreciation, avoids the fees of mutual funds, and allows the investors to get on with their lives secure in the knowledge that just as they get up every morning and go to work, so do the employees who work for them at the companies they own. It all builds wealth if you let it.

Times Square   *Ben Aronson 2006*
Oil on linen   *48 x 48 inches*

Chapter 13
Portfolio Construction

In this chapter I will present portfolio construction and provide a listing of stocks to provide the characteristics needed to meet diversification goals. But first a word on diversification. As described later in this chapter, Modern Portfolio Theory (MPT) was developed to dampen volatility by calling for allocation across multiple companies selected for their cyclical, semi-cyclical, non-cyclical, and counter-cyclical characteristics. Of course, cyclicality to what is a fair question.

Typically, market volatility is managed by balancing portfolio constituents across a spectrum from cash and near cash, through bonds, then low-beta big capitalization stocks and then moving successively toward high-beta low capitalization stocks eventually to several positions in emerging markets expected to mushroom with time though in the meantime exhibiting great volatility.

Diversification by Time

If the portfolio under consideration has a time horizon of say 20 years or more, diversification is really not an issue unless you want to make accommodation for emergencies and keep a portion in near cash. Or a portfolio may be constructed as described above in a spectrum of cyclicality with the idea that whenever an emergency arises, in a well-diversified portfolio one of the positions is bound to be in positive territory and a ready candidate for harvesting, or if dollar-cost-averaging, discrete shares in a narrowly diversified portfolio are likely to be always in positive territory. In any case, "diversification" typically means diversification by position and is designed to tamp down risk, but takes no note of diversification by time and the performance penalty such diversification imposes on a portfolio.

Many wealthy more sophisticated investors who are not concerned with unplanned cash demands, due to cash on hand or borrowing capacity, select portfolio constituents strictly on anticipated performance expectations and have no interest in Modern Portfolio Theory or diversification. In fact, as described in the chapter on taxes, the wealthy prefer borrowing over stock liquidation to head off a capital gains tax event, so for them diversification is a distraction from two main themes: liquidity and growth. Liquidity comes in bonds or borrowing, sometimes against their stocks and growth in stocks.

This chapter on portfolio construction is presented more to inform than to advise. For those with little interest in investment per se, they are well served by just dollar-cost-averaging into an accumulation of the common stocks of the Dow 30 or the most iconic 20 to 25 members of the S&P500, or,

even better, a select group from a global 100.
Although the United States has a disproportionate
membership in the top global 100 companies, membership is
not exclusive to this country, and there are many fine non-U.S.
firms to choose from as well. If the reader does this, maxing out
their Roth IRA contributions in doing so, there will be as good
a result as anybody may achieve using the most sophisticated
portfolio construction methodology.

Elasticity to the Business Cycle

As economies ebb and flow, companies fall into line
following cyclicality in various degrees of elasticity. Companies
that are highly elastic to economic expansion and contraction,
which might be providers of luxury goods like Tiffany or
LVMH (Moet, Hennessy, Louis Vuitton, etc.) will quickly
prosper in good times and just as quickly founder in bad.
Lower elasticity companies would be quite resistant to
economic cycles because of the prosaic nature of their products,
such as dishwashing liquid and soap provided by Procter &
Gamble. These would be non-cyclical. Then there are those
companies that are semi-elastic like automobile tires or
products whose lives may be extended in bad times but will
ultimately have to be replaced. And finally there are products
that are counter-cyclical in that they thrive in bad times by
providing alternative lower-cost solutions. Such companies are
Wal-Mart, Family Dollar, McDonald's and any other company
that traditionally caters to the budget-conscious but in bad
times, reels in the formerly well-to-do as well.

So as Modern Portfolio Theory would counsel, a well-
diversified portfolio would contain both elastic and inelastic
companies and within the elastic group some semi-cyclical and
counter-cyclicals with the objective of dampening volatility in
overall portfolio value. A little perspective needs to be injected
here however. When markets tank, often all companies, even
counter-cyclicals, go in the tank too. This is meant not to

discourage assembling a low-correlation portfolio, but to do so with the understanding that markets are like floods -- when trouble comes there is nothing good about it except the opportunity to acquire cheap shares of whatever it is you are accumulating. But it is always a bad time to disinvest, that is, sell shares. Also, you can be sure that stock price will be more volatile than the fortunes of the company the stock represents. In other words, don't judge the fortunes a company only by the behavior of its stock price movements.

The Role of Beta

Another measurement tool helpful for examining diversification is "Beta" for volatility. Beta is like Specific Gravity used in physics to denote density. In physics, water was chosen randomly as the standard and assigned a specific gravity of "1" and all other compounds are defined by densities that are greater or less than that of water. For example lead has a specific gravity of 11.35 because it is 11.35 times heavier than an equal volume of water and balsa wood has a specific gravity of 0.2 because it is 20% as dense as water of an equal volume.

The standard in investing "Beta" is the S&P 500 which is assigned a volatility of "1." All stocks are then measured for volatility against the S&P 500 varying from, for example, 2.28 (more volatile) for Dow Chemical to 0.35 for Southern Company, a power generation utility. A few other Beta examples are: Coca-Cola 0.60, McDonalds 0.48, Tiffany 1.74, S.L. Green, a New York City REIT 2.43, and the current winner is, iShares Gold Trust, which mimics gold at a Beta of 0.05. But beware, just as stock prices change so do Beta numbers. One would think that gold is quite volatile, but a recent check on the beta of iShares Gold Trust (IAU) found the newer beta to be 0.15. Gold apparently is not a volatile commodity.

Like all company metrics perspective is needed to understand just how to apply the data point. Beta values may be measured over one-year or many years. If over many years the figure may incorporate so much data that it is meaningless and if using too short a time span may be just reflecting a transient condition that soon will no longer be relevant. So Beta can be a useful measure but should be used with an understanding of its ephemeral nature. For example, during placid times the top 50 stocks in the S&P 500 by capitalization will have low correlations among each other, 10% to 40% according to a December 31st 2011 article in *The New York Times*. During market upset that correlation for the top 50 moved to 90%, that is, they were in lockstep in their price behavior and would have all had similar Beta values during that period.

Also, be aware that while water may be thought of as quite a neutral compound and a good stand-in for a baseline specific gravity standard, this is not the case with the S&P 500, which is quite a volatile standard. Witness the historical fluctuations of the S&P 500 over a 30-year period below. As you will see, it can hardly be compared to water unless you want to conjure up a roiling ocean.

YEAR	S&P 500	YEAR	S&P 500
1980	32.5	1995	37.6
1981	-4.9	1996	22.9
1982	21.5	1997	33.4
1983	22.5	1998	28.6
1984	6.3	1999	21.0
1985	31.7	2000	-9.11
1986	18.7	2001	-11.9
1987	5.3	2002	-22.1
1988	16.6	2003	28.7
1989	31.7	2004	10.9
1990	-3.1	2005	4.9
1991	30.4	2006	15.8
1992	7.6	2007	5.5
1993	10.1	2008	-37.2
1994	1.3	2009	27.1

As you can see the S&P 500 is pretty volatile but generally in a favorable direction. An investment would have multiplied 28.39 times over the 1980-2010 thirty-year period, well ahead of inflation.

A negative Beta would describe a stock that moves opposite to the market, a stock that becomes volatile in placid markets and calms down in roiling markets, a perfect diversification stock.

Companies may be sliced and diced in many different ways besides Beta, for example by capitalization size, years in business, industry sector, dividend payers and non-payers, growth or defensive (which is to say cyclical or non-cyclical) leveraged/un-leveraged, life-cycle position, global or domestic currency, conglomerate or single product, and legal structure, for example C- corporation or Partnership. One of the best websites to help you with your portfolio construction is www.advfn.com with free membership. The corporate data available at this site for stock selection is the most complete and accessible I have ever seen. Yahoo is another very good site.

Capitalization size and years in business does not require much elaboration and only serves to provide a sense of safety in size and longevity, but the following list of bankruptcies by year of incorporation, year of the bankruptcy, and capitalization may dispel some complacency:

Largest U.S. Bankruptcies:

o Texaco founded in 1901 and bankrupt in 1987 - $34.9 billion

o Bank of New England, founded in 1831 and bankrupt in 1991 - $29.7 billion

o Enron, founded in 1932 and bankrupt in 2001 - $65.5 billion

o Pacific Gas & Electric, founded in 1905 and bankrupt in 2001 - $36.1 billion

o WorldCom, founded in 1983 and bankrupt in 2002 - $103.9 billion o Refco, founded in 1969 and bankrupt in 2005 - $33.3 billion

o Calpine, founded in 1984 and bankrupt in 2004 - $27.2 billion

o Washington Mutual, founded in 1889 and bankrupt in 2008 - $327.9 billion

o Lehman Brothers, founded in 1850 and bankrupt in 2008 - $691 billion

o General Motors, founded in 1908 and bankrupt in 2009 - $91 billion

o Lyondell Chemical Company, founded in 1985 and bankrupt in 2008 - $27.4 billion

o General Growth Properties, founded in 1954 and bankrupt in 2009 - $29.6 billion

Sectors

The next qualifier is industry sector, which itself may be sliced and diced in many ways. For example one list of sectors is as follows:

Basic Materials
Conglomerates
Consumer Goods
Financial
Healthcare
Industrial Goods
Services
Technology
Utilities

But the list is not very helpful because the subcategories may behave quite differently from one other during market upset. For example, Industrial Goods may include cement and textiles. It is obvious that cement is a cyclical industry because during periods of low interest and rapidly growing economy cement will be demanded for construction. But textiles are a more evenly demanded commodity being better classified as non-cyclical – depending, of course, on the kind of textiles, carpeting or towels. In fact, the above nine sectors can each be further subdivided into about 20 subsectors yielding 180 sub-subsectors, which is not very helpful in constructing a diversified portfolio. On the other hand, using cyclical and non-cyclical is not definitive enough either, forcing us to rely on either the BCG life-cycle or the Morningstar 9-box matrix of capitalization and market growth, but these too are perhaps not enough guidance. The idea of diversification is an old one, as evidenced by the often cited rule, Don't put all your eggs in one basket.

Modern Portfolio Theory (MPT)

In the investment world, Dr. Harry Markowitz is thought to have advanced the concept of diversification to its logical and scientific end. Markowitz postulated that assets in a portfolio should be uncorrelated to one other as much as possible. This was dubbed "Modern Portfolio Theory" by Wall Street actors seizing upon a new tool to reel in investors. Markowitz himself called it merely Portfolio Theory, saying there was nothing modern about it. Incidentally, Markowitz was a professor at the University of Chicago, also the home of Milton Friedman, and today the university is cited for its unique flavor of economic theory called "The Chicago School." This "Chicago School" borrowed heavily from the "Austrian School," which was heavily influenced by Friedrich Hayek, a critic of John Maynard Keynes and author of an economics classic, *The Road to Serfdom*. In any case, MPT is now pretty much accepted as the gold standard of portfolio management, but saying so does not provide much direction in finding what is uncorrelated or what is elastic and inelastic.

Correlation or co-relation, refers to the effect events have on a population of components. If an event like rain, for example, on occasion causes floods, you can say they are correlated, and in some flood prone areas of the world that correlation may be very high, whereas in drought areas, the correlation is low. Some correlations are very obviously non-existent, for example: Do people who eat peanuts drive more expensive cars? Probably not necessarily. In other words, there is probably no correlation at all. So according to Markowitz, putting peanuts and expensive cars in the same portfolio would be a good diversification move. But this neglects the case for a diversification qualifier: Both peanuts and expensive cars will not do well in a down economy, so in that case they may not be so uncorrelated after all. They are both luxuries people indulge in when times are good.

So what is the variable we are finding correlations for? Most agree that periods of economic expansion and contraction are the key parameters, but during such market movements, all stocks seem to expand and contract with the market. For example, in the depths of the Depression, what industry thrived? Perhaps peanuts. As hard times hit, many families turn to peanut butter as a staple to take the place of more expensive foods. But this example makes the point that even in a single product there are holes in the conventional wisdom about their market behavior -- in bad times peanut butter may go up but honey roasted peanuts will go down. So be careful in deciding what is elastic and what isn't and how elastic.

Additionally, as markets take off or plunge, all assets start to move in lockstep as investors liquidate all positions regardless of their cyclicality, up or down, so you might begin to think about other forces that might offer diversification during periods of market upset So the correlation game is really looking at how to insulate against incvitable market downward spirals. Using cyclical and non-cyclical stocks is only a start of a good palette.

Another easy correlation factor involves global currency movements, which lead to appreciating and depreciating currencies. As U.S. residents, we are mostly concerned with the U.S. dollar (USD) and some of us may be completely insulated from the global currency market, but that would neglect a very good source of inflation fighting because while the USD might be inflating against the Euro and other currencies, stock positions in those currencies would be appreciating against the USD increasing investor returns. Larger companies are typically involved in global business and are therefore operating in many currencies and in so doing are a good portfolio position against U.S.-dollar-only companies. For example, a power generation utility is probably earning only USD whereas a global franchisor like McDonald's, which is in over 119 countries, is a great currency hedge against the USD. If the USD goes in the tank, McDonald's stock will probably not be too affected. Also as the USD tanks, McDonald's performance will be enhanced relative to other less globally diversified companies. This alone makes McDonald's a good diversification move in most portfolios worldwide. Also, since food is a non-cyclical commodity (people have to eat) food companies make good portfolio non-cyclical constituents.

McDonald's indeed has been an unusually good performer during periods of economic upset. During the down period of 2007-'09, while the S&P 500 turned in a negative performance of -15.6%, McDonald's turned in a positive gain of 15.5%. Some of that may well have been because of global currencies strengthening against the USD. Nevertheless, this is what Harry Markowitz had in mind in portfolio theory. Also keep in mind, global investing is not only spreading currency risk, but macro-economic risk as well, because you are spreading country risk.

You can think about other upsets that are likely to affect global markets and think about diversifying, or hedging, against them. Some upsetting events can be war, inflation, floods, droughts, earthquakes, storms, commodity shortages, water shortages, disease, and changes in economic hegemony as is occurring now between the United States and China, which may be called regional rotations, like sector rotation. The main point is to set diversification parameters and then make diversifying selections on that parameter. For example during periods of disorder like inflation and war, people flock to gold as a store of value, so in placid times when there is no war or inflation, gold might not be looked upon as a diversification move, but that is exactly what gold is at that point in time. Remember, investment is for an uncertain future, we don't invest for the present. In serene times gold will be at a low and will be perceived as an asset class without a future because periods of disorder cannot be predicted. That is the time to buy gold as a diversifier against an uncertain future that may include war and other public disorder. When that disorder comes, your stock positions will sink but your gold position will soar.

By uncorrelated we mean responding to different forces. For example, drought might drive up the price of commodities but not affect the steel supply, so grains and steel are two commodities that would seem to be uncorrelated because they respond to different forces. What Harry Markowitz had in mind was a portfolio that might look like a Ferris Wheel, where some positions were at the top, others at the bottom, and the rest spread around evenly at all points in between. Some might debate the wisdom of this, preferring to be overweight at the top, but the problem Markowitz was solving was not avoiding losses in the market; he was solving the problem of volatility and panic selling that volatility prompts. A much better long-term investment result might proceed from a non-diversified portfolio, but the volatility might tax the stamina of even the most ardent investor.

Legend has it that the young Markowitz, a doctoral candidate in mathematics at the University of Chicago, was waiting outside his advisor's office to get approval of his doctoral thesis on some aspect of number theory. Also sitting and waiting to see the same professor was a stockbroker. The two fell into conversation and when Harry described his thesis project, the stockbroker suggested a different thesis project. He suggested the topic of removing volatility from portfolios, presumably because volatility prompted panic selling, which most stock brokers had great difficulty stopping, and, of course, which they did not like because it led to an exodus of assets to manage and charge fees on. So the objective was not to find the *optimal* portfolio strategy, but to find the *most serene* portfolio strategy.

What this means is that MPT is an important tool, but not necessarily the end-all in portfolio management. For example, MPT neglects the diversifying action of dollar-cost-averaging, wherein one could have a portfolio of just one company's stock, but being purchased at intervals over a long period of time. Doing so might well yield liquidity in even the most depressed markets, because the cheapest shares would still show a profit in such times. If I had to choose, I would prefer to diversify by time rather than position. Of course, combining the two is the optimal strategy.

As mentioned earlier, MPT was developed to dampen volatility not necessarily improve performance. The reason volatility is undesirable in an overall portfolio is that it might lead to panic selling. But another favorable attribute of MPT is that during periods of market upset a well-diversified portfolio may be down overall but have some positions still in positive territory. If this is the case, it can be said that the portfolio still has liquidity; in other words it is possible to liquidate from profits rather than principal.

There's an old trust-fund rule, "Never dip into principal." Principal is your dry-powder, or as in old cowboy movies, it is your grubstake. It is what makes investment possible and you don't want to reduce it. In fact, you should increase principal at the rate of inflation. So if in a market downturn you need money, pray that you are diversified to the extent that you can draw out some profit without cutting into principal.

Now here is the key concept of diversification to understand: If you have a pool of retirement money that you don't need to raid even during transient personal upset (in other words, liquidity is not an issue) that pool does not have to be subject to the same diversification criteria as a more near-term portfolio. Such a portfolio may be, and should be, just as diversified, but not necessarily so driven by off-correlation. This frees you up to giving greater weight to expected long-run performance over non-correlation. For example, a longer-run portfolio will naturally be diversified by time if you are dollar-cost-averaging, which should always be the case. So while a well-diversified portfolio might have 25 or 30 constituents to manage risk and liquidity, a longer horizon portfolio may reasonably have as few as 10 constituents, but all aggregated over time. Chances are such a portfolio will have just as much liquidity, but will react in concert to market euphoria or panic – exactly what MPT seeks to avoid. And again, the core problem being attacked is panic selling.

Investor sentiment might be thought of as occupying one of three realms: euphoria, neutrality, or fear. During periods of euphoria or fear, clear thinking has been hijacked by the emotional state of either focusing on once-in-a-lifetime riches or conversely the thought of being wiped out altogether. Euphoria or fear creep in and displace rational thought. MPT seeks to head that off by providing the emotional investor with an overall result that should have a calming effect. Buying into euphoria will inevitably lead to the buying of overpriced shares and selling on fear will inevitably result in sales of expensive shares at fire-sale prices, because after all, isn't the worst offender the one stock causing the problem and the one that must be sold. The advantage of dollar-cost-averaging over MPT is that it is harder to identify a "bad actor" if some shares are still in positive territory during market upset – what do you sell and why? In the meantime, market upset is a good time to buy cheap shares that will produce future profits. But the best strategy of all is to just set an automated purchase routine and forget the market, including leaving quarterly brokerage statements un-opened.

Going Against the Grain

Benjamin Graham pointed out in *Security Analysis* that securities are not necessarily speculative in kind -- stocks vs. bonds vs. mutual funds -- but derive their risk dimension from the soundness of the firm issuing the security. Consequently one might assemble a very speculative mutual fund from a basket of very speculative stocks and at the same time assemble a much less risky position of, say, nothing but Procter & Gamble common stock acquired incrementally over a period of time. In such a case, the mutual fund would be speculative whereas the diverse position in the single stock (PG) would be low risk. Of course, many on Wall Street would object to my characterization of a single holding as being low risk, but that is what this book is about, separating Wall Street nonsense from common sense. Of course, if you divide your investments into two stocks, you have just reduced your company risk by 50%, which is a good thing.

The reason Wall Streeters would object to calling diversification by time, and not position, "safe" is that they want to charge fees on their magic formula for "managing" assets, including their highly magical diversification stratagems -- some American Funds, a little Fidelity Contra Fund, some Davis New York Venture fund and a little Cohen & Steers for real estate diversification, plus maybe a smidgeon of PIMCO Total Return Fund to add a little bond content. Such a "balanced" portfolio with the MPT chatter to go with it can't help but impress and reassure an adoring client.

Sometimes you will read such statements as: "Buy and Hold doesn't work." Well, for what term are we talking? One year, three years, ten-years? The statement never comes with that qualifier. The market, ever since performance data has been collected, has done nothing but rise with time – that is a 100% correlation - time = profit. People who make such silly statements such as "Buy and Hold" doesn't work," have invariably purchased positions (I won't use the word "invest") with the intention of holding on to them for a longer period than is their usual practice, and then along comes a dip in their otherwise smooth road and they sell out in a panic, proclaiming "Buy and Hold" doesn't work. If you check in with these same people ten years later, you might very well hear; "If only I had hung on."

Bragging is a big part of investment life for many and the mother-of-all-brags is that against all prevailing sentiment, somebody bought a position due to his or her great brilliance and prescience and later cashed in for millions. Of course this is loudly proclaimed until it comes into the hearing of somebody collecting for a charity, at which point the oxygen goes missing and the braggart disappears. This is the standard water-cooler chatter for public braggarts. But coming in for a close second is the "one that got away." In this brag, the practitioner bought the position but then sold out and was cheated out of his due by some nefarious rumor or other countervailing condition out of his control. Bragging is just as pernicious as the media in disempowering otherwise rational people from hewing to a sound investment process. Inuring yourself from bragging is part of becoming an investor.

Sometimes when I pick up a ringing phone I am confronted with a telemarketer who is particularly effective in blowing past my objections and continuing to deliver his script. I then default to my anti-telemarketer script and ask him if I might discuss variable annuities with them. This works almost 100% of the time. Similarly when subjected to investment bragging, that is the time to roll out your favorite charity. It should be tear-jerker though, like widows struggling to get nutrition for their emaciated infants.

Reversion to the Mean and Dow Theory

But for the non-braggarts, the general theory of stocks eventually recovering is very generally accepted on Wall Street and is even captured in a more generic way with the theory of "Reversion to the Mean." This theory is that a stock price will gyrate above and below "intrinsic" value and one should plot the historical mean price of a stock and buy when the price is below the mean, with the idea that the price will ultimately return to the mean and even above the mean. A common technical analysis tool is to compare, say, the 50-day moving average with the 200-day moving average and when the 50-day crosses above the 200-day it is time to buy, or even better, buy when the 50-day reverses direction and starts moving up. But be careful, the relative position of the 50-day below the 200-day tells the trader that the stock is merely recovering though not making new highs and may therefore be a premature signal.

This needs a fuller explanation. Tracing daily stock price movements will create a jagged line. If the same data points are consolidated into moving 50-point averages, the jagged line gets smoothed, taking out daily meaningless gyrations. A moving average created from 200 points will be even smoother. Since the 50-day line and the 200-day line are created from the same data, the lines will be on top of each other. Sometimes the 50-day line will cross down over the 200-day line and this is considered a bearish or unfavorable sign for investors going long on the stock. When the 50-day line crosses up through the 200-day line this is felt to be a bullish sign and a good time to go long and buy the stock with the expectation that the upward momentum of the 50-day line will continue its upward ascent. The 50-day/200-day SMA (Simple Moving Average) is a popular technical analysis tool.

Whether you call it rebalancing, Dow Theory, or Reversion to the Mean, it all may be captured in dollar-cost-averaging, which biases a position with a disproportionate number of cheaper shares. So dollar-cost-averaging is a form of rebalancing, but to put that process on steroids by rebalancing existing positions is generally a good thing. And remember, dollar-cost-averaging is carried out not by selling out positions, but by redirecting cash flows to out of favor positions already held. Perhaps the core concept here, however, is that when the market is down and shares are cheap, it is difficult to develop the will and discipline to buy. The reason is that the media will be broadcasting fear -- it is how they make money, getting you to listen -- and if you listen to the fear they are dispensing you either miss your opportunity or lose money by panic selling. Dow Theory helps the wobbly-kneed stay the course and even "cowboy-up" and buy the out of favor shares. A Warren Buffet aphorism fits here: "Be fearful when others are greedy and be greedy only when others are fearful."

Paranoia

Something like this once happened to me. I was a broker at a major firm when in 2008 the bottom dropped out of the housing market followed by a collapse of securitized mortgage bonds. The iconic Wall Street firm is Goldman Sachs. Whether you love it or hate it, it is head, shoulders, and torso above every other firm. I cannot tell you how many times I heard people in my own firm, assert their primacy with the statement: "Oh, I came over from Goldman." That was the imprimatur that was always cited if available.

I had never bought any Goldman (GS) stock because I thought it was overpriced. That is the case with some high-profile iconic brands, they are always overbought. So when the entire market caved in at the end of 2008, Goldman dropped from about $225 a share to about $85. I was talking to a prospect over the phone about it, and mentioned that I saw this as a rare opportunity to buy into Goldman and was thinking about a pretty good-sized trade for my own account. My prospect, jaded on all of Wall Street over the mess, declared that Goldman was no different than the other failing firms and they had a lot farther to drop. I couldn't see it, but the fear infecting all discourse infected me as well and I was cautious so didn't buy, abandoning in fear an opportunity to buy into a perennial iconic brand.

The argument in favor of Goldman is that it, like P&G, is the undisputed leader, and it is because the brightest always flock there. So buying a company that attracts the top tier of the top business schools in the country may not be without risk, but at $85 vs. $225 a share, GS was solidly below its long-term moving average and decidedly more opportunity than risk. By the same time the following year, Goldman stock had climbed back up to about $200 a share, taking it out of my investment universe. Since then a general economic downturn has seen Goldman stock plunge again so I may yet find an iconic brand within reach.

This was a case where I succumbed to the paranoia and missed an opportunity to own a stock I badly wanted. Goldman Sachs is running into headwinds, but when there is a company that is so prominent within its market, it is the kind of company you want to own. Whatever comes their way, they have the talent to work it out. For all practical purposes, in my view, Goldman Sachs like other iconic companies, doesn't have competition. But there are missteps, such as the cautionary tale of the poor performance on the Libya sovereign investment. Goldman lost, as was reported, 98% of a $1.3 billion stake of sovereign wealth invested with them by Libyan authorities.

Big financial institutions often labeled "too big to fail," have also been characterized as "too big to manage" by Amar Bhide, an economist worth reading on the subject. Bhide has built a credible and logical argument that finance today has replaced human interaction and judgment, which is to say Loan Officers with computer modeling programs that parse risk on numerical variables and then securitize that risk by offloading it onto investors. Bhide points out that when Goldman Sachs was a partnership, the custody of the Libya funds would have had to have passed the inspection of the partners who would then have been on the hook for losses. But in the new, modern, publicly-owned Goldman Sachs, the investments were selected by a computer program that would be beyond the capability of the former partners to even understand -- too big to fail and too big to manage, according to Bhide.

The Dow 30

Below is the present Dow Jones Industrial group.

	Symbol	Name
1	**AA**	Alcoa Inc.
2	**AXP**	American Express Company
3	**BA**	Boeing Company (The)
4	**BAC**	Bank of America Corporation
5	**CAT**	Caterpillar, Inc.
6	**CSCO**	Cisco Systems, Inc.
7	**CVX**	Chevron Corporation
8	**DD**	E.I. du Pont de Nemours
9	**DIS**	Walt Disney Company (The)
10	**GE**	General Electric Company
11	**HD**	Home Depot, Inc. (The)
12	**HPQ**	Hewlett-Packard Company
13	**IBM**	International Business Machines
14	**INTC**	Intel Corporation
15	**JNJ**	Johnson & Johnson
16	**JPM**	JP Morgan Chase & Co.
17	**KFT**	Kraft Foods Inc.
18	**KO**	Coca-Cola Company (The)

19	MCD	McDonald's Corporation
20	MMM	3M Company
21	MRK	Merck & Company, Inc.
22	MSFT	Microsoft Corporation
23	PFE	Pfizer, Inc.
24	PG	Procter & Gamble Company (The)
25	T	AT&T Inc.
26	TRV	The Travelers Companies, Inc.
27	UTX	United Technologies Corporation
28	VZ	Verizon Communications Inc.
29	WMT	Wal-Mart Stores, Inc.
30	XOM	Exxon Mobil Corporation

The Dow industrial index was created by Charles Dow in 1896, and, of course, published. Charles Dow started *The Wall Street Journal* and Dow Jones & Company. Today the DJIA is composed of 30 stocks but the original Dow was only 12 stocks, of which GE is the only one still in the index intact; the others were usually bought out except Laclede which survives. The originals were:

1. American Cotton Oil - Predecessor of Bestfoods
2. American Sugar - Evolved into Amstar Holdings
3. American Tobacco - Broken up in 1911 by antitrust actions
4. Chicago Gas - Now part of Peoples Energy
5. Distilling & Cattle Feeding - Evolved into Millennium Chemicals
6. Laclede Gas - Still in operation as Laclede Group
7. National Lead - Now known as NL Industries
8. North American - Utility broken up in the 1940s

9. Tennessee Coal, Iron and Railroad Company - Bought by U.S. Steel
10. U.S. Leather - Dissolved in 1952
11. U.S.Rubber - Now part of Michelin
12. General Electric

The purpose of stock ownership is to beat inflation in accumulating a retirement nest-egg. The purpose of a portfolio is to manage that nest-egg accumulation. Given those criteria, one could accomplish the mission by just using the Dow Jones industrials and diversifying over time with dollar-cost-averaging, which will succeed as well as any "sophisticated" asset allocation strategy being touted by a Wall Street professional in search of assets to charge fees on.

A not insignificant component of wealth creation will come from dividends, which I call free money because stock price seems to move independently of dividend distribution. In other words, the market doesn't seem to care about dividends, but there is a small subset of the market that cares very much about dividends and engages in a strategy called "Dividend Capture."

Dividend Capture

Instead of just distributing dividends un-announced, companies announce dividend distributions typically two days before the "Record Date," which is the day on which those owners of the stock are identified as recipients of the dividend earned over the preceding quarter. On the record date, the stock price is reduced so that new buyers, who will not receive the dividend, will be treated equally with dividend receivers. This is called stock price going "ex-dividend." After the dividend distribution, the stock gradually recovers that deficit in expectation of the next dividend in the stock price. The reason for the price adjustment is that if the stock is sold shortly after going ex-dividend, the dividend distribution still goes to the earlier owner of record who receives along with a slightly lower stock price, the dividend. The buyer pays a little less for the stock but does not receive the dividend. The "Dividend Capture" strategy calls for purchasing the stock just before the ex-dividend date and then selling the following morning. In some cases the dividend drop is less than the dividend and other factors may drive up the price overnight. In the meantime, the dividend capturers are guaranteed a dividend.

Let's take a $50 stock with a yield of 5% which would be $2.50 parsed into 4 quarterly dividend distributions of 75¢ each. A thousand shares would realize $750, and 10,000 shares would yield $7500, which would be a pretty good day's return. But, there are trading costs and risks that the stock will drop 75¢ or more.

Nevertheless there are actors who focus on this strategy and move very big money around doing it. I present this so when you hear of this strategy you will be inoculated against it.

Most dividend-paying stocks pay their dividends quarterly or on some regular schedule, so those wishing to game the system can do so by anticipating the dividend announcement. The more important aspect of dividends is that they are generally not reflected in stock price movements. In other words, when stock price moves in response to demand shifts created by news, the amount of the change is typically reflected only in stock price without accounting for the contribution of dividends. Theoretically, dividend-paying stocks should not see their stock price move as much, up or down, because part of the payoff will come in the dividend. But the market ignores the contribution of dividends in valuation, and the stock gets bid up without any thought to dividends. This stock price behavior without respect to dividends makes dividends a source of free -- and often overlooked -- money. Consequently overweighting dividends in portfolio stock selection is a good move. Elsewhere in this book I model the dividend boost by comparing the same asset base over a 40-year compounding period at 9% and 12% (3% dividend). Try it yourself and see what you get – you will be amazed.

The Wall Street Weir

Most investors will have some knowledge of perhaps 25 stocks and some recognition of perhaps another 100. But there are roughly 10,000 stocks traded in the U.S. and the Russell Global Index referred to earlier will have about 10,000 U.S. and non-U.S. issues. The number of U.S. companies in the Russell Global Index is about 3,000, leaving 7,000 non-U.S. companies in the Russell Global index. This adds up to a population of 17,000 common stocks of global corporations notable enough to make an index, 10,000 Russell Global constituents and 7,000 U.S. constituents not in the Russell Global index. This means that the population of common stocks an investor can reasonably draw ideas from is 17,000. Obviously a thorough study of those 17,000 to make an informed selection of perhaps 25 will never occur; it is too much work. Most investors just depend upon the serendipitous encounter of stocks worth researching. Into this vacuum comes Wall Street.

As soon as you start researching a stock being touted by Wall Street you are hooked because a little bit of research leads to more research and by the time you are finished you are buying it because a good case can be made for any stock.

Every stock, no matter how obscure has a following and by investing in it, you are the new kid on the block going up against the veterans. And if the stock is being touted by Wall Street it is already in play and floating on a cushion of investor sentiment. Ignore Wall Street chatter and just use your everyday life to spot investment candidates and do your research from there.

Managing the Client

Burnishing the core message of this book that Wall Street is not an essential component of investment I wish to relate the following story that took place in my final interview to become a stock broker at a major firm. I was both very excited or as excited as a 60 year-old man can get and awed by the world of wealth I was possibly about to enter. I of course wore a conservative suit to this meeting, meaning a dark suit, white shirt and not too garish a tie. I was shown into the office manager's office which was wall-to-wall mahogany and brass, all working in concert with the dark red carpeting to set a tone of wealth and privilege. The manager was dressed pretty much as I was with the exception of a crisper white shirt, obviously more costly tie and the obligatory French-cuffs with cuff-links. I was impressed.

During the course of the interview the phone rang and the manager took the call, giving me my first lesson: When a client calls, the call is taken no matter what. I was also a bit surprised that the manager had personal clients he was managing directly. I would have thought that all client contact work would have been left to lesser mortals. Of course, I learned later that clients are the life-blood of a stock broker's business regardless of position and that afloat on a turbulent sea, no manager will give up his or her clients unless assured of a permanent seat somewhere. This manager took his client's call and immediately began responding sympathetically to the client's worry over a transient market downturn. With a few mouse-clicks the client's portfolio was displayed on the manager's two-screen workstation. The manager then began to suggest candidates to sell in this small stock market storm. The client approved, and with a few more mouse-clicks the positions were sold.

After three or four sales, the manager gave some reassuring sounds that the client was then in a "safe" place and "crisis" had been averted. The client seemed satisfied and rang off.

I have always been one to enunciate my thoughts and pondered whether to ask the manager if selling in a falling market was a good idea. Fortunately I bit my tongue and, incidentally, got the job. Biting one's tongue I have long ago learned is an important skill, unless you are writing a book, of course. In any case, as I began my new career mixing with experienced stock brokers I was given a client management rule that was crucial to success. If a client calls with a bad investment idea, accept it with measured hesitation: *"Hey, if you say so Herb, I can do that for you."* Never, ever dispute the idea. And the "Mother-of-all Rules" is: Don't ever suggest an alternative stock. The reason is that if the broker talks the client out of his or her stock pick, and the stock goes up, even momentarily, the broker is branded an obstruction to wealth creation. If the broker suggests an alternative and the client's pick goes up and the broker's goes down, even momentarily, the broker will probably lose the client. If the broker doesn't debate the client and just buys the stock, no matter what happens, the broker will rise in the estimation of the client because good service was provided. This is the client-broker interface in the real world. It has nothing to do with investment and all about keeping a client, for better or for worse.

You the reader should take away from this and the saga of Bernie Madoff, his feeder funds, and his clients, that all the mahogany along with the brass and the cuff-links and the assets under management are just trappings designed to reel in clients. Just focus on the word "trappings" -- does that suggest anything?

Investors who judge their positions solely on stock price, are the pawns of buy/sell decisions of a small subset of the entire roster of stockholders for that stock, and the most impulsive subset, floating mindlessly on the winds of optimism or pessimism on the prospect of the company over the next quarter, even on companies that have been doing business since the 19th century. It is like judging a person's longevity on their day-to-day complaints of aches and pains or lack thereof. It is meaningless noise. Have you ever heard the term "loose cannon?" Well, that is what drives stock prices, loose cannons going off all over the place. The best response is to duck.

Investments in the Weather

Another highly differentiated and interesting stock class is the property and casualty insurance sector from Bermuda. Bermuda is quite vulnerable to storms and has no natural water supply; water comes only from the sky and must be used very thoughtfully. With no water to support industry, Bermuda has apparently turned to services, namely property & casualty insurance, perhaps as a result of seeing many ship wrecks wash up on its shores from storms.

The way this business works is that a long period of storm-free seasonal changes will lead to declining revenue as subscribers thin out and premiums are reduced. Then there will be a huge storm with gargantuan losses and the survival of some of these insurers will be questioned. The industry survives and immediately charges higher premiums which everybody is happy to pay with the recent storm in sharp focus. The insurer then enjoys some years of very attractive profits that starts the whole cycle all over again.

The nice thing about this sector is that it tends to be cyclical like Wall Street, but driven by weather storms rather than investor storms. They also typically pay a nice dividend. I have listed 10 Bermuda property & casualty insurers below, but in reviewing them, think about market structure. Their core competency is underwriting, which means pricing risk, which is a learned skill with statistics characteristics. For some reason this core competency related to storms is centered in Bermuda. So in choosing one or more of the companies, what you are choosing is Bermuda casualty underwriting because you can be sure they are all talking to each other if they are not all related to each other. Also keep in mind that the numbers that you see are all floating on air, as soon as the next storm hits you can be sure there will be big changes.

What is on display on the next page, is outsized profits and very strong financials no doubt due to the ferocity of recent storms and the raising of not only premiums to provide adequate cover but also plenty of earlier victims and witnesses ready to pay. Expect some volatility in these numbers, which are likely to be as volatile as the storms they cover, keeping in mind that global warming is being blamed for increasingly more frequent outlier storms.

Referring again to our discussion of normal distributions, storms are categorized by the frequency of their likely occurrence, 50-year storms are bigger than 5-year storms and used to reside in one of the tails of a normal distribution, the trailing tail possibly – 2½% probability. With global warming, it looks like 50-year storms have moved in-board to occupy a more probable position in the distribution.

Stock	Symbol	Beta	Dividend	Rev	Profit	Assets/ Revenue
Ace	ACE	0.69	2.20%	$15.86 Billion	16%	515.37
PartnerRe	PRE	0.43	3.50%	$5.49 Billion	16%	429.01
EverestRe Group	RE	0.54	2.36%	$4.75 Billion	13%	404.76
Axis Capital Holdings	AXS	0.76	2.87%	$3.66 Billion	24%	482.75
Aspen Insurance Holdings	AHL	0.62	2.20%	$2.16 Billion	17%	382.89
Validus Holdings Ltd.	VR	0.35	3.67%	$1.91 Billion	35%	420.60
Alterra	ALTE	0.86	2.10%	$1.58 Billion	14%	710.25
Maiden Holdings Ltd.	MHLD	0.24	3.00%	$1.34 Billion	9%	415.68
RenaissanceRe Holdings Ltd.	RNR	0.53	1.46%	$1.21 Billion	39%	540.06
Platinum Underwriters Holdings Ltd.	PTP	0.61	0.92%	$955 Million	23%	394.50

Other Places to Look for Investment Candidates

I've made many references to the Dow 30 and the S&P 500 as being good places to look for strong companies but that leaves out many foreign issues and in a multi-national world it only makes sense to put companies in a global rather than just a national competition. Below is a list of the top multi-nationals sorted by profit. The companies from totalitarian countries have been removed as well as those that cannot be accessed through U.S. markets. Nevertheless what is left is all you need to create a great portfolio. Keep in mind that profit, yield and beta are constantly changing values.

Rank	Company	Revenues ($ millions)	Profits ($ millions)	Symbol	Yield	Beta
3	Exxon Mobil	$284,650	$19,280	XOM	2.80%	0.50
4	BP	$246,138	$16,578	BP	5.10%	1.22
54	Petrobras	$91,869	$15,504	PBR	5.09%	1.45
96	Barclays	$66,533	$14,648	BCS	2.00%	2.64
1	Wal-Mart Stores	$408,214	$14,335	WMT	2.30%	0.31
80	Vodafone	$70,899	$13,782	VOD	7.20%	0.73
66	Procter & Gamble	$79,697	$13,436	PG	3.80%	0.45
48	International Business Machines	$95,758	$13,425	IBM	1.80%	0.66
21	AT&T	$123,018	$12,535	T	5.00%	0.57
2	Royal Dutch Shell	$285,129	$12,518	RDS.B	5.30%	1.28
37	Banco Santander	$106,345	$12,430	SAN	17.54%	1.76
46	Wells Fargo	$98,636	$12,275	WFC	2.68%	1.31
14	Total	$155,887	$11,741	TOT	6.90%	1.00
25	J.P. Morgan Chase & Co.	$115,632	$11,728	JPM	3.33%	1.32
27	E.ON	$113,849	$11,670	EONGY	6.55%	
13	General Electric	$156,779	$11,025	GE	3.43%	1.56
68	Telefónica	$78,853	$10,808	VIV	4.40%	0.65
11	Chevron	$163,527	$10,483	CVX	3.58%	0.77
44	Nestlé	$99,114	$9,604	NSRGY	1.60%	0.62
18	BNP Paribas	$130,708	$8,106	BNPQY	7.96%	
28	Berkshire Hathaway	$112,493	$8,055	BRK.B		0.25

26	Hewlett-Packard	$114,552	$7,660	HP	0.67%	1.21
38	General Motors	$104,589	$7,600	GM		1.36
32	Samsung Electronics	$108,927	$7,562	SSNGY	1.18%	
60	Enel	$89,329	$7,499	ENLAY		
15	Bank of America Corp.	$150,450	$6,276	BAC	0.50%	2.28
29	GDF Suez	$111,069	$6,223	GDFZY	7.51%	
24	ENI	$117,235	$6,070	ENI	4.72%	0.66
20	Allianz	$125,999	$5,973	ALIZF	7.00%	
39	HSBC Holdings	$103,736	$5,834	HBC	4.10%	1.21
31	Nippon Telegraph & Telephone	$109,656	$5,302	NTT	3.80%	0.35
9	AXA	$175,257	$5,012	AXAHY	3.40%	2.30
17	ConocoPhillips	$139,515	$4,858	COP	4.94%	1.12
100	WellPoint	$65,028	$4,746	WLP		0.06
42	Lloyds Banking Group	$102,967	$4,409	LYG		2.07
61	UnitedHealth Group	$87,138	$3,822	UNH	1.50%	0.90
45	CVS Caremark	$98,729	$3,696	CVS	1.42%	0.76
58	Tesco	$90,234	$3,690	TESO		1.99
35	Verizon Communications	$107,808	$3,651	VZ	4.55%	0.52
73	Munich Re Group	$74,764	$3,504	MURGY	4.00%	
83	Zurich Financial Services	$70,272	$3,215	ZURVY		
40	Siemens	$103,605	$3,097	SI	4.72%	1.57
74	Statoil	$74,000	$2,912	STO	4.00%	1.19
51	Honda Motor	$92,400	$2,891	HMC	2.10%	0.85
23	Ford Motor	$118,308	$2,717	F	1.96%	2.36
97	Home Depot	$66,176	$2,661	HD	2.20%	0.78
98	Target	$65,357	$2,488	TGT	2.50%	0.87
5	Toyota Motor	$204,106	$2,256	TM	1.20%	0.73
81	BASF	$70,461	$1,960	BFFAF		
88	Archer Daniels Midland	$69,207	$1,707	ADM	2.40%	0.46

53	Aviva	$92,140	$1,692	AV	11.90%	1.37
36	Crédit Agricole	$106,538	$1,564	CRARY		
49	Dexia Group	$95,144	$1,404	DXBGY		
95	CNP Assurances	$66,556	$1,396	CNPAY		
90	Legal & General Group	$68,290	$1,346	LGGNY		
16	Volkswagen	$146,205	$1,334	VLKAY	2.24%	
91	Boeing	$68,281	$1,312	BA	2.40%	1.21
34	McKesson	$108,702	$1,263	MCK	0.87%	0.80
67	LG	$78,892	$1,206	LPL		1.56
43	Cardinal Health	$99,613	$1,152	CAH	2.28%	0.80
79	Costco Wholesale	$71,422	$1,086	COST	1.20%	0.66
72	Prudential	$75,010	$1,054	PRU	3.10%	2.37
62	Société Générale	$84,157	$942	SCGLY		
86	Deutsche Post	$69,427	$895	DPSGY		
76	AmerisourceBergen	$71,789	$503	ABC	1.40%	0.71
59	Deutsche Telekom	$89,794	$491	DTEGY		
63	Nissan Motor	$80,963	$456	NSANY		1.73
22	Carrefour	$121,452	$454	CRERF	8.68%	
82	BMW	$70,444	$284	BAMXY		
99	ArcelorMittal	$65,110	$118	AMSIY		
70	Kroger	$76,733	$70	KR	2.00%	0.4
89	Toshiba	$68,731	-$213	TSHTF		
69	Sony	$77,696	-$439	SNE	2.20%	1.48
65	Panasonic	$79,893	-$1,114	PC	1.70%	0.84
47	Hitachi	$96,593	-$1,152	HTHIY	0.38%	
85	Fiat	$69,639	-$1,165	FIATY		
12	ING Group	$163,204	-$1,300	ING		2.77
33	Citigroup	$108,785	-$1,606	C	0.14%	2.56
94	Peugeot	$67,297	-$1,614	PEUGY		
84	Valero Energy	$70,035	-$1,982	VLO	2.60%	1.43

30	Daimler	$109,700	-$3,670	DDAIF	6.07%	1.98
55	Royal Bank of Scotland	$91,767	-$4,167	RBS		2.53
41	American International Group	$103,189	-$10,949	AIG		3.43

Time Horizon

The platform on which a portfolio is constructed is the life term of the portfolio. Young people, those in their 20s just beginning their careers, are lucky in that they can create a 50-year portfolio that is overweight in positions selected only for their long-term prospects without too much regard for cyclicality. Of course they do need some near cash assets to cover emergencies. But if they leave those long-term positions alone, and add to them over time using dollar-cost-averaging at a rate of 5% of their income, they will never have a need for particularly sage stock selection because any stocks will do from the global 100 or S&P 500.

As the time horizon shortens, progressively more attention must be paid to cyclicality to force results over an abbreviated time frame, making sure the portfolio is always liquid to some degree and to stage dis-investment with the least disruption to continued growth.

You can ignore all of this discussion and most of this book and just buy the discrete common stocks that make up the Dow 30 or select a subset from the S&P 500 or the S&P Dow Jones S&P 500 High Quality Rankings Index or the global top 100 companies, and that strategy will probably outperform any portfolio you put together no matter how well uncorrelated or thought out. Or to be even more passive, select several index funds based on the S&P 500 indices and the Russell indices. If you are more likely to leave your investments alone using index funds over discrete common stocks, do that. *The main ingredient to wealth creation, is not in the stock selection, but in stamina to stay the course after the stock selection is made.*

Down Lexington   *Ben Aronson 2003*
Oil on linen, 68 x 82 inches   Tibor de Nagy Gallery

Chapter 13a

A Model Portfolio

I am putting together a model portfolio just to give a sense of how you might go about putting a portfolio together. There is no mystery to it, but a model is always useful. First, I'm going to set some diversification parameters, as follows:

(1) Basic Materials – (cyclical)
(2) Retail - (cyclical)
(3) Automobile – (cyclical)
(4) Industrial – (cyclical)
(5) Energy – (semi-cyclical)
(6) Financial – (semi-cyclical)
(7) Consumer Staples – (non-cyclical)
(8) Utilities – (non-cyclical) –
(9) Telecom – (non-cyclical) –
(10) Water – (non-cyclical) –

(11) Medical – (non-cyclical) –
(12) Counter-Cyclicals –
(13) Military – (non-correlated) –
(14) High-Yield – (multi-correlated) –
(15) Small-Cap Fund –

Now I'm going to populate that rough diversification table with investment candidates.

(1) Basic Materials – (cyclical) – Alcoa, PPG, LaFarge, Arcelor Mittal, BASF
(2) Retail - (cyclical) – Costco, Tiffany, Walt Disney
(3) Automobile – (cyclical) – BMW, Hyundai, Toyota
(4) Industrial – (cyclical) – Cummins, Eaton, ITW
(5) Energy – (semi-cyclical) – Exxon Mobil, Shell, Chevron
(6) Financial – (semi-cyclical) – Citigroup, Aetna, Cigna, NYSE Euronext, ACE
(7) Consumer Staples – (non-cyclical) – Campbell Soup, Nestle, P&G, Kraft, Ambev
(8) Utilities – (non-cyclical) – Southern Company, PP&L, Dominion
(9) Telecom – (non-cyclical) – Vodafone, Verizon
(10) Water – (non-cyclical) - Veolia
(11) Medical – (non-cyclical) – JNJ, Merck, Pfizer
(12) Counter-Cyclicals – Yum, McDonald's, Wal-Mart,
(13) Military – (non-correlated) – Boeing, General Dynamics
(14) High-Yield – (multi-correlated) – Annaly Capital, Blackstone, Vornado, SL Green
(15) Small-Cap Fund – Alger Small Cap Growth Fund, Templeton Frontier Markets Fund

Now I am going to construct the final portfolio. Yields are shown in parentheses.:

(1) Basic Materials – (cyclical) –
Alcoa (1.30%), Arcelor Mittal (4.10%)
(2) Retail - (cyclical) –
Walt Disney (1.20%)
(3) Automobile – (cyclical) –
Hyundai (0.00%)
(4) Industrial – (cyclical) –
Cummins (1.60%), ITW (2.70%)
(5) Energy – (semi-cyclical) –
Exxon Mobil (2.70%), Royal Dutch Shell (4.70%)
(6) Financial – (semi-cyclical) –
NYSE Euronext (4.70%), ACE Ltd. (2.70%)
(7) Consumer Staples – (non-cyclical) –
Nestle (0.00%), P&G (3.70%), Ambev (3.80%)
(8) Utilities – (non-cyclical)
Southern Company (4.20%), Dominion (3.90%)
(9) Telecom – (non-cyclical)
Vodafone (7.00%), Verizon (4.50%)
(10) Water – (non-cyclical)
Veolia (6.50%)
(11) Medical – (non-cyclical)
JNJ (3.60%), Merck (4.00%)
(12) Counter-Cyclicals –
Yum (1.80%), McDonald's (3.10%),
(13) Military – (non-correlated) –
General Dynamics (3.10%)
(14) High-Yield – (multi-correlated) –
Annaly Capital Management (13.00%), Blackstone Group
(3.00%)
(15) Small-Cap Fund –
Alger Small Cap Growth Fund (0.00%)

The final portfolio with 26 stocks yielding 3.50%:

	STOCK	SYMBOL		YIELD	BETA
1	Alcoa	AA	Cyclical	1.30%	2.04
2	Arcelor Mittal	MT	Cyclical	4.10%	2.13
3	Walt Disney	DIS	Cyclical	1.20%	1.15
4	Hyundai	HYMTF	Cyclical	0.00%	
5	Cummins	CMI	Cyclical	1.60%	1.99
6	ITW	ITW	Cyclical	2.70%	1.17
7	Exxon Mobil	XOM	Semi-cyclical	2.70%	0.51
8	Royal Dutch Shell	RDS-A	Semi-cyclical	4.70%	1.02
9	NYSE Euronext	NYX	Non-cyclical	4.70%	1.66
10	ACE Ltd.	ACE	Non-cyclical	2.70%	0.73
11	Nestle	NSRGY	Non-cyclical	0.00%	0.62
12	P&G	PG	Non-cyclical	3.70%	0.44
13	Ambev	ABV	Non-cyclical	3.80%	1.00
14	Southern Company	SO	Non-cyclical	4.20%	0.26
15	Dominion Resources	D	Non-cyclical	3.90%	0.45
16	Vodafone	VOD	Non-cyclical	7.00%	0.72
17	Verizon	VZ	Non-cyclical	4.50%	0.53
18	Veolia	VE	Non-cyclical	6.50%	1.75
19	Johnson&Johnson	JNJ	Non-cyclical	3.60%	0.52
20	Merck	MRK	Non-cyclical	4.00%	0.65
21	Yum Brands	YUM	Counter-cyclical	1.80%	
22	McDonald's	MCD	Counter-cyclical	3.10%	0.39

23	General Dynamics	GD	Non-cyclical	3.10%	1.26
24	Annaly Capital Mgmnt.	NLY	Semi-cyclical	13.00%	0.25
25	Blackstone Group	BX	Semi-cyclical	3.00%	2.26
26	Alger Small Cap Growth	ALSCX	cyclical	0.00%	

I invite you to just copy this portfolio or use similar diversification methods and populate those with your favorites. The Beta numbers are not offered as selection criteria but to acclimate the investor to differences in expected volatility across portfolio constituents. It could be argued that two less volatile basic materials stocks should be substituted for Alcoa and Arcelor-Mittal, but when you are dollar-cost-averaging, volatility is your friend: cheapening shares going down, cheap shares at the bottom and cheaper shares on the way back up.

Always dollar-cost-average your way to filling out this or any other portfolio. The best strategy is to automate your purchases wherever you can using DRIPs or CapitalOne ShareBuilder.

This portfolio does not conform to the discussion on the Morningstar style-boxes, ignoring for the most part all the boxes except "big-cap value" and perhaps some smaller capitalization "value" stocks. The absence of "growth" stocks is a fair criticism. I have a strong preference for dividends because they help to further insulate the stock from panic selling, which I view as the leading cause of investment failure in not only beginners, but seasoned investors as well. To address this lapse, I would use a mutual fund or funds to fill the lower-right style boxes of the Morningstar matrix. I have already mentioned Alger funds work in this sector. Franklin-Templeton and Cohen & Steers would be other recommendations. For this book I found some funds that could fill these style-boxes. For small cap growth you can look at Alger Small Cap Growth Fund (ALSAX) and Alger Growth Opportunities Fund (AOFCX). For global, look to Franklin Templeton funds managed by Mark Mobius, PhD a prominent globe-trotting analyst: Templeton Frontier Markets (FFRMX) and Templeton Emerging Markets Small Cap (TEMZX). For hard assets look at Cohen & Steers Emerging Markets Real Estate (APFCX) and Cohen & Steers Global Infrastructure Fund (CSUCX). In buying these funds, make sure you are acquiring "C" class shares.

The only style-box left unfilled is the lower left small-cap value. I consulted Forbes contributing analyst John Buckingham who talked up the Greek tanker stock Navios Maritime Holdings (NM) which was yielding 6.5%. Navios also issues what looks like Master Limited Partnership units (NMM) yielding around 13% but in that issue, prefers to be treated as a "C" corporation for tax purposes meaning that you get a typical 1099-Div earnings statement and probably long before tax day. Again, this is Greek shipping, which is a good place to look for tanker stocks. The USA for software, South Korea for electronics, Australia for mining, Italy and France for fashion, Germany for machinery and cars, Canada for banking and Greece for shipping to name a few highly correlated national identities.

If at some point you must take a look at what you have, hopefully you will discern your stock holdings arrayed in a Ferris Wheel, some positions up, some sideways, and some down. The order will change with time and the seasons of the economy but the effect will be the same, all growing at different rates, all responding to the aggregate effort of the employees, your neighbors, in trying daily to make their lives more secure within the companies that employ them. In the end their effort will be rewarded with rising stock price, maybe not right away, but in the long-run their effort will be reflected in stock price. These people, your neighbors, are the real market. Oh. And I almost forgot. Regardless of market action, you can almost certainly expect to collect your 3½% dividend. Price may decline but this does not cause dividends to decline.

Street in Genoa   Ben Aronson 2009
Oil on panel, 24 x 24 inches   Private Collection

Chapter 14
Insurance and Annuities

Earlier in this book I listed a number of asset classes that was meant to be exhaustive, but isn't because new asset classes are being thought up all the time. At the same time, it was the intent of this book to hew strictly to common stocks, venturing into other asset classes more or less just to inoculate the reader from having to experiment with them. Asset classes that have a reputation for being exotic are often thought of as being superior, but rarely if ever has an asset class trumped plain old common stock for the opportunity to consistently beat inflation. For one thing, few of the other asset classes lend themselves to dollar-cost-averaging, one of the most powerful tools in the world of building retirement income. Two asset classes, however, warrant discussion, and these are both life insurance products: life insurance and variable annuities.

The History of Life Insurance and Annuities

The Roman republic was built on public virtue that began to erode when money from a growing empire of tax collection and trade led to the ascendancy of a mercantile class and that class then began to successfully bribe the Senate to resist legislation that would challenge their growing wealth and influence. Sound familiar? In response, there arose occasional public officials who challenged this corruption of the Roman state, notably, the Gracchi brothers who were assassinated for their intransigence and later two military figures: Marius and his son-in-law Gaius Julius Caesar. Both were accomplished generals. Up until the time of Marius, the army ranks were filled with citizens doing their patriotic duty. Not all citizens could be soldiers, however, because a soldier had to outfit himself, and as the republic grew in wealth many could not afford to do so. They could not serve because they were dispossessed by the wealthy. Does this sound familiar?

The Romans felt that soldiers who didn't have enough in assets to equip themselves would make poor soldiers and so were more of a liability than a fighting asset. A soldier without assets, so went the theory, would cut and run, because he had nothing to fight for. But by 100BC when Marius was in power, the income inequality was so great that staffing the army became a problem, so Marius created a professional army and from then on soldiers were hired and outfitted by the state. This, however, did not solve the problem of proper burial, which was beyond the resources of most soldiers. So a common fund was started, a burial club, with regular small payments into the fund to provide for a proper burial and perhaps even a small stipend for the widow. This is cited as the start of life insurance.

So life insurance has been around for about 2,100 years. Incidentally, another life insurance product not covered in this book also had its origin in Rome and in the military – pensions. The Roman legionnaire, perhaps with the start of the professional soldier, earned a pension, which was then formalized by Augustus (the first emperor) in 13BC. It granted every soldier a pension after 20 years of service.

It should be pointed out that many Americans have grown up with the idea that the United States is the wealthiest state to come into existence thus far. As a rough guess, the Roman military during the imperial period was paid well over twice and perhaps thrice what the American military personnel are paid today. When Julius Caesar was assassinated his will was publicly read and in it, he awarded to each and every Roman citizen, somewhere between 1 and 2 million citizens, about $200 in today's money. But this was not even the bulk of his estate; the bulk he left to his nephew Octavian (Augustus). Don't look for that to happen in the U.S. anytime soon, just to apply a little perspective.

A characteristic central to life insurance is the triggering event – death. The irrefutability of death means there is no room for argument whether a settlement is due or not. This means that life insurance is not plagued with the eruption of conflicting opinion about whether a payoff event has occurred and who gets the money. Death triggers a payoff to a named beneficiary, case closed.

This leads to a corollary characteristic, namely insurable interest. You cannot purchase life insurance on a person's life unless you can prove that you will suffer loss upon the person's death. Without this provision, anybody could insure any life. Soon you would have speculators hanging around doctor's offices to learn who had been given an attenuated life prognosis. That would be followed by a mad rush to the nearest life insurer to insure that life, with the expectation of paying a few premiums before the bonanza comes in – or if the bonanza didn't come in soon, it could be hastened along. This is stopped in its tracks by the "insurable interest" provision.

Another life insurance product that was banned for similar reasons is the Tontine. In a Tontine, you pay premiums that build an accumulating and concentrating pool of assets as participants die off, leaving their contributions to survivors. Many years later the few survivors reap a big return. It was felt that easing aging survivors into a premature exit before the payoff date was too tempting a proposition and a challenge to public order. But all is not lost, because life insurance is a sort of tontine in reverse.

The common pile gets richer as people drop out of their life insurance pools due, usually, to the exertions of financial advisors trying to win their business. What these advisors do is point out to their targets that having lived through the formative years of their children and other family responsibilities, life insurance is no longer needed, and why not drop the unneeded expense, investing those premiums instead. I will not argue the wisdom or lack thereof of that argument, but merely point out that up until the moment the policy is cancelled, the insurance company had collected money for a liability that is suddenly removed with the cancellation. That is like the bank unexpectedly advising you that your mortgage has been cancelled and no further payment is necessary. Whoppeeeee! If the policy is "whole life," there is a cash value that must be returned, but it is a fraction of what was paid in or what would eventually be paid out. So the insurance company collected a stream of rich payments that lasted for years for doing . . . a little recordkeeping. What a great business, and how good for the remaining beneficiaries that get a bigger pile to draw from or lower premiums to pay in the meantime. And unlike a tontine, it is perfectly legal and does not create public disorder beyond that caused by financial advisors in search of clients.

In the section of inflation, I characterized cash flows over time as diminishing in purchasing power, roughly cut in half every 25 years or so. Illustrated below is a typical inflation-adjusted cash in-flow to the life insurer over the life of the policy. Note the diminishing purchasing power eroded by inflation of the premium in-flow to the insurer.

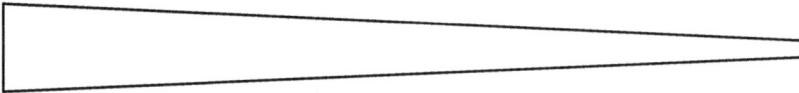

Next, you see what the insurer does with that cash-inflow. The premiums get invested.

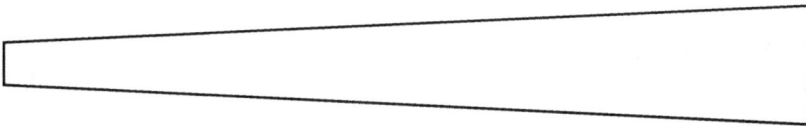

Illustrated below is roughly what the pay-off is.

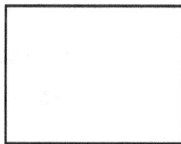

Illustrated below is the life insurer's pay off on a cancelled policy.

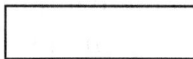

The above figures are not to scale, but are used to show the fundamental relationships of cash flows and investment returns under inflation in a life insurance policy. For one thing the value of the insurance company payoff will be determined by where along the timeline of the insured's life the payoff comes. It could come even between policy issue and the second premium payment.

The Value of Life Insurance

I believe life insurance is an excellent asset class under even the most negative outcome, which is very long life with a settlement to a widow/widower that is a fraction of the purchasing power of the face value at inception. First of all, the widow/widower is provided for during the life of the policy. Also, inflation is not guaranteed; had there been deflation, the pay-off would have much greater purchasing power than the original face amount – though this is a very unlikely event.

The purchasing power of the premiums decline over time at the same rate as the pay-off declines, but the pay-off is given better tax treatment than other cash inflows to the beneficiary. However, the real benefit of life insurance is that it provides protection during the life of the policy, and the policy is made stronger by late-term cancellations by other persons, and in the case of whole life, there is a growing cash value that can be raided in an emergency. Also, the growing cash value can be used to purchase additional death benefit and restore the purchasing power of the life policy. Here is life insurance as an inflation fighter.

Finally, with funeral costs running to $10,000 and more, life insurance takes care of final expenses without burdening the family left behind. But the purpose of this book is not to discuss life insurance, but rather beating inflation, and life insurance clearly is not the best tool for doing that. As a matter of fact, life insurance can be a poster child for why investing to stay ahead of inflation is urgent for all, except the wealthy, whose financial cares are not how to increase their wealth, but how to hang on to the wealth they have.

The reason for my detour into life insurance is to lead up to another life insurance product, an inflation beating one – variable annuities. Variable annuities are life insurance products because of trusteeship and custody issues that are routine for insurers, and because of beneficiary guarantees tied to longevity for lifetime payouts that require actuarial calculations. The longevity aspect of variable annuities comes in the pay-off, which is calculated based on the expected life of the beneficiary. There is, however, one very important distinction between life insurance longevity and variable annuity longevity and that is: there is no underwriting in variable annuity sales.

Underwriting

Underwriting? A strange term. According to legend, there was a coffee shop in London where merchants would gather in the morning for their cup of joe. The coffee shop may have been named Lloyds. On the wall was a blackboard, a very large blackboard, that listed the outbound ships by name, (this was in the days of sail), the captain's name, and other pertinent facts, such as destination, cargo, etc. Merchants, sipping their coffee, were invited to insure ships and cargoes and thereby earn a premium for undertaking risk for others, the ship owners. If after scrutinizing the board, an individual saw a "well found" ship, a well-regarded captain and a destination that did not involve "going around the Horn," he would realize his premium cash in-flow by writing his name under the ship of his choice – thus the term underwriting as it came to be called.

Today, careful scrutiny of risk as in medical examinations, is standard for all life policies that are underwritten. If a life policy is obtained at work, then there is group underwriting, as in employees of a coal mining company paying higher premiums than employees of a publishing house, for example. In variable annuities, there is no individual underwriting, but unlike life insurance this loophole is exploitable only by the very healthy and long lived.

We again turn to Rome for the origin of annuities, wherein

citizens could make a lump sum payment and in exchange receive an annual stream of payments that lasted as long as they lived. The payments were called (in Latin) *annua*, for the Latin word for "years," thus annuities.

Annuities have survived to the present day and the unique service they offer is the same: an aging person with a lump of money trying to decide how to meter the dis-investment so it will be entirely used upon drawing one's last breath. As you might imagine, this is a very difficult calculation to make, thus the *annua* or annuity. Let the longevity experts meter your money for you, spreading the risk over a pool of participants – some will die sooner while others will die later, but all are provided for.

Individual underwriting is not done, as far as I know. The insurance company asses risk strictly by age and the general population and then gives you a fixed lifetime income that will last, unchanged, whether you die the next day or in a hundred years.

Variable Annuities

For young people investing in the stock market, there is one source of uncertainty and that is the market return from year-to-year. We know that over a 40-year period for example, the market will have a total return of about 9½% per year annualized but that on an annual basis the results will not be so smooth. But young people won't be retiring for another 40-years or longer, so market volatility is really not an issue for them.

Older people nearing retirement have another source of uncertainty – how long are they going to live. As you get into the range of retirement planning longevity becomes a consideration, and longevity usually means periods that could be much shorter than 40 years and that makes volatility an issue. For young people building wealth, volatility is good. For older people planning retirement, volatility is bad.

below is a chart from an earlier chapter showing the volatility in S&P 500 returns over a 43-year period. The S&P 500 returns for the first half of 2013 were around 12%. I am guessing the chart is total return and not merely price return.

1970	3.95%	1984	6.25%	1998	28.58%
1971	14.31%	1985	31.74%	1999	21.04%
1972	19.02%	1986	18.67%	2000	-9.09%
1973	-14.00%	1987	5.26%	2001	-11.89%
1974	-26.48%	1988	16.61%	2002	-22.10%
1975	37.22%	1989	31.68%	2003	28.69%
1976	23.92%	1990	-3.10%	2004	10.88%
1977	-7.15%	1991	30.46%	2005	4.91%
1978	6.56%	1992	7.64%	2006	15.80%
1979	18.61%	1993	10.08%	2007	5.50%
1980	32.49%	1994	1.32%	2008	-37.00%
1981	-4.89%	1995	37.57%	2009	26.45%
1982	21.55%	1996	22.96%	2010	15.06%
1983	22.55%	1997	33.38%	2011	2.11%
				2012	15.83%

There are five years in which the S&P 500 experienced double-digit declines. If an investor decided to allocate $100,000 to a retirement income fund and the fund lost 22% in the first year, one would have to realize a 29% gain just to get even and a 41% gain to get to a point where the fund should be had it realized the annualized 10% gain from the start. In other words, the order in which the gains and losses are realized can play a very big role.

It may take years to make up for early losses in a retirement fund and the lost revenue is gone forever. If a retiree is taking a fixed percentage from savings say 10% annually, the withdrawals will be disproportionately determined from performance during the early years. See table below modeling the same S&P 500 returns in reverse order and taking a 10% withdrawal income rate.

	DECLINES EARLY IN TERM				DECLINES LATE IN TERM		
YR	Return	Principal	Income		Return	Principal	Income
1		$100,000				$100,000	
2	-14.00%	$86,000	$8600		22.50%	$122,500	$12,250
3	-26.48%	$56,904	$5690		21.55%	$134,008	$13,400
4	37.22%	$70,276	$7027		-4.89%	$126,181	$12,618
5	23.92%	$78,378	$7837		32.49%	$165,506	$16,550
6	-7.15%	$65,497	$6549		18.61%	$194,344	$19,434
7	6.56%	$62,815	$6281		6.56%	$206,023	$20,602
8	18.61%	$67,055	$6705		-7.15%	$188,451	$18,845
9	32.49%	$79,958	$7995		23.92%	$231,194	$23,119
10	-4.89%	$68,444	$6844		37.22%	$314,073	$31,407
11	21.55%	$74,874	$7487		-26.48%	$231,707	$23,170
12	22.55%	$82,583	$8258		-14.00%	$197,276	$19,727
		$74,326				$177,549	
	TOTAL INCOME		$79,273		TOTAL INCOME		$211,122

As you can see, the cash flow from the two scenarios and the ending capital value were vastly different, while the S&P 500 returns were identical, just in reverse order.

This is both a dramatic demonstration of the randomness of the market, the power of the market to deal very different results to different players and the power of the market to handily beat inflation.

Examining the chart, you can see that even under adverse market conditions, $79,273 was taken out and you still have $74,326 left. The stock market turned $100,000 into $153,599 in 11 years under adverse market conditions. This is not a bad result. The other result, of course is mind boggling, but again under totally random conditions of the market, just as likely as the first result. The best modeling outcome is perhaps a point in between the two – about $150,000 in income and about $150,000 in ending capital. But in the stock market over short periods, anything can happen.

For some people, this would not work. Look at the chart on the left again and ask yourself, at what point does an investor give up and look for a different solution. I suspect when the principal gets down to $56,904, most investors would throw in the towel.

The Role of Variable Annuities

Because throwing in the towel would be a disaster, there are variable annuities and plenty of people to buy them. What is a variable annuity?

A variable annuity is a product sold by an insurance company that puts a floor under investment performance – investments can go up but they can't go down. Wow! What a product. Where can I line-up for this?

Not so fast. There are high fees and lots of gotchas. Still variable annuities are an important asset class and should be understood by any investor.

Let's start out with immediate annuities. These are annuities where you turn a retirement lump sum over to an insurance company and in return they give you a cash-flow out that will never stop as long as you live. This sounds rather amazing until you consider that if the same lump were put into an S&P 500 index fund, you should derive a lifetime income as well. But as in the illustration above, that income might decline dramatically over the short-term and take your principal with it. An immediate annuity guarantees you a level cash-flow that is determined before you buy the annuity and for life. The upside is the stability, the downside is that over time, inflation will eat away the purchasing power of your level cash-flow and your principal is gone, the insurance company has it.

An immediate annuity for a 70-year old typically pays about 7% per year from the initial principal, level for life. In the above illustration, this would have beat the market cash-flow in five of the eleven years. Not too bad, but then the loss of the principal is significant. So immediate annuities are not a very good deal but they do provide certainty and for many people, if the cash-flow is adequate, even with inflation effects, the certainty is worth a lot.

In addition to immediate annuities, there are deferred annuities. In this flavor of annuity, you invest your money in mutual-like funds offered by an insurance company and they provide principal protection, where your annuity value can only go up and never down, but you defer taking an income, perhaps for many years. This deferral time is called the "accumulation period."

The first thing to understand about annuities is that they are contracts: you provide money and the insurance company provides contractual services like principal protection. Most annuity contracts have terms of time and early termination is discouraged with high termination fees. Also, principal protection comes with a fee, a high fee. But now the fun starts. Providers of annuities are well aware of the price people will pay for certainty and so they add all sorts of features to jazz up the annuity contracts and reel in more clients. The jazzed up components of a variable annuity contract are given the general name of "living benefits," in other words these are benefits for the living that operate during the accumulation phase or the withdrawal phase.

GMIB

First up are Guaranteed Minimum Income Benefits (GMIB). These are devices that extend principal protection throughout the accumulation period or for shorter definite terms, depending on the contract. Simple principal protection produces two values in your quarterly statements: Actual account value from market action, and the minimum guarantee from which withdrawals will be calculated, which is your original principal. If the market has been in an uptrend, the actual account value will be higher than the guarantee value. If the market has been trending down, the actual account value will be lower.

The first GMIB feature that might be part of your contract is a "ratchet," or "step-up." A ratchet/step-up resets the guarantee on each anniversary if the actual account value is higher at that point in time than the original investment. If the actual account value is higher, you now have a higher guarantee withdrawal base than your original principal. Contracts may vary the ratchet period from ten years on up to until withdrawals begin.

Another GMIB is called a "roll-up." In a roll-up, the insurance company agrees to credit your account with a percentage increase, treating your principal like a savings deposit that earns interest. In such a case, your statement might list four contract values: Principal protection of the original investment amount, actual account value, guaranteed (ratchet/step-up) withdrawal base and guaranteed roll-up withdrawal base. If the "surrender" period was up, usually ten years, you could surrender your contract at no-charge and just take the actual account value. Or you could just continue the contract and let it accumulate, protecting you from a down market. Or you could, if you were 59½ years old, begin withdrawals which would then be calculated from the highest of the four values. At 59½ the likely annuitization rate might be around 5%, meaning you would receive 5% of the highest value for life. Of course when you 'turn-on" the annuity all accumulation stops and you have a level fixed income for life that will erode with inflation.

All variable annuity contracts offer principal protection, beyond that, ratchets and roll-ups may be purchased as options. Most if not all contracts also provide life insurance that will pay a beneficiary in the event of the death of the annuitant. In some contracts, the owner can purchase a doubling of the life benefit and the life benefit is calculated on the highest of values between actual account value and any living benefit values that are part of the contract.

GMWB

Since inflation is a reality for which variable annuities may be thought of as vulnerable and an unattractive asset class for that reason, insurance companies have introduced an inflation fighter – a Guaranteed Minimum Withdrawal Benefit (GMWB).

In a GMWB contract, there may be ratchets/step-ups and

roll-ups but the withdrawal benefit is that the principal remains the property of the annuity owner even after withdrawals have begun. Withdrawal percentages may be lower than annuitized withdrawals but they will keep pace with inflation and grow with time. As long as the actual account value is higher than any living benefit base value, then surrender is always an option provided you are beyond the surrender penalty period. If the living benefit values are higher, then taking the variable annuity guaranteed withdrawals may be a better option. And in a GMWB contract, you retain the assets, meaning that something will be left for heirs.

In a GMWB contract, the most likely scenario is that withdrawals will mostly come from market performance, leaving your principal pretty much intact. But should the actual account value ever go to zero due to taking withdrawals in a persistently down market, the withdrawals will continue based on the highest value the account ever reached, but from that point on, the withdrawals will be level. The only way for withdrawals to increase is due to an increase in actual account value. However given the history of the broader market, one can expect market advances and increases in withdrawals for the entire withdrawal period, up to death.

A Real-Life Example

After I was licensed broker, I asked a gentleman in our office to manage my wife's account so I could watch what he did and learn. One of the investments he suggested was a variable annuity. So my wife invested $100,000 in a GMIB variable annuity contract with a ratchet/step-up and a 7% roll-up.

Six months after that I was fired for not bringing in enough clients but in a move that puzzled me, I was hired by another brokerage firm. I had to move our assets over to the new firm and that meant managing my wife's variable annuity. At that time, the market was heating up and I decided to move her entire account into an international real estate fund. It seemed pretty risky, but since the account had principal protection, I thought "Why not?"

I was at this new firm when the market crashed in 2008 and many brokers started leaving the firm and in one case it resulted in my losing a partner on a large account I was part of, so I joined another firm. When I opened my wife's variable annuity statement, because I had to move it again, I was horrified to find that the actual account value had fallen to $63,000. What was I going to tell my wife!

I then noticed, and I was new to variable annuities and really didn't know how they operated in detail, but I noticed that the guaranteed withdrawal base was $150,000 and the death benefit, to me, was $150,000. What is going on here, I wondered? After further study, I saw that the international real estate fund had taken the account up to $150,000 before crashing down to $63,000 and that value got locked-in as a ratchet/step-up. I then very proudly showed my wife how she had benefited from my investment prowess.

I changed the investments to a much more mainstream allocation but with the passage of time, that $150,000 withdrawal base wasn't really all that attractive any longer and the actual account value was just recovering to the original amount - $100,000.

Then after another several years the actual account value had only risen to $103,216 but the roll-up withdrawal benefit and death benefit had risen to $173,819, while the ratchet/step-up base remained at $150,000. This was a much better result. Still the only way to realize that value is to turn on a lifetime income which would be about possibly 7% a year when my wife reaches 70. When that happens, the principal will be lost.

Nevertheless, it would be useful to model what actually happened inside the annuity with what could have been outside the annuity. The table on the next page shows three values: the annuity ratchet/step-up value, the roll-up value, the actual account value and S&P 500 returns over the same period. As you can see, the variable annuity option, even with the loss of principal, might not be too bad an option. Some attention would have to be paid to longevity expectations based on family longevity history but just the certainty of the annuitized cash-flow out for life, regardless of the length of that life, will be decisive for some, perhaps those with no other financial or family resources.

YEAR	ANNUITY RATCHET VALUE	ANNUITY ROLL-UP VALUE	ANNUITY ACTUAL ACCOUNT VALUE	S&P500 EQUIVALENT VALUE
2005	$100,000	$100,000	$100,000	$100,000
2006	$125,000	$107,000	$125,000	$104,910
2007	$150,000	$114,490	$150,000	$121,485
2008	$150,000	$122,504	$100,000	$128,167
2009	$150,000	$131,079	$63,000	$80,745
2010	$150,000	$140,255	$70,000	$102,102
2011	$150,000	$150,073	$80,000	$117,479
2012	$150,000	$161,578	$90,000	$119,958
2013	$150,000	$173,818	$103,216	$138,948

Annuitizing the roll-up value would produce an annual income of 7% at age 70 or $12,167 per year for life. Alternatively my wife could surrender her annuity and with favorable market conditions take out 10% per year from $103,216, the cash value. Let's say for a twenty-year period, to age 90, modeling the additional years from the most recent S&P 500 data. See table below. The annuitized cash flow total ($12,167 x 20) comes to $243,340. The 10% annual distribution from an S&P 500 index portfolio would be a range between $119,771 and $195,822.

10%	DECLINES EARLY IN TERM				DECLINES LATE IN TERM		
YR	Return	Principal	Income		Return	Principal	Income
1		$103,216				$103,216	
2	-14.00%	$88,765	$8876		22.50%	$126,491	$12,649
3	-26.48%	$58,734	$5873		21.55%	$138,375	$13,837
4	37.22%	$72,537	$7253		-4.89%	$118,448	$11,844
5	23.92%	$80,900	$8090		32.49%	$141,239	$14,123

6	-7.15%	$67,604	$6760	18.61%	$150,773	$15,077
7	6.56%	$64,835	$6483	6.56%	$144,597	$14,459
8	18.61%	$69,212	$6921	-7.15%	$120,833	$12,083
9	32.49%	$85,529	$8552	23.92%	$134,763	$13,476
10	-4.89%	$70,359	$7035	37.22%	$166,431	$16,643
11	21.55%	$74,874	$7487	-26.48%	$110,124	$11,012
12	22.55%	$76,971	$7697	-14.00%	$85,236	$8523
13	10.88%	$69,274	$6927	10.88%	$76,713	$7671
14	4.91%	$65,408	$6540	4.91%	$72,431	$7243
15	15.80%	$68,169	$6816	15.80%	$75,488	$7548
16	5.50%	$64,727	$6472	5.50%	$71,677	$7167
17	-37.00%	$36,701	$3670	-37.00%	$40,641	$4064
18	26.45%	$41,767	$4176	26.45%	$46,252	$4625
19	15.06%	$43,253	$4325	15.06%	$47, 896	$4789
20	2.11%	$39,749	$3974	2.11%	$44,017	$4401
21	15.83%	$41,438	$4143	15.83%	$45,887	$4588
		$37,295			$41,299	
	TOTAL INCOME	$119,771		TOTAL INCOME	$195,822	

Optimizing Cash-Flow

Strangely enough, those incomes can be raised by reducing the withdrawal income to 7% from 10% , yielding $143,566 instead of $119,771 in the adverse market condition modeling and raised to $210,110 from $195,822 in the favorable market modeling. This demonstrates that optimizing withdrawals means striking a balance between withdrawals and leaving money in to grow with the market. If you take more out, there is less left to grow tomorrow's income. A withdrawal rate of 7% seems to be a pretty optimal figure. See chart below.

7%	DECLINES EARLY IN TERM				DECLINES LATE IN TERM		
YR	Return	Principal	Income		Return	Principal	Income
1		$103,216				$103,216	
2	-14.00%	$88,765	$6213		22.50%	$126,491	$8854
3	-26.48%	$61,517	$4306		21.55%	$142,987	$10,009
4	37.22%	$78,504	$5495		-4.89%	$126,475	$8853
5	23.92%	$90,472	$6333		32.49%	$155,837	$10,908
6	-7.15%	$84,139	$5889		18.61%	$171,900	$12,033
7	6.56%	$83,383	$5836		6.56%	$170,354	$11,924
8	18.61%	$91,978	$6438		-7.15%	$158,430	$11,090
9	32.49%	$113,331	$7933		23.92%	$182,583	$12,780
10	-4.89%	$100,244	$7017		37.22%	$233,003	$16,310

11	21.55%	$113,317	$7932		-26.48%	$161,479	$11,303
12	22.55%	$129,149	$9040		-14.00%	$129,151	$9040
13	10.88%	$133,176	$9322		10.88%	$133,170	$9322
14	4.91%	$129,935	$9095		4.91%	$129,928	$9095
15	15.80%	$139,932	$9795		15.80%	$139,924	$9794
16	5.50%	$137,294	$9610		5.50%	$130,130	$9109
17	-37.00%	$80,440	$5630		-37.00%	$121,021	$8471
18	26.45%	$94,597	$6621		26.45%	$142,319	$9962
19	15.06%	$101,225	$7085		15.06%	$152,289	$10,660
20	2.11%	$96,126	$6728		2.11%	$141,629	$9914
21	15.83%	$103,549	$7248		15.83%	$152,565	$10,679
		$96,301				$141,886	
	TOTAL INCOME		$143,566		TOTAL INCOME		$210,110

Still, taking the 7% from the roll-up base yields 20 x $12,167,or $243,340 and that is only for 20-years and not life as is guaranteed by the contract. So in this particular case, as of this date, the variable annuity may be the better choice for some retirees.

Abuse in VA Sales

There are frequent abuses of VA sales, particularly upon the elderly who are concerned with outliving their money. Their plight is exacerbated by the fact that VA commissions are some of the highest in the industry and a good way for a Financial Advisor to lock in a good pay day. When I was selling VAs, I had a prospect in California, and I was required to get a California license to sell them, and this required me to take a California course on VAs and get tested on California laws enacted to protect against exploitation of the elderly. I'm glad I took the course, because the California curriculum included information on annuity strategies I had not been exposed to up to that time.

I was taught , among other things, to layer multiple VAs with different characteristics to better hedge a client against unplanned events. Rather than say getting one $100,000 variable annuity, better to buy four $25,000 annuities with different characteristics, that way when you need income in retirement, you can turn on only as much as you need, and leave the rest at work in the market. Also, if you have an emergency you need to only cash in one of the four.

How to Buy a VA

There is great variation among companies, and it would be typical to find the most generous living benefits being offered by companies with the most restricted menu. You are better off to put investment menu near the top of the list of selection criteria, because it is exactly the opportunity to invest aggressively that you are paying high fees for. Restricted menus may require some fraction of the investment be in fixed-income.

The selling of VAs always focuses on the scare that the market will tank and the investor will be wiped out, and VAs are a way to protect against that. VA critics are right to attack this practice. Although it can happen, over the term of a VA contract the likeliest scenario by far is that the value will advance with the market. But the advance may be very uneven as seen above. If a VA contract guarantees you 7% a year but then restricts you to funds that are 25% fixed income, your account value will be muted in its growth.

What you want, since the insurance company is taking all the risk, is to get as much growth as you can by selecting not several funds, but one fund in the most expectant sector you can find without a requirement to include a fixed-income selection as well. This will depend upon your being offered such an option and it is that option that will pretty much determine what that annuity does for you, and not the living benefits that are mostly sales tools. So pay attention to menu, not living benefits. The only living benefit you really need is that your account value can never decline and all VAs provide that. But be aware, it is difficult to impossible to beat the S&P 500.

In layering annuities, it may be optimal to divide your

purchase between accumulation benefits and withdrawal benefits if you can't get all in the same contract – GMIB and GMWB. Remember, this election is made at the start and cannot be changed. Later, you can turn on the GMWB first because it will rise with inflation. Save the GMIB cash flow for later so it can work in the market longer.

There are also other options for managing payout and that is to select terms that are shorter than life expectancy. For example, if you have, say, four Variable Annuities to draw from in retirement, you may wish to turn on the first one that provides only a payout for, say, 10-years, period certain. In this payout flavor, the insurance company calculates a payout over only 10 years and not life and therefore the cash flow will be higher. If you don't live the entire ten years, then the remaining Variable Annuities payments are made to heirs. If you do live ten years, you can then turn on a second larger cash stream with a second VA with period certain.

Most Annuities are Surrendered

Unfortunately the VA story doesn't end there. Most VA clients forget why they bought them, and upon being challenged by a prospecting advisor on why they are paying such high fees for funds they can get much cheaper, don't know the answer, and cash them in, often at a loss. There are heavy penalties in most cases for cashing in a VA during the first ten years, and the sad fact is, most VAs get cashed in prematurely. It is the minority that are actually held to term and then used to fund a retirement that can't run out.

The core concept of VAs is to put a floor under retirement assets to protect them from market upset, which occurs with some regularity. But over a very long period of time, say 30 years, the living benefit guarantees offered by annuities are really not useful because in a long span of time, the market will have plenty of opportunity to recover from various upsets along the way, so the ending value in VAs held over a long period is almost certainly going to be the result of market advances and not guaranteed minimums and the fees saved will be better off invested. Variable annuities as investments are better utilized for the mid-term, when market uncertainty and volatility might prompt counterproductive panic selling and destroy a retirement. It is only when retirement is in sight, that VAs make sense as investments – for security and to head off panic selling. Also remember to layer VAs to structure the payout.

VAs for Aggressive Investment

But VAs may also be used earlier as a vehicle for aggressive investing or investment by very skittish investors, which they might never do without the principal protection feature offered by VAs.

For example my father was very risk averse. He worked for the U.S. government and had a pension, and he left an estate worth about $1½ million all in municipal bonds. Interest from muni bonds are free of federal income tax that goes to pay federal workers, but he may have missed that dimension in his planning. In any case, he might have better managed his risk-averse nature in his savings program by using variable annuities. Just a guess on my part would forecast at least a doubling the size of his estate had he done so. So here was a case where VAs would have been a good life-long investment strategy. Unfortunately he was so risk averse, I doubt that anybody, including Abraham, would have been able to talk him into a VA.

If you wish to diversify into an aggressive sector using a VA, don't be distracted by "living benefits." Instead, concentrate on investment menu. For example, some insurance companies offer juicier "living benefits" and then limit the investment menu to a mix of stocks and bonds, as already described. This is a waste of time and should be avoided. What you want in a long-term VA, is the freedom to invest in discrete stock funds that are entirely devoted to mid-cap and small-cap funds. These are funds or stocks in funds that I would otherwise recommend against as offering too much risk for the return.

When you buy a variable annuity and pick the most aggressive investment option offered, you can sit back and watch your annuity provider go on a roller coaster ride while you go just take a smooth ride up, and if you do it in a Roth, so much the better. Of course, as in all investment, you will have to leave it alone and let the market, and not you, decide what the current market value is. If you touch it, then all is lost and there was no point in having the VA in the first place. Also keep in mind that over the long-term, it is very difficult to beat the S&P 500. But as in the case of someone like my father, who would not invest in the S&P 500 without principal protection, VAs are a good choice and keep in mind, locking-in a high the S&P 500 reaches over a 30-year or 40-year term might wind up making a significant contribution to retirement income. Bad things happen. VAs mitigate those bad things.

When to Buy a VA

But there is some timing of VA purchases you should pay attention to. Each VA is an individual contract between the insurance company and the annuity owner that spells out both the payoff conditions and the investment limitations.

In turbulent times when everybody is feeling vulnerable to market upset VA sales rise because people are responding to the guarantees provided. At such times, investment returns for insurers are down and they are getting squeezed and so cut back on the investment choices allowed in their VAs, thus forcing participants into conservative allocations that dampen future outsized liabilities like the one my wife became entitled to. Also at such times, living benefits are reduced. For this reason turbulent times are not good times to buy VAs.

In placid times, VA sales are down as people feel insulated

from turbulent markets and find the VA thesis less compelling. VA providers then respond by opening up the menu, and generally making the contracts more attractive and increasing living benefits. In the case of a client of mine, in 2007 I got him and his wife into two $100,000 VAs that guaranteed a doubling of account value if held for ten years. When the market tanked in 2008, this guarantee was removed on future sales, but my clients had contracts and were locked in on the guarantee that amounted to a guaranteed growth rate over ten years of about 7.15% annually. And that 7.15% guarantee is over and above all fees, and allows the client to invest the money any way he or she wishes, including putting it all into Asian real estate. And if the Asian real estate does better than the 7.15%, then the 7.15% becomes only a floor that the account return cannot go below.

I am also a staunch champion of variable annuities for children. If you have a child interested in investment, get them a VA and let them play.

Third-Parties to VAs

Variable Annuities also have another dimension that makes them an important asset class and this is the flexibility to name three people as participants to the annuity: owner, annuitant and beneficiary. That may come into play when you want to provide for someone upon the death of another. Let's say you have a sibling who gives up a career to care for a parent. When the parent dies you want the sibling to be provided for. In such a case whoever buys the annuity is the owner, the parent is the annuitant, and the caregiver is the beneficiary.

Parsing annuity participation can get tricky as in the following scenario that led to a lawsuit, a successful lawsuit apparently. A husband had just married for the second time to a woman who had two sons, whom the groom was not very fond of.

He loved his wife, however, and bought an annuity to take care of her in case of his death. Well, the woman, who pre-deceased the husband named her sons beneficiaries. Upon her death the annuity paid the sons the proceeds. The problem was, the groom was then out the money that he might have used to purchase an annuity for a third wife and that money was now, legally, in the hands of the sons with whom the groom had an increasingly tense relationship. Even when people come into a mistaken windfall, they are loath to give it up.

Seeing the futility of clawing back the money from the sons, the groom sued the annuity provider for not alerting him to the hazard of losing control of the annuity if his wife, the annuitant, pre-deceased him. Reportedly, he won. So annuities are a very interesting asset class whose main benefit is providing an income right up to the point of death, but are very complex to understand on three levels:

- Accumulation and payout rules
- Investment options
- Custody between owner, annuitant, and beneficiaries

These issues are difficult enough within themselves, but then add in a competitive analysis across multiple providers and you are looking at spaghetti and don't expect much help from a financial advisor. If you are serious about purchasing a variable annuity, figure out first how you are going to get your money out, staging the draw-down across both non-annuitized and annuitized cash flows. Then back into some annuity choices using a spreadsheet, and finally model the various life events across owner, annuitant, and beneficiary or beneficiaries to come up with the best mix.

Inevitably you will be better off layering your annuity assets into several discrete annuity contracts. Also keep in mind that by the time the annuity payout is needed, the owner and the annuitant may not have the faculties to do the turning on. If that occurs, the beneficiary will need to have the power and the will to do it. But this gets beyond the scope of this book, which is providing a retirement nest-egg. Just remember there are two groups of people who have income for life that can never run out, people who have more money than they know what to do with and annuity participants.

See *The AARP Retirement Survival Guide*; Jason, Julie; 2009

Selling on the News   Ben Aronson 2010
Oil on panel, 12 x 12 inches   Tibor de Nagy Gallery

Chapter 15

Exotics

As I ride up to the top of the mountain at a ski resort, I sit in the chair-lift with nothing to do but look around and muse. And what inevitably catches my attention are the ski tracks where skiers coming down the mountain have found all manner of off-trail routes that bring them out through the woods back onto the main trail, in some cases skiing down impossible inclines and around daunting obstructions. But in the end, they all get down. When I see these terrain defying ski tracks I wonder to myself at the unlimited creativity of man;

always pushing the envelope, always finding new and unimaginable ways.

It should come as no surprise then that the unlimited creativity of man and money would become fast friends. And so it is, and for the reason that asking the broad population to make judgments on all things, has been found to be the most accurate in arriving at all manner of solutions. The classic case used in the investment world took place in England where fair goers were challenged to guess the dressed weight of a huge live steer on display. An enterprising statistician, after the game was over, recovered all of the tickets submitted for the prize and calculated the mean (average) value and found that the mean value of all the tickets was almost exactly the final dressed weight of the steer. The people had been right in the aggregate. This outcome of collective wisdom is then used to cite the intelligence of the broad market in pricing stocks.

I'm sure there have been many additional examples of similar calculations but one other one must be presented to show the range of applications. Back in the 1960s or '70s or the Cold War days, a U.S. Air Force bomber lost a nuclear bomb accidentally as it was approaching the coast of Spain from the south. The bomb fell into the Mediterranean and was lost. After much futile searching a population of players were given altitude, speed, and other characteristics of the flight and asked to guess the final resting place of the bomb. Someone triangulated all the responses, and that is where the bomb was found. So man in the aggregate usually comes up with the answer.

Derivatives and Other Securities

Getting back to the core subject, man's creativity and money, there is a proliferation of ways to make money from the central activity of man, commercial activity. Just to name a few, there are, options, convertibles, warrants, unit trusts, credit default swaps, collateralized mortgage obligations, hedge funds, private equity, and structured products. And given the creativity of man, it is just not possible to name all of the ways Wall Street has devised to offer adventurous individuals a "work-around" to avoid colluding with the unwashed masses, in fact, to fleece the unwashed masses; that is the central idea.

Before briefly describing most of these, they must as a class be characterized as bets rather than investments. One invests in a phenomenon that will play out over many cycles and into a future that is not visible and must be taken pretty much on trust, instinct, stamina and experience. The myriad of derivative products are mostly bets that will play out over one or several cycles that offer the owner some visibility, but in the end, mostly take the money from the neophyte. Remember there are always two players, sellers and buyers, winners and losers. Most annuities are surrendered prematurely and most options expire worthless.

Options

Let's start with options, something that roped me in earlier in life. First, although options sound exotic, most people use options every day as a matter of routine – note the frequency of hearing the question: "What are my options?" Options are very simply a way to get in on the action for what one might call "earnest money," a deposit. When you go to buy a house, you will be asked to submit an offer and put down some earnest money. That is an option. If later you discover something about the house you don't like, you can get out of the deal. The most you can lose is your earnest money. In a house purchase you initially buy an option and the house seller sells an option. If you bail out the seller may get to keep your money. So for putting up the money, your option gives you the freedom to proceed or bail out – your position is voluntary. You can do whatever you want. The seller, on the other hand, is obligated to sell you the house if you want it. The seller has an obligation while you don't. So that if an oil well is discovered on the property while you have a contract (option) the seller has no choice but to sell to you for the agreed upon figure before the well was found, a fraction of what the property is now worth with the newly discovered oil well on it.

Of course, what would happen in such a case, is a savvy oil prospector would make an assessment of the property and offer to buy the option (contract) from the buyer at some price more closely approximating the new value of the property. Options are bought and sold in the secondary market all the time.

What is described above is a commodity option; real estate or oil. So in the above case, real estate and oil are referred to as the "underlying" or the source of the real value upon which the options are constructed. You will probably not be surprised to learn that options may be constructed on almost any underlying. Two come to mind that demonstrate the creativity component of mankind, particularly greedy mankind, quite aptly. At one time the idea was floated and then immediately shot down of selling options on terrorist activity. It was observed that since people in the aggregate are very accurate, people buying and selling options would be able to accurately forecast terrorist activity. One reason it was shot down was for the same reason tontines were shot down many years ago: Lucrative positions might inspire action to take the uncertainty out of the position. In other words, the mere presence of wagers would drive terrorism acts for profit. The idea was abandoned.

Another "pushing-the-envelope" idea also never went anywhere. Ken Lay and his minions at Enron, at the height of their power, conceived of the idea of constructing options on the weather. Since weather is perennial and requires no effort to produce, it is the ideal "underlying." All Enron had to do was hold a market for weather option buyers and sellers and just take a commission on trades. It never happened, but you will be amazed to learn that during this period, the arrogance at Enron rose to a level that even Wall Street was offended.

Now that takes some doing.

The more usual "underlying" components are commodities and stocks. This may have begun with commodities, because non-farmers would not want actual possession of corn or hogs, so just opted to buy options which they could then just buy and sell, profitably if the "underlying" rose if they were buyers or lose if they were sellers. Today, many farmers buy options to hedge their real crops so that whatever they lose at the real market where they sell their produce they gain in the options market with the offsetting bet against themselves (buying rather than selling), but at a fraction of the price of the underlying.

Stock options are typically used as leverage to increase the profitability of stock price movement. Let's say XYZ was trading at $30 a share and expected to rise to $40/per share in short order. The cost to acquire 1,000 shares is $30,000, a good bit of money. You can buy an option on 1000 shares instead for say $1,500 with 60-day strike-price of say $35. If the stock never makes it to $35 within 60 days, the option expires worthless and you lose $1,500. But if the stock goes to say $38, then the option is worth $3 per share or $3,000. You could let the option expire and exercise your right to buy 1,000 shares of XYZ for $35,000 instead of the $38,000 the position is worth, but most option players close out their position ahead of expiration and just take the $3,000 which is a 100% return on their $1500 bet. Buying the underlying stock for $30,000 and selling for $38,000 would have returned $8,000/$30,000 = 26.6%.

As an interesting footnote, Thales of Miletus (624BC-546BC) is credited with pioneering options. Thales forecast that if the olive crop was particularly good in the coming year, he might get shut out from the few olive pressing services available and generally scaled to meet normal market demands. In a bumper crop year, there would not be enough capacity. So Thales contracted with one press owner to make a deposit and be guaranteed press time. If Thales crop failed or was smaller than forecast, he would lose his deposit or overpay for pressing his sub-ordinary crop. So, it seems, options were invented.

Since most market participants feel more comfortable with common stocks than agricultural products, the preferred option "underlying" is common stock. You can go to the Yahoo finance site and for every stock you bring up by symbol, you will be greeted on the left with a column of possible information searches from "Summary" giving a snapshot of company performance to "Options" giving the price for various option "Chains." An option "Chain" is required because options are sold by "strike price" and expiration date. Because there are multiple strike prices and expirations possible – after all, you have to select one specific price from a range of prices – it is necessary to price each option individually. This gives rise to multiple option choices called "Chains," because they are presented in a logical chain of expiration and strike-price choices.

As you might suspect, the more likely a price is to be exceeded by events, the more expensive the option. To buy an option cheaply, you have to select a strike price unlikely to be topped. This would be an "Out-of-the-Money" option as opposed to an "In-the-Money" option. The hope is that by the time the option expires, it will be "in-the-money." But, most options expire worthless, which means it is better to be a seller of options rather than a buyer. But be careful: Because stock price can go anywhere, seller's losses can go anywhere. For safety it is better to be a buyer.

If you feel that the near-term is too difficult to predict, there are long-term options called "Leaps" which go out a year. I have lost a fair amount of money on Leaps thinking that surely in a year the stock would rise sufficiently to push the strike price into the money. Sadly, no. And when that would happen I would always remember the observation of John Maynard Keynes: "In the long run, we are all dead." In other words, anomalies in security pricing can last a very long time, often more than a year.

As already mentioned, in order to buy an option there must be a seller of options. What options markets do is bring buyers and sellers together, and just like stocks, they are evenly matched in number by adjusting price up and down until everyone is satisfied. In trading common stocks a buyer is said to be opening a position and going "Long" on the particular stock. The seller is merely closing out a position. There are also buyers who feel the stock is about to take a dive and so they open a position by selling the stock or going "Short" on the stock. So stock buyers can either be "Long" or "Short" the position. If the "Shortseller" is correct and the stock price takes a dive, the stock may then be purchased not to be "Long" the position, but to close out the short position at a profit.

Calls and Puts

In the case of options, buyers – those who think the option price will rise – purchase what are called "Call" options. The seller of that "Call" feels the stock is going to go down, so he sells "Call" options, which is the other side of the same option the buyer purchased. If the stock price rises higher than the strike price, the owner of the "Call" gets to buy the underlying stock at the strike price, which is lower than – or at a discount to – the market price of the stock. He buys from the seller of the option. The purchaser then may immediately sell the stock and realize a profit. In reality the option position is closed out ahead of maturity and the profit is taken on just the move in option pricing. This eliminates unnecessary trading costs.

Now in comes a little more creativity. Why not have options that make money going down as well going up, because after all doesn't price move in both directions? Done. If you think an underlying is going to crater, you would find a seller who thinks you're nuts and he will gladly sell you a "Put" option, an option that pays the buyer when the underlying drops below a "Strike Price." In this case, you get to buy the stock at the new lower price and sell it back to your counterparty at the strike price. In reality, just the option is normally closed out at a profit before maturity.

Just to keep options straight they had to be named; otherwise there would be a great deal of confusion in sorting out what was wanted, up or down. Accordingly, options intended to make money for the buyer – the enabling player – as they rise are named "Calls." Options intended to make money for the buyer on the way down are named "Puts." Sometimes to help sort them out the phraseology is used: "Called away" and "Put it to the seller." When a stock is called away, it is won by an option buyer because the Strike Price has been exceeded. When an option buyer "Puts it" to a seller it is because a stock price has dropped below the Strike Price and the option buyer reminds the seller that the stock must be purchased at the higher-than-market strike price.

"Calls" and "Puts" may be bought or sold, giving rise to the matrix below. The shaded boxes show those positions that profit if stock price rises. The unshaded boxes represent those positions that profit from a fall in price.

Buyer	Calls	Puts
Seller	Calls	Puts

In portraying options there is also one other important matrix: liability. A buyer of Puts or Calls risks loss of the premium only, like not following through on the purchase of a house and losing your earnest money. A seller of a Call might wind up needing to sell a stock he doesn't own at the strike price which will trigger a need to purchase it at some new stratospheric market price it skyrocketed to on "good news." In such a case, the seller of the Call has unlimited liability. The seller of a Put might be required to buy a stock at the strike price while the stock went to zero on "bad news," or "very bad news." The seller of a Put also has liability but his liability has a floor because stock price can only plummet to zero. The matrix on the following page shows the liability exposure between buyers and sellers of options. The liability of buyers is limited to the price of the option. The liability of sellers is limited by the spread between the strike price and the market price of the underlying at option expiration or the point at which the option buyer closes his position. The shaded boxes indicate high liability.

Buyer	Calls (premium)	Puts (Premium)
Seller	Calls (Unlimited)	Puts (Strike Price of Underlying)

I must relate an option play that I wanted to engage in but couldn't because my accounts were being transferred and unavailable at the time. Delta Airlines was in a very bad way and facing both bankruptcy and demise, although they were still flying and a major air carrier. The stock was trading at around $3. I came to the opinion that Delta would not go out, and asked my soon to be boss at the brokerage that had just hired me to sell Puts on Delta in my account for me at a strike price of perhaps $2.50. As I recall, I was looking to sell maybe 1,000 Puts. I would receive a nice premium for taking this position which ordinarily would be very high risk. But at $2.50 a share, my total risk was only $2500 minus the Premium I would have received. I cannot report the result because the option position was never acquired but this illustrates the liability limit of selling Puts on very low-priced stocks.

When you buy an option, your payment is called a Premium, perhaps because you may not be buying anything. If the underlying doesn't break or fall through the Strike Price, you have nothing. So a buyer of options has limited their liability to the loss of their premium money. That is the worst that can happen. Now suppose the buyer of an option sees the underlying break through Strike Price and in the case of a Call, rise up into the stratosphere, which could happen with an option on a major breakthrough at a pharmaceutical company. That option buyer is in the money big time, but where is that money going to come from? Well, from the option seller, who for a mere pittance, the premium for selling an option, is now on the hook for very big money, something he didn't think would be possible. No matter; time to mortgage the house and pay up. Had the same seller sold a "Put" instead of a "Call," liability would have stopped when the underlying hit zero. It may be a long way down, but it does eventually put a stop to the carnage. Because of the great amount of havoc to be created by such positions, they are called "Naked" options. Perhaps because sellers of such options are likely to have to go naked after they have paid up.

The fact that there are "Naked" options suggests that there are clothed options as well and so there are: "Covered," options.

"Covered" options refers to the sale of options for which positions in the underlying are held, hence the position is covered.

Now comes a bit of complexity that will be a challenge to get your mind around. Calls are manufactured so that optimistic buyers may leverage their bet by controlling many more shares than if they just bought the underlying. For the same amount of money, buyers of Calls may control perhaps ten times as much of the underlying than if they bought the underlying directly instead. For example, say GE was trading at $20 a share, so a round-lot of 100 shares would cost $2000 plus commission. For $2000 one could buy Call options instead on perhaps 10,000 shares. Of course, the Call option would have a strike-price of perhaps $24. If by the end of the option term GE stock hits, say, $26, then the round-lot buyer would have a profit of $6 X 100 = $600. The Call option buyer would have a profit of $2 X 10,000 = $20,000. But the more likely outcome is that the strike price would not have been broken through, in which case the round-lot buyer has his position intact while the option buyer is out $2000 plus commissions. The seller of the Call option pockets the $2000.

Sellers of "Puts" are betting that the stock is going to go up and if it does, they get to keep the premium they were paid by the buyer. If the stock falls below the Strike Price, however, the seller must then become a buyer and buy the underlying at the Strike Price from the buyer of the option while the underlying may be purchased in the market at a lower price. Of course, what usually happens is that the seller just pays the buyer the new higher value of the option. Regular options buyers and sellers usually close out a position ahead of maturity.

There are buyers of stocks who routinely acquire positions they wish to own by selling Puts on them. Let's say IBM was trading at $185.24 and you wished to acquire 100 shares. You could either spend $18,524 for your position or you could "Write," (sell) a "Put" option with a "Strike Price" of $175 and take in $31.00 in premium.

If IBM doesn't break the Strike Price you just keep the $31.00. If on the other hand IBM drops to say $170.00, you are obligated to buy 100 shares of IBM from your buyer at $175 per share. So instead of spending $18,524 to acquire your position, you have spent $17,500 - $31 = $17,469 to acquire the same position. Of course the position is only worth $17,000, but you have avoided the original higher price which you were quite willing to pay. During my stock broker days I struck up a conversation with a young woman who told me she routinely acquired her stock positions in this way. It may sound too complicated to many readers, but by focusing on a strategy over time, it is mastered and becomes "second-nature." Complexity comes from lack of familiarity. Nobody dabbles in options. Options buyers tend to be just that, options buyers and nothing else, except for Covered Call writers.

The term "Covered" for options usually refers to the practice selling or "Writing" Covered Calls on underlying positions that are already owned. Options are bought and sold in 100-share increments, so a Covered Call would be "covered" by ownership of 100 shares or more. The practice of "Covered Call Writing" is so benign that it is permitted in IRA accounts. And there are people who routinely write covered calls as a source of income. If an investor holds multiple 100+ share positions in low Beta, non-volatile stocks, that investor may routinely sell Calls on those positions at a Strike Price say 10% above the current value. They then receive a premium payment from the option buyer. If the Strike price is never breached – the usual case because most options expire worthless – the seller just keeps the premiums.

Now comes the good part, the win/win part. If the stock breaches the Strike Price, you are obligated to sell your stock to the buyer of your option at the Strike Price, which is higher than the market price at time of option writing – in other words your stock is "called away" at a profit. There are people who do this year-in and year-out all while their stock positions are advancing with time and the market. It is like putting their stocks on steroids and it can be done in IRA accounts. But remember, low volatility means low premiums. For the fat juicy premiums, you must sell Calls on high-beta stocks – these are stocks you might not wish to own.

This has been a very inadequate review of options that does not begin to describe the complex structures that can be formed, using multiple options, to make almost any kind of bet you want to make from winning if nothing happens to winning if the almost impossible happens – and for very low cost. But long story short: It is not investing, it is betting, and many of the bets that look like sure things turn out to be sure losers. But remember, even Granny can get good at selling Covered Calls on her Blue Chip stocks and you would be surprised at what some of those benign looking grandmas are doing.

Convertibles and Warrants

Man's penchant for creativity seems to be matched only by man's penchant for gambling, and for that we have convertibles and warrants. Companies have a perpetual need for money to grow and so they are continuously faced with the conundrum of offering either debt or ownership. If a company decides on debt, then bonds will be issued that will obligate the company to many years of debt repayment that cannot be offloaded or delayed without damaging the company's ability to raise more money. To avoid this fate, companies opt for issuing more ownership, selling stock for money. But this angers the existing stockholders because they now own a smaller fraction of the company in a process known as dilution.

The company can reasonably point out that the company has grown by the inflow of cash, but investors are not mollified and much prefer when a company announces a share repurchase, whereby cash goes out for incoming stock and each investor sees his fractional share in the company rise. But from the company's point of view, issuing equity is free in that they don't take on monthly debt payment obligations. All companies wind up balancing equity and debt in what is called capital structure and reported as the Debt/Equity Ratio. Direct stock purchase plans are one way companies can source cash for ownership.

Of course, the treasury people at corporations are as creative as the rest of Wall Street and so they are quite capable of devising "hybrid" money-raising instruments that offer the public new ways to make new bets, something the public likes to do. Here's how it works. Would you rather have a stock or a bond? Well, I like the "safety" of bonds in that if the company remains solvent I will eventually get back the face value. But wait a minute, what about the inflation penalty? I would rather have a stock that keeps pace with inflation. But wait a minute, the stock might go down. Well, for such a bi-polar investor, there are convertibles and warrants. If the stock price goes down it's a bond if stock price rises, it's a stock.

Quoting an opening scene from a popular '50s era TV show *Superman*, "It's a bird, it's a plane, no it's Superman." Well, it sounds wonderful and Warren Buffet has used these instruments very profitably in financing Goldman Sachs and GE through the 2008 storm. Goldman, however, was smarter than GE and wrote in an exit clause to get out of them before it cost them too much money. GE as far as I know, is still paying dearly and will pay dearly to term.

Why would a company offer such an instrument? To save money, of course. If a bond is convertible to stock, then the interest paid on that bond doesn't need to be very high. The investor gets a little bit of interest and the opportunity to cash in if the stock price takes off. And like options, the convertible usually has a strike price at which the conversion may take place at the investor's discretion. People who buy convertibles and warrants are like option buyers, they tend to specialize in their narrow area of expertise.

So if you are interested in these instruments you can either dip in carefully on your own or locate a specialist that concentrates on them. When I was a stockbroker, I briefly worked with the former head of the options desk of a major firm. He began by trading options for a very large Mexican trader and eventually opted to "go into production" and handle the gentleman's account on a personal basis, earning commissions rather than a salary. In his case, the Mexican client got a very knowledgeable advisor and the brokerage house was okay with it. But most brokerage houses don't like retail brokers working in options because, for one thing, the possibility of suits.

I must also digress to share this story on options trading and options traders. When I first became a stockbroker, I got into conversation with an options trader at our firm and because I was studying options at the time, learning the Black-Scholes pricing formula, I asked if I could visit him and watch him trade. He agreed. I arrived on a Friday after Thanksgiving to his trading area, which he shared with three or four other options traders. I was immediately surprised to see these most extraordinary traders, dressed pretty much in sweat suits, one with Daffy Duck on the front, lounging around in front of their screens waiting for the market to open. They were exceedingly friendly and anxious to help, but looked like they just got off the New York subway system from a homeless shelter and blew into this office to keep warm. They also all had three screens in front of them to follow the action.

I learned that the trader I was working with had been a commercial fisherman from Massachusetts but had abandoned that occupation with the decline of the Northeast fishing industry although he was looking forward to getting back into it. Meanwhile he was instructing me on how options work and the pricing of options using the Black-Scholes formula. He broke off suddenly when the market opened, announcing to all within earshot that: "It's off to the races."

He picked up the action for a client he was working with who was millions of dollars in the money but wanted to make just one more increment of profit to cover the commission – $45,000. By the time I was getting ready to leave, that gentleman was down almost a $250,000 trying to pay for that $45,000 commission. The trader just got a chuckle out it and I left. Options clients are like gamblers; they have a disease. Looking back on this episode I wonder when in that fisherman's life he recognized his talent for options – options I surmise are far removed from fishing, but maybe not.

Other Exotics: Unit Trusts, Credit Default Swaps, Hedge Funds, and Private Equity, and Structured Products

Unit Trusts are not difficult, they are just a basket of stocks put together for a fixed term at which point they are sold and the investors paid off. From the investor's side they pay a unit trust amount that reflects their share of the basket and if the person putting the basket together is correct, at expiration everybody walks away with a profit. If you like that sort of thing it is there and always with a very compelling sales thesis. This was perhaps the original mutual fund product developed back in Holland of the 17th century, right after the start of joint stock companies selling stock to the public.

Credit Default Swaps are a new instrument devised undoubtedly by, as George Corley Wallace used to call them, "Northeastern Pointy-Heads," or PhDs from Northeastern academia. They are very simply option-like instruments designed to put a floor under buyers of Collateralized Mortgage Obligations (CMOs). If the housing market collapses, all those banks who were holding CMOs didn't have to worry because they had Credit Default Swaps. Of course, a la Enron, no one expected that once the housing pillow had been fluffed up that it would ever lose its air. But it did, big time, and it turned out, those CDSs had to be sold too cheaply. Not to worry, however, because the U.S. government rode to the rescue with TARP, the Troubled Asset Relief Program. So those are Collateralized Mortgage Obligations and Credit Default Swaps.

One last word on this asset class is warranted. You will notice that really big pools of money get a lot of attention. Well, a house is usually the largest investment a homeowner makes, plus there is also commercial and industrial real estate and there is land. So real estate is a very big pool of money and it will always attract a concentration of activity figuring out ways to monetize all that value.

After WW I and the ruinous Versailles Treaty that John Maynard Keynes railed against, Germany could not keep up simultaneously with their loss of production assets to the victors and outsized reparations payments – something had to give, and give it did. The German government printed more money, which eventually sparked out of control "hyper-inflation."

There are many amusing stories from this time of hyper-inflation, such as concert pianists wishing to be paid in sausages rather than in a currency that would lose most of its value by the time it could be spent buying sausages. Finally some German visionaries replaced the hyper-inflated Mark with the new Renten Mark that was backed by land and that brought the hyperinflation to an end. Land had become the final backstop to valuing the currency of the German state. This is a testament to both the vastness of real estate wealth and its ultimate valuation. Gold is usually the flight-to-safety commodity in troubled times but you can't grow food or build a house on it. So real estate will always be a store of value on which new "investment" products will be conceived.

The various Acts passed by Congress in the 1930s and '40s in response to the stock market crash of 1929 were meant to protect investors against unscrupulous practices and one thing they did was regulate mutual funds by first of all requiring that each investor be sent a prospectus detailing objectives, methodologies, and fees. The upside is that mutual fund investors know how their money is invested, more or less, but the downside is that mutual funds don't have the flexibility to chase the latest and greatest – they must adhere to their "style." When large-cap funds start to include too much small cap, it is called style drift. The small cap is added to add return giving the fund more pizzazz.

Accredited Investors and only Accredited Investors wishing to chase potential larger gains can invest in hedge funds. Hedge funds have no restrictions on style and are not required to provide a conventional prospectus, only "Offering Documents," which are regulated but mainly written to protect the fund from investor suits. Accredited investors are individuals or couples who have a net worth of greater than

$1million excluding primary residence or individuals with incomes greater than $200K or together with a spouse, greater than $300K. Supposedly such individuals are sophisticated enough not to be taken advantage of, but as the Bernie Madoff episode makes clear, accredited investors are no more sophisticated than average investors – both are pretty lazy when it comes to investigating financial instruments and are willing to sign on to whatever sounds good.

In essence, a hedge fund is just a collective bundle of cash given to a hedge fund manager who has Carte Blanche to do whatever he wants with it, typically charging a 2% management fee and a 20% performance fee on any gains. The sales literature provided is usually long on the resume of the fund manager and short on anything else and even road shows will provide little insight in how the money is invested. Perhaps the most notable hedge fund is Steve Cohen's SAC Capital Advisors that reportedly charges a 5% management fee and a 50% performance fee, but has apparently delivered the expected performance. Many other hedge funds have not outperformed the wider market.

Hedge funds also have rigid rules on selling out positions and are therefore somewhat illiquid. You can't pull your money out just because you need it.

Another playground for the wealthy is Private Equity. In this asset class, investors sign up to provide a sizeable investment in scheduled chunks and then the Private Equity Manager looks for a project like a turnaround situation like JC Penney or a promising start-up. The investors then meet their scheduled capital requirements and the Private Equity management team goes to work making whatever company they have taken over and privatized into a success. At the optimum time the company is then taken public again and the investors are paid off. An early example of Private Equity is The Carlyle Group that has done extremely well by employing well-placed people close to government and industry and using that knowledge to guide their proxy companies to success, enabling them to exit with a nice profit for all. As you might imagine, Private Equity is the most illiquid asset class and is not a good fit for people who might need access to their Private Equity assets in an emergency.

Hedge Funds and Private Equity are fairly recent developments undoubtedly driven by lackluster performance within the mutual fund industry and the totally disconnected asset valuation found in the stock market, which just cycles between euphoria and panic. Retail stock brokers able to both outperform the market and enunciate the methodology for that outperformance are rare to non-existent, and if they do exist would require a level of investor prescience not found in the general population – and I include myself in that group.

Hedge Funds and Private Equity managers are larger-scale retail stock brokers able to package their products for general consumption. That is the difference – scale, and working with more sophisticated investors who won't bolt at the first hiccup. And there are retirement funds and pension pools that are buying into the Hedge Fund/Private Equity model, notably CalPERS, the California Public Employees Retirement System that provides retirements to 1.6 million members. However, as must be stated over and over, it is doubtful that Hedge Funds or Private Equity deliver an end result for a retail or institutional investor that is dramatically better that the result provided by dollar-cost-averaging into the individual stocks of the Dow 30 over a 30-year term.

The final "Exotics" covered are structured products, which take two forms: 1) Almost anything you want them to be and 2) options. Structured Products are bets on things like a basket of stocks or a basket of currencies, or a basket of anything that enough buyers think will rise in value. You bet on a basket over a fixed term and, like Unit Trusts, if the basket rises you walk away with a profit. Structured Products may be segmented by possible outcome, which generally offer two choices: full market exposure or limited upside with protection from downside.

Let's say an analyst believes that owing to economic challenges felt in the United States, Europe and China the Japanese Yen will appreciate dramatically against the U.S. Dollar (USD) or against a basket of currencies. Such a bet sounds pretty good but Japan has some problems of its own and that currency could come in for some heavy selling. So the institution the analyst works for decides to offer a structured product that offers the investor (read bettor) 75% of the upside on the Yen vs. Euro/U.S. Dollar with a floor on the downside – if the Yen collapses, the investors just walks away. Let's say the analyst turns out to be right, the Japanese Yen goes through the roof, and his institution cashes in all the shares; they just pay out 75% of the rise to the share-holders who took no risk. What if the Yen crashes instead? The institution has hedged their position with opposite Structured Products. People I know who play this game play many positions, don't lose on any, and occasionally profit on some.

This chapter does not begin to describe the vast population of financial instruments devised by man to appeal to "investors." There is no end to what can be valued and played. The point in writing this chapter has not been to inform in order to empower but rather to discourage. All of these products are high-impact products that must be studied carefully but can only be mastered by very expensive experience all while foregoing the much more fruitful exercise of developing a holistic overall process for attaining a life-goal of well financed retirement.

Options are too much work. Why not let the market do the work for you and just invest, in the best sense of the word. You can lie back and let the market do its magic and revalue your shares upward with the advancing value spurred on by employees' natural inclination to want to keep their jobs and maybe even advance in the organization by creating more value. Why bet on transient blips when you can invest in a process based on man's need to make tomorrow better than today, a process that has five million years of evolution behind it. Remember common stocks are ubiquitous and prosaic because they work.

The Secret   *Ben Aronson 2008*
Oil on panel, 36 x 36 inches   Private Collection

Chapter 16
Taxes

In economic speak, externalities are penalties or benefits that cannot be linked to any single user and so are made public for everyone's shared benefit or liability. Roads are externalities unless they are toll roads, in which case users pay for the road. Taxes are meant to pay for externalities. They are societal arrangements for paying for public goods and services that cannot be delivered any other way, like the interstate road system that connects our country and makes possible the automobile industry with its attendant byproduct industries like gas stations, lodging chains, etc. Taxes also provide for the national defense.

But in another sense, taxes are a barometer of how well the society is doing balancing productivity and need. This balancing act may result in annual surpluses that lead to a lowering of taxes or to deficits that will require the raising of taxes. Raising taxes is unpopular and produces drag on productivity, so deficits are often dealt with by borrowing.

Some Tax & Spend History

In our country, I am sure you know, our balancing act has not been so good and years of deficit spending has led to enormous debt that is not only reaching a worrisome level, but also is on auto-pilot to bankrupt the country, but with fiat currency, bankruptcy is hard to define. One projection is that by 2030 total tax receipts will be just enough to pay Social Security, Medicare, Medicaid, some pensions, and that is about it. Like it or not, taxes will have to be raised and even with that, services will undoubtedly have to be cut as well. Perhaps there will be a miracle of productivity to save us, but there is nothing on the horizon as of yet.

The reason for the debt is that dollars can be sticky or slippery. Dollars earned as wages tend to be sticky in that if business falls companies tend to just postpone raises rather than cut wages which most households need to meet a carefully worked out budget that spends almost all of the incoming wage dollars. So you could say that sticky dollars are those that defy gravity.

Slippery dollars are those that also defy gravity but are generally not visible – that is why they are slippery. Former President George Herbert Walker Bush was known for making frequent pleas for the "Line Item Veto." When a bill in Congress is being prepared for a vote, Congressmen routinely add pet projects to the bill and if other Congressmen want the bill to get voted into law, they must accept the riders, which is to say others' pet projects. President Bush wanted the power to strip bills of the pet projects but he never succeeded and so you have a very good example of slippery dollars in everyday Congressional legislation. The pet dollars are voted in along with the core purpose of the bill.

The combined action of sticky dollars and slippery dollars results in a U.S. economy that has no problem going up in good times but cannot contract in bad times and so must plug the hole with borrowing, and because borrowing is painless, borrowing has become the default rubber band that expands with any need. Taxing is painful while borrowing is painless, so borrowing is the default way to reconcile tax collection shortfall relative to federal spending.

To give some visibility into the tax trend it may be useful to look at the federal Surplus/Deficit history since say 1901. From 1901 to 1916 surplus years pretty much equal deficit years and the amounts seem to range from 10% to 15% of the budget or thereabouts, resulting in an aggregate national debt of zero. Then our entry into WWI produces three years of deficits with outlays running about 300% of receipts. But receipts ramp up to meet the challenge of war. Interestingly you cannot tell by looking at the data that income tax began in 1913. Apparently it mostly just replaced tariff income to promote trade. But the war seems to have been the catalyst to ramp up income taxation to finance a larger more active government.

After WWI, apparently with the new source of revenue of income taxation, there is a long string of surplus years with surpluses ranging up to about 125% of outlays. The surplus years end in 1931 at which, no doubt due to the Great Depression, receipts drop and expenditures really ramp up, producing deficits that range up to 135% of receipts up until 1940. Our entry into WWII in 1941 sees deficits go from 150% of receipts up to 200% and then back down to 150% right after the war. Then for the next ten years (1948-1957) surpluses more or less match deficits.

Then 1958 marks the start of systemic deficit spending that pretty much ranges between 110% up to 120% and reaching over 175% in 2009 to fight the Great Recession. But within this dreary unending string of out-of-control government spending there is an eight-year respite thanks to the reign of President William Jefferson Clinton that saw deficit spending get drawn down and producing several years of surplus, up to an 11% surplus in 2000. That was quickly halted though by the "fiscally responsible" Republicans who restored "order." I must make an admission here – I'm a Republican and have been since I first voted for Richard Nixon in 1968. But I must make another admission – I have given up – Republicans outspend Democrats. I don't see anything in the Republican character, the national character, or national demographics that will reverse deficit spending, and because ultimately the strength of a currency depends on confidence in that currency, fast moving global shifts will inevitably call the U.S. dollar into question, at which point taxes will have to be raised. That is one pillar of my Roth recommendation. The other is the onset of senility makes tax accounting and preparation a challenge that Roths circumvent. Roth not only means no tax, it means no tax accounting.

Tax Loopholes

Tax policy has as its mantra to extract as much tax as possible without disturbing productivity, and years of that balancing act have given us a myriad of "loopholes" through which various populations are taxed but small population subsets escape because they are deemed to be unusually productive, or would have their productivity reduced if taxed. For example, General Electric paid no tax on earnings for 2010, because they created a tax avoidance department as a profit center, and being the very capable GE employees they are, they did their jobs. This is all perfectly legal and just exploits the tax code with all its loopholes. Of course GE is expected to deliver up the goods in value creation, but that will probably not be audited, at least anytime soon.

Individuals do the same thing because there are loopholes for everybody. For example, very few people, if any, pay the default tax rate. Rather they engage professional tax-preparation services to find every single legitimate loophole and claim a deduction. So between all the loopholes and ramped up slippery and sticky government spending, we have a deficit budget dealt with by borrowing. Who do we borrow from? The Chinese and the Japanese are by far the largest buyers of U.S. sovereign debt. But wealthy individuals and endowments serving individuals and families are also big buyers of U.S. debt securities which they see as being almost riskless except for inflation. They along with the Chinese and Japanese want to be paid regularly and so we borrow more to make those interest payments.

There are several loopholes you should be concerned with as an investor. The first is the difference between short-term and long-term capital gains. The government, for some reason, wants you to hang on to your investments once you make them, and to inspire you to do so has dramatically reduced the capital gains tax rate on investments held over a year. The short-term rate is the same rate applied to Ordinary Income, which is the highest rate, or the default rate for your situation given the loopholes you use.

But if you hold your investment for over a year before cashing it in, the long-term rate – as of this writing – is for most people half the Ordinary Income rate. The default tax rate range is 10% to 35% and the long-term capital gains rate as of this writing is rising from 15% to 20%. So the first loophole is long-term capital gains rate. But notice that the tax is rising and not declining.

It is necessary here to make a short digression. Many wealthy investors feel there should be no capital gains tax, because the gains are taxed at the corporate level. So if you owned stock in a company that had earnings and those earnings were taxed, the theory is that your dividends and capital gains tax was paid for by the corporation and to then tax you on those same gains is double taxation. Further, those arguing this point claim the elimination of the capital gains tax would spur investment needed to stimulate productivity.

Apparently the taxing authorities don't agree and it is doubtful, given our deficit, that capital gains taxes are going away anytime soon. But there is a loophole: Invest in corporations whose profits are not taxed at the corporate level. These are Publicly Traded Partnerships such as REITs, Business Development Companies and Royalty Trusts discussed in Chapter 7. Capital gains in these corporate structures are only taxed once and at the investor level, but the tax rules are quite complex.

A digression on this loophole is also in order because you will be hearing more about it. Partnerships are legal structures that like C-corporations come into existence to make money but unlike C-corporations their profits are not taxed at the corporate level. Profits are distributed to the partners and taxed at the individual level but at the more favorable long-term capital gains rate. Hedge funds are usually organized as partnerships. As more and more wealthy investors migrate to hedge funds they ramp up the hedge fund industry. Hedge Fund managers do not have income per se but are invested in their jobs and so pay the lower long-term capital gains rate on their outsized incomes and not the ordinary income rate.

This loophole is gaining more scrutiny and may have been the prompt for a letter printed in *The New York Times* by Warren Buffett urging legislators to close this outsized loophole. In making the argument that taxation does not stifle investment, Buffet pointed out that investment analysis must by its nature include the impact of taxation and any project with positive after-tax return will get investment. Perhaps the most urgent characteristic of investment is not the tax burden but risk.

Buffet asserted that tax rates do not regulate investment at least to the degree legislators have been claiming and that any worthwhile investment must clear taxing hurdles to become viable and that normal income tax rates on the wealthy will not dampen investment. Buffet also pointed out in the letter that he paid around $6 million in income tax and at a much lower rate than his secretary which he underscored was extremely unfair. Also, as Ed Easterling's book, *Unexpected Returns*, reports, investors bid up stocks during periods of stability, and a tax policy that underweights tax on the wealthy probably will not lead to stability let alone prosperity. But those benefitting from those loopholes make big political contributions and that is what drives legislation.

Another loophole created for the individual investor is the tax-deferred account. I have some reservations about the attractiveness of this loophole and regard it as more of a loophole for the federal government. Here is how it works. If you wish to put aside a portion of your earnings as savings for your future retirement, which the government wants you to do in order to relieve the strain on Social Security and other government-provided services, you may skip paying income tax on those earnings used for retirement "deferrals," thus making Uncle Sam a partner in your retirement nest egg – you give some, he gives some. Then, many years later, in retirement you pay tax on the withdrawals. The withdrawal tax rate, however, is the Ordinary Income rate, the highest rate, on both contributions and gains. In this scenario you forego the much lower long-term capital gains rate on the gains, which over time will be the majority portion of the overall retirement nest-egg.

Also, when non-retirement or non-tax deferred stock is inherited, the taxable gain is reduced by what is called a "Step-up" valuation, as already discussed. Inherited stocks inside tax deferred accounts are not eligible for step-up. So government inspired tax-deferred accounts are a mixed bag but do accomplish the very important object of getting people to save for retirement through payroll deductions.

Defenders of this deferral "loophole" point out that in

retirement your income bracket goes down and you wind up paying less tax, maybe even less than the long-term capital gains rate. If during your work life, Uncle Sam contributes 25% (your tax rate) and then in retirement only taxes 15% back, that sounds like a good deal. But you have to break your retirement nest egg down into its constituent parts – contributions and capital gains – to see if it is advantageous.

Contributions are what you put in and gains are what the market puts in. In a non-tax deferred account – an account wherein the contributions have already been taxed – only the gains will be taxed on withdrawal and at the more favorable long-term capital gains rate. However, each case is different and difficult to predict due to deductions unique to each case. For example, mortgage interest deduction taken during working years may not be available in retirement. The largest question mark, however, is the default tax rate, which must surely rise to meet the growing deficit and national debt of a country that is spending itself into poverty while concurrently reducing its productivity. The money has to come from somewhere and that somewhere will inevitably be your pocketbook in the form of taxes. So look for higher taxes going forward.

For those who see a growing disconnect between taxing and spending in this country, there is what I believe to be the Mother of all tax loopholes – the Roth. Roth accounts are retirement accounts. In one sense they are like regular IRAs and other tax-deferred retirement accounts that levy penalties for early withdrawal before the age of 59½ – unless for medical emergencies, education or a first house, all tax loopholes designed to stimulate specific activities. But otherwise the Roth is very different. Uncle Sam takes his cut up-front at Ordinary Income tax rates and then collects no tax on all later withdrawals, which means no tax on earnings or gains. That's right, the Roth is a tax-free account. Of course there are critics, who point out that by not getting a deferral – Uncle Sam's share – you have less to invest. In other words, retirement account deferrals are made with untaxed dollars so the amount otherwise destined for Uncle Sam goes to your account instead – a gift from your rich uncle. Later, tax on all withdrawals from tax-deferred accounts are at the ordinary income tax rates for both contributions and gains. But another very compelling feature of Roth IRAs, in my view, is that heirs inheriting Roth IRAs are also exempt from income tax on the inheritance. Plus contributions to Traditional IRAs must stop at age 70½ whereas there is no age limit on Roth contributions.

Required Minimum Distributions (RMDs)

Another counter argument to Roth critics is: taxes are going up and in old age you are going to be too infirm to deal correctly with the tax laws. Here's an example. When I was a stockbroker I inherited an account owned by an elderly gentleman who was infirm and living in a decaying neighborhood in a house he had owned for many years that was also in a state of decay. He had a son helping him, but the son was barely working and instead depended on the father's savings for support. This was a very troubling case.

Tax law requires that tax deferred retirement accounts be liquidated, so all those pent up tax dollars can be released and collected. That is the bargain you make with Uncle Sam for his share of your investment nest-egg. The penalty for not meeting minimum withdrawals is 50%. The withdrawals are called Required Minimum Distributions (RMDs).

The calculation of the RMD is quite burdensome and is based on age, marital status, balance in the account and other factors designed to withdraw the entire amount prior to death. While I used to do the calculations, the home office of our brokerage firm also began doing it for us, and often I found I had made errors in my calculation. You can imagine how this elderly gentleman was going to deal with that on his own.

The RMD also must be taken before the end of the year. So

in the case of my elderly client, I received an advisory in December from the home office that this client had not met his RMD requirement. I contacted the client who had no notion of such a requirement, discussed various options for treating the RMD, opening another account for example, or putting it into his checking account for the son to raid. When all that was settled, I had to have him sign a form authorizing the distribution.

He missed several appointments because his son couldn't bring him in and so in the last week of December, I found myself searching out his house in the worst neighborhood of a small city. There was a problem with the form and I never got out to him before the end of the year and so he was liable for a 50% federal penalty on the entire annual distribution. I think in his case, the Feds probably would have taken pity because he was very obviously quite limited in his awareness of his surroundings, but maybe not. And going forward you can be sure that the mercy exhibited by IRS officials is on a downward trend as the government struggles to meet its obligations.

By contrast, a Roth avoids all the pain of Required Minimum Distributions, penalties, and tax accounting associated with withdrawals. So in addition to avoiding rising taxes, a Roth allows you to avoid much bookkeeping and learning of tax regulations – no tax, no regulations to be aware of and no RMDs to worry about.

While on the subject of the tax saving opportunities of the Roth, I relate an episode that occurred during my days as a stock broker prospecting for business. I conceived the idea of opening up Roth accounts for kids. I investigated the tax laws, labor laws, and products designed to help kids, like college savings plans. But there are problems with college savings plans. They are complex, and they have issues such as who controlled the assets and what would happen if the kid didn't want to go to college, etc., etc. There could be a solution to this.

Babies, I thought, get a social security number at birth. So next I thought, why not put those babies to work? Of course, there are labor laws against that, but parents could employ their children so long as the work is not too burdensome. Then if children had earned income, they could open up a Roth IRA. The IRA would have to be in a custodial account, but that isn't a problem. And the advantage of an IRA is that early, penalty-free withdrawals may be taken for college, for a first house, and for medical emergencies. And if the IRA were a Roth, there would be no tax consequences on distributions.

Roth IRAs for College Savings Plans

Armed with this strategy, I began calling business owners and asking them if they had children and if they had a college savings program. I got one prospect interested, a woman who owned a furniture showroom and had pre-teen children. I told her she could hire her children to do some light dusting around the showroom, limited to the number of hours the labor laws allowed, pay her children handsomely, and put it all into their Roth IRAs. Presto, there is your tax-free college funding. There is a wrinkle, however, a small one. Children's incomes are combined with those of the parents and are taxed at the parent's default tax rate, or some such tax law that prevents the children from earning tax-free income because they are below the tax threshold for reporting income and paying tax, then withdraw tax-free for college. The Feds do not like totally tax-free.

At any rate the woman, totally befuddled by the complexity and not knowing me from Adam, never acted on my idea, at least not with me. This is another example of the futility of selling financial advice. But all business owners with children should be investigating this loophole. It is the ideal college savings program and one in which the kids start participating in at an early age. This is presented at a time when college loans are being characterized as the next "debt bomb" to strike our country, the first one being the mortgage blowup of 2008.

Today aggregate national college debt exceeds credit card debt. Economics professor at Smith College, Randall Bartlett, has a very effective way to help his children – he will give them a $1million if they let him. He agrees to put $100 per month into his two daughters' stock market accounts every month for life. If they touch it, the contributions stop. If they don't touch it, they will each have $1 million to retire on from these accounts. This is a very reasonable calculation Professor Bartlett makes on the cash-flow into the market and the growth of that cash flow over time in the market. But the most compelling part for me is that if his daughters raid the accounts, it all stops abruptly and what could have been, won't be. A very powerful lesson in failing to let the market work for them.

Some people, often due to their work life, accumulate large holdings of company stock inside tax-deferred employer sponsored retirement accounts and will face the Ordinary Income tax rate upon withdrawal. If those holdings are the result of a lifetime of work and represent perhaps 20 years or longer of accumulation, it is quite possible that the larger proportion of the accumulation is due to capital gains rather than contributions.

For example, say a person deposits $6,000 into a brokerage retirement account, and adds $6000 every year for 20 years, the contributions add up to 21 X $6,000 or $126,000. The total value of the account if it grew at an average rate of 7% would be about $270,000. Over a 20-year period a single stock of an employing company might yield closer to 10% and perhaps higher, resulting in an accumulation of about say $385,000. In the latter case, most of the accumulation ($259,000) is gain while contributions only add up to $126,000.

There are three choices in the way taxes will be managed in distribution: (1) just take the RMDs and pay the Ordinary Income tax rate; (2) Rotherize by paying tax on the $126,000 contribution if this is allowed; or (3) Net Unrealized Appreciation (NUA) by distribution to a taxable account by paying the Ordinary Income tax rate on the $126,000 and paying long-term capital gains rate on the remainder or 67% of the account value. Obviously, Rotherizing is the best solution, if government tax rules permit it, but this year the Roth limit is $6,000 per year. The limits in a Roth 401(k) are substantially greater than in a Roth IRA: $17,000 for 2013 and $23,000 for those 50 or older by the end of the year. These rules are constantly changing. But Rotherizing part of it is certainly a good option.

Net Unrealized Appreciation (NUA)

NUA may be a good option also. If an investor is in a 25% tax bracket, all distributions from a retirement account will be taxed at that rate. NUA allows a retiree to pay the 25% tax rate on only the original contributions and then withdraw the gains at the more favorable 15% or 20% long-term capital gains rate.

The subject of NUA also raises another issue that you should be aware of – liability. Anybody can sue anybody at any time for damages that only exist in the eye of the "victim" – in other words, we live in a litigious society where a significant proportion of the population strive to gain their assets through litigation rather than saving and investment. This dangerous landscape would rob many people of their retirement funds, throwing them upon the charity of the government, which means you and me.

Since this outcome would be too burdensome to public policy, retirement accounts are blocked from attachment. A doctor, for example, may through negligence cause great injury, and justifiably be sued, and if he or she had $1million in a retirement account and $10,000 in non-retirement assets, the plaintiff could only hope to realize a portion of the $10,000. If, however, the doctor, wishing to reduce the tax burden on retirement savings, transferred the retirement assets to a taxable account by NUA, those assets become unblocked and subject to seizure resulting from court awarded damage claims.

I learned this when I was a stockbroker and almost talked a wealthy client into NUA. In the course of the proceedings I discovered this loss of protection detail, learned that NUA is irreversible, and cancelled the transaction. The client, of course and justifiably, lost faith in my advice.

During the accumulation period, retirement accounts such as 401(k) plans take before-tax deferrals from regular salary for participants. This usually results in Uncle Sam's help with your retirement with the understanding you will pay Uncle Sam back in the form of tax on distributions from the account and that the rules will require you to entirely liquidate the account by the end of your actuarial life by RMDs. This means that in a tax-deferred account, you will pay Ordinary Income tax on both the deferrals you elected to make and the gains those deferrals produced.

What NUA does, is change the tax status of just the gains from fully taxable at Ordinary Income tax rates to the lighter tax status accorded to long-term gains, which obtains a dramatic easing of the tax burden on that fraction of the asset pool. The contribution fraction of the asset pool is taxed at ordinary income rates just as they would had they not gone into a tax-deferred plan in the first place. In order to exercise the NUA option, however, you must pay the tax on the contributions. The advantage is that you don't pay tax on the much larger fraction, the gains, until you take them as a distribution, and then at the lower long-term capital gains rate. The loss of asset protection from NUA may be solved with an even better tax strategy – converting to a Roth, if possible.

Tax Treatment of Tax Deferred Assets

Converting tax-deferred assets to a Roth means paying tax on both contributions and gains up to the time of conversion and at the Ordinary Income tax rates, but you do duck the 10% penalty for early withdrawal (if you are under 59½) though by paying the tax from assets outside of the IRA. If you elect to pay taxes from assets inside the IRA then you will pay a 10% early withdrawal penalty on just that tax amount if you are under 59½. Sometimes you might get a two-year formula, depending on the rules at the time of conversion.

Once the tax is paid, and the assets are in a Roth, they cannot be distributed without a penalty for five years, but after that, all distributions are tax-free.

A disclosure is appropriate here. This year, I suggested to my wife that she Rotherize some assets to acquire a number of Roth DRIPs. We went to her bank, which is one of the big four: Citigroup, Chase, Bank of America or Wells Fargo. Her advisor asked if she wanted to pay tax on the Rotherization at that point, or deal with it on her tax return. I was sitting next to her and we both agreed to do what sounded like the conservative thing and pay tax then at the time of the conversion. Of course that tax came out of the assets in the account and would trigger a 10% penalty for early withdrawal of the amount of tax. Had we selected instead to have taken care of the tax liability on our tax return, the tax would have been paid from outside of the account and the 10% penalty would have been avoided.

But here is the point. Both I as a past financial advisor writing a book on the subject and her mega bank advisor failed to appreciate the difference. This was incompetence on the part of two professionals. It points out the subtle complexities that must be mastered and yet often fall through the cracks owing to the present compensation of financial advisors – commissions on assets under management. Unfortunately this is a very typical example of the incompetence of generalized professional financial advice. Whenever there is a tax question, go to a tax professional. My wife wound up paying a 10% penalty with the help of two financial advisors!

The advantage of a Roth in place of a tax-deferred account or Traditional IRA, is the amount of tax paid on the gains; in a Roth, gains are not taxed at all. But all is not lost for those wishing to Rotherize but are put off by the big tax bill – Wall

Street to the rescue. As has been described throughout this book, stock price has a life of its own following the ups and downs of that free for all party in what we call the market, and you can pretty much count on that party eventually leading to a huge blowout followed by a crash and ensuing hangover.

The hangover will be a period when stock prices and your tax-deferred account are in the proverbial tank. They will recover of course, because after an extended hangover people start to recover and before you know it, it's party time again. During the depths of the hangover period, however, you may want to consider converting a portion of your assets to a Roth. The depressed valuations will mean a tax break on assets that are almost certainly going to recover, giving you a tax-free recovery. Also the hangover period may see a drop in your own fortunes and you may be going through a lower-tax period due to lower Adjusted Gross Income, making a conversion in a financial storm even more attractive. When your Rotherized assets recover with the market, they will have done so entirely free of taxation.

There is an important distinction that needs to be drawn between conversion of tax-deferred assets to a Roth IRA versus conversion to NUA (Net Unrealized Assets), which you might do in order to recharacterize the gains as long-term capital gains rather than tax-deferred gains taxed at the Ordinary Income tax rate. The distinction is that in a Roth conversion all tax-deferred assets, contributions, and gains up to the time of conversion, are liberated at the Ordinary Income tax rate. Tax-deferred assets converted to NUA are liberated by paying Ordinary Income tax on contributions only. Then all gains on positions held over one-year (which should be all the gains) are taxed at the long-term capital gains rate. But again to repeat, Roth assets are protected from creditors and NUA assets are not. Also Roth assets are not eligible for step-up valuation of cost-basis at time of death while NUA assets are. There is a lot to think about.

I prospected during the depths of the crash with the idea of Rotherizing tax-deferred assets while they were depressed but got no takers except my wife and I. It seemed that the people I spoke with were so spooked by the crash they couldn't even think about any account activity. Of course, most didn't understand what I was proposing and viewed it as just more Wall Street shenanigans designed to get their money.

This also reinforces a point that many savvy investors make, that most people don't do well in the market because they are paralyzed with fear when they should be acting and then act at times when they should be paralyzed with fear. I believe this aphorism was first enunciated by Warren Buffet. Most non-savvy investors are 180 degrees out of sync. This also is another reason why making regular fixed-dollar investments automatically is such a good idea – it takes the investor and investor emotion out. Ask yourself, how many 401(k) plan participants would have continued to buy shares during the 2008 crash? Fortunately it wasn't an issue – their continued contributions were automatic and they accumulated a good number of very cheap shares during the bust.

This episode also reinforces the futile nature of prospecting for asset management business among strangers – even good advice is rejected. I did have one client who accepted without question every stock recommendation I gave him, but when I presented him with the Roth conversion idea at the depths of the 2008 crash he said he would get back to me. About a week later he called and told me his attorney had dissuaded him from acting on my recommendation because the positions he would be Rotherizing might not recover. "Ever?" I wondered.

This was another data point that inspired me to write this book. This good client of mine did not act on my advice about stocks because he understood my advice to be good or bad; he acted because he trusted me. But on matters of taxation he trusted his lawyer more. At some future time when he is faced with RMDs from a fully recovered market, he may think back that instead of paying taxes on RMDs he could have instead realized a nice tax-free gain with no accounting requirements.

This prompts me to relate another Wall Street story concerning this client. When the crash of 2008 was well underway I took this client, with his approval, completely out of the market. I still had his account but it was all in cash for which fees could not be levied. Now markets never go down smoothly as they don't go up smoothly – market action is in fits and starts. In fact, when the market reaches bottom there is always the last death throe known on Wall Street as the "Dead Cat Bounce." This is the last opportunity investors have to get out with something before their accounts hit bottom. The accounts will recover, however, so if an investor didn't get out it is not a problem – you just wait for the market to recover, which it will do as long as the general population is looking forward to their next meal.

So in this storm I got this client out and the market continued to gyrate down and, of course, I was totally freaked out because I was supposed to make money for my clients and not lose it. In a financial storm when you look ahead you are only peering into the abyss, so it was a very difficult time for me. During one of the upward gyrations I received an e-mail from what in a police department would be called "Internal Affairs." These were the firm's cops. The e-mail asked me what I was going to tell my client when he pointed out to me that on this transient recovery he lost out on recovering $8,000. I was freaked out already and now this really set me off. The firm, of course, was upset because they couldn't charge fees on cash. I called the client and told him about the email but he blew it off saying he was better off citing losses already avoided.

Today I would use such a storm to urge clients to Rotherize when getting to the bottom, after the Dead Cat Bounce.

Loss Carry Forwards

In considering tax issues one should also pay attention to the complexities of tax preparation. We have already discussed the burden of RMDs for the most vulnerable people in our society – the elderly. Another issue is Loss Carry Forwards. In a regular taxable account, tax is due only on gains. Some accounts may go for many years without an overall gain and so are not subject to any tax. This is achieved by applying prior year losses against current gains with the use of Loss Carry Forwards. It is not until all losses have been made up that tax liability begins. But since retirement accounts are not taxed until distributions begin, there are no Loss Carry Forwards in retirement accounts. Any money lost in an IRA or 401(k) account is lost forever. For this reason, more speculative investing should be done in a taxable account.

Taxable Cost-Basis

Another big advantage of a Roth IRA and the elimination of the need to report is the calculation of gain from the difference between the acquisition cost (cost basis) and selling price. Keeping records of major stock purchases is routine for many investors and some brokerage firms, but what do you do about keeping cost-basis records for dollar-cost-averaging and then accounting for reinvested dividends? This is too burdensome. If the occasion arises where you have to calculate gains on multiple purchases with fluctuating cost-bases and if you don't have records, the IRS seems to accept average year-by-year valuations. Just look up the beginning and ending price for each year and average the figure and use that for your cost-basis for shares acquired that year. Also note, the IRS wants you to use FIFO (first in, first out) method of accounting. In other words, cheaper shares are sold first for a bigger gain and a bigger capital gains tax.

If you keep careful records, you can duck FIFO and designate specific shares for sale and reduce your tax burden. Tax planning for example, is selling your most expensive shares first, thus reducing taxable gain. The proceeds are the same, the current price of the stock at liquidation. The choice is liquidating cheap shares or expensive shares. If you choose to liquidate expensive shares, you get a lower tax bill. But you must keep careful records.

The last tax issue dealt with in this book is the tax treatment of mutual funds. When I first became a stockbroker, I was encouraged to put my clients into mutual funds, I think, for a very good reason – avoiding lawsuits. Somebody new to the business would undoubtedly be seduced by the allure of the "undiscovered stock set to take off." The more likely outcome would be, take off to oblivion, but not before a quick burp to justify its press release. Indeed, my early purchase of a Chinese coal mine for a Chinese client, my first client, was just such an event.

For some reason, investing is subject to the promise of undiscovered gems, which really is against all reason. First, there are a lot of smart greedy people in the market – that's what the market is, and the possibility that some gem went undiscovered is just not plausible. Second, if it is an undiscovered gem, why not share the news? More likely, it is a pump and dump scheme, where somebody found a plausible story (read investor ignorance and gullibility), invested in it in its undiscovered phase, and now wishing to cash in, will pump it up and then unload.

The allure is irresistible to new brokers who are on the lookout for the undiscovered gem with which they can reel in new clients. So to avoid being sued I studied mutual funds and was struck by two things: the frequency of trading (very high) and the lackluster performance (low). How can I possibly sell these, I thought to myself, and embarked on a career of individual common stock picking instead.

Tax Treatment of Mutual Funds

Of all the brokers I met, less than 10% were stock pickers, preferring to operate in the world of mutual funds. This together with the almost exclusive use of mutual funds in 401(k) plans make mutual funds ubiquitous, so understanding the tax issues of funds is important. Of course, in a Roth IRA there are no tax issues and in a traditional IRA all taxes are at Ordinary Income rates. But for taxable accounts, mutual fund tax issues may be important.

Very simply, all that mutual fund trading will generate gains that are subject to capital gains tax. The gains are not taxed at the mutual fund level, but, like Master Limited Partnerships, tax liabilities flow out to the individual fund investors. There is a timing issue, however. Since mutual fund investors are trading in and out of the fund with abandon, who gets the tax bill? It has been decided that the tax bill goes to the investors who are in the fund at the time the tax bill is presented. This gives rise to people selling out to duck taxes and blithe new investors getting tax bills for gains they never realized.

As you already know, gains are taxed as either short-term or long-term. The difference is the holding period. Positions held longer than one year are subject to the lighter tax treatment accorded long-term capital gains. But in mutual funds, there are differences between the fund holding period and the individual investor holding period. In the case of mutual funds, it is the holding period at the mutual fund level that prevails, so if there is a long-term capital gains distribution and you have held the fund for less than a year, you get the long-term tax rate on the gain and hopefully the gain, too. If the gain is short-term at the mutual-fund level, your distribution may be characterized as a "dividend" and you will be taxed at Ordinary Income rates, but if you got the gain, you are still probably ahead.

If you have loss carry forwards from losses in previous years, you may apply those to offset long-term mutual fund gains and reduce your tax burden accordingly, but loss carry forwards may not be applied against short-term mutual fund gains. And here is the rub: It is possible for a new mutual fund investor to enter the fund just as the tax liabilities are being distributed for gains realized before he got there. This is bad enough, but imagine the consternation upon learning that the tax bill is for short-term gains and loss carry forwards can't be applied. Many stockbrokers are acutely aware of these calendar issues and are careful to shield their clients from most of the damage. If you don't use a stock broker or a Registered Investment Advisor (RIA), you should look up the mutual fund you are interested in buying and learn the date of their tax liability allocation and then buy in after that date.

If all of this tax complexity has you spooked on figuring your own taxes, remember that with tax-deferred accounts much of the complexity goes away because you are only taxed on withdrawals and, without regard for the holding period of the stock. Moreover, with a Roth no taxes on withdrawals means no tax calculations period.

An important consideration in tax-deferred accounts and in Roth accounts is that there are no loss carry forwards because taxes are deferred until withdrawal, and of course, no step-up valuation upon death.

In a regular taxable account, if you have losses, those losses are offset against future gains, shielding those gains from tax until the account is profitable as a whole. This is a significant disadvantage to using aggressive individual stocks in tax-deferred accounts where losses cannot be used to offset tax on gains. On the other hand, aggressive mutual funds held in tax-deferred accounts can offset gains with loss carry forwards before allocating gains to the individual mutual fund investor. So if you are not using mutual funds inside tax-deferred accounts, it is best to invest conservatively. But remember, by dollar-cost-averaging your way into sound companies these issues will probably never materialize for you. Loss carry forwards are for Wall Street traders jumping in and out of positions looking for those short-term gains to reel in new clients.

Tax Treatment of Variable Annuity Distributions

Variable annuities are usually purchased with after tax

dollars and then accumulate tax-deferred afterward. Upon distribution, typically a calculation is made on the fractions of contribution and gain and distributions are taxed at ordinary rates on the only the gain fraction.

The Future of Taxation

A longer view on taxation must accompany any discussion of investment taxation because investment by its nature is forward looking. As pointed out earlier and in the section on inflation, the way nation states deal with soaring debt is by inflating it away, which may be done by market forces, plain old inflation, or by fiat - currency devaluation. In any of these cases, the effect is the same, market-based assets will rise with inflation and fixed assets will get crushed by inflation and that includes the national debt. So those Japanese and Chinese holding the U.S. national debt will get crushed. And you can be sure they are thinking about that and looking for ways to bring about a soft landing.

It is unclear, at least to me, how we are going to get from here to there by triangulating, national debt, inflation, and taxes, but you can be sure it will be a very big part of the investment landscape and one that you should pay attention to - keep your eye on the spread between coupon and yield of the U.S. Treasury 30-year "long" bond. Right now the coupon is 3.125% and the yield is 2.92%, meaning it is trading at a small premium which implies global confidence in the U.S. dollar. When the "long" bond starts trading at a discount, investigate or ask someone to investigate it for you. It is time to plan your next move.

Finally let me give you the standard disclaimer: I am not a tax professional. In fact I am not even a tax amateur. I don't even prepare my own returns. The person who prepares my tax returns tells me that almost daily she receives updates on new tax rules and it is more than she can do to keep up. In tax matters, no decision should be taken without consulting a knowledgeable tax professional.

The Rumor   *Ben Aronson 2010*
Oil on panel, 12 x 12 inches   Private Collection

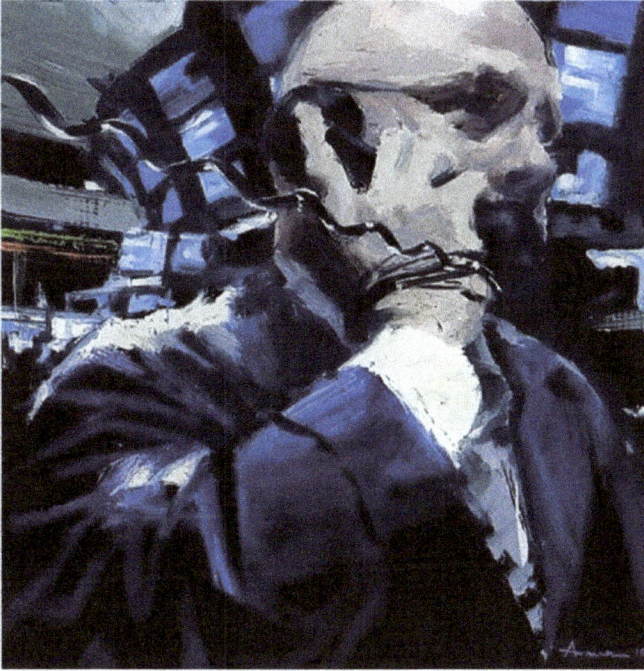

Chapter 17

Disinvestment

Up to now this book has been dedicated to building a retirement nest-egg, which, as has been pointed out, is fraught with distractions likely to lead to a very small nest-egg. Hopefully, the reader has at this point committed to developing a process that will in the end result in an accumulation that will permit retirement.

In drawing down what has been built up there are also good and bad practices that help or hurt, and as has been implied earlier the gradual accumulation of a lifetime is likely going to fund a much longer disinvestment period thanks to modern medicine.

Budgeting by Shares Rather Than Dollars

Much space was given to describing dollar-cost-averaging and how it worked to the advantage of the investor with an overweighting of cheap shares and an underweighting of expensive shares. One way to think about this phenomenon is like a car driving across the country. On level ground the car may be travelling at 60 miles per hour. When the car gets to a hill, it is slowed perhaps down to 30 mph. Then when reaching the top of the hill, the car begins to speed up as it goes down the other side. Dollar-cost-averaging works the same way. During placid times you will acquire an average number of shares for your investment. When the markets get riled up, like going uphill, your investment slows and you only buy a few high-priced shares. Then when the stock tanks in response to market upset, it's like going down a hill – your investment increases speed to gobble up all the cheaper shares on the way down. In this way, dollar-cost-averaging accumulates a disproportionate fraction of cheap shares. Fewer shares on the way up and more shares on the way down.

Why does this synergistic phenomenon occur? It's because you are using a fixed screen to act as gatekeeper to a random and volatile process. Dollar-cost-averaging is a fine mesh filter that screens out expensive shares. Once you have your screen in place, all you need is a volatile stream of stocks moving against it and the market is happy to supply that. The screen does the rest, biasing in favor of cheap shares. Volatility is your friend and your best friend when markets tank during the accumulation phase. In the distribution phase, however, volatility is not your friend.

A common mistake is to use the same process during the disinvestment phase as during the accumulation phase. But this would be a mistake precisely for the same reason that it works in building up the nest egg: the inordinate withdrawal of shares when they are cheap. In investment, you want to accumulate as many shares as possible, and dollar-cost-averaging tilts the table in the investor's favor, overweighting cheap shares during the accumulation phase. Using the same process in disinvestment you will see the liquidation of mostly cheap shares with market volatility. So that at the end of the day, when total liquidation has been achieved, hopefully upon drawing one's last breath, or financing life to the last breath, most of the liquidated shares will have been cheap shares. If you regularize the investment going in, the majority of accumulated shares will be cheap shares. If you regularize the investment going out, most of the liquidated shares will be cheap shares. This is not what you want in the disinvestment phase.

If you have an accumulation of say 12,000 shares of a particular stock or portfolio of stocks, in order to make the most of the accumulation, you should switch away from dollar-cost liquidation and elect to meter you disinvestment by shares or percentage of assets and not by fixed dollar amounts. This means if you are targeting 120 months of liquidation, you must divide your number of shares by 120 and draw down only that number of shares a month regardless of their current value or 7% of assets per year regardless of the balance. In the above example of 12,000 shares, that means 100 shares a month regardless of their current value. This flies in the face of custom, which calls for making a budget and then adhering to that fixed number. If you need that fixed number then you should be investigating in annuities, which provide the characteristic of regularized cash-flow.

In Chapter 8 we discussed how dollar-cost-averaging results in the accumulation of a disproportionate number of cheap shares as illustrated below by a skewed curve.

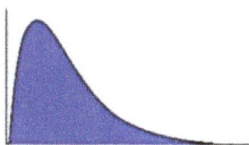

When you disinvest, what you really want you can't have and that is a curve skewed toward more expensive shares, as seen below.

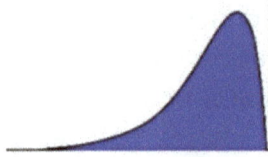

The best you can hope for is to regularize by taking out a fixed percentage monthly rather than a fixed amount. If the asset base is up, you get more, if the asset base is down, you get less.

Given the long-term history of S&P 500 return, setting a withdrawal rate of 7% per year seems do the best job of balancing income with asset base to power growth for optimal future income. (See the tables in the variable annuity section). If you take out too much, you deplete your asset base and your income will decline. A withdrawal rate of 7% seems to get the maximum, over time, from an asset base. This is a case where less is more. Also, drawing off dividends in retirement, rather than reinvesting them, might be a viable way to supplement a 7% income from a price return calculation.

Once a withdrawal rate is established, opportunistically selecting stocks for liquidation that are at or near historic highs will help drive a dis-investment curve that looks more like a normal distribution.

Of course with time, there should be some skewing to the right as the market advances and this would argue for liquidating evenly across all stocks rather than drawing down first one stock and then another. And giving more thought to disinvestment might well yield a better end result than might be achieved with having had a better investment result but scattershot disinvestment. Indeed, disinvestment, the conversion of stock to cash, is not so different as the conversion of cash to stock, that is, investment.

Recently there has been an attack on what are called life-style funds inside 401(k) plans. Life-style funds are the result of a strategy developed for the very passive 401(k) plan participant who felt befuddled by the need to pick funds. Funds were put together for specific investment horizons like 10-year, 20-year and 30-year funds. These were typically named after the year at which dis-investment would start, like the 2030 fund and the 2040 fund for people retiring in 2030 and 2040. In this way, very passive plan participants didn't have to wrestle with picking funds whose style and capitalization was difficult to discern. That is done for them. All the plan participant has to do is pick his retirement date and match that up with the related fund. These funds were constructed to gradually move money out of common stocks and into near-cash instruments to begin to provide cash flow but over an extended horizon.

As the retiree ages and draws down his or her account, a larger fraction of the account must be moved closer to cash to provide the cash flow from a diminishing pool. During the market upset of 2008 many of these funds went in the tank along with the broader market. Of course, this was fodder for the media that began publishing article with titles such as: "*The Failure of Life-Style Funds.*"

The assumption made in the articles attacking life-style funds was that on Day One of retirement, the entire accumulation is in a near cash position and therefore insulated from market upset. This is not the case. On Day One you are only starting a cash stream and whatever is not needed for income must remain invested in the broader market. So a life-style fund for the year 2010, for example, would still have most of the positions in the broader market and would be expected to follow the broader market, up, down or sideways. And given the longevity that one would have to plan for at this time, it would be quite appropriate to meter the near-cash portion to a minimum necessary to meet near-term cash flow requirements.

The Role of Annuities

Metering assets to fill an uncertain lifetime is not a problem for the wealthy, because they will inevitably have a surplus, which will be bequeathed to beneficiaries. But for those of middling accumulation, metering becomes crucial to meet longevity targets as well as provide for infirmity, when sound decisions are no longer possible.

We have already discussed the use of Roth IRAs to head off any tax problems. And we have discussed the operation of annuities in providing a lifetime income that cannot run out. Annuities may be either immediate or deferred. In immediate annuities, the life insurance company takes a lump sum and in return provides a lifetime income that can't run out. Of course, what the life insurance company does is calculate a life expectancy based on actuarial tables. But unlike life insurance, you are betting that you are going to live, which is much more difficult to game than if you are betting that you are going to die. A untimely prognosis from the doctor might well alert you to the imminent need for life insurance, something the insurers are well aware of and for which they have a solution – underwriting. On the other hand, longevity cannot be gamed other than to get a favorable health report from a doctor and that means that you just fall into the general population for which underwriting is not required – standard actuarial tables will do. Accordingly, if a retiree is in poor health, they will probably not do well with an annuity that assumes a long life and meters a lower monthly life payout accordingly.

So the first component of a disinvestment plan must assess the health and longevity of the retiree. People with a family history of long-lived ancestors might do well to think along the lines of an annuity, particularly with a non-annuitized cash flow expected to keep pace with inflation. Of course, as stated in the chapter on annuities, be sure to layer multiple annuities to provide a better match-up with cash flow requirements.

For annuitants of poor health with limited life-expectancy it may be more useful to select a payout other than for a lifetime. For example the beneficiary can specify something like Ten Years Period Certain. In this case the annuity will stop in either ten years or death, whichever occurs sooner. Multiple layered annuities can then be "turned-on" as needed in stages, and if death occurs during the term of the first annuity the other annuities can then be left to heirs.

Let's take an example. At age 65 a $100,000 annuity purchased in 2012 will have a monthly payout of about $600 for one life or $500 for either you or your spouse's life – a joint-life annuity. If you elect a 10-year period certain, you can expect about $1,000 per month or around $900 for a joint-life. You can see from this illustration that cutting an annuity in half and selecting a 10-year period-certain over life payout may be a better option because if you make it past the first ten years, the other half will have grown with inflation and will pay out in a succeeding 10-year period certain a cash flow that has kept pace with inflation. Now compare the erosion of a level payout after 10 years of inflation with a new inflation-adjusted payout. The difference is dramatic. But to make it even more dramatic, acquire the annuities with Roth assets. Annuities purchased with Roth assets are Rotherized and free of tax and tax accounting.

The retiree must be very careful with the purchase of annuities because they are very complicated and are issued as contracts that cannot be vacated and there are steep penalties for premature surrender. The problem is that very few financial advisors are conversant enough with the intricacies of just one brand, let alone familiar enough with multiple brands to steer a client toward an optimal solution. The other option of dealing directly with the issuing company is also off the table because they want to distribute through agents and brokers only.

In most cases, a broker will bring in a provider to discuss the detail of a given annuity product and that information will be very reliable but restricted to just the one brand. This is not to blame the financial advisor community unnecessarily, because the products are very complicated, and mastering just one flavor of a brand is a big job. Moreover, the bells and whistles inside each annuity product are constantly changing in response to competition and actuarial experience and, in addition to all that, most annuity providers offer a stable of choices.

If a benefit is offered and results in an unanticipated level of claims, that benefit will no longer be offered or at best offered with new conditions, such as, say, for ages 70 and older. How is a financial advisor supposed to keep up with all of that? It won't happen. The best antidote is for the retiree to begin researching annuities long before they are needed and as part of that research, developing a spreadsheet to isolate those characteristics that really matter, mainly getting the most payout.

The Role of Life Insurance

Another end-of-life asset that is often overlooked is life insurance. Life insurance is not just for spouse and children. Spouse and children are certainly the beneficiaries you have in mind when a life insurance policy is first purchased but at some point those contingent liabilities are going to fade or disappear altogether. And it is the practice of some financial advisors to talk clients into surrendering their policies with the observation that with changed conditions, those policies are no longer serving their intended purpose – which is largely true and true enough to gain a few clients. But those who hang on to their policies may find a new purpose for them, such as naming an end-of-life caregiver as beneficiary in return for terminal care or selling a life policy in a viatical settlement.

I had a related experience with an older gentleman who was renting a nice carriage house on an estate of an even older and quite wealthy landlord who was beginning to talk about vacating the property in anticipation of his own changing circumstances. This created a dilemma for the renter: Should he move while he still could or should he stay and hope for the best? I asked him if he had a life insurance policy and if he had heirs who needed the proceeds. He did have a policy but the heirs were his children with whom he had only a formal relationship, perhaps due to a divorce many years earlier, and accordingly the heirs did not expect to inherit. I suggested he offer to make the landlord, or the landlord's estate, the beneficiary of his life policy. In return he could negotiate a rental for life at a lower rent than he was currently paying, and the arrangement could follow the property to a new owner in the event of the landlord's death. At the same time, he would reduce his monthly expenses. He loved the idea and thought the landlord would as well, because like an insurance company, the landlord would probably come out ahead. As it turned out, the renter died prematurely about five years later, and I don't know if he ever changed the beneficiary on his life policy. But the core lesson is that life insurance is an asset like any other that requires thoughtful dis-investment.

Other Securitization Strategies

In recognition of growing longevity issues, entrepreneurs have come into the marketplace offering disinvestment products for both life insurance and real estate, and these products are, conceptually at least, very useful. The life insurance product is called a Viatical Settlement and allows you to sell your policy to a buyer who then makes the premium payments and waits for your exit. The amount of the settlement will be driven by the amount of death benefit, the monthly premium and health of the insured. Of course, like any other financial product you can buy or sell a viatical settlement. But by buying you are taking on a certain negative cash flow for a very uncertain pay off. The way companies offering Viatical Settlements succeed is the same way life insurance companies succeed – spreading the risk over many lives. Nevertheless, Viatical Settlements are just another way to monetize a life insurance policy. Also keep in mind that while in general the need for life insurance diminishes with aging, for many the loss of a life may mean a financial hardship right up to the end. Each case is different and once a life policy is vacated, you are done; it's over and there is no reinstatement. So think carefully before vacating a life policy.

In addition to disinvesting in a life insurance policy, you can disinvest in your house with a Reverse Mortgage. This is a sale of your house that allows you to remain in the house for the term of your life and will give you a monthly cash flow in the meantime, or you can take a lump sum and buy an annuity, or meter it yourself. I did a quick calculation on my own life just to get a rough idea on what the possibilities are. I modeled a house value of $300,000 and age of the homeowner and spouse at 67 years old. The lump sum available on a fully paid up $300,000 house is $175,000. That $175,000 may be taken in a number of ways: a line of credit that grows at the rate of 4% per year guaranteed, or a monthly cash-flow of $1,017 for life, or a variety of combinations of the above. Just as with annuities, you can select a period certain after which all payments stop. Also at your death the residual value of your reverse mortgage is calculated and distributed to your heirs.

But a word of caution needs to be sounded on reverse mortgages. Just as with annuities, the payout is lower for joint-life. Unscrupulous sales people have been known to push single-life settlements with the argument that the elderly couple will get a bigger payout. If the single-life spouse dies, the contract is terminated and the survivor must move or buy out the contract. This has resulted in elderly surviving spouses getting what they were trying to avoid in the first place – loss of their assets, their domicile and their way of life. Couples should always select joint-life reverse mortgages.

Estate Planning

Another disinvestment end-of-life issue constantly debated is the use of estate planning and trusts rather than just defaulting to a will and to probate. When I was a stockbroker I spent a period going through probate court files, which are all entirely public, including an audit of the deceased's estate right down to contents of the house. While none of my business, I was able to discover all of the assets contained in the estate of any deceased whose estate comes into probate court. This public display of one's assets and accompanying will containing desired distribution is all available to the public. The way to head this off is to have a trust and name a trustee, often a bank or an attorney.

A trust avoids probate and doing so has several advantages for the heirs. First, a trust is a higher order of custody not susceptible to being hijacked. This has been disputed by an attorney I consulted.

A probate judge serves at the pleasure of the people and this means mostly untouchable. In my stockbroker days I met a few probate judges and they inhabit a rarefied atmosphere as evidenced by a level of cavalier behavior that took my breath away. I don't recall the specific issue but I do recall clearly that reality was what the judge said it was, and it may or may not have been consistent with a will. A will is a ticket to probate court.

The other advantage of trusts is that they are private and circumvent any public reporting of assets, and public reporting of assets is likely to bring forth creditors real and imagined.

During that same period I was prospecting at Probate Court, I came upon a very interesting case which was fully documented in a probate file. A woman had died leaving her estate to be divided equally among two nieces and a nephew. One niece lived nearby, another niece lived several towns away, and the nephew lived in Florida, a plane flight away. The nephew wanted to stay in the aunt's house for the funeral to save lodging costs and the nearby niece, named executor, denied the request with an excuse that didn't make sense. The nephew became suspicious because it was known that the aunt, although a very plain living woman, had a good sized but undisclosed estate. When the nephew arrived in town, he broke into the aunt's house and discovered an opened safe in the basement that had been emptied as well as a variety of stock certificates – this is not fiction – stuffed under sofa cushions, all not acknowledged by the niece executor who probably didn't know what a stock certificate was. He called his sister who was the more distant niece and confided in her. The sister was just as surprised and drove over to the aunt's house and became just as suspicious as her brother and immediately joined him in his search of other assets that might not be reported.

The more distant niece and her husband eventually became my clients and I heard the rest of the story. The nearby niece was named executor despite challenges by her siblings and co-inheritors, and was never required to account for the missing assets. She then hired her husband to make "repairs" around the house to prepare it for sale. The dispossessed niece and nephew objected but got nowhere. The contents of the safe never became part of the public record and the two disenfranchised heirs eventually gave up the fight. They waited for the sale of the house and the final distribution of their share after the very expensive "repairs" were completed.

Had the aunt in the above case elected a trust, a trustee would have been named, either by the aunt or a bank, and any apparent larceny would have been the subject to police arrest and prosecution in a criminal court. But, despite any prosecution, the trustee would still distribute the estate as directed by the trust. No probate judge would be involved. Of course, a trust is vulnerable to not being populated with assets and in the aforementioned case had the aunt not placed all her assets inside a trust, perhaps by reason of infirmity, any assets outside the trust would have been handled by probate.

I once observed a very capable man delivering investment training for a company that had hired him as a third-party to discharge their training mandate for sponsoring a 401(k) plan under the Department of Labor and ERISA. He did the training in about 10 modules and the module I attended included a discussion of trusts vs. probate. He stated unequivocally that unless you lived in Florida or California, probate was the preferred venue for distributing assets to heirs. Apparently Florida and California have quite high probate fees calculated as a percentage of the assets, making those states unfriendly for probate solutions. I asked him if it wasn't possible for a probate judge overseeing the settlement of an estate to show partiality and hire favorites for expensive auditing services. He said he had never seen it.

The one other data point I have on this issue is a statement made to me by an attorney turned stockbroker who was in training with me. On the subject of probate, he said, and I quote: *"Everyone knows probate court is corrupt."* I advise people with any complications at all to their estates to opt for a trust. Trustees themselves normally set the trust option threshold at $300,000 in combined assets as a figure that would trigger need for a trust.

Even where probate court tries to do a good job the problem arises from the judge having no knowledge of the case versus a trustee who has custody and a record of the assets. Often a probate court must appoint an auditor to examine an estate and prepare a report on the nature and quantity of assets. This may further trigger a real estate appraisal, and these services, together with the audit, are carried out by people with no incentive to turn in a reasonable fee. In the case of a trust however, a trustee who needs these services turns to service providers who must earn his business in a competitive environment. And while it is possible for trustees to abuse their position, what is at stake is the reputation of the bank or law firm that make trustee work a core service. Also, questionable behavior by a trustee is subject to a suit and nobody is more easily aggrieved and more anxious to sue than heirs. Trustees understand this and are very careful to carry out the wishes of the deceased to the letter. Of course, winning more business is not a problem faced by a probate court judge.

The list of potential services that may have to be hired to settle an estate are daunting. These include real estate repairs, asset searches, searches for heirs, settlement of debts and so on, all at premium prices. If an estate goes to probate, the first step is publication of the opening of an estate case and a search for heirs and creditors, giving them so much time to make their claim. You can imagine what comes out of the woodwork from these public announcements. As James Carville once said, if you troll a $100 dollar bill through a community you are likely to get anything, or words to that effect.

In the case of a trust, all the assets, heirs and creditors are named in the trust to the trustee and nothing is made public. The trustee has a duty to distribute exactly as stated in the trust and only to whom is named in the trust. There may be legitimate creditors, but if they never learn of the passing of the debtor and the debtor has a trust, that creditor is unlikely to get paid.

It should be noted that trusts often fall short of expectations because of the failure to put all assets into a trust. Assets not specifically placed in a trust then get distributed by probate.

There is one additional reason to consider a trust: people. When I first began looking for clients at the probate records office, I was astounded at the disintegration of sibling relationships over money in an estate. I have already related one story but there were many stories, although none quite as dramatic. I mentioned this to one of the administrators in the office and he said I hadn't seen anything yet. So what looks like family during the life phase, quickly turns in many cases to war after death. Of course people leaving sizable estates sense this and keep all heirs at arm's length. This sets the stage for misplaced assets as the aging benefactor forgets where everything is. It is far better to start a trust early and populate that trust with all the assets so that as infirmity sets in, all the assets are accounted for and distributed without prompting the breakout of war among heirs. War can still break out but it won't affect carrying out the directions of the benefactor.

When a person dies, their property will transfer by any combination of four methods:

1. Contract
2. Title
3. Trust
4. Probate

Contract is the highest form of asset transfer and is used wherever beneficiaries and contingent beneficiaries are named. Retirement accounts such as IRAs, 401(k)s, pension plans, annuities and life insurance policies all transfer assets by contract and cannot be overturned by wills or trusts as far as I know, although there could be an intervention by court order, as in divorce, where a Qualified Domestic Relations Order (QDRO) may require naming a particular beneficiary in a life policy. This is more prone to occur in workplace sponsored benefit plans like 401(k), pension and life insurance purchased through the workplace.

Another issue here is keeping beneficiary designations current. It is not unheard of for a surviving spouse to learn too late that because beneficiary designations were not updated, the hated former spouse gets a big payday and current spouse gets nothing despite trusts and wills to the contrary.

Title is the next highest order of asset transfer. Brokerage houses regularly offer non-retirement accounts in two flavors of title, with and without TOD (Transfer on Death). You can add a TOD provision to many assets, such as brokerage accounts, bank accounts, houses and cars, or anything that is titled. Rules will vary from state-to-state, but this option is usually free and keeps consideration of the asset transfer out of probate. Upon death of the owner, the assets transfer automatically to the TOD designated person. The drawback is that the assets are frozen to the heir until a death certificate can be produced.

A trust is useful for all other assets that cannot be transferred by contract or title and the main purpose is to assure that the wishes of the benefactor will be carried out. Trusts keep asset transfers out of probate but only if the assets are inside the trust.

The function of a will is to override default formulas various states have for distributing assets of decedents who are intestate (without a will). These formulas will typically distribute to parents and children in addition to the spouse. To transfer all assets not already provided for by contract, title or trust, use a will.

In all cases, don't rely solely upon what you read in a book. The foregoing is only a prompt for you to see an attorney to discuss your arrangements in detail. Also keep in mind, laws can be challenged upending that age old phrase: "written in stone."

There are tax implications on leaving common stock in an estate, or even in probate. The present tax code allows for what is called "Step-up" valuation upon the death of the benefactor leaving common stock to heirs. The heirs inheriting the stock will see the Cost Basis (price at which the stock was originally purchased) stepped up to the price on day of death, I presume closing price on date of death. Well if stock was purchased for $10 per share, and by the date of death had split several times and risen to say $50 per share, none of that matters, the new Cost Basis for heirs is $50 per share for all the shares in the estate. All that tax on the splits and appreciation prior to date of death is foregone. This being the case, many wealthy investors borrow against the collateral offered by their common stock rather than selling stock, which triggers capital gains tax. By borrowing, the tax is avoided and heirs and creditors acquire the stock at stepped-up valuation. The avoided tax can then go a long way toward repaying the debt. Step-up does not apply to tax-sheltered assets such as 401(k) plan assets.

The objective of this chapter is to prompt rather than to replace, a visit to a tax professional and attorney by pointing out the complexity that arises in the distribution of assets.

*72nd **Street Station***   *Ben Aronson 2008*
Oil on panel 12 x 12 inches   *Private Collection*

Chapter 18
401(k) Plans

Otto von Bismarck was a Junker – landed Prussian gentry – who turned to politics, and eventually became German Chancellor from 1862 to 1890, and created modern Germany. My introduction to Bismarck came from reading about an episode when he was presiding over a howling Congress objecting to some issue he was asking them to vote on. Rather than taking their objection seriously, Bismarck sat in his chair reading the paper, apparently oblivious to the pandemonium around him. He later unified Germany, which up to his time was, like Italy, a collection of fiefdoms.

In 1889 Germany, under Bismarck, installed a program which is the forerunner of Social Security. As you can imagine, a personality like Bismarck's would have attracted a lot of vitriol anyway but it really ramped up when he introduced the need for social insurance with the following statement: *"...those who are disabled from work by age and invalidity have a well-grounded claim to care from the State."* This triggered a new general howling with the accusation that Bismarck was a closet communist. Bismarck replied: *"Call it Socialism or whatever you like. It is the same to me."* And so Social Security came into being in Germany in 1889.

The Start of Social Security

It took the Depression to prompt the U.S. to adopt a similar measure and accordingly Franklin Delano Roosevelt signed the Social Security Act on August 14, 1935. FICA (Federal Insurance Contribution Act) taxes began to be collected in 1937 and Social Security payments began in 1940.

Since 1940 there has been a gradual cultural shift in the U.S. away from self-reliance to reliance upon the state, making the state, or the population at large, responsible for fixing whatever ails us. Accordingly, like a lone lifeboat in the vicinity of a sunken ship, all manner of survivors are clambering aboard the Social Security lifeboat and threatening its stability. Perhaps the best example is the recent action by the FDA to pull approval of a breast-cancer drug that was costing publicly provided health care around $90,000 per year per patient. FDA defended their action with test results that indicated the treatment was ineffective. This produced an outcry from patients who have no other hope and demanded that coverage be continued anyway, which it was.

As was mentioned in another chapter, Social Security was intended as a backstop for all workers who were expected to plan and save for their old age, but who often didn't, or otherwise there would be no need for Social Security. In an earlier era the family farm was the resting place for Mom and Pop, but industrialization had pretty much put an end to that venue and the security it provided.

The Growth of Pension Plans
After WWII there was an economic boom in the U.S. as returning soldiers and wartime workers began to spend their accumulated savings resulting from wartime rationing, and the U.S. economy went into overdrive. Finding enough loyal workers to staff rapidly growing businesses then became a challenge and, perhaps borrowing from the military, companies began offering pension plans, or savings and investment plans that guaranteed lifetime retirement incomes commensurate with years of service; pension payments would be over and above Social Security. If you left a company before retiring, you lost your retirement income from that plan. That, as was intended, would produce loyalty and solve a nagging staffing problem.

The 401(k) Solution
As years passed and growth flagged, particularly with offshoring of manufacturing, the Social Security boat was getting swamped by outsized disability and medical claims. Of course, those same medical claims were keeping people alive and on their Social Security benefits a lot longer than originally imagined and so the Social Security boat began to swamp badly. Company pension plans felt the same effect and because pensions were elective and not a Federal mandate on business, companies began to "freeze" their pension plans, freezing out ongoing contributions and new employees. The swamping of both the Social Security boat and the pension boats created a looming crisis. Something had to be done or the Social Security boat would go under. The solution was the 401(k) plan introduced in 1978.

The premise for the 401(k) plan is that workers are unable to plan ahead and so will not provide for their old age on their own. Accordingly the workplace was selected as the place to defer a portion of a person's weekly income and apply it toward a retirement nest egg. To head off worker objection, the deferrals were pre-tax, making the U.S. government a contributor toward workers' retirement incomes. The government would tax the money later on and recoup its investment. Also, payroll deferrals would not be missed by the workers unable to save any other way because they wouldn't see the deferrals that were made before the paycheck is issued.

The United States has a savings rate of 5% in good times, which is among the lowest savings rates in the world. China at about 40% has one of the highest savings rates. Savings rates are largely driven by the perceived public safety net. China has little if any public safety net, hence high savings rates that lead to low consumption and an economy dependent on American consumers whose consumption is financed by loans from China.

While the 401(k) concept sounds simple enough, it raised numerous issues, not least of which was making the employer a financial advisor to the employees, a role most companies are unwilling and unable to fill. This dimension was offloaded onto "professionals" who were then tasked to create plans that would provide retirements, and, even more urgently, get the companies out of the participant's cross-hairs should the hoped for retirement not materialize in a voluntary non-government plan.

But the Achilles' Heel of this program remains. It is that the employer is gatekeeper to the employee's fortunes, and that is a role that ultimately replays the same old broken interface of non-financial types trying to buy a financial solution but with the added burden of culpability and vulnerability to lawsuits. This is a very big problem and, as in the Madoff affair, what counts is AUM (Assets Under Management) and one other dimension, indemnification from lawsuits.

Everyone has heard of the outlandish settlement McDonald's had to come up with for a woman who spilled hot coffee on herself, so this exposure to employee law suit is a very big issue, really a driving issue in 401(k) plan sponsorship.

Five elements are important for understanding 401(k) plans.
1. Recordkeeping. At the end of each trading day all trades must be settled and accounted for and because brokerage houses are the only conduit for trading, they have an extensive recordkeeping infrastructure that allows clients no later than the following morning to see the current value of their holdings. When you think of the billions if not trillions of trades executed every day, this is a daunting task, yet it is carried out flawlessly. Similarly, every participant in a 401(k) plan can access their account information and get up to the most recent close valuation on their account. Where plans can differ is in the range of assets they will record-keep. A mutual fund company managing a 401(k) plan routinely record-keeps its own funds and can add a few outside funds and record-keep those for a low price. Some record-keepers are more flexible and will record-keep almost anything, including hedge funds, and will charge a higher price for the more custom service.
2. Trustee. Although recordkeeping can keep track of where assets are supposed to be, that alone does not guarantee custody. Ordinary brokerage accounts have no super custodial requirements beyond providing a quarterly statement. Retirement funds, however, are not so casually handled and therefore require a trustee to guarantee that assets are secure.
3. Asset Management. Asset management involves putting together an investment menu that captures the imagination and aspiration of all participants

without allowing access to investments that are likely to take a nosedive and squash a participant's retirement. The typical menu includes only mutual funds and typically those that mimic the S&P 500. Most menus also include some bond funds and a few international offerings and perhaps a more aggressive fund or two, like an emerging markets or technology fund. Given the passivity of most participants there has been a recent move toward what are called "life-style" funds or "target-date" funds. These funds are typically given a target year as a name, like the 2030 fund and actively change the constituents inside the fund to gradually move the composition of the fund from aggressive growth to enough of a lower-yielding near-cash position in anticipation of the onset of withdrawals on the retirement "target" date. The character of the participant pool drives investment menu. Where the participant pool is highly educated and young, a more aggressive menu is offered and perhaps even a self-directed channel where participants can open a brokerage account inside their 401(k) plan and purchase individual stocks. The employer "sponsor" of the plan is on the hook for getting the participants a good result, so self-directed features are considered very carefully and seldom offered for fear that a participant employee will engage in losing trades and then sue the employer for allowing it to happen.

4. Compliance. There are both ERISA (Employee Retirement Income Security Act) and DOL (Department of Labor) regulations that the plan must meet to be eligible for tax deferral. In general, ERISA and DOL want to make sure employees receive fair treatment and therefore will not allow tax-deferral on plans operated only for executives, as an example. If

the executives want to a tax-deferred savings plan, it must be offered to the employees as well. A core concept of 401(k) and IRA pre-tax deferrals is that the 20% -30% share Uncle Sam is supplying is ultimately going to be paid back as a 10% - 20% share of a reduced income stream in retirement that is taxed at a lower rate. I question this concept but many big investors embrace it, perhaps because they are in very high tax brackets and can find a way like a trust to minimize taxes later on. If they had their way, the theory goes, they would craft a 401(k) plan that only the executives or highly paid employees would have access to and would then defer a large fraction of their outsized salaries that they don't need to live on anyway. DOL and ERISA prevent this self-dealing in corporate retirement plan sponsorship.

5. Education. Given the unwanted exposure to employee suits from retirees with insufficient retirement savings, sponsors are eager to obtain indemnification and can do so by following ERISA/DOL guidelines. If an investment menu in any of its components or in the aggregate allows participants to mimic the S&P 500, the sponsor is off the hook if the participants are able to make selections from the menu to meet their retirement needs. Given the passivity of most participants, "target-date/life-style" funds are a good choice. There are also employees who never become participants by procrastination, and recently this problem was addressed by regulations that offer plan sponsors the option of automatically enrolling all employees and then requiring an employee to opt out if they don't want to participate. Early results from studies indicate most employees don't opt out probably again owing to procrastination. And for those that despite all the

education still can't make selections from the menu, like the people who were automatically enrolled, they are then automatically invested in a QDIA (Qualified Default Investment Alternative). The QDIA is not an all bond fund as might be suspected, because ERISA and DOL recognize that a bond fund will not get the participant where they need to go. QDIAs are more like target-date funds.

"Safe-Harbor"

Deferrals are limited by law and as of this writing 401(k) plan deferrals are limited to $16,500 a year with additional "catch-up" deferrals possible for older participants. But these limits may be out of reach of the most highly compensated employees if the rank and file employees don't participate in the plan. There are tests that compare rank and file deferrals with highly compensated deferrals. If the plan fails one of these tests – that is, found to be "top-heavy" – then larger deferrals must be scaled back. And this would be to the consternation, theoretically, of the highly compensated. There is a work around, however, called "Safe Harbor" by which all employees, whether participating or not, can have accounts opened and then involuntarily funded for them at the rate of 3% of their compensation. If the sponsoring company does this, then the executive deferrals can be maxed out.

ERISA has written the rules, and DOL audits plans for compliance. I was always amazed at executive's reluctance to supply 3% of worker compensation since to me it seemed a pittance that could easily have been repaid by thinner annual raises. But corporate management was by and large dead set against making any 3% of compensation contributions for employees.

In addition to "Top-Heavy" testing, compliance requires that deferrals be deposited into employee accounts in a timely manner, that statements be provided quarterly, that the plan be audited by an outside firm if there are more than 110 employees and that employee participants receive training needed to make investment decisions from the menu they are offered.

Documentation Requirements

ERISA and DOL also require the sponsor to prepare a Plan Document and a Summary Plan Document. These lay out details on how the plan is to be constructed and managed and then summarize that for participants who are given a Summary Plan Document by law. Plan documents must be approved by ERISA/DOL and to head off an expensive review process, most sponsors just adopt a "Prototype" plan usually developed by a financial services firm and pre-approved by ERISA/DOL.

It is also possible to craft a custom plan that can call out investment menu and restriction to that menu. For example, the menu may contain several volatile funds such as a nano-technology fund and then restrict access to only participants with, say, $100K or more in the plan and restrict even these persons to placing to no more than 10% of their 401(k) funds in the volatile fund.

Sponsors, as has been described, are anxious to offload as much exposure to law suit as possible and one way to do this is to chop up a plan into many pieces with many actors and that way head off any hint of self-dealing or collusion. One area that gets some collusion is when the entity that provides the investment menu comes in to present an annual "audit" they have done on themselves and they report that the results met all market standards, they therefore having had a successful plan year, may expect to continue the engagement. This very obvious self-dealing passes over the heads of most plan sponsors who are impressed with the quality of the report, the quality of the paper it is printed on, and the results. I have personally been the recipient of such "glowing" reports delivered by HR people who are usually the gatekeepers of the 401(k) plan.

More sophisticated plan sponsors break up the asset management and auditing into separate functions performed by separate entities and even engage a third party to do the training. In this way, if anything goes wrong, the sponsor can say it eliminated all possibility of self-dealing. But these more sophisticated actors are a small fraction of the 401(k) landscape. Most sponsors just want to offload the whole thing onto one entity and be done with it.

Packaged Plans

These five parts are the key dimensions to sponsoring a 401(k) plan: Recordkeeping, Trusteeship, Asset Management, Compliance, and Education. In "packaged plans," such as those provided by mutual fund or insurance companies, the "Provider" does it all. Most packaged plans are sold by stock brokers or Registered Investment Advisors (RIAs) and they function as a third-party by hiring and firing the Provider. But it is the Provider who is paying commissions directly to the broker, so it is often not an arm's-length relationship. The key gatekeeper is the plan trustee at the employer, who does not receive incentive pay. In many cases, however, the trustee has a personal relationship with the broker and often as well a brokerage account. This situation does not pass fiduciary rigor but is very common.

Sometimes a broker will leave a brokerage firm for another firm and will be unable to move the 401(k) plan because the new firm does not have a selling agreement with the 401(k) plan provider. In such a case, the broker will move the plan to another provider. This is often done with the ready assent of the employer if it is felt that the broker is particularly effective in helping with the plan, such as in auditing the provider.

A key parameter is, of course, fees and for very small plans or start-up plans that are just being established and have little in the way of assets, fees are high, perhaps 1½% or more, and investment menu is restricted. When plans get up over

$5million in assets they usually have access to a wider investment menu that often includes outside funds. At the other end of the size spectrum, mega plans of, say, over $100 million can carry fees closer ¼% or less. But ¼% of $100,000,000 is $250,000 which is more than sufficient to cover all the recordkeeping, asset management, compliance, and training.

Despite the vastness of the 401(k) plan market and the huge amount of money involved there is very little differentiation among providers. This is because if one plan markedly outperformed another, there might be reasonable grounds for a suit. But there is a more reasonable explanation: Many plans although competitive with each other on the outside use many of the same funds on the inside.

As it is, any participating employee is likely to get a result that mimics the S&P 500 and that is not an actionable result. Even if the entire market craters as it did in 2008 and some actors escaped the damage, the S&P 500 is the unwritten but agreed upon standard and the only actionable results are those that fall far short of the S&P 500, where the investment menu was too narrow, and/or training wasn't offered. This will not happen with a packaged plan. That is the guarantee most sponsors are looking for and get from the very large and wealthy field of packaged plan providers.

Non-Packaged Plans

Unpackaged plans come about when more sophisticated plan sponsors break up the recordkeeping, trusteeship, asset management, compliance ,and training into five pieces and dole them out to five unrelated parties. This is a very small fraction of the 401(k) landscape but it does occur.

I am reminded of an incident when I was prospecting a plan sponsor who had a $7 million plan. I was with a major brokerage at the time and the prospect felt I would be unable to put together an investment menu in which I didn't have an interest, which was true – I would get paid a commission on any and all funds in the menu. He then went on to describe a "consultant" he was working with who was going to ask a number of packaged plan providers to provide bids from which he and the "consultant" were going to select a winner and then the "consultant" would act as a fiduciary to the plan, overseeing the operation and performance. My partner at the firm was doing the same thing, holding himself out to be a "consultant" and he didn't want me to "rain on Bob's parade."

At any rate it was a parade and the client was bringing up the rear. It seems that the word "consultant" is the magic that plan sponsors are looking for to give them fiduciary cover. Incidentally, fiduciary cover doesn't mean they are looking after the participant's interests, but rather that should something go wrong they can't be successfully sued – they have cover, fiduciary cover. In the case just described, the "consultant" would help the client select a packaged plan which would then pay the "consultant" commission and, of course, the "consultant" would audit the plan performance.

The 401(k) Football

A brief digression is worthwhile to discuss the role 401(k) plans play in corporate life. The default gatekeeper is usually the Director of HR but in larger companies there may be a "Benefits Manager" who takes the role. These people are always non-financial types and mainly act as gatekeepers. Some catalyst will then prompt a company to undertake a search for alternative providers. Sometimes they will use a real consultant who will put together a Request for Proposal (RFP) and invite a small field of suitable candidates to bid on the work. Because the consultants are in the business, they know who the players are. They spreadsheet the responses, usually ask the top three candidates in for a presentation, and in concert with their client make a selection. This is a pretty clean process but is subject to the bias of the consultant and usually limited to the consultant's acquaintances in the business, who are acquaintances, however, because they do good work.

What often happens in mid-sized company plans is that the HR person will select a field of perhaps five providers to make proposals. This eventually comes to the notice of the Board of Directors who up until this time had no particular interest in the plan.

Suddenly it is learned, one of the directors has a friend in the business and that friend then looks over the same proposals and points out to the board that the friend is able to provide a better plan at lower cost. The plan is then moved to the friend. There are many derivatives of this scenario, including the one where in the 11th hour the plan cannot be moved because as it turns out the plan is with a friend of someone on the board and the friend is going to do better job and alleviate any concern that others in the company had. The bottom line is that assets are never orphans.

I have attended numerous presentations to 401(k) plan committees, mostly on the losing side but occasionally on the winning side. And these meetings are all marked by the same clueless questions and answers as advisors functioning as sales people try to build rapport knowing there is no substantive issue that can be raised that will position the provider ahead of the competition. In one case, to a construction products firm whose business my team was attempting to win, the provider we brought in described delivering a quarterly educational session to another construction products firm, and in order to do so to a large assembly, was lifted up above the crowd in a crane. This produced instant credibility and we won the engagement.

I was told of another case. A household name in asset management sent a guy and a gal out to address a union group on what is called a Taft-Hartley plan for unions. The next day five guys from Goldman Sachs showed up with American flag pins in their lapels. Goldman got the engagement. It was the five guys and the lapel pins that won the job, according to the gatekeeper who told me the story. Don't go to a union pension selection meeting without an American flag in your lapel, and bring in lots of guys to mimic the union penchant for "creating" jobs. That's the unwritten rule for union plans according to this woman gatekeeper who related this episode to me. At Goldman Sachs they know this.

The Power of 401(k) Savings

If markets were placid there would be little value in dollar-cost-averaging because all the shares would cost about the same amount, varying only by the gradual upward march in value with time, value creation, and inflation. But markets are not placid; they gyrate wildly even in the best of times and so dollar-cost-averaging becomes a powerful tool for accumulating a disproportionate fraction of cheap shares.

It is in the wild gyrations of the market plus the vast amount of 401(k) plan money dollar-cost-averaging a disproportionate fraction of cheap shares into plan accounts of working Americans that has the best chance of doing what Congress originally intended, namely, replacing broken pensions with robust individual retirement portfolios. Just imagine the boost those 401(k) plan accounts got in the crash of 2008, accumulating all those cheap shares on the way down, grabbing some more at the bottom and continuing the accumulation on the way back up gradually closing down the valve as the shares reassumed their previous higher valuations. The crash of 2008 was a disaster for many, but for 401(k) plan participants it was money from heaven.

So the 401(k) plan landscape, as self-serving as it is, still creates a lot of value for the participants and perhaps adds a stabilizing force to the market as panic selling sends share prices into the cellar restrained only by those gazillion shares locked up in 401(k) plans under the control of people whose only concern in the 2008 crash was if they would keep their jobs. Most people, dreading to open their quarterly 401(k) plan statements, just threw them in a drawer and forgot about them. That is the magic of 401(k).

Throwing statements into a drawer and forgetting about them is perhaps the epitome of investment wisdom and in large part, I believe, it comes about because participants feel that their plan is under the control of competent professionals.

Those professionals managing these assets don't get paid unless the assets are being managed and that means invested somewhere. A mutual fund would have a difficult time charging a fee on a fund that was temporarily in an all-cash position although attaining that all-cash position took some doing. What happens is that the mutual fund rides the market all the way down and then all the way up on the other side, charging a percentage fee on assets throughout. Remember the mutual fund gets paid on fees that are tied to the value of the assets and as such is not in a position to lose – they can see their fees get thinner, a lot thinner, but they are always in positive territory. Not so their investors who may be suffering dramatic paper losses. So it is easier for the fund manager than the fund investor to stay the course. But staying the course is crucial to investment success and if mutual funds help people do this, it is a good thing. Keep in mind that dollar-cost-averaging works best in volatile markets and that means does well going down as well as up.

The magic of 401(k) plans is fourfold: (1) total management of participant assets for a fee, which heads off selling by both asset managers and participants; (2) returns that mimic the S&P 500; (3) dollar-cost-averaging; and (4) custom matching of asset allocation to participant's needs for cash in the disinvestment stage.

401(k) vs. Pension (Defined Contribution vs Defined Benefit)

This last point was discussed earlier on asset pools being allocated first on the need for cash. The closer an asset gets to cash the less it earns. People whose retirement is many years off should be invested as far away from cash as they can get, which might be a mutual fund of start-up companies that won't see profits for many years but whose profits, when they come, could be big. Young people have that luxury. People nearing retirement can't have a sizable fraction of assets in negative territory and must be close to cash with enough assets to help fund a retirement. Such a portfolio will be ready to spin off cash but will have very little growth, though as long as the liquidity of the portfolio matches the liquidity requirements of the participant, that participant is well served.

The problem with pensions and other shared asset pools is that the liquidity position may be optimal for a small fraction of the older pool participants while short changing the younger ones who need growth to build a retirement sized nest-egg. Pension plans are sometimes not managed optimally and fail or become underfunded. Although in the same market arena as 401(k) plans, pension plans guarantee a good retirement whether or not the market or management of the plan has produced the needed return. After several highly publicized large pension plan failures, the Pension Benefit Guaranty Corporation (PBGC), a U.S. government agency came into existence fill in the gap.

The PBGC claims it can meet all the pension liability it holds by combining assets in pools it takes over, plus assets it realizes in the closing of distressed companies, plus premiums it receives from companies that insure their pension plans through PBGC, and, of course, gains on the investment of its capital, which for the year 2010 was 12% closely approximating the S&P 500's 12.87%. Of course that is an exceptional return given that a substantial cash position must be maintained to meet retiree claims. These are retirees incidentally who are insulated from market outcomes by the intervention of PBGC, which spreads the risk over a larger pool of participants.

PBGC insures pension outcomes up to a maximum monthly income of $4,500 ($54,000 a year). A quick comparison with an immediate annuity for a 65-year-old male single-life would value that income stream as equivalent to about an $800,000 lump sum. A joint life annuity for husband and wife aged 65 would require a $925,000 lump sum. A joint-life pays $4,500.00 per month to end of life of either spouse.

In both cases – PBGC and an annuity – there is no COLA (Cost of Living Adjustment) or inflation adjustment. I suspect however that those benefit levels are adjusted from time to time.

These figures don't sound too difficult to achieve until you look at a person's earnings history over his or her entire life. While a person may start out with a lower income in his or her 20s, salary is expected to grow to a maximum in his or her 60s. Using a nice round number like $50,000 per year for a 40-year period, total compensation comes to $2 million.

Saving 10% of $2 million provides a $200K nest egg or a life annuity monthly payment of about $1100 for a single 65-year-old male life. More typically a husband and wife might accumulate together $350K providing about $1,700 monthly for a joint-life annuity. And this is all if they actually save 10%, which is not the norm. The American norm is 5%, but with a 10% market return, all you need is 5% if you start in your 20s.

Divergence of Income Growth and Investment Growth

Although the above savings figures are optimistic at 10% of income, they seem a little anemic from a retirement perspective. But once again 401(k) to the rescue. Salaries even with promotions for most people, don't keep up with the S&P 500. Up until the 2008 crash, aggregate S&P 500 total-return corrected for inflation was 9.28% per year. Very few people work for 40 years and even with promotions realize a 9.28% annual increase over 40 years. That would be a mind boggling result.

Just to provide an example, in 1972 I got my first company car and expense account working for a very fine Virginia company named Solite. My job was to travel around New York State and eastern Pennsylvania calling on architects and engineers promoting the use of the company's lightweight aggregate (stone) in concrete and concrete masonry units. My salary was about $12,000. Well had I remained at Solite for 40 years and gotten a 9.28% annual increase, last year, 2010, I would have realized an astonishing salary income of $382,180.05. As it is, my income was closer to $40,000.

Such is the power of that scary thing called the stock market. And what is that power? It is work that everyday people do every day, day in and day out, year after year; creating value which the stock market attempts to put a price on. In a famous quote, Benjamin Graham said: *"In the short run the stock market is a voting machine, but over the long run it is a weighing machine."* The implication is that the company valuation is not set by the stock market but by rank and file employees building value over the term of their careers.

There is another lesson in the divergence between wage growth and investment growth – the power of savings. If I had saved 5% of my wages in 1972 and invested the $600 in S&P 500 equivalents, at the end of 40 years the result would be $18,845 today. If I did this every year, saved and invested 5% of my wages for 40 years, the accumulated savings plus gains would be $323,490. This is calculated on wage growth of 4% and investment growth of 9%. The magic comes from two sources: the difference between wage growth and investment growth; and time. You absolutely cannot overestimate the role of time and that means setting an investment process and then forgetting it. Leave the investments alone and let the market, which is to say the general working population, do the work.

In the above case, if $323,490 had been the ending accumulation, that would buy an annuity with a lifetime payout of about $1,900 per month on a single life or about $1,600 per month on a joint life. And in this illustration, we are just using a low 5% savings rate for one person, not a couple.

So the process for those not inheriting wealth should be a 5% savings rate invested in S&P 500 equivalents to meet minimum retirement needs.

Examine the chart on the next page which compares the difference in wage growth rate at 4% and investment growth rate at 9% over a 40-year period. What you see is the magic of an investment process and a commitment to that process. What you see is a retirement nest-egg from humble beginnings and a humble process.

This chart is a very tangible demonstration of the power of savings and investment to build wealth over time if invested in just the S&P 500 and left alone – a very passive strategy. Owning a subset of the common stocks of the individual constituents of the S&P 500 would add dividends and perhaps splits, easily another 2%.

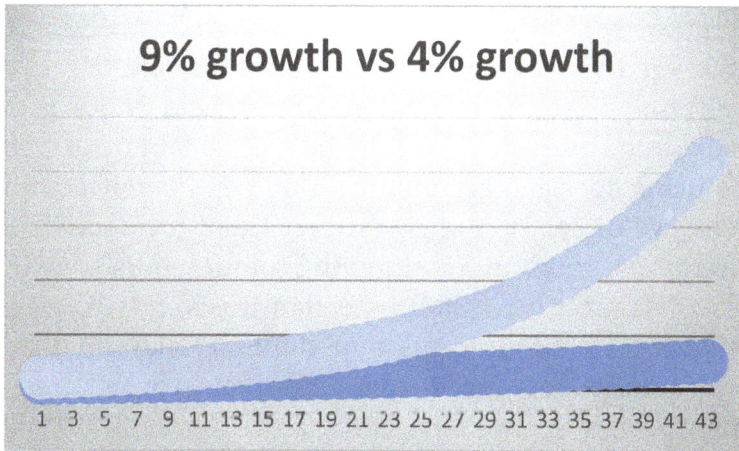

9% growth vs 4% growth

Comparison of 4% annual wage growth vs. 9% annual market growth.

The S&P 500 is an index made up mostly of America's largest and most widely held stocks and therefore most notable corporations plus notable global corporations. The aggregate result of the S&P 500 of 9.28% over a long period of time is a mean value of 500 common stocks over a long period of time. A mean value of 9.28% means that about 250 stocks did better and about 250 stocks did worse than the 9.28%. It would be interesting to see if just a random sampling of, say, just 25 constituents of the S&P 500 would produce a dramatically different result.

Beating the Market

In manufacturing operations, quality is guaranteed by testing a sampling of the products at random. QA (quality assurance) rules call for sampling rates that are some percentage of total production. If in that sample defects are found, a larger sample must then be taken and inspected. Then there are rules that dictate what further action is to be taken if no defects are found in the larger sample or if the defect rate is the same as in the original sample or if the defect rate is larger. In very few cases is 100% inspection required because it would be cheaper to just deal with the failures in the field, although this might not apply to some manufacturing like NASA rocket projects where I am sure 100% inspection is the rule.

So selecting 25 stocks at random from a field of 500 is a 5% sampling rate, which would be acceptable in some manufacturing to establish quality. But we are not sampling duplicates, we are sampling constituents that try very hard to be different, so a random 5% sampling might tell us something else. What I suspect it will tell us is that it is very easy to pick stocks that are in the upper 250 of the S&P 500 and thereby select out stocks in the lower 250 that are a drag on performance.

On the following pages is a complete listing of the S&P 500 constituents. I am going to pick out 25 constituents by what I consider to be their prominence in the American cultural landscape. The 25 I select are in blue and bold. I will select first from the top of the list, then from the bottom and then from the middle until I have a pretty good dispersion across the whole list. But there are some selections that are not random only because I consider them to be iconic American companies, like

P&G, Clorox, Exxon Mobil and some others.

Ticker symbol	Company	Portfolio Selection
MMM	3M Co.	1
ACE	ACE Limited	
ABT	Abbott Laboratories	
ANF	Abercrombie & Fitch Company A	
ADBE	Adobe Systems Inc	
AMD	Advanced Micro Devices	
AES	AES Corp	2
AET	Aetna Inc	
AFL	AFLAC Inc	
A	Agilent Technologies Inc	
APD	Air Products & Chemicals Inc	
ARG	Airgas Inc	
AKS	AK Steel Hldg Corp	
AKAM	Akamai Technologies Inc	
AA	Alcoa Inc	
ATI	Allegheny Technologies Inc	
AGN	Allergan Inc	
ALL	Allstate Corp	
ALTR	Altera Corp	
MO	Altria Group Inc	3
AMZN	Amazon.com Inc	
AEE	Ameren Corp	
AEP	American Electric Power	
AXP	American Express Co	
AIG	American Intl Group Inc	

AMT	American Tower Corp A	
AMP	Ameriprise Financial	
ABC	AmerisourceBergen Corp	
AMGN	Amgen Inc	
APH	Amphenol Corp A	
APC	Anadarko Petroleum Corp	
ADI	Analog Devices Inc	
AON	Aon Corporation	
APA	Apache Corporation	
AIV	Apartment Investment & Mgmt	
APOL	Apollo Group Inc	
AAPL	Apple Inc.	
AMAT	Applied Materials Inc	
ADM	Archer-Daniels-Midland Co	
AIZ	Assurant Inc	
T	AT&T Inc	
ADSK	Autodesk Inc	
ADP	Automatic Data Processing	
AN	AutoNation Inc	
AZO	AutoZone Inc	
AVB	AvalonBay Communities, Inc.	
AVY	Avery Dennison Corp	
AVP	Avon Products	4
BHI	Baker Hughes Inc	
BLL	Ball Corp	
BAC	Bank of America Corp	
BK	The Bank of New York Mellon Corp.	

BCR	Bard (C.R.) Inc.	
BAX	Baxter International Inc.	
BBT	BB&T Corporation	
BDX	Becton Dickinson	
BBBY	Bed Bath & Beyond	
BMS	Bemis Company	
BRK.B	Berkshire Hathaway	
BBY	Best Buy Co. Inc.	
BIG	Big Lots Inc.	
BIIB	BIOGEN IDEC Inc.	
BLK	Blackrock	
HRB	Block H&R	
BMC	BMC Software	
BA	Boeing Company	
BXP	Boston Properties	
BSX	Boston Scientific	
BMY	Bristol-Myers Squibb	
BRCM	Broadcom Corporation	
BF.B	Brown-Forman Corporation	
CHRW	C. H. Robinson Worldwide	
CA	CA, Inc.	
CVC	Cablevision Systems Corp.	
COG	Cabot Oil & Gas	
CAM	Cameron International Corp.	
CPB	Campbell Soup	
COF	Capital One Financial	
CAH	Cardinal Health Inc.	
CFN	Carefusion	

KMX	Carmax Inc	
CCL	Carnival Corp.	
CAT	Caterpillar Inc.	5
CBG	CBRE	
CBS	CBS Corp.	
CELG	Celgene Corp.	
CNP	CenterPoint Energy	
CTL	CenturyTel Inc	
CERN	Cerner	
CF	CF Industries Holdings Inc	
SCHW	Charles Schwab	
CHK	Chesapeake Energy	
CVX	Chevron Corp.	
CB	Chubb Corp.	
CI	CIGNA Corp.	
CINF	Cincinnati Financial	
CTAS	Cintas Corporation	
CSCO	Cisco Systems	
C	Citigroup Inc.	
CTXS	Citrix Systems	
CLF	Cliffs Natural Resources	
CLX	Clorox Co.	6
CME	CME Group Inc.	
CMS	CMS Energy	
COH	Coach Inc.	
KO	Coca Cola Co.	7
CCE	Coca-Cola Enterprises	
CTSH	Cognizant Technology Solutions	
CL	Colgate-Palmolive	

CMCSA	Comcast Corp.	
CMA	Comerica Inc.	
CSC	Computer Sciences Corp.	
CPWR	Compuware Corp.	
CAG	ConAgra Foods Inc.	
COP	ConocoPhillips	
CNX	CONSOL Energy Inc.	
ED	Consolidated Edison	
STZ	Constellation Brands	
CEG	Constellation Energy Group	
GLW	Corning Inc.	
COST	Costco Co.	
CVH	Coventry Health Care Inc.	
COV	Covidien plc	
CSX	CSX Corp.	
CMI	Cummins Inc.	8
CVS	CVS Caremark Corp.	
DHI	D. R. Horton	
DHR	Danaher Corp.	
DRI	Darden Restaurants	
DVA	DaVita Inc.	
DF	Dean Foods	
DE	Deere & Co.	
DELL	Dell Inc.	
DNR	Denbury Resources Inc.	
XRAY	Dentsply International	
DVN	Devon Energy Corp.	
DV	DeVry, Inc.	
DO	Diamond Offshore Drilling	

DTV	DirecTV	
DFS	Discover Financial Services	
DISCA	Discovery Communications	
D	Dominion Resources	
RRD	Donnelley (R.R.) & Sons	
DOV	Dover Corp.	
DOW	Dow Chemical	
DPS	Dr Pepper Snapple Group	
DTE	DTE Energy Co.	
DD	Du Pont (E.I.)	
DUK	Duke Energy	
DNB	Dun & Bradstreet	
ETFC	E-Trade	
EMN	Eastman Chemical	
ETN	Eaton Corp.	
EBAY	eBay Inc.	
ECL	Ecolab Inc.	
EIX	Edison Int'l	
EW	Edwards Lifesciences	
EP	El Paso Corp.	
ERTS	Electronic Arts	
EMC	EMC Corp.	
EMR	Emerson Electric	
ETR	Entergy Corp.	
EOG	EOG Resources	
EQT	EQT Corporation	
EFX	Equifax Inc.	
EQR	Equity Residential	
EL	Estee Lauder Cos.	

EXC	Exelon Corp.	
EXPE	Expedia Inc.	
EXPD	Expeditors Int'l	
ESRX	Express Scripts	
XOM	Exxon Mobil Corp.	9
FFIV	F5 Networks	
FDO	Family Dollar Stores	
FAST	Fastenal Co	
FII	Federated Investors Inc.	
FDX	FedEx Corporation	
FIS	Fidelity National Information Services	
FITB	Fifth Third Bancorp	
FHN	First Horizon National	
FSLR	First Solar Inc	
FE	FirstEnergy Corp	
FISV	Fiserv Inc	
FLIR	FLIR Systems	
FLS	Flowserve Corporation	
FLR	Fluor Corp.	
FMC	FMC Corporation	
FTI	FMC Technologies Inc.	
F	Ford Motor	
FRX	Forest Laboratories	
BEAM	Beam Inc.	
BEN	Franklin Resources	
FCX	Freeport-McMoran Cp & Gld	
FTR	Frontier Communications	
GME	GameStop Corp.	

GCI	Gannett Co.	
GPS	Gap (The)	
GD	General Dynamics	10
GE	General Electric	
GIS	General Mills	
GPC	Genuine Parts	
GNW	Genworth Financial Inc.	
GILD	Gilead Sciences	
GS	Goldman Sachs Group	
GR	Goodrich Corporation	
GT	Goodyear Tire & Rubber	
GOOG	Google Inc.	
GWW	Grainger (W.W.) Inc.	
HAL	Halliburton Co.	
HOG	Harley-Davidson	
HAR	Harman Int'l Industries	
HRS	Harris Corporation	
HIG	Hartford Financial Svc.Gp.	
HAS	Hasbro Inc.	
HCP	HCP Inc.	
HCN	Health Care REIT	
HNZ	Heinz (H.J.)	
HP	Helmerich & Payne	
HES	Hess Corporation	
HPQ	Hewlett-Packard	
HD	Home Depot	
HON	Honeywell Int'l Inc.	
HRL	Hormel Foods Corp.	
HSP	Hospira Inc.	
HST	Host Hotels & Resorts	

HCBK	Hudson City Bancorp	
HUM	Humana Inc.	
HBAN	Huntington Bancshares	
ITW	Illinois Tool Works	
TEG	Integrys Energy Group Inc.	
INTC	Intel Corp.	
ICE	Intercontinental Exchange Inc.	
IBM	International Business. Machines	11
IFF	International Flav/Frag	
IGT	International Game Technology	
IP	International Paper	
IPG	Interpublic Group	
INTU	Intuit Inc.	
ISRG	Intuitive Surgical Inc.	
IVZ	Invesco Ltd.	
IRM	Iron Mountain Incorporated	
XYL	Xylem Inc.	
JBL	Jabil Circuit	
JEC	Jacobs Engineering Group	
CBE	Cooper Industries	
JDSU	JDS Uniphase Corp.	
JNJ	Johnson & Johnson	12
JCI	Johnson Controls	
JOYG	Joy Global Inc.	
JPM	JPMorgan Chase & Co.	
JNPR	Juniper Networks	
K	Kellogg Co.	13

KEY	KeyCorp	
KMB	Kimberly-Clark	
KIM	Kimco Realty	
KLAC	KLA-Tencor Corp.	
KSS	Kohl's Corp.	
KFT	Kraft Foods Inc-A	
KR	Kroger Co.	
LLL	L-3 Communications Holdings	
LH	Laboratory Corp. of America Holding	
LM	Legg Mason	
LEG	Leggett & Platt	
LEN	Lennar Corp.	
LUK	Leucadia National Corp.	
LXK	Lexmark Int'l Inc	
LIFE	Life Technologies	
LLY	Lilly (Eli) & Co.	14
LTD	Limited Brands Inc.	
LNC	Lincoln National	
LLTC	Linear Technology Corp.	
LMT	Lockheed Martin Corp.	
L	Loews Corp.	
LO	Lorillard Inc.	
LOW	Lowe's Cos.	
LSI	LSI Corporation	
MTB	M&T Bank Corp.	
M	Macy's Inc.	
MRO	Marathon Oil Corp.	
MAR	Marriott Int'l.	15

MMC	Marsh & McLennan	
ACN	Accenture PLC	
MAS	Masco Corp.	
ANR	Alpha Natural Resources	
MA	Mastercard Inc.	
MAT	Mattel Inc.	
MKC	McCormick & Co.	
MCD	McDonald's Corp.	16
MHP	McGraw-Hill	17
MCK	McKesson Corp.	
MJN	Mead Johnson	
MWV	MeadWestvaco Corporation	
MHS	Medco Health Solutions Inc.	
MDT	Medtronic Inc.	
WFR	MEMC Electronic Materials	
MRK	Merck & Co.	
MET	MetLife Inc.	
PCS	MetroPCS Communications Inc.	
MCHP	Microchip Technology	
MU	Micron Technology	
MSFT	Microsoft Corp.	
MOLX	Molex Inc.	
TAP	Molson Coors Brewing Company	
MON	Monsanto Co.	
MWW	Monster Worldwide	
MCO	Moody's Corp	
MS	Morgan Stanley	

MOS	The Mosaic Company	
MMI	Motorola Mobility Holdings Inc.	
MSI	Motorola Solutions Inc.	
MUR	Murphy Oil	
MYL	Mylan Inc.	
NBR	Nabors Industries Ltd.	
NDAQ	NASDAQ OMX Group	
NOV	National Oilwell Varco Inc.	
NTAP	NetApp	
NFLX	NetFlix Inc.	
NWL	Newell Rubbermaid Co.	
NFX	Newfield Exploration Co	
NEM	Newmont Mining Corp. (Hldg. Co.)	
NWSA	News Corporation	
NEE	NextEra Energy Resources	
GAS	NICOR Inc.	
NKE	NIKE Inc.	
NI	NiSource Inc.	
NE	Noble Corp	
NBL	Noble Energy Inc	
JWN	Nordstrom	
NSC	Norfolk Southern Corp.	
NTRS	Northern Trust Corp.	
NOC	Northrop Grumman Corp.	
NU	Northeast Utilities	
CMG	Chipotle Mexican Grill	
NVLS	Novellus Systems	
NRG	NRG Energy	

NUE	Nucor Corp.	
NVDA	Nvidia Corporation	
NYX	NYSE Euronext	
ORLY	O'Reilly Automotive	
OXY	Occidental Petroleum	
OMC	Omnicom Group	
OKE	ONEOK	
ORCL	Oracle Corp.	
OI	Owens-Illinois Inc	
PCAR	PACCAR Inc.	18
IR	Ingersoll-Rand PLC	
PLL	Pall Corp.	
PH	Parker-Hannifin	
PDCO	Patterson Companies	
PAYX	Paychex Inc.	
BTU	Peabody Energy	
JCP	Penney (J.C.)	
PBCT	People's United Bank	
POM	Pepco Holdings Inc.	
PEP	PepsiCo Inc.	
PKI	PerkinElmer	
PFE	Pfizer Inc.	
PCG	PG&E Corp.	
PM	Philip Morris International	19
PNW	Pinnacle West Capital	
PXD	Pioneer Natural Resources	
PBI	Pitney-Bowes	
PCL	Plum Creek Timber Co.	
PNC	PNC Financial Services	

RL	Polo Ralph Lauren Corp.	
PPG	PPG Industries	
PPL	PPL Corp.	
PX	Praxair Inc.	
PCP	Precision Castparts	
PCLN	Priceline.com Inc	
PFG	Principal Financial Group	
PG	Procter & Gamble	20
PGN	Progress Energy Inc.	
PGR	Progressive Corp.	
PLD	ProLogis	
PRU	Prudential Financial	
PEG	Public Serv. Enterprise Inc.	
PSA	Public Storage	
PHM	Pulte Homes Inc.	
QEP	QEP Resources	
PWR	Quanta Services Inc.	
QCOM	QUALCOMM Inc.	
DGX	Quest Diagnostics	
RSH	RadioShack Corp	
RRC	Range Resources Corp.	
RTN	Raytheon Co.	
RHT	Red Hat Inc.	
RF	Regions Financial Corp.	
RSG	Republic Services Inc	
RAI	Reynolds American Inc.	
RHI	Robert Half International	
ROK	Rockwell Automation Inc.	
COL	Rockwell Collins	
ROP	Roper Industries	

ROST	Ross Stores Inc.	
RDC	Rowan Cos.	
R	Ryder System	
SWY	Safeway Inc.	
SAI	SAIC	
CRM	Salesforce.com	
SNDK	SanDisk Corporation	
SLE	Sara Lee Corp.	
SCG	SCANA Corp	
SLB	Schlumberger Ltd.	
SNI	Scripps Networks Interactive Inc.	
SEE	Sealed Air Corp.(New)	
SHLD	Sears Holdings Corporation	
SRE	Sempra Energy	
SHW	Sherwin-Williams	
SIAL	Sigma-Aldrich	
SPG	Simon Property Group Inc	
SLM	SLM Corporation	
SJM	Smucker (J.M.)	
SNA	Snap-On Inc.	
SO	Southern Co.	
LUV	Southwest Airlines	
SWN	Southwestern Energy	
SE	Spectra Energy Corp.	
S	Sprint Nextel Corp.	
STJ	St Jude Medical	
SWK	Stanley Black & Decker	
SPLS	Staples Inc.	

SBUX	Starbucks Corp.	21
HOT	Starwood Hotels & Resorts	
STT	State Street Corp.	
SRCL	Stericycle Inc	
SYK	Stryker Corp.	
SUN	Sunoco Inc.	
STI	SunTrust Banks	
SVU	Supervalu Inc.	
SYMC	Symantec Corp.	
SYY	Sysco Corp.	
TROW	T. Rowe Price Group	
TGT	Target Corp.	
TEL	TE Connectivity Ltd.	
TE	TECO Energy	
TLAB	Tellabs Inc.	
THC	Tenet Healthcare Corp.	
TDC	Teradata Corp.	
TER	Teradyne Inc.	
TSO	Tesoro Petroleum Co.	
TXN	Texas Instruments	
TXT	Textron Inc.	
HSY	The Hershey Company	
TRV	The Travelers Companies Inc.	
TMO	Thermo Fisher Scientific	
TIF	Tiffany & Co.	
TWX	Time Warner Inc.	
TWC	Time Warner Cable Inc.	
TIE	Titanium Metals Corp	
TJX	TJX Companies Inc.	

TMK	Torchmark Corp.	
TSS	Total System Services	
TSN	Tyson Foods	
TYC	Tyco International	
USB	U.S. Bancorp	
UNP	Union Pacific	
UNH	United Health Group Inc.	
UPS	United Parcel Service	22
X	United States Steel Corp.	
UTX	United Technologies	
UNM	Unum Group	
URBN	Urban Outfitters	
VFC	V.F. Corp.	
VLO	Valero Energy	
VAR	Varian Medical Systems	
VTR	Ventas Inc	
VRSN	Verisign Inc.	
VZ	Verizon Communications	23
VIA.B	Viacom Inc.	
V	Visa Inc.	
VNO	Vornado Realty Trust	24
VMC	Vulcan Materials	
WMT	Wal-Mart Stores	
WAG	Walgreen Co.	
DIS	Walt Disney Co.	25
WPO	Washington Post Co B	
WM	Waste Management Inc.	
WAT	Waters Corporation	
WPI	Watson Pharmaceuticals	
WLP	WellPoint Inc.	

WFC	Wells Fargo	
WDC	Western Digital	
WU	Western Union Co	
WY	Weyerhaeuser Corp.	
WHR	Whirlpool Corp.	
WFM	Whole Foods Market	
WMB	Williams Cos.	
WIN	Windstream Corporation	
WEC	Wisconsin Energy Corporation	
WYN	Wyndham Worldwide	
WYNN	Wynn Resorts Ltd	
XEL	Xcel Energy Inc	
XRX	Xerox Corp.	
XLNX	Xilinx Inc	
XL	XL Capital	
YHOO	Yahoo Inc.	
YUM	Yum! Brands Inc	
ZMH	Zimmer Holdings	
ZION	Zions Bancorp	

So for better or for worse, the 25 stocks for my 401(k) plan are:

Ticker symbol	Company	Portfolio Selection
MMM	3M Co.	1
AES	AES Corp	2
MO	Altria Group Inc.	3
AVP	Avon Products	4
CAT	Caterpillar Inc.	5
CLX	Clorox Co.	6

KO	Coca Cola Co.	7
CMI	Cummins Inc.	8
XOM	Exxon Mobil Corp.	9
GD	General Dynamics	10
IBM	International Business. Machines	11
JNJ	Johnson & Johnson	12
K	Kellogg Co.	13
LLY	Lilly (Eli) & Co.	14
MAR	Marriott Int'l.	15
MCD	McDonald's Corp.	16
MHP	McGraw-Hill	17
PCAR	PACCAR Inc.	18
PM	Philip Morris International	19
PG	Procter & Gamble	20
SBUX	Starbucks Corp.	21
UPS	United Parcel Service	22
VZ	Verizon Communications	23
VNO	Vornado Realty Trust	24
DIS	Walt Disney Co.	25

Now let's look at how these 25 companies did relative to the S&P 500. But before moving directly to that, be aware that owning these stocks outside of a mutual fund and if held for the life of the 401(k) plan, will in addition to capital gain, provide stock splits and dividends.

What will be presented is the stock chart for these selected stocks, compared with the S&P 500, and a chart showing splits where applicable and a chart showing dividends. Dividend yields will also be shown.

The lighter line is the S&P 500. These thumb-nail charts are meant to show how just picking iconic companies from within the S&P 500 universe, you are able to easily select 25 that are mostly in the upper half or upper quartile ranking by performance. Stock charts are best viewed relative to an index like the S&P 500. To get a much better picture, on the Internet just go to Big Charts and select "Interactive Chart," then chart a stock against an index. You can also display splits and dividends – splits are in the left column denoted by yellow dots and dividends are shown in the right column denoted by black squares.

		3M Company MMM Split 4th Q 2003 Yield 2.89%
		American Electric Power AES no splits Yield 4.92%
		Altria MO No splits Yield 5.11%
		Avon Products AVP Split 3rd Q 2004 Yield 5.72%
		Caterpillar CAT Split 4th Q 2005 Yield 2.12%
		Clorox CLX No splits Yield 3.75%

Coca-Cola
KO
No splits
Yield 2.90%

Cummins
CMI
Split 3rd Q 2007 &
2nd Q 2008
Yield 1.86%

Exxon-Mobil
XOM
Split 4th Q 2002
Yield 2.54%

General
Dynamics
GD

International Bus.
Mach.
IBM

Johnson&Johnson
JNJ
Split 3rd Q 2001
Yield 3.72%

Kellogg's
K
No splits
Yield 3.53%

Eli Lilly
LLY
No splits
Yield 4.77%

		Marriott Corp MARsplit 3rd Q 2006 Yield 1.43%
		McDonalds MCD No splits Yield 3.04%
		MHP (McGraw-Hill) No splits Yield 2.29%
		Paccar PCAR Splits 02,04,06 and 08 Yield 1.93%
		Philip Morris PM No splits Yield 3.61%
		Procter & Gamble PG Split 3rd Q 2004 Yield 3.44%
		Starbucks SBUX Splits early on Yield 1.25%
		United Parcel Service UPS No splits Yield 3.13%

	Verizon VZ 2 splits Yield 4.83%
	Vornado Realty VNO No splits Yield 3.90%
	Walt Disney DIS 1 split Yield 1.35%

Beating the Market With Stocks

As you can see, although all 25 stocks are members of the S&P 500 they mostly outperformed the total index. This is because the index contains 250 stocks that mostly underperformed the mean of the index. In a 401(k) plan, offering 25 stocks as an alternative to the mutual fund menu may offer the promise of better performance but at some risk and risk that most plan sponsors are unwilling to accept because their objective is to head off lawsuits.

Many investors are not cognizant enough of the power of dividends, although they may respect that dividends make a contribution. To get an idea, I modeled a 40-year growth period using an Excel spreadsheet, assumed a 9% annual growth rate in capital gains as one set of outcomes and then added 3% as a stand-in for dividends. I modeled a 12% annual growth rate (9% plus 3%) to reflect dividend reinvestment. After 40 years, $100 with no additions turned into $3,140 as a result of capital gains at 9% and turned into $9,305 with 3% dividend reinvestment. There is just no other way to say it: Dividend reinvestment is very powerful; it needs to be near the top in stock selection criteria and in 401(k) plans.

One advantage of a portfolio of stocks in a 401(k) plan is the cash flow produced by dividends. A $1 million portfolio might be expected to produce $30,000 annually in dividends and there are many, many elderly who depend heavily on their dividend checks.

Unfortunately very few, if any, 401(k) plans offer the choice of holding a portfolio of stocks. Some plans offer what is called a "self-directed" channel, but most sponsors are leery of this option because they are afraid some participants will move their entire account into a self-directed plan and then hurt themselves through a combination of the volatility of the market and investor volatility, the latter of which will inevitably produce losses and possibly even catastrophic losses. It won't be long before an attorney will see in that scenario an opportunity to blame a plan sponsor for providing the freedom and not the education to prevent catastrophe.

For the plan sponsor, self-directed accounts are all downside. And this is so because there is no education that can be effective. Investment success is the result of hard earned experience. To the neophyte the stock market looks like a money machine with no thought of loss, and it is only with some hard knocks – more for some and fewer for others – that a more balanced view begins to emerge. One hopes this balanced view may with further refinement eventually morph into a successful investment discipline. Investment is a personal journey and not something that is going to be taught in the context of a 401(k) plan education session.

I am reminded of an episode in 1935 when Hitler wished to add to his political gravitas and bring an iconic German general into his coterie by offering him the highest level of command, that of Field Marshal. General Erich Ludendorff reportedly regarded Hitler with contempt and when he was made the offer became incensed. He shouted at Hitler: *"Field Marshals are born, not made!"* Well, successful investment is the same way; it comes from the inside, and is not something picked up in the context of a 401(k) plan.

Creating the New "Family Farm"

Nevertheless, with the loss of the family farm as a source of employment, income, and security, the only thing left is the stock market. And therefore it is not the opportunity, but the duty of people to become successful investors and pass that realization onto their children. As has been shown, savings alone from a job cannot provide security, those savings must be successfully invested to do so. This is particularly critical as public sector and union retirees continue to claim a dis-proportionate share of public wealth that is increasingly not there because the value was never created. Corporate produced wealth in the form of advancing stock price, on the other hand is not reserved for the state or for the politically connected or for the organized; it is for everybody, and it is there for the taking by those who know how to take. It is investment. It is putting money in so that corporations can put that money to work for you so that you can be provided for in old age. This is not a voluntary exercise; it is a duty as a citizen sharing resources in common with others.

As suggested here previously, Wall Street has hijacked the investment landscape, convincing people who otherwise might be inclined to study the stock market that it is a dangerous and complicated place that can only be understood and negotiated through a stock brokerage firm. Actually, the opposite is true that ignorance and misadventure await the unsuspecting client new to the world of brokerage. It's true, of course, that you must use a broker to buy and sell stock, but the service ends there. The client needs instead to examine his or her own experience with investments: the family house, investments employers have made, what's in the newspapers, personal experience and so on, to learn investment. Another good source is reading books on economics.

When Adam Smith wrote about the pin factory he purposefully left out the part about betting on the daily valuation changes of the pin business because it was irrelevant. Businesses succeed or fail on the basis of their ability to adapt to changing markets. The pin factory succeeded because somebody got the idea of dividing labor into discrete repetitive tasks that would add efficiency and bring down the cost of a pin. This is economics, the downward spiral of cost and the upward spiral of value, revenue and profit where creative minds are at work.

As the beginning investor begins to cultivate the economics view, the process will snowball and build upon itself and produce over time the ability to assess and manage risk. He or she will ultimately see that investing in just the 25 or 30 largest capitalization constituents in the S&P 500, or simply in the Dow 30, or a subset of the global 100, will provide a dramatically better result that investing in mutual funds that mimic the S&P 500. These provide the illusion of safety and fiduciary cover for a 401(k) plan sponsor while robbing the participants of the opportunity to both do better and see how the stock market really works.

401(k) plans lie at the intersection of Wall Street and Main Street and highlight the intractable problem of managing traffic from both directions for the benefit of both. As it stands, Wall Street is there in the service of those wishing and hoping for a quick buck in a short-term trade with the expectation that repeating that process will build wealth sooner rather than later and in predictable ways. This notion was best quashed by Burton Malkiel in *A Random Walk Down Wall Street*, who pointed out that random processes cannot be gamed for very long and stock price moves are random. Burton Malkiel did admit that there are actors who through superior intuition and intelligence are able to engage in the trading game and win more than they lose, but they are not looking for clients and certainly not retail clients (my view) – plus they can't be identified by the public anyway.

The point of this book is that you don't have to lose. You don't have to buy into the Wall Street mantra that trading in and out of stocks on short-term or transient information billed as "research" is synonymous with investment. If anything that is more like trading than investment. Investment is characterized by a more thoughtful approach coupled by a longer term process that seeks to build wealth by the owning a piece of productivity that the world depends upon.

From employee to the Lord of the Manor

The investor is like the Lord of the Manor, going out each day and regarding his serfs at work and marveling at both their great skill and contentment with their lot. They just want to work. And that is what the corporate world wants – they want to work for you.

The corporate world does not like trading and traders, that is why they offer DRIP plans, because they know that DRIP plan investors are in it for the long haul. By cultivating investors rather than traders, corporations cut out the counterproductive trading culture that breeds erratic stock price which itself shifts the focus of management from the core business of the company to the distraction of answering for daily investor sentiment.

When I was a stock broker I picked up one client who was a nut-case, but a nice nut-case. He would get trading ideas from a man who owned three luxury car dealerships and had worked himself into meeting a $200,000 per month payment for financing them. He was described to me as being manic, starting out with sedatives in the morning, mixing in alcohol at lunch, and ending each day totally toasted. He was also trying to acquire a fourth dealership, which he felt would take the pressure off due to its success. In between he was on the phone with his investor network and would take huge positions on the most transient news. I heard about these when my client wanted me to buy those same issues for him. One was a heavy vehicle aftermarket manufacturer who was building heavily armored vehicles for the military to provide protection from Iraqi road mines. That stock took off like a rocket and soon after came down at the same velocity – pump and dump. The reason I know is that I was a loser along with my client. It was just another lesson along the way to my education as an investor.

This same client described losing money in the internet bubble and with a stock broker which I found to be an unbelievable data point. I could see retail investors losing money in the internet bubble trading on their own, but not a professional. Nevertheless with a healthy dose of amnesia from his first Wall Street brokerage experience he gave me his account. The first thing I bought for him was the Singapore Fund. This is a closed end fund that was trading at a deep discount on an economy I have a great deal of faith in, Singapore incorporated. I bought it at around $16.50. My client called up about 3 days later and without even introducing himself, asks: *"Where's it at?"* I had to focus for a moment on who this was who was calling and then with a great deal of irritation, I stopped what I was doing to see where the Singapore Fund was trading at: *"$16.26,"* I replied. *"It's not supposed to do that,"* he shot back. *"Not supposed to do that?"* I then gave him a lecture that surprised even me.

Nevertheless, the client continued the relationship and my fellow brokers in the cubicles surrounding mine would always get ready for a chuckle whenever I answered a ringing phone with: *"Hey Lon, how ya doin',"* and a note of boredom in my voice. His outrageous pronouncements with the belief that he could game the market would always elicit from me a stern lecture describing the market as nothing more than a carnival wheel where anything could and did happen. He always took the lectures good naturedly apparently with the thought that maybe I was trying to help him. But people like him and his Quaalude friend cannot be helped; it's a disease. It's a disease because they just can't let go in the face of the fact that the randomness of the market cannot be gamed. They are like people who inadvertently touch a high voltage wire and then can't let go.

Lon's world is one end of the market, the frantic end that provides liquidity. Participants in 401(k) plans are at the other end, so passive they don't even know what they are invested in. Nevertheless 401(k) plan participants do better. But there is a middle ground where 401(k) plan participants would be able to have the choice between mutual funds mimicking the S&P 500, a portfolio of the 30 top capitalization constituents of the S&P 500, or the Dow 30. This "top 30" portfolio would outperform the S&P 500 index and perhaps offer organic training as participants would see the effects of dollar-cost-averaging, stock splits and dividends.

The shift away from stocks into mutual funds I believe was triggered by "May Day" May 1st 1975 when the SEC discontinued fixed commissions and opened stock trading commissions to competition. Within the first month commissions were cut in half.

The idea may have been to reduce the cost of market participation but if anything it may have raised the cost. From the founding of the NYSE in 1792 up until "May Day, 1975" stock trading commissions were fixed and once a client paid for a trade there were no more charges for having the account beyond perhaps a very small administrative fee. Today very few brokers do what is called stock picking and instead put their clients into mutual funds which charge ongoing fees for commissions, trading, management and marketing. The clients never see the fees because they come off the top. If a fund earned 11% in a given year, the performance of the fund is reported as around 9½% and that is what the client sees. As explained in the chapter on mutual funds there are different share "classes" for the same fund and each class earns a return consistent with its fee structure.

Mutual funds have replaced trading commissions as a source of revenue for brokers who are now incentivized to promote mutual funds and, of course, the mantra is safety. And it works. I have had many prospects tell me that stocks are dangerous and they only want funds. And what has even been more remarkable to me is that I have had stock brokers recoil in terror when I tell them I use stocks. Very dangerous they feel.

I will tell you how dangerous it is. It is as dangerous as living, which is dangerous, I admit. People die every day. But to understand how dangerous common stocks are, consider the top 10 stocks of the S&P 500 by capitalization, how soon are they going to close up shop? Here they are, the top 10:

1. Exxon Mobil
2. Microsoft
3. Wal-Mart
4. Johnson & Johnson
5. Procter & Gamble
6. IBM
7. AT&T
8. Apple
9. JP Morgan Chase
10. Google

If a 401(k) plan participant had a portfolio of these 10 stocks, they would outperform any mutual fund found in any 401(k) plan. Just elimination of fees would be a 1½% boost. Then there's another increase of about 2% for dividends. So you have an estimated 3½% boost in performance.

We have shown that the long-term return of the S&P 500 is about 9½ % while wage growth is closer to 4%. So putting money to work in the S&P 500 at the rate of 5% of income will produce a viable retirement income if started when just entering the workforce as a youth. In this respect 401(k) plans have filled a vital need in the American economy. 401(k) plans are also tailored to the individual, allowing better asset allocation to balance the need for growth with the need for cash flow. Nevertheless if some method could be found to allow participants to buy discrete company common stock from a narrow menu at low enough trading costs, a significant boost to the S&P 500 outcome could be achieved. The key challenge is trading costs which are entirely circumvented by mutual funds.

POSTSCRIPT:

In an April 27, 2012 editorial in *The New York Times*, Joe Nocera lamented the results of his reliance on his 401(k) plan for retirement. Before feeling too bad for Joe, be aware that he has since written a book and hopefully will repair his retirement nest-egg.

In his own words, here is what happened to Joe's 401(k) plan assets:

"The bull market ended with the bursting of that bubble in 2000. My tech-laden portfolio was cut in half. A half-dozen years later, I got divorced, cutting my 401(k) in half again. A few years after that, I bought a house that needed some costly renovations. Since my retirement account was now hopelessly inadequate for actual retirement, I reasoned that I might as well get some use out of the money while I could. So I threw another chunk of my 401(k) at the renovation. That's where I stand today."

Joe then goes on to quote an economist who focuses on retirement, Teresa Ghilarducci: *"People tend to be overconfident about their own abilities., They tend to focus on the short term rather than thinking about long-term consequences. And they tend to think that whatever the current trend is will always be the trend. That is why people buy high and sell low."* Ghilarducci has been cited as stating that 401(k) plans are a failed experiment.

There are obvious holes in Joe's tale, although it could happen I suppose. A "tech-laden" portfolio should not be a possibility in a 401(k) plan because the menu would be limited to S&P 500 equivalents and maybe one or two slightly more aggressive funds, but it may be possible that Joe's plan permitted lopsided allocation or he may have had a brokerage channel.

Nevertheless, Joe's story is a stand-in for the calamitous intersection of Wall Street and Main Street. As Ms. Ghilarducci points out, relying on untutored mainstream American workers to make investment decisions is a recipe for failure. But the problem wasn't Joe Nocera's 401(k) plan, it was Joe Nocera.

Mainstream untutored American workers do fine when they stay out of the way, and that is because in the entire American landscape there is nothing that will create as much value for Americans as the stock market. Their jobs will degrade or go away; their salaries will dwindle as what they do becomes more of a commodity and competition ramps up; and their health will decline. In short, the trend in life is generally down, down for everything except for the stock market. The stock market is the only feature in American life that goes up with time.

Now how do you connect untutored mainstream America to the stock market? If you put everybody into the same pool (pensions) then the younger experience the drag of paying older workers. The best option is tailoring offered by individual accounts, and payroll deduction is a no-brainer. The weakness of 401(k) plans is the self-directed part.

The challenge in a 401(k) plan is to obtain the needed growth while heading off self-destructive trading that leaves the sponsor vulnerable to participant disappointment and failure that then produces liability. Nevertheless it should be possible to allow participants to select pre-selected portfolios of 20 or 30 stocks with some variability in trade-off between expected capital gain (NASDAQ issues) and dividend payers (NYSE issues). The challenge then becomes keeping trading costs down, that is one area where mutual funds are hard to beat – trading costs are very low even for small incremental purchases such as in a 401(k) plan.

But either way, mutual funds, index funds or individual common stocks, the key ingredient is making the deferrals and staying the course. It is the process that is decisive in determining what kind of a retirement people will have or even if they will have a retirement.

North Over Madison *Ben Aronson 2008*
Oil on panel, 30 x 30 inches *Private Collection*

Afterword

*"Gooseberries, wild plums and lobsters, as well as eels "trod"
from the nearby salt marsh, completed a meal intimately bound
to the surrounding land and water. Though corn prompted the
celebration, and was doubtless included in pottages and stews,
the centerpieces were all products of the bountiful yet intensely
threatening natural world."*

A 17th century description of the first Thanksgiving.

Like the pilgrims who landed at Plymouth Rock in 1620, we
are beset by the need to secure our futures. However, unlike
the plight of the Pilgrims, we don't know the way. For the

Pilgrims the course was clear: clear the land, plant crops, build a house, hunt, trap, fish, and harvest timber, all going back to the mother country in trade. After 30 years, the future was theirs with ample wealth in cropland, animal husbandry and the family farm to sustain them right up to the end. That freehold and the imperative that went with it along with the natural bounty that it produced is no longer available and in its place people have uncertain jobs, which take care of only today if all goes well, which it often doesn't. The land has been turned into factors of production and the only way to secure a future is to work those factors. But the imperative is not clear and Wall Street is the gatekeeper. The Pilgrims had the Indians to teach them to plant and fish; we have Wall Street brokers.

It has been the intention of this book to demystify investment and show that it is no more difficult that planting, building, and harvesting though it does require education. The education is not of an arcane kind with esoteric formulas but rather devoted to gaining confidence in your own judgment in determining what is useful work and can be relied upon to earn a profit. Just general observation is required to see that investing in a company is no more dangerous that accepting employment at that same company and that the fortunes of that company are pretty much mirrored in the fortunes of our country and of our world.

You can visit a re-creation of the original Plymouth Plantation and then take a drive downtown into modern-day Plymouth and see for yourself what almost 400 years of man's labor has done. What would the Pilgrim's think if they could see how people live today? The production of man-made wealth is everywhere. Not only are companies not dangerous to invest in, without them we are back living in caves. Companies are the safest investment, in fact you can't keep them down, they will overcome all obstacles to produce wealth, just as the Pilgrims did.

The wealth that companies produce is there for anybody

who wants it. One would think such a boon would be reserved for the elite or for the connected, perhaps only employees, but no, it is there for anybody who wants it. All you have to do is buy shares and you are on board and suddenly your life is not bound by the 3%-4% wage growth you can expect in your work life, but you are now attached to a 9+% growth engine and if you put away just 5% of your earnings all the emoluments of the family farm are there for your old age – a soft landing.

However, the big advantage the Pilgrims had was that if a storm came and blew down their crop, they couldn't bail out, they would have to hunt or trap or fish, or beg or borrow, but they couldn't give up. Giving up was not an option, they had to soldier on. But then there would be sunshine and good times and plentiful harvests to give them faith and the strength to keep going even inducing them to clear more land. In the end they were delivered by the lack of exits, no ships in the harbor waiting to take them back to England.

Today's Pilgrim is not so fortunate. There are not only multiple exits but exits so alluring they don't look like exits at all, just new entrances to greater and greater wealth all accompanied by their carnival barkers: "This way to the Egress." And being constantly subject to such seduction it is not surprising that many people give up except they won't know they gave up until it's retirement time and there is no farm and then they understand that they gave up. They lost their faith not in their own humanity but in the inevitability of wealth proceeding from people just going to work to do their jobs. They lost faith in Main Street and listened to the carnival barkers on Wall Street. Don't do it. Pick 15 or 20 great companies, any companies, buy shares every payday, 5% of your pay, and hold on as if there were no exits. Close your eyes if you have to, but hold on. You will be rewarded. If you don't believe me, look up the price of the stocks you are interested in and see what they were trading at 30 years ago, or 40 years ago. If you do that, you will have a view into building an estate you can retire on.

I looked up growth in GE from 1972 to 2012 (40 years) at

Yahoo under historical prices. In 1972 GE stock was trading at a split-adjusted 36¢ and in 2012 at $19.87. That is a gain of $19.51 or 10½% per year. But wait, dividends added another 1½% for a total gain of $33.61 or 12% per year overall. Or to give perhaps a better perspective, purchasing a share of GE stock today at $19.87 and adding in an annual yield of 3.40%, in 40 years that one share would reach a value of $2,424.55. That means a 100 share investment of just $1987 today would yield in 40 years, $242,455.00 if the next 40 years are anything like the last 40 years. Of course purchasing power will only be about $100,000, but we are only talking about $1987 in today's dollars. Do you think you can put away more? Have faith, you can do it and you don't need any professional help, just be a Pilgrim. And after a while you will own a nice chunk of Main Street like the Lord or Lady of the Manor and you will enjoy the wealth that your serfs are producing for you. All you have to do is let them. Don't interfere and you'll be fine.

INDEX

	546, 552
Viatical Settlement	557-558
Volatility	70, 74, 85, 105, 147, 150, 153, 155, 191, 203, 251, 259, 264, 266, 268, 271, 277, 340, 343, 353, 357, 378, 406, 413, 421, 437-440, 447-448, 463, 473, 484-485, 497, 514, 550-551, 610
Von Hayek, Friedrich	21, 22, 38, 444
Waksal, Sam	147-148, 166
Wal-Mart	274, 348, 368, 429, 433, 439, 456, 464, 470, 603, 616
Wasting Assets	67, 74, 268
Wrap Account	151
Zero-Coupon bonds	54

Bibliography (grouped by subject):

General guides:

Graham, Benjamin & Dodd, David L., *Security Analysis: Principles and Technique*, McGraw-Hill, 1940

Malkiel, Burton G., *A Random Walk Down Wall Street: A Time-Tested Strategy for Successful Investing*, W.W. Norton & Company, 2007 (1973)

Hooke, Jeffrey C., *Security Analysis on Wall Street: A Comprehensive Guide to Today's Valuation Methods*, John Wiley & Sons, Inc., 1998

Khoury, Sarkis Joseph; Pal, Poorna; Zhou, Chunsheng; Karayan, John, *Wealth Forever: The Analytics of Stock Markets*, World Scientific, 2003

Helfert, Erich A., *Techniques of Financial Analysis*, Irwin, after 1977 (1963)

Brealey, Richard A., *An Introduction to Risk and Return from Common Stocks*, The M.I.T. Press, 1969

Gibson, Roger C., *Asset Allocation: Balancing Financial Risk*, McGraw-Hill, 2000 (1990)

Stein, Ben & DeMuth, Phil, *Yes, You Can Time the Market*, John Wiley & Sons, Inc., 2003

Strachman, Daniel A., *Essential Stock Picking Strategies: What Works on Wall Street*, John Wiley & Sons, Inc., 2002

Cohen, Bejamin J, *The Geography of Money*, Cornell University Press, 1998

Easterling, Ed, *Unexpected Returns: Understanding Secular Stock Market Cycles*, Cypress House, 2005

Carlson, Charles B., CFA, *Winning with Dow's Losers: Beat the Market with Underdog Stocks*, Harper Business 2004

Off the Rails:

Lowenstein, Roger, *When Genius Failed: The Rise and Fall of Long-Term Capital Management*, Random House, 2000

Chancellor, Edward, *The Devil Take the Hindmost: A History of Financial Speculation*, Plume (Penguin Group), 2000

Vines, Stephen, *Market Panic: Wild Gyrations, Risks, and Opportunities in Stock Markets*, John Wiley & Sons(Asia) Ptr. Ltd., 2003

Shiller, Robert J., *Irrational Exuberance*, Princeton University Press, 2005

Surowiecki, *The Wisdom of Crowds*, Anchor (Random House), 2004

Mandelbrot, Benoit & Hudson, Richard L., *The (Mis)Behavior of Markets: A Fractal View of Risk, Ruin & Reward*, Basic (Perseus), 2004

Skousen, Mark, *Economics on Trial: Lies, Myths and Realities*, Business One Irwin, 1991

Sheimo, Michael D., *Stock Market Rules: 70 of the Most Widely*

Held Investment Axioms Explained, Examined and Exposed, McGraw-Hill, 1999

Personal Investment Ghosts:

Kahneman, Daniel; Slovic, Paul; Tversky, Amos, *Judgement Under Uncertainty: Heuristics and biases,* Cambridge University Press, 1982

Mamis, Justin, *The Nature of Risk,* Fraser Publishing Company, 1999 (1929)

Trone, Donald B; Allbright, William R. & Taylor, Philip R., *The Management of Investment Decisions,* McGraw-Hill, 1996

Mauboussin, Michael J., *More Than You Know: Finding Financial Wisdom in Unconventional Places,* Columbia University Press, 2006

Shleifer, Andrei, *Inefficient Markets: an Introduction to Behavioral Finance,* Oxford University Press, 2000

Hagstrom, Robert G, Latticework: The New Investing, Texere, 2000

Eadington, William R and Cornelius, Judy A., *Gambling Behavior & Problem Gambling,* Institute for the Study of Gambling and Commercial Gaming, University of Navada, Reno, 1993

Inside Wall Street:

Levitt, Arthur with Dwyer, Paula, *Take on the Street: How to Fight for Your Financial Future,* Vintage Books, 2003 (2002)

Little, Jeffrey B. and Rhodes, Lucien, *Understanding Wall Street*, Liberty Hall, 1991 (1978)

Faber, David, with Kurson, Ken, *The Faber Report: How Wall Street Really Works – And How You Can Make It Work For You*, Little, Brown & Company, 2002

Winslow, Edward, *Blind Faith: Our Misplaced Trust in the Stock Market and Smarter, Safer Ways to Invest*, Berrett-Koehler, 2003

Perino, Michael, *The Hellhound of Wall Street: How Ferdinand Pecora's Investigation of the Great Crash Forever Changed American Finance*, Penguin, 2010

Personalities:

Boik, John, *Lessons from the Greatest Stock Traders of All Time: Proven Strategies Active Traders Can Use Today to Beat the Markets*, McGraw-Hill, 2004

Boik, John, *How Legendary Traders Made Millions*, McGraw-Hill, 2006

Lowe, Janet, *The Man Who Beats the S&P: Investing with Bill Miller*, John Wiley & Sons, Inc., 2002

Tanous, Peter J., *Investment Visionaries, Lessons in Creating Wealth from the World's Greatest Risk Takers*, Prentice Hall, 2003

Buffett, Mary & Clark, David, *Buffetology: The Previously Unexplained Techniques That Have Made Warren Buffett the World's Most Famous Investor*, Rawson Associates, (Scribner, Simon & Schuster, Inc.), 1997

Yield Investing:

Tigue, Joseph and Lisanti, Joseph, *The Dividend Rich Investor: Building Wealth with High-Quality Dividend Paying Stocks*, McGraw-Hill, 1999 (1997)

Peters, Josh, CFA, *The Ultimate Dividend Playbook: Income, Insight, and Independence for Today's Investor*, John Wiley & Sons, Inc., 2008

Klugman, Roxann, J.D., L.L.M., *The Dividend Growth Investment Strategy: How to Keep Your Retirement Income Doubling Every Five Years*, Citadel Press, 2001

Schreiber, Don Jr. and Stroik, Gary E., *All About Dividend Investing: The Easy Way to Get Started*, McGraw-Hill, 2005

Miller, Lowell, *The Single Best Investment: Creating Wealth with Dividend Growth*, Independent Publishers Group, 2006

Stein, Ben & DeMuth, Phil, *Yes, You Can Be a Successful Income Investor: Reaching for Yield in Today's Market*, New Beginnings Press, 2005

Lehman, Richard, *Income Investing today: Safety and High Income Through Diversification*, John Wiley & Sons, Inc., 2007

Fixed Income Investing:

Temel, Judy Wesalo, *The Fundamentals of Municipal Bonds. (The Bond Market Association)*, John Wiley & Sons, Inc.,2001 (1981)

Little, Jeffrey B. (Samuelson, Paul A.), *Bonds, Preferred Stocks, and the Money Market*, Chelsea House, 1988

O'Higgins, Michael B., with MaCarty, John, *Beating the Dow with Bonds: A High-Return, Low-Risk Strategy for Outperforming the Pros even when Stocks Go South*, Harper Business, 1999

LeDu, Doug K., *Cdx3 income engine: Preferred Stock Investing*, Booklocker.com, Inc., 2007

Prendergast, S.L., *Uncommon Profits Through Stock Purchase Warrants*, Dow Jones-Irwin, Inc. 1973

McHattie, Andrew, *The Investors Guide to Warrants*, F.T. Pitman, 1992

Investment Strategies:

Holton, Lisa, *How to be a Value Investor: Essential Guides to Today's Most Popular Investment Strategies*, McGraw-Hill, 1999

Ellis, Joseph H., *Ahead of the Curve: A Commonsense Guide to Forecasting Business and Market Cycles*, Harvard Business School Press, 2005
Port, Michael and Marshall, Elizabeth, *The Contrarian Effect*, John Wiley & Sons, Inc., 2008

Brooke, Christopher D., CFM, *Wealth Shift, Profit Strategies for Investors as the Baby Boomers Approach Retirement*, Perigee, 2005

Mathews, Bill, *Winning Big with Bargain Stocks: How to Invest Successfully in New Issues, Warrants, and Stocks of Turnaround Companies Under $10*, Dearborn, (ca 1992)

Mauldin, John, *Bull's Eye Investing: Targeting Real Returns in a Smoke and Mirrors Market*, John Wiley & Sons, Inc.,2004

Dorsey, Pat, *The Five Rules for Successful Stock Investing:*

Morningstar's Guide to Building Wealth and Winning in the Market, John Wiley & Sons, 2004

Dorsey, Pat, *The Little Book That Builds Wealth: The Knockout Formula for Finding Great Investments,* John Wiley & Sons, Inc., 2008

Swensen, David F., *Unconventional Success: A Fundamental Approach to Personal Investment,* Free Press, 2005

Ferri, Richard A., CFA, *All About Asset Allocation,* McGraw-Hill, 2006

Morningstar, *How to Get Started in Stocks (1,2 & 3),* John Wiley & Sons, Inc.2005

Gerstein, Marc H., *Screening the Market: A Four-Step Method to Find, Analyze, Buy and Sell Stocks,* John Wiley & Sons, Inc., 2002

Gerstein, Marc H., *The Value Connection: A Four-Step Market Screening Method the Match Good Companies with Good Stocks,* John Wiley & Sons, Inc., 2003

Darst, David M., *Mastering the Art of Asset Allocation: Comprehensive Approaches to Managing Risk and Optimizing Returns,* McGraw-Hill, 2007

Prestbo, John A., & Sease, Douglas R., *The Wall Street Journal, Book of International Investing: Everything You Need to Know About Investing in Foreign Markets,* Hyperion, 1997

Insana, Ron, *Trend-Watching,* Harper Business, 2002

Case, Samuel, *The First Book of Small Stock Investing,* Prima, 1998

Clements, Jonathan, *25 Myths you've Got To Avoid If You want to Manage Your Money Right: The New Rules for Financial Success*, Simon & Schuster, 1998

Taulli, Tom, *Investing in IPOs, Version 2.0*, Bloomberg Press, 2001

O'Neil, William J. with Morales, Gil, *How to Make Money Selling Stocks Short*, John Wiley & Sons, Inc., 2005

Porter, Michael E., *Competitive Advantage: Creating and Sustaining Superior Performance*, The Free Press (Macmillan), 1985

Block, Ralph L., *Investing in REITS: Real Estate Investment Trusts*, Bloomberg Press, 2006

Lee, Kenneth, *Trouncing the Dow; A Value-Based Method for Making Huge Profits*, McGraw-Hill, 1998

Gelman, Steve and the Editors of Money, *Investing Moves for Today*, Money Books (Time Inc.), 1999

Root, Jack B. & Mortensen, Douglas L., *The 7 Secrets of Financial Success: How to Apply Time-Tested Principles to Create, Manage & Build Personal Wealth*, McGraw-Hill, 1998 (1996)

Niederhoffer, Victor & Kenner, Laurel, *Practical Speculation*, John Wiley & Sons, Inc., 2003

Simon, W. Scott, *Index Mutual Funds, Profiting from an Investment Revolution*, Namborn, 1998

Biderman, Charles with Santschi, David, *Trim Tabs Investing: Investing Using Liquidity Theory to Beat the Stock Market*, John Wiley & Sons, Inc., 2005

Retirement Planning:

Jason, Julie, *The AARP Retirement Survival Guide*, Sterling Publishing Company, 2009

Dellinger, Jeffrey K., *The Handbook of Variable Income Annuities*, John Wiley & Sons, Inc., 2006

Lane, Michael F., *Guaranteed Income for Life: How Variable Annuities Can Cut Your Taxes, Pay You Every Year of Your Life, and Bring You Financial Peace of Mind*, McGraw-Hill, 1999

Slott, Ed, *Your Complete Retirement Planning Road Map: A Comprehensive Action Plan for Securing IRAs, 401(k)s, and Other Retirement Plans for Yourself and Your Family*, Ballantine, 2007
Garner, Robert J., Coplan, Robert B., Nissenbaum, Martin, Raasch, Barbara J., Ratner, Charles L., *Ernst & Young's Personal Financial Planning Guide*, John Wiley & Sons, Inc., 2000

DRIPS & DSPPs

Carlson, Charles B, CFA, *Buying Stocks Without a Broker*, McGraw Hill, 1992

Fisher, George C., *All About DRIPs and DSPs*, McGraw Hill, 2001

Fischer, Jeff, *Investing without a Silver Spoon*, The Motley Fool Inc., 1999

Options, Currencies, Commodities and Trading:

McMillan, Lawrence G., *McMillan on Options*, John Wiley & Sons, Inc., 1996

McMillan, Lawrence G., *Options as a Strategic Investment*, New York Institute of Finance, 2002

Wasendorf, Russell R. & McCafferty, Thomas A., *All About Commodities: From the Inside Out*, McGraw-Hill, 1993

Fink, Robert E., Feduniak, Robert B., *Futures Trading: Concepts and Strategies*, New York Institute of Finance, 1988

Luca, Cornelius, *Trading in the Global Currency Markets*, New York Institute of Finance, 2000

Horn, Frederick F., and Farah, Victor W., *Trading in Commodity Futures*, New York Institute of Finance, 1979

Carter, John F., *Mastering the Trade: Proven Techniques for Profiting from Intraday and Swing Trading Setups*, McGraw-Hill, 2006

Rogers, Jim, *Hot Commodities: How Anyone Can Invest Profitably in the World's Best Market*, Random House, 2004

Teweles, Richard J. & Jones, Frank J., *The Futures Game: Who Wins, Who Loses, Why*, McGraw-Hill, 1987 (1974)

Technical Analysis:

Copsey, Ian, *Integrated Technical Analysis*, John Wiley & Sons (Asia) Pte Ltd, 1999

Du Plessis, Jeremy, *The Definitive Guide to Point and Figure: A comprehensive Guide to the Theory and Practical Use of the Point and Figure Charting Method*, Harriman House, 2005

Corporate Governance:

Monks, Robert A.G. and Minow, Nell, *Corporate Governance, 2nd Edition*, Blackwell Publishers Ltd., 2001

Miscellaneous:

Mallach, David A., *Dancing with the Analysts: A Wall Street Novel About the Ultimate Financial Challenge*, Penhurst, 2003

Stanley, Thomas J, PhD and Danko, William D., PhD, *The Millionaire Next Door: The Surprising Secrets of America's Wealthy*, Barnes & Noble, 1996

www.ingramcontent.com/pod-product-compliance
Lightning Source LLC
Chambersburg PA
CBHW060823220326
41599CB00017B/2262